The Shaolin Monastery

The Shaolin

Monastery

History, Religion, and the Chinese Martial Arts

Meir Shahar

University of Hawai'i Press
Honolulu

18 17   9 8 7 6 5

Library of Congress Cataloging-in-Publication Data

Shahar, Meir.
    The Shaolin monastery : history, religion, and the Chinese martial arts / Meir
Shahar.
        p. cm.
    Includes bibliographical references and index.
    ISBN 978-0-8248-3349-7 (alk. paper)
    1. Shao lin si (Dengfeng xian, China)—History. 2. Martial arts—China. I. Title.
II. Title: History, religion, and the Chinese martial arts.
    BQ6345.T462S52275 2008
    294.3'657095118—dc22

                                                                    2007032532

Designed by University of Hawai'i Press production staff

For Noga Zhang Hui

Contents

Maps and Figures

Acknowledgments

Two FRIENDS have contributed most to this study: A'de guided me at the Shaolin Monastery and generously shared with me his intimate knowledge of its history and epigraphic treasures; Gene Ching revealed to me the complexities of the contemporary martial world. His dedication to his art has been a source of inspiration.

I have troubled no fewer than five scholars to read my manuscript, and I am deeply grateful for their comments and suggestions. They are Bernard Faure, Barend ter Haar, Valerie Hansen, Patrick Hanan, and John Kieschnick. For advice, rare materials, and/or hospitality, I am also indebted to Carl Bielefeldt, Susan Bush, Stanley E. Henning, Wilt Idema, Paul Katz, Li Fengmao, Liao Chao-heng, Wu Jen-shu, Zhou Qiufang, Zhou Weiliang, and Robin Yates. Invaluable help with the maps and the illustrations was provided by Dina Shahar, Gideon Zorea, and Patrick Lugo. Patricia Crosby of the University of Hawai'i Press has been helpful and encouraging throughout.

My research benefited from an Israel Science Foundation Grant (no. 851), and the leisure for writing was provided by the generosity of Yad-Hanadiv Foundation, Jerusalem.

Introduction

AT THE BEGINNING of the twenty-first century, the Shaolin Monastery has arguably become the most famous Buddhist temple in the world. The reason lies neither in its contribution to Chinese Buddhist evolution nor in its art treasures that have been accumulated in the course of its fifteen-hundred-year history. Not even the legends associating the monastery with the mythic founder of Chan (Zen) Buddhism, Bodhidharma, are the source of its renown. Rather, the Shaolin Monastery is world-famous because of its presumed connection to the Chinese martial arts.

The Westward dissemination of Chinese fighting techniques is among the intriguing aspects of the cultural encounter between China and the modern West. Featuring a unique synthesis of military, therapeutic, and religious goals, the Chinese martial arts appeal to millions of Western practitioners. Often presented as if they had originated at the Shaolin Monastery, these fighting techniques spread the temple's fame among large populations not necessarily familiar with the Buddhist faith. Moreover, nonpractitioners have been exposed to the Shaolin myth as well; beginning with Bruce Lee's (Li Xiaolong) (1940–1973) legendary films in the 1960s and culminating with Li Lianjie's (Jet Li) (b. 1963) spectacular features, the Shaolin Temple has been celebrated in numerous kung fu movies, which have played a major role in the propagation of its legend.

Is Shaolin's fame justified? Did its monks ever practice the martial arts? If they did, their military practice would give rise to numerous questions: religious, political, and military alike. The Buddhologist, to start with, would be struck by the obvious contradiction between monastic military training and the Buddhist prohibition of violence. How could Shaolin monks disregard a primary tenet of their religious faith that forbade warfare? Didn't they feel uneasy heading to the battlefield? Did they try to vindicate their transgression of Buddhist monastic law?

It could be argued, of course, that individuals and collectives alike have always found ways to justify violating their professed ideologies, in which sense the *contradiction* between Buddhism and martial practice is less interesting than the *connection*. Are the Shaolin martial arts inherently related to Buddhism? Nowadays, Shaolin monks emphatically claim that their martial regimen is a form of spiritual training. Shaolin's Abbot Yongxin (b. 1965) refers to his monastery's military tradition as "martial Chan" (*wuchan*), meaning that the physical exercises are a tool for the cultivation of religious awareness. Some practitioners argue further that it is possible to perceive a Chan logic within the Shaolin fighting method (as distinct from other Chinese martial styles such as Taiji Quan). The Shaolin sequence of fighting postures, they explain, creates patterns only to destroy them, thereby liberating the practitioner from preconceived notions. Such claims should not be belittled; on the contrary, the historian should trace their origins.

Other connections between Buddhism and military practice may also exist. As early as the medieval period, the Shaolin Monastery owned a large estate, which in chaotic times needed military protection. Shaolin martial training might have derived, therefore, from economic necessity: the safeguarding of the temple's property. Practical needs might have been sanctioned by divine precedents. It is striking that a religion as intent on peace as Buddhism arrived in China equipped with an entire arsenal of military gods. Buddhist iconography flanks the Buddha with heavily armed, ferocious-looking deities who trample demons underfoot. Such guardian deities might have provided a religious excuse for monastic violence; if the world-honored one required the protection of martial gods, then his monastic community certainly needed the defense of martial monks.

No investigation of Chinese monastic martial practice would be complete without reference to the possibility of native influences. Gymnastic and breathing exercises, coupled with techniques for the internal circulation of vital energy (*qi*), have been practiced in China as early as the first centuries BCE. Considered useful for longevity and spiritual self-cultivation, these exercises were incorporated during the early medieval period into the emerging Daoist religion, where they became an integral element of the faith's search for immortality. It is possible that this ancient tradition of religiously oriented gymnastics influenced Shaolin fighting techniques, in which case the Chinese Buddhist martial arts could be interpreted as yet another example of the sinicization of Buddhism.

The implications of Buddhist martial practice are not merely religious; monastic armies might have played a political role as well. Chinese imperial regimes of the past, like their contemporary Communist successors, have always been suspicious of the presumed rebellious intents of religious organizations. How could they tolerate monastic military training? The political historian would investigate, therefore, whether the state attempted to suppress Shaolin martial practice, or, on the contrary, employed fighting monks for its own military ends. As the following chapters demonstrate, the answer varied from one period to another. Whereas Shaolin monks rendered loyal military service to the Ming dynasty (1368–1644), for which they were handsomely rewarded with state patronage, their relations with the Qing (1644–1911) were ambivalent. Qing officials feared—probably not without reason—that some Shaolin affiliates would join sectarian revolts.

Practitioners and martial arts historians alike would be more interested in the evolution of *techniques* than in their religious or political implications. When did the Shaolin martial arts emerge? To address this question we must distinguish between military *activities* and fighting *techniques*: As early as the Tang dynasty (618–907), Shaolin monks engaged in warfare, but there is no evidence that at that time they specialized in a given martial art, let alone developed their own. The monks presumably carried to battle common Tang weaponry, practicing the same military tactics as other medieval soldiers.

As to the monastery's own martial arts, they evolved in two stages that lasted several centuries each. In the first phase, which likely began around the twelfth century and reached its apogee in the sixteenth, Shaolin monks specialized in staff fighting. By the late Ming, their techniques with this weapon were considered the best in China. In the second phase, from the sixteenth century to the present, the monks have been perfecting their unarmed techniques, which gradually eclipsed the staff as the dominant form of Shaolin martial practice. By the twenty-first century, the Shaolin method of hand combat (*quan*) has spread all over the world. It needs be emphasized that throughout the monastery's history, the monks have also practiced fighting with swords, spears, and other sharp weapons, which in real battle were more effective than either staff or hand combat.

Beginning with Tang Hao's (1897–1959) pioneering research in the 1930s, significant progress has been made in the study of martial arts history. Nevertheless, the evolution of Chinese fighting techniques is not yet fully charted, and important lacunas remain to be explored. The development of Shaolin fighting could potentially shed light on martial arts history in general. Significantly, Shaolin hand combat emerged during the same period—the late Ming and early Qing—as other familiar bare-handed styles such as Taiji Quan and Xingyi Quan. As shown in the following chapters, the Ming-Qing transition was a pivotal period in martial arts history, in which Daoist gymnastic and breathing techniques were integrated with bare-handed fighting, creating a synthesis of fighting, healing, and self-cultivation. Arguably, this unique combination of military, therapeutic, and religious goals has been the key to the martial arts' appeal in their native land and the modern West as well.

This book is concerned then with these problems: military, political, and religious. However, before they could have been addressed, a fundamental question had to be answered: Did Shaolin monks practice fighting, and if so since when? During the late imperial period an enormous body of legends grew around the Shaolin Temple. The Chinese martial arts were wrapped in an elaborate mythology that ascribed them to Buddhist saints and to Daoist immortals. Propagated the world over by training manuals, as well as by novels and movies, this mythology has become part of our own. To examine the evolution of Shao-lin fighting, it was necessary therefore to separate—as far as possible—myth from history. The result is a chronological account that spans fifteen hundred years, from Shaolin's founding in the late fifth century through the monastery's Tang military campaigns, the military services it rendered the Ming dynasty, the evolution of its staff techniques and later its bare-handed techniques, and its un-easy relations with the Qing, which lasted through the nineteenth century.

Any attempt to investigate the history of monastic fighting is confronted by the reluctance of Buddhist authors to record it. Even though some eminent monks criticized monastic warfare—providing us important information on it—the typical Buddhist response has been silence. In the vast historiographi-cal corpus of the Chinese canon, no reference is made to Shaolin military ac-tivities, which contradicted Buddhist monastic law. In this absence, epigraphy has proven to be an invaluable source. The Shaolin Monastery boasts dozens of inscriptions, which shed light on its military activities from the seventh through the nineteenth centuries. Whereas Tang and Ming steles record imperial gifts, which were bestowed on the monastery in recognition of its military services, Qing inscriptions warn the monks not to engage in rebellious activities. Other information was also recorded in stone. The burial stupas of Ming-period Shaolin fighting monks are inscribed with epitaphs that list individual battles in which the clerics had participated.

Whereas all through the fourteenth century, epigraphy is our most im-portant source of Shaolin military activities, beginning in the mid-Ming the situation changes dramatically; the Shaolin martial arts are lauded in every genre of sixteenth- and seventeenth-century Chinese literature, and fighting monks figure in dozens, if not hundreds, of late Ming and Qing texts. There were probably several causes for the burst of late Ming interest in monastic fighting, which lasted through the ensuing Qing period.

The first reason was the decline of the hereditary Ming army, which forced the government to rely on other military forces, including monastic troops. The late Ming was the heyday of monastic armies, the martial arts being prac-ticed in temples across the empire. Fighting monks were drafted for numerous military campaigns, and their contribution to national defense was recorded in official histories such as the *Ming Veritable Records* (*Ming shi lu*) and the *Ming History* (*Mingshi*). The bravery and fighting skills of clerical troops—Shaolin's and other's—were similarly lauded in chronicles of individual battles. The con-tribution of monastic armies to the sixteenth-century piracy campaign, for ex-ample, was repeatedly praised in treatises on coastal defense.

A second cause for the wealth of sixteenth- and seventeenth-century sources on Shaolin fighting was the publishing industry's growth. The Shaolin martial arts were featured in new genres, which were first printed during the late Ming, as well as in old ones, which proliferated in that period. They figure in military treatises and martial arts manuals; local gazetteers and monastic histories (which, unlike general histories of Chinese Buddhism, did mention fighting monks); household encyclopedias, travel guides, and memoirs; as well as a great variety of fiction in both the classical and vernacular idioms.

The Manchu conquest of 1644 furnishes a third important factor in the historiography of Shaolin fighting. The humiliating defeat turned the attention of the literati elite to the popular martial arts, which had been earlier considered unworthy of documentation. Renowned literati such as Gu Yanwu (1613–1682), Huang Zongxi (1610–1695), and the latter's son Huang Baijia (1643–?) acknowledged becoming interested in folk fighting techniques because their scholarly Confucian education had failed in the nation's defense. These scholars were not motivated by a naïve belief that bare-handed fighting could overthrow the foreign conquerors, but rather looked for the martial arts as a means for restoring national confidence, not unlike nineteenth- and twentieth-century Chinese attempts to restore the nation's political body by invigorating the corporal bodies of individual citizens.[1]

The great medievalist Marc Bloch has commented that knowledge of the present is necessary for an understanding of the past.[2] On several occasions contemporary Shaolin practice has illuminated for me aspects of the temple's history. This is especially true as regards the fluidity of the Shaolin community, of which resident monks constitute no more than a core minority. In addition to ordained clerics who dwell inside the temple, numerous Shaolin practitioners —monks and laymen alike—have been trained at the monastery but have left it to pursue an independent career, often opening up their own martial arts schools. These Shaolin alumni often disregard monastic regulations (especially the dietary law prohibiting meat), just as their late imperial predecessors might have joined in sectarian revolts. During the Qing period, government officials censured the criminal activities of the itinerant Shaolin community rather than blame the monastery itself for seditious intents. The Shaolin Temple was suspect not because of its own insubordination, but because of its intimate connection to an unruly and fluid martial community, which *was* deemed potentially dangerous.

Thus, where the elucidation of a historical problem requires reference to contemporary conditions, I have ventured into ethnographic observation. Nevertheless, Shaolin's modern history will have to await another study. Beginning in the mid-nineteenth century, Shaolin's martial evolution has been intimately related to the fate of the modern Chinese martial arts. The traumatic encounter with the modern West and the attempt to save the race by martial training; the emergence of the modern media—newspaper, film, and television industries— and their respective roles in spreading the martial arts; the promotion of standardized martial arts sports in the People's Republic of China and the government's attempt, on which national pride hinges, to include them in the Olympic games—even though I have commented on them, these topics will require the attention of the specialist in modern Chinese history.

PART I

Origins of a
Military Tradition
(500–900)

CHAPTER 1

The Monastery

SHAOLIN'S HISTORY spans fifteen hundred years. The monastery was founded during the last decade of the fifth century by an Indian-born monk, who is referred to in the Chinese sources as Batuo, or Fotuo. It is situated in mountainous Dengfeng County, Central Henan, some thirty miles southeast of Luoyang, the former capital of the Northern Wei dynasty (386–534), and forty-five miles southwest of Zhengzhou, the modern capital of Henan Province (map 1). The peaks of the lofty Mt. Song rise above the temple. Today they are largely barren, but during the period when the monastery was established the entire county was covered with forests.[1]

In terms of its population, which approaches a hundred million, Henan is today the largest Chinese province. Removed from China's prosperous coast, it is also one of the poorest.[2] Dusty villages line the road from the Zhengzhou airport to the Shaolin Monastery. The air is heavily polluted by coal that is carried in open trucks from nearby mines. The poverty of its surroundings highlights the Shaolin Monastery's significance for the region's economy. By the late 1990s the temple attracted more than a million tourists a year. The lodging, food, and transportation these modern pilgrims require spurred the emergence of a tourist industry, which plays a major role in Dengfeng County's economy; the sale of entry tickets to the temple alone brings in US $5 million annually.[3]

From the county's perspective, students are even more valuable than tourists. Dengfeng is home to some seventy thousand aspiring martial artists, who study in dozens of fighting schools that mushroomed around the monastery beginning in the 1980s. Admitting boarding students aged six and up, the schools offer a comprehensive martial training coupled with such required scholastic skills as math, language, and the like.[4] Only a fraction of their prospective graduates are ordained as Shaolin monks. Most become professional martial artists, earning a living as instructors of physical education, as soldiers

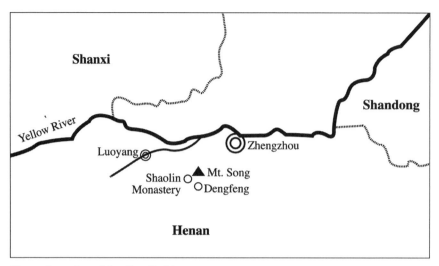

MAP 1. Location of the Shaolin Monastery.

in elite military units, or as freelance bodyguards for affluent businessmen. The very best may be handpicked for the Chinese national team, whereas others may hope for a career in the film industry; at least one Dengfeng student, Shi Xiaolong (b. 1988), became an international movie star before reaching the age of fifteen. Young Shi has starred in more than ten Hong Kong kung fu movies, as well as in several of his own television serials.[5]

The economic benefits of the Shaolin Temple are felt throughout Henan, not only in Dengfeng County. In the early 1990s provincial authorities capitalized on the monastery's international renown. In association with Shaolin's abbot, they initiated the biennial Shaolin Martial Arts Festival (Shaolin wushu jie), which is held simultaneously at the temple and the provincial capital. The festival brings to Henan athletes and enthusiasts from around the globe. It is celebrated in the Chinese national media and advertised by the China National Tourism Administration the world over.[6]

Shaolin's intense commercialization perplexes some of its devotees. Devout Buddhists and committed martial artists aspire to the serenity of self-cultivation. The temple strikes them instead as a martial arts supermarket that caters to the uninitiated. Their disappointment was shared by pilgrims centuries ago. As early as the Ming period some believers were disturbed by Shaolin's excessive wealth, which they considered contrary to Buddhist ideology. In the early seventeenth century a Dengfeng County magistrate named Fu Mei (fl. 1610) lamented that "Shaolin's lofty mansions and splendid furnishings are reminiscent of a government official's residence. Truly, the decline of the Buddhist teaching is far-reaching. Thinking of the Buddhist sages of old, one can only sigh deeply!"[7]

Even though his first impression of Shaolin was disappointing, Fu was well aware that the monastery made an enormous contribution to the evolution of Chinese Buddhism, and—it could be argued—to Chinese culture at large. Indeed, he himself proceeded to write a history of the temple, titled—in reference to the peaks above it—*Song Mountain Book* (*Song shu*).[8] His history includes detailed biographies of eminent Shaolin monks belonging to every Buddhist sect from Chan to Pure Land. It also includes transcriptions of Shaolin steles, some of which date back to the sixth and seventh centuries. The Shaolin Monastery boasts a priceless collection of some two hundred carved inscriptions, which were bestowed upon it by powerful patrons ranging from Empress Wu (r. 684–705) to the Qianlong emperor (r. 1736–1795). These provide the historian with invaluable information on the religion, economy, and government of imperial China.

Fu's book on the Shaolin Monastery was neither the first nor the only one. In its millennium-and-a-half history, the monastery has been celebrated in countless literary compositions, ranging in length from individual poems to full-length monographs. Emperors, officials, and poets have extolled in verse and prose the beauty of Shaolin's halls and towers. The monastery's masterpieces of art make it uniquely important for the historian of Chinese painting and sculpture.[9] Its Stupa Forest (Talin) is a treasure of Buddhist architecture, containing more than two hundred—the largest number in China—stupas (pagodas). Usually housing the cremated remains of eminent monks, these elegant stone structures are inscribed with important texts on the history of medieval Buddhism.[10]

Why did the Buddhist tradition accord Shaolin such a prominent position? What were the sources of the monastery's wealth? Why did its monks practice the martial arts? We begin our investigation with the monastery's location on the slopes of the sacred Mt. Song.

Sanctity

"In China, the mountains are divinities," wrote one of the pioneers of Western sinology.[11] Indeed, the Chinese religious tradition has accorded peaks numinous powers. Chinese pilgrimage sites—regardless of religious affiliation—are almost invariably located in alpine landscapes.[12] Situated on the slopes of Mt. Song, the Shaolin Monastery is no exception. The name "Song" does not allude to a single peak, but to an entire range of mountains, which runs east to west across Dengfeng County. This range's highest elevations are Mt. Taishi in the east (1,440 meters or 4,724 feet above sea level) and Mt. Shaoshi in the west (1,512 meters or 4,961 feet above sea level). The Shaolin Monastery is nestled underneath the latter. Its name probably reflects its location in Mt. *Shao*shi's ancient *lin* (grove), hence *Shaolin*.

Mt. Song occupied a prominent position among Chinese sacred mountains long before the Shaolin Monastery was founded. As early as the first centuries BCE it was chosen as one of the Five Holy Peaks (Wuyue), which served as divine protectors of the state.[13] In accordance with Five-Phases Cosmology, these deified mountains faced north (Mt. Heng), south (Mt. Heng), east (Mt. Tai), west (Mt. Hua), and center (Mt. Song). In 110 BCE, Emperor Han Wudi (reigned 140–87 BCE) climbed the Central Holy Peak (Mt. Song) and offered sacrifice to the mountain's god.[14] Thus, he began a tradition that lasted through the seventh century, when Empress Wu performed there the most elaborate of all imperial legitimation rites: the *fengshan* sacrifice. On that occasion, the empress changed the surrounding county's name—as well as her own reign title—to Dengfeng (literally, "mounting the *feng* [sacrifice]").[15]

Mt. Song's significance in imperial cults was reflected during the first centuries CE in the sacred geography of the emerging Daoist religion. The mountain became the object of Daoist pilgrimages, real as well as imaginary. Whereas eminent Daoists such as Zhang Daoling (fl. 142), Kou Qianzhi (365–448), and Sima Chengzhen (647–735) resided on the mountain,[16] mystics arrived there without ever leaving their studios. Using as aids for the imagination spiritual charts such as the *Map of the Five Peaks' True Shape* (*Wu yue zhen xing shan tu*), they reached the mountain by meditation. Early in the medieval period the enormous Daoist Temple of the Central Peak (Zhongyue miao) was established on Mt. Song. It is among the largest and most ancient Daoist temples in China. Nowadays it houses monks—and, in a separate wing, nuns—belonging to the Perfect Realization (Quanzhen) Sect.[17]

Religions tend to appropriate each other's sacred places (Jerusalem is one example). Thus, when Buddhist missionaries arrived in China in the first centuries CE, they quickly perceived the religious potential of Mt. Song. As early as the third century a Buddhist monastery was established on the mountain, which by the early sixth century featured no fewer than six Buddhist temples.[18] The mountain's "Buddhist conquest" (as Bernard Faure has termed it) involved the creation of a new mythology, which tied the Chinese peak to the Indian-born faith. It centered on the legendary founder of the Chan (Japanese: Zen) School: Bodhidharma.[19]

The eighth century witnessed the flowering of a new school of Chinese Buddhism, which as indicated by its name stressed the significance of meditation (*chan* in Chinese; *dhyāna* in Sanskrit). One of the Chan School's novel traits was the belief that the truth revealed by the Buddha could be directly transmitted from master to disciple. At least in theory, it was no longer necessary to study the scriptures. Instead, the unmediated mind-dharma (*xinfa*) could be handed from teacher to student. To legitimize this claim, Chan masters had to show that *their* mind-dharma had been transmitted to them through a lineage going back all the way to the Buddha himself. Therefore, in the course of the eighth century, Chan authors furnished their school with a past. They manufactured a genealogy of Chinese—and, further back, Indian— patriarchs who connected them to the source of the Buddhist faith.[20]

Chan authors paid particular attention to the patriarch they claimed brought the teachings from India to China. They assigned this role to the obscure Bodhidharma (Chinese: Damo), whom they venerated as the founder of their school. In the course of the twentieth century, Bodhidharma has been the subject of intense scholarly research. Chinese, Japanese, and Western scholars usually accept the historicity of this Indian (or, according to another version, Persian) missionary, who arrived in China around 480 and propagated the Dharma in the Luoyang region until ca. 520. However, scholars are skeptical as to Bodhidharma's role in the Chan School (which emerged at least a century after his death). Even if Bodhidharma preached a doctrine that influenced Chan thinkers, the attribution of the school to him is considered a legend by most historians.[21]

For our purpose here, the significance of the Bodhidharma myth is its association with Mt. Song. During the last decades of the seventh century, this mountain became an important center of Chan learning, as eminent masters such as Faru (638–689) and Huian (?–709) took up residence at the Shaolin Monastery. These early Chan practitioners were probably responsible for connecting Bodhidharma to the Central Holy Peak.[22] It was on Mt. Song, they claimed, that the aged Indian patriarch (he was said to be more than a hundred years old) had transmitted the Dharma to his Chinese disciple—the first native patriarch—Huike (ca. 485–ca. 555). Thus, Mt. Song became the symbolic crossing point between the realm of the Buddha and China.

The evolution of Bodhidharma's Mt. Song legends can be traced through medieval Buddhist literature. In the sixth-century *Record of Buddhist Monasteries in Lo-yang*) (*Luoyang qielan ji*) (ca. 547), the saint is said to have visited the city, but no allusion is made to the nearby Mt. Song. Approximately a century later, the *Continuation of the Biographies of Eminent Monks* (*Xu Gaoseng zhuan*) (645), describes him as active in the "Mt. Song–Luoyang" region. Then, in such early eighth-century compositions as the *Precious Record of the Dharma's Transmission* (*Chuanfa baoji*) (ca. 710) Bodhidharma is identified not merely with Mt. Song but more specifically with the Shaolin Monastery, where supposedly for several years he faced the wall in meditation. The *Precious Record* also mentions the trials undergone by Huike when, at the Shaolin Monastery, he sought Bodhidharma's instruction. To express his earnestness, Huike cut off his arm and offered it to the Indian patriarch, who in response led him to enlightenment.[23]

Tang legends are elaborated upon in Song hagiographic collections. The eleventh-century *Jingde Period Record of the Transmission of the Lamp* (*Jingde Chuandeng lu*) (1004) embellishes eighth-century Bodhidharma stories with dramatic detail. It was an ice-cold night, we are told, when Huike sought the saint's guidance at the Shaolin Monastery. The Chinese disciple stood motionless in the freezing snow, waiting for Bodhidharma's attention. Then, in a surge of religious zeal, he cut off his arm. "My mind is not at peace," he disclosed. "Please pacify it for me." "Bring your mind here and I will pacify it for you," replied Bodhidharma. "I have searched for my mind," Huike conceded, "but I cannot find it anywhere," at which point it was only necessary for Bodhidharma to conclude with: "I have now completely pacified your mind for you."[24]

Bodhidharma's association with Shaolin, which is traceable in canonical scriptures, is equally attested to by archaeological evidence at the temple itself. Shaolin steles reveal the gradual process by which the Indian saint had been linked to the Chinese temple. A stele inscription dated 728 is the earliest to have Bodhidharma residing on Mt. Song, and another, dated 798, already has Huike performing the dramatic gesture of severing his arm.[25] Then a plethora of thirteenth- and fourteenth-century steles feature the complete myth as it appears in such Song-period hagiographies as the *Jingde Period Record of the Transmission of the Lamp*. The latter is cited, for example, in the following Shaolin stele:

> After nine years had passed, Bodhidharma wished to return to the west, to India, so he commanded his disciples saying, "The time is near; each of you should say what you have attained." At the time the disciple Daofu replied, "As I see it, the function of the Dao consists in not attaching to scriptures and not being apart from scriptures." The master said, "You have gotten my skin." The nun Zongchi said, "My understanding now is that it is like the joy of seeing the Buddha-land of Akṣobhya: it is felt at the first glance, but not the second glance." The master said, "You have gotten my flesh." Daoyu said, "The four elements are at root empty, and the five *skandhas* have no existence; from my point of view, there is not a single dharma that could be attained." The master said, "You have gotten my bones." Finally Huike, after making a prostration, just stood at his place. The master said, "You have gotten my marrow."[26]

In this Song-period text, Bodhidharma's ranking of his students is expressed metaphorically: Huike's silent answer earns him the saint's "marrow" (*sui*), namely, the essence of Bodhidharma's teachings. Centuries later the saint's words were given a radically different interpretation. With the growth of the Shaolin martial tradition, the "marrow" was taken literally as the name of a secret manual—the *Marrow-Cleansing Classic* (*Xisui jing*)—which Bodhidharma supposedly had handed to his chosen disciple. Treasuring the saint's arcane gymnastics, this treatise had remained hidden for more than a millennium. Then during the seventeenth century it miraculously emerged to influence the late imperial martial arts.

Charting the development of the Bodhidharma myth, Shaolin steles also unravel the evolution of his visual representations. An engraving dated 1209 depicts the barefoot saint holding a shoe in reference to the legend of his resurrection (figure 1).[27] After Bodhidharma's death, the legend goes, a Chinese emissary to central Asia met the saint, who was walking barefoot and carrying a single shoe. Bodhidharma explained to the startled diplomat that he was heading back to his native India. When the emissary returned to

FIG. 1. The Shoe-Holding
Bodhidharma on his way to the
West (1209 Shaolin stele).

China and told his story, Bodhidharma's grave was promptly opened. It was
found to be empty except for the other shoe.[28]

The shoe-holding Bodhidharma became a standard motif in Chan art.
Another thirteenth-century image that became ubiquitous showed him riding a fragile stalk across the Yangtze River's mighty waves (figure 2).[29] Icons
of the Reed-Floating Bodhidharma tend to portray the saint quite humor-
ously. He sports a beard and an earring, and the artist has taken care to
highlight his foreign features: the large nose and bushy eyebrows. This image
betrays a common Chinese perception of the saint as eccentric. The pot-bel-
lied Maitreya Buddha, the divine clown Daoji, and the idiosyncratic arhats
(*luohan*) are all depicted in Chinese art and literature as holy fools, whose divinity is masked behind an eccentric facade.[30]

FIG. 2. The Rush-Leaf
Bodhidharma on a 1624
Shaolin stele.

Bodhidharma's veneration at the Shaolin Monastery culminated in
1125 with the construction of a special temple in his honor. Since the patriarch was believed to have spent most of his time in solitary meditation, his
shrine was built approximately a half-mile northwest of the monastery
proper. Commonly known as the "First Patriarch's Hermitage" (Chuzu an),
it has been preserved to this day. Gaily ornamented with reliefs of birds, fish,
and Buddhist deities, it is considered a masterpiece of Song stone carving.[31]

With the establishment of Bodhidharma's shrine, "a kind of pilgrimage
or sight-seeing circuit" emerged on Mt. Song.[32] It included the sites associated with the saint: the Shaolin Monastery, the "First Patriarch's Hermitage,"
and—most sacred of all—the cave where Bodhidharma had supposedly
meditated. Since he was said to have sat motionless for nine years, Bodhidharma's shadow was even imprinted on the cave's wall, where his image had

remained visible for centuries.[33] Today visitors to the Shaolin Monastery are shown—inside the temple—a large stone carved with the figure of the meditating saint. Supposedly, this stone was brought to the temple from Bodhidharma's cave, where his shade had been engraved upon it.[34]

When Shaolin monks constructed Bodhidharma's shrine, Chan was gaining in popularity. During the Song period it became the most influential school of Chinese Buddhism. Chan's growing significance elevated its putative founder into a central position in the Buddhist pantheon. The saint's intimate association with Shaolin had significant implications therefore for the monastery's standing: Bodhidharma bolstered Shaolin's sanctity. Half a millennium later—during the Ming-Qing transition period—he also became associated with the monastery's martial tradition.

Patronage

Bodhidharma granted Shaolin charisma; emperors endowed the monastery with wealth. Some thirty miles northwest of Shaolin, the city of Luoyang had served as the seat of government during much of the medieval period. It was capital of the Eastern Han (25–220), the Wei (220–265), the Western Jin (265–316), the Northern Wei (495–534), and the Sui (581–618), and it was chosen as secondary capital by the Tang (618–907). Shaolin's relative proximity to this administrative hub enabled it to enjoy imperial munificence, securing the monastery's fortunes.

The first patron of the Shaolin Monastery was the devout Emperor Xiaowen (r. 471–499), who in 495 transferred the capital of his Northern Wei Tuoba dynasty (386–534) from Pingcheng (today's Datong, Shanxi) to Luoyang. The following year, the monarch provided the Indian-born monk Batuo with funds to establish the Shaolin Temple. Batuo, also referred to in the Chinese sources as Fotuo, had met the emperor several years before. He had enjoyed Xiaowen's sponsorship ever since he arrived in Pingcheng via the silk route around 490.[35]

Batuo was a teacher of Buddhist doctrine as well as a painter of Buddhist scenes.[36] Under his able leadership Shaolin became a center of religious education. The foreign missionary invited experts in monastic law such as Huiguang (487–536) and Daoping (488–559) to Shaolin.[37] He established there a Sutra Translation Hall (Fanjing Tang), where sixth-century scholars such as Ratnamati (Lenamoti) and Bodhiruci (Putiliuzhi) rendered Sanskrit scriptures into Chinese. Indeed, the fame of Shaolin's translation academy was such that in 645 the great scholar Xuanzang (596–664) asked Emperor Taizong (r. 627–649) for permission to reside there. In his petition—which was denied by the emperor, who wished to keep the eminent monk near him—Xuanzang cited the achievements of Bodhiruci as the reason for his choice of the Shaolin Monastery.[38]

Shaolin was but one of numerous monasteries established by the Northern Wei in their new capital. Emperor Xiaowen and his successors ushered in a period of spectacular Buddhist growth in Luoyang. Within decades of the court's being established there, the city featured more than a thousand Buddhist temples, whose golden roofs, we are told, dazzled the eyes.[39] The generosity with which these temples were appointed is vividly rendered in the contemporary *Record of Buddhist Monasteries in Lo-yang* (547):

> Princes, dukes, and ranking officials donated such valuable things as elephants and horses, as generously as if they were slipping shoes from off their feet. The people and wealthy families parted with their treasures as easily as with forgotten rubbish. As a result, Buddhist temples were built side by side, and stupas rose up in row after row. People competed among themselves in making or copying the Buddha's portraits. Golden stupas matched the imperial observatory in height, and Buddhist lecture halls were as magnificent as the [ostentatiously wasteful] E-bang [Palaces of the Qin dynasty (221–207 BCE)].[40]

The magnificent golden-roofed monasteries of Luoyang no longer survive. In 534, with the fall of the Northern Wei capital, most of its temples were destroyed. However, another expression of the Tuobas' religious fervor has remained intact. During the same years in which the Shaolin Monastery was established, work began on what was to become one of the largest monuments of Buddhist sculpture in Asia. Thousands of Buddha images were carved into the rock at Longmen, on the outskirts of Luoyang. These gigantic statues—some are more than two hundred feet tall—still gaze majestically out upon the flowing waters of the Yi River, unaffected by the ravages of time.[41]

Xiaowen's patronage of the Shaolin Monastery was continued by devout emperors of the following medieval dynasties. Two notable examples are the Sui emperor Wendi (r. 581–604) and the Tang empress Wu Zetian (r. 684–705). The former endowed the monastery with a 1,400-acre estate, which included a water mill.[42] (During the medieval period mills were a common source of monastic income.)[43] The latter felt so attached to Shaolin that she built there a ten-story stupa for the deliverance of her mother's soul. In addition, the empress graced the monastery with a poem, which was engraved on a Shaolin stele. Both can be admired at the monastery to this day.[44]

The proselytizing efforts of devout emperors such as Xiaowen have transformed central Henan into what could be described as a "Buddhist Land." To this day, the road from Shaolin to Luoyang is dotted with villages that bear such Buddhist names as Foguang (Buddha's Light). Some twelve miles from Shaolin, at Xuanzang's native village, one encounters a temple for the famed pilgrim. Further up the road is the enormous White Horse Temple (Baima Si), which, dating back to the Eastern Han, is reputed to be the oldest Buddhist monastery in China. As one approaches Luoyang, the monumental Buddhist caves of Longmen become visible. It was within this Buddhist realm that, during the medieval period, the Shaolin Monastery prospered.

Situated on a venerable mountain within range of an imperial capital, the Shaolin Temple benefited from sanctity and patronage alike. Its elevated location above a government center also had military implications. The monastery controlled the mountain road leading from Luoyang to Dengfeng and further southeast. This strategic significance served as the background for the Shaolin monks' earliest involvement in warfare.

CHAPTER 2

Serving the Emperor

BUDDHISM PROHIBITS VIOLENCE. Binding the clergy and laity alike, the first of the Five Buddhist Precepts forbids killing a living being (*bu sha sheng*). The prohibition applies to all sentient beings, humans as well as animals. However, the moral burden of murder differs in accordance with the being involved; killing a big animal is usually considered more serious than injuring a small one. The murder of a human being is the greatest offense; it receives the heaviest retribution in the afterlife, and if committed by a monk, it involves permanent expulsion from the monastic order.[1]

The Buddhist prohibition of violence has had significant implications for the religion's attitude toward war. Buddhism has been less inclined than other faiths to sanction warfare. Some exceptions notwithstanding, most Buddhist authors have refused to condone the social or political obligation of soldiers to fight. Unlike Hinduism, for example, which allows for warriors going to heaven, many Buddhist scriptures have them punished in hell. The Buddhist philosopher Vasubandhu (fl. fifth century) goes as far as to argue that even if they are pressured to fight, soldiers should not do so, for it is better to die than to kill. In warfare, Vasubandhu emphatically states, responsibility is collective, meaning that it is shared—not divided—by all participants. The soldier who kills and his comrade who happens not to kill are equally guilty, for they have enlisted for the same purpose of slaughter.[2]

The religion's objection to war was translated into its monastic code. The *vinaya* regulations of all the Indian Buddhist schools go into great length to prevent monastic participation in warfare. Monks are forbidden to carry arms or join an army. They are not allowed to fight themselves, nor to incite others to fight. Even as passive spectators they are not permitted to enter a battlefield, for they should neither hear the sound of war nor witness its horrors.[3] Chinese biographies of eminent monks reveal specific instances in which they heeded these laws: In 454, Guṇabhadra (Qiunabatuoluo) refused to take part in the military operations of his patron, the prince of Nanqiao, exclaiming that "a monk should not be involved in warfare," and in 645, Xuanzang declined Emperor Taizong's invitation to join him on the Korean campaign, citing the *vinaya* interdiction against monks entering the battlefield.[4]

Whereas most Chinese monks doubtless observed the prohibition of warfare, there were some who—despite Buddhist attempts to gloss over the issue—did not. During the medieval period, some monks fought, but information on them in Buddhist sources is scarce. Buddhist authors were reluctant to record transgressions of the monastic code, preferring to ignore fighting monks. The canon's vast historiographical corpus contains only scant references to monastic involvement in warfare. In those rare cases where Buddhist participation in war is mentioned, it is explained by coercion on the part of secular authorities. We are told, for example, that the fifth-century Northern Liang monks who fought the Northern Wei invaders were sent forcibly to battle.[5]

If we were to rely on their own testimony, we would thus be under the impression that medieval monks rarely, if ever, fought. However, what Buddhist authors tend to hide, other writers reveal. The Confucian compilers of the Chinese histories recorded with relish instances of Buddhist involvement in armed revolts—they proved the dangers inherent in the foreign faith. For the chaotic decade of Sui-Tang transition alone (the 610s) they noted no fewer than five revolts in which monks were involved.[6] This rebellious activity—often with messianic overtones—continued well into the Tang period (618–907). In 815 a monk named Yuanjing (ca. 735–815) from a monastery adjacent to Shaolin, the Monastery of the Central Peak (Zhongyue si), played a leading role in Li Shidao's (?–815) attempted coup d'état. When the revolt failed, Yuanjing was subjected to the customary torture. A soldier tried to break his shinbones with a sledgehammer, but for some reason failed. The fierce monk then offered assistance by spreading his legs, at the same time sneering scornfully: "You can't even break a fellah's shin, and you call yourself a tough guy, bah!"[7]

And then there is archaeological evidence. Late Tang manuscripts discovered at the famed Dunhuang Caves in Gansu reveal that monks had taken an active role in fighting along China's northwestern borders. Dunhuang monks were drafted for military service under Chinese and Tibetan rule alike.[8] One manuscript, for example, discloses that monks played a major role in the "Return to Allegiance Army" (Guiyi jun) which, under the command of the Chinese adventurer Zhang Yichao (fl. 850), brought Turfan under Chinese rule.[9]

As to Shaolin, its martial aspect is first attested to by another archaeological source: epigraphy. Engraved steles dating from the medieval period record at least two instances in which Shaolin monks resorted to arms: The first was in the last years of the Sui dynasty (ca. 610), when they warded off an attack by bandits. The second was approximately a decade later, when they assisted Emperor Li Shimin (600–649) in the campaigns leading to the founding of the Tang dynasty (618–907). Their heroic assistance to the dynasty earned Shaolin monks property rights that the steles were erected to safeguard.

The significance of Shaolin's military service to the Tang should be evaluated in the context of the dynasty's Buddhist policies. Unlike rulers of the preceding Northern Wei and Sui dynasties, "Tang emperors for the most part did not exhibit much enthusiasm for Buddhism."[10] Devout Buddhist monarchs such as Empress Wu notwithstanding, Tang history was marked by attempts to curb the economic and political clout of the Buddhist church. These attempts culminated, under Emperor Wuzong (reigned 841–846), in a major purge of the Buddhist faith; hundreds of monasteries were destroyed and thousands of monks forcibly returned to lay life. Following this religious persecution, Chinese Buddhism never recovered the institutional strength it had enjoyed in medieval times.

If it were not for Shaolin's military contribution to the dynasty's founding, the monastery might have fared like countless others that at best received no government support and at worst were demolished. By contrast, the Shaolin stele inscriptions attest that the monks' assistance to Li Shimin earned them the patronage of his successors, many of whom were far from sympathetic to the faith. Evidently, the monks' disregard of the Buddhist prohibition of violence secured their monastery's fortunes under the Tang.

The Shaolin monks' heroic assistance to Li Shimin was not recorded by Buddhist historians, who were doubtless disconcerted by it. Indeed, it was engraved in stone at the monastery not to influence the behavior of future Buddhists, but to remind Tang officials of their indebtedness to the monastery. As such, the Shaolin inscriptions exemplify the significance of epigraphy as a source for Buddhist historiography. Gregory Schopen has observed that in the Indian case, "inscriptional materials tells us not what some literate, educated Indian Buddhist wrote, but what a fairly large number of practicing Buddhists actually did."[11] His insight is applicable to China: Shaolin steles reveal a story untold in Chinese Buddhist historiography, one of Buddhist monks who served an emperor on the battlefield.

The "Shaolin Monastery Stele" of 728

More than a hundred engraved steles embellish the Shaolin Monastery, monuments that span the entire history of the monastery. Whereas the oldest ones date from the sixth and seventh centuries, new ones are continuously being carved. In 2001, a Shaolin inscription was dedicated by the best-selling novelist Jin Yong (1924–), whose martial arts fiction extolled the monastery's heroic lore. Within the bewildering array of Shaolin stone documents, the so-called "Shaolin Monastery Stele" ("Shaolin si bei") of 728 stands out as the gem of the entire collection. This large monument—11.3 feet tall and 4.2 feet wide—has been studied by generations of scholars.[12] It is engraved with seven different texts, which were authored between 621 and 728. Despite their diverse dates, the seven texts all concern the contribution of Shaolin warriors to one of the early Tang military campaigns.

When in 618 Li Yuan (566–635) (Emperor Gaozu) proclaimed in Chang'an the establishment of a new Tang dynasty, he was far from the only contender to the throne of the defunct Sui dynasty. Before Tang rule was firmly established, Li Yuan had to overcome several military leaders who vied for power. One was the Sui general Wang Shichong (?–621), who in 619 declared himself emperor of a new Zheng dynasty. Wang, like his Sui predecessors, established his capital at Luoyang and at the height of his power controlled virtually all of Henan Province.

Li Yuan's second son, Li Shimin (600–649), was charged with the war against Wang. At the time, Li Shimin was titled Prince of Qin (Qin Wang). Five years later, after a successful coup in which he eliminated his elder brother, he was to succeed his father to the imperial throne. As an emperor, Li Shimin laid the foundation for Tang civil bureaucracy as well as the dynasty's military might. He rationalized the administration, implemented a new legal code, and led the Tang army to unparalleled military victories in central Asia. In the traditional histories, which refer to him by his posthumous temple name of Taizong, Li Shimin's reign is portrayed as a golden age of civil virtue and military might.[13]

Li Shimin's war against Wang Shichong lasted almost a year, from August 620 to June 621. Li instructed his generals to refrain from attacking Wang's capital outright. Instead, they were to disrupt the food supply to Luoyang by occupying strategic junctions along the waterways leading to it. Only after several months of fighting did Li Shimin gradually tighten his siege of Luoyang, which by the spring of 621 was reduced to famine.

At this point another Sui rebel, Dou Jiande (?–621), came to Wang Shichong's rescue. Dou, who had established his power base in the Shandong-Hebei border region, feared that a victory by Tang forces would be detrimental to his own imperial ambitions. Therefore he accepted Wang's plea to form at least a temporary alliance against the Tang, and in May 621 marched his army toward Luoyang. Li Shimin decided to confront Dou Jiande first and deal with Wang Shichong later. On May 28 he personally led his armies to a great victory over Dou Jiande at the strategic pass of Hulao, some sixty miles northeast of Luoyang (map 2). Following Dou's defeat, Wang Shichong had no choice but to surrender, and on June 4, 621 Luoyang fell into Li Shimin's hands. Shortly afterwards, Dou Jiande was executed and Wang Shichong was murdered on his route into exile.[14]

The "Shaolin Monastery Stele" reveals that Shaolin monks participated in Li Shimin's campaign against Wang Shichong. The texts inscribed on it attest that shortly before the Hulao victory, Shaolin monks defeated a contin-

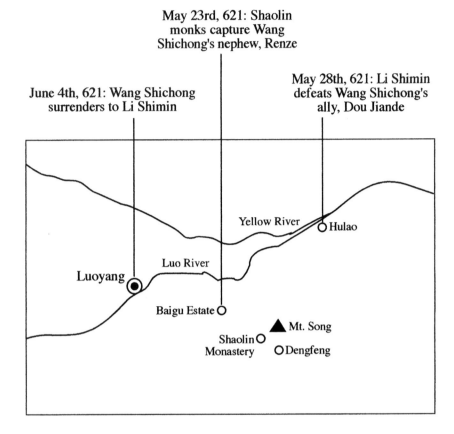

May 23rd, 621: Shaolin
monks capture Wang
Shichong's nephew, Renze

May 28th, 621: Li Shimin
defeats Wang Shichong's
ally, Dou Jiande

June 4th, 621: Wang Shichong
surrenders to Li Shimin

Yellow River   Hulao

Luo River
Luoyang

Baigu Estate

Mt. Song
Shaolin
Monastery   Dengfeng

MAP 2. Shaolin's contribution to Li Shimin's campaign against Wang Shichong.

gent of Wang Shichong's army that occupied the strategic Mt. Huanyuan, where the monastery's Cypress Valley Estate (Baigu zhuang) was situated (map 2). Moreover, the monks took Wang Shichong's nephew, Wang Renze, captive.[15] In gratitude, the future emperor Li Shimin bestowed upon them anew the estate they had liberated and appointed one of them general-in-chief (Da Jiangjun) in his army.

The seven texts inscribed on the "Shaolin Monastery Stele" include a history of the monastery, a letter of thanks from Li Shimin, and several Tang legal documents. They shed light on the monks' military activities from different angles:

Text 1: Pei Cui's Shaolin Monastery History

The longest of the seven texts inscribed on the "Shaolin Monastery Stele" is a detailed history of the monastery, authored in 728 by a prominent official in Emperor Xuanzong's (r. 712–755) government, minister of personnel (Libu shangshu) Pei Cui (ca. 670–736).[16] Pei alludes to two instances in which Shaolin monks resorted to arms, the first in the last years of the Sui Dynasty, when their monastery was attacked by bandits, and the second approximately a decade later, when they participated in Li Shimin's war against Wang Shichong:

> During the last years of the Daye reign period (605–616) the empire disintegrated. Bands of robbers plundered the population, clergy and laity alike. This monastery (Shaolin) was pillaged by roving bandits. The monks resisted them, whereupon the bandits set fire and burned the stūpas and courtyard. Within an instant all the buildings in the court perished in the flames. Only the Spirit Stūpa (Lingta) remained, visible afar, as lofty as ever. The heavenly beings protected it. The mountain spirits blessed it. What divine power was able to accomplish [in this case] surpassed anything known before.
>
> Fifty *li* (approximately seventeen miles) to the monastery's north-west is the Cypress Valley Estate (Baigu shu). Crowded peaks are arrayed there together. Deep valleys curve to and fro. Piled up stone steps lead to the clouds' edge. It overlooks the imperial capital (Luoyang). Its highest peak reaches the sun. Its slopes preside over the birds' route. During the Jin period (265–420) a fort (*wu*) was built there. During the Qi period (479–502) it served as the site of a commandery (*jun*). When Wang Chong (Wang Shichong) usurped the imperial title he established there a prefecture called Yuanzhou. Taking advantage of the site's strategic location, he placed there a signal tower as well as troops. He assembled an army at Luoyi (Luoyang), and was planning to seize the Buddhist Temple (Shaolin).
>
> The august Tang dynasty resonates with the halcyon days ordained by the five phases. It is blessed with the grand mandate of a thousand years. It wipes out the calamities caused by the evil tyrant's insatiable avarice. It delivers the people from disasters of extreme adversity. Emperor Taizong Wenhuang [Li Shimin] majestically arose at Taiyuan.[17] His army encamped at Guangwu.[18] He opened wide the commanding officer's tent [for counselors' advice]. He personally led his troops.
>
> The monks Zhicao, Huiyang, Tanzong, and the others examined to which of the contending parties divine grace was directed. They realized who deserved hymns of praise. They led the multitude in fighting the rebel army. They petitioned the emperor to express their complete submission. They captured [Wang Shi] chong's nephew, Renze, thereby pledging their allegiance to this dynasty.
>
> Taizong commended the monks' loyalty and courage. He repeatedly issued official documents expressing his support [of the Shaolin Monastery]. He graced the monks with a royal letter of praise, at the same time that he patronized the monastery with imperial almsgiving. He bestowed on the monastery forty *qing* of land [approximately 560

acres], and a water mill. These constitute the Cypress Valley Estate
(Baigu zhuang).[19]

Pei's history highlights the significance of Shaolin's Cypress Valley
(Baigu) Estate as the location, the cause, and the reward for the monks' participation in Li Shimin's campaign. Medieval monastic estates were usually
situated not in the intensely cultivated alluvial plains but rather in the high-
lands. In addition to arable lands, they comprised "woods, copses, pastures,
mountain gardens, and orchards."[20] The Shaolin farm was no exception. Bestowed on the monastery by the Sui emperor Wendi (Yang Jian) (r. 581–604),
the estate was located southeast of Luoyang, at the western edge of the Song
mountain range (map 2).[21] The steep Winding Path Mountain (Huanyuan
shan)—so named because of the curved trail leading to its peak[22]—towered
above the estate. "Crowded peaks are arrayed there together," writes Pei Cui.
"Deep valleys curve to and fro. Piled up stone steps lead to the clouds' edge.
It overlooks the imperial capital [Luoyang]."

The estate was named after a deep valley, lined with cypress trees, which
ran across it. The road from Luoyang to Dengfeng passed through this valley,
which was so narrow and overgrown with trees that according to medieval
sources, vehicles could not turn around in it.[23] Thus, Shaolin's estate commanded a crucial pass on the road to the eastern capital. Indeed, its military
significance had been recognized centuries before it was bestowed on the
monastery. As early as the Jin period (265–420), a fort (*wu*) was established at
Cypress Valley, and it was the site of bitter warfare all through the seventh century.[24] To this day the local village is named Cypress Valley *Fort* (Baigu wu).[25]

The strategic significance of Shaolin's Cypress Valley Estate explains why
both Wang Shichong and Li Shimin were eager to capture it. Pei Cui emphasizes that Wang "took advantage of the [estate's] strategic location" (*cheng qi di
xian*), placing a signal tower and troops there. In addition, the Sui rebel employed Cypress Valley for local administration. He established a county seat
there named, like the mountain above it, Huanyuan.[26] It was this military and
administrative center that the Shaolin monks conquered, earning the gratitude of the future Tang emperor.

Pei Cui does not allude to a Tang government request that the monks confront Wang Shichong. His chronicle suggests that it was their initiative to attack
the Sui rebel. The monks certainly resented Wang, who had robbed them of
their estate. However, strong as their resentment was, political calculations also
contributed to their military action. Pei notes that "monks Zhicao, Huiyang,
Tanzong and the others examined to which of the contending parties divine
grace was directed." The Shaolin clerics probably did not debate the respective
spiritual merits of the Tang rulers and Wang Shichong, but rather who was
more likely to win the war. Had they wagered on the wrong party this would
have been detrimental to their monastery. Instead their choice of the Tang dynasty guaranteed the prosperity of the Shaolin Temple for centuries to come.

What could have befallen the monastery had its monks made the wrong decision is suggested by events that took place more than a millennium later. In the early twentieth century Shaolin monks became embroiled in the war-lords' feuds that swept the north China plains. They sided with General Fan Zhongxiu (1888–1930) against Shi Yousan (1891–1940). As a boy, Fan had stud-ied the martial arts at the Shaolin Monastery, for which reason, presumably, its monks lent him their support. The results were disastrous. Fan was defeated, and on March 15, 1928, Shi set fire to the monastery, destroying some of its an-cient towers and halls. The flames partially damaged the "Shaolin Monastery Stele," which recorded the politically astute choice made by other Shaolin cler-ics fifteen hundred years earlier.[27]

Text 2: Li Shimin's letter of May 26, 621

Li Shimin himself confirmed that Shaolin monks had contributed to his campaign. On May 26, 621, three days after the monks captured Mt. Huanyuan,[28] Li Shimin addressed them a letter of thanks. Li was in the field, preparing his troops for the showdown with Dou Jiande two days later. Presumably he dic-tated the letter to one of his secretaries. The Prince of Qin did sign the letter though, and his autograph was later copied onto the Shaolin stele (figure 3):[29]

[FROM]: The Defender-in-Chief, Director of the Department of State Affairs, Director of the Branch Departments of State Affairs in the Shaandong Circuit and the Yizhou Circuit, Metropolitan Governor of Yongzhou, Military Marquis of the Left and the Right, General-in-Chief, Area Commander in Chief Commissioned with Extraordinary Powers

FIG. 3. Li Shimin's autograph "Shimin" as copied onto the 728 Shaolin stele.

for Liangzhou, Supreme Pillar of State (*shang zhuguo*), Prince of Qin, [Li] Shimin,

To: The Cypress Valley Fort (Baigu wu) Shaolin Monastery's Dean (*shangzuo*), and Abbot (*sizhu*), and their disciples, as well as to the military and civil leaders, officers, common people, and the rest:

Recently, there has been chaos under heaven. Nowhere in the land is there a lord, and the world is falling apart. The Way of the Three Vehicles (Buddhism) is declining. This has caused the Jambudvīpa (Yanfu) Continent to disintegrate. Warhorses sweep through the land. The Central Kingdom is boiling, and the devils are all contending.

This court [the Tang dynasty] has received the heavenly omens of government. It upholds the correct Buddhist truth. Riding the phoenix and turning the wheel (*lun*; Sanskrit: *cakra*), it glorifies the Great Treasure [of the Buddhist faith]. Therefore, virtue will reach the common folk, education will instruct the monastic community. Thus, the people will enjoy the grace of release from suffering, and all will be favored with the benefits of the other shore.

Wang Shichong usurped other people's position. He dared oppose the heavenly principles. He coveted the Dharma-Realm (Shaolin's Cypress Valley Estate). He acted recklessly, disregarding the laws of Karma.

Now, the winds of virtue are blowing far, and the beacon of wisdom is glowing near. The Buddhist eightfold path[30] is being opened, and throughout the land the Buddhist sanctuaries are being restored. Shaolin's Master of the Law (*fashi*), together with the other monks, deeply comprehended the changing circumstances and adapted to them. The monks immediately realized which action would yield the Buddhist fruit, and they succeeded in drawing an excellent plan. Together, they returned to the Earthly Paradise (*fudi*). They captured that evil bastard (Wang's nephew, Renze), and they cleansed the Pure Land (*jingtu*). The results of their respectful observance and expressed loyalty have become known at court. Their way of attainment and self-cultivation adds further glory to their Buddhist temple.

We heard [of Shaolin's contribution] with pleasure and appreciation. It surpasses imagination and words. The monastery should be supported, and its monks generously rewarded. Regardless of changing circumstances, the monastery should be provided with fixed income.

The crisis at the eastern capital will be resolved shortly. At the same time we should urge people to exert themselves and make a contribution, so that they provide example to future generations. Everyone should peacefully resume his previous vocation, forever enjoying heavenly blessings.

> Therefore I am sending to you the Supreme Pillar of State, the Dynasty-Founding, Commandery Duke of Deguang, [Li] Anyuan (?–633)[31] to express my appreciation. You may send here one or two commanders who made a contribution, so that I meet them. I will elaborate no more.
>
> THE THIRTIETH OF THE FOURTH MONTH [of the Wude reign period fourth year] (May 26th, 621).[32]

On the face of it, Li Shimin's letter expresses nothing but gratitude. In ornate parallel prose, characteristic of his later writings,[33] the Prince of Qin elaborates on the monks' courage and loyalty, which, he promises, would be amply rewarded. However, a closer reading reveals a subtler tone in the prince's dispatch. Even as he was praising their heroic spirit, Li Shimin warned the monks to desist from further military action. "Everyone should peacefully resume his previous vocation" (ge an jiu ye) is a reminder to the Shaolin clerics that their vocation is Buddhist learning. The Prince of Qin, who was absolutely certain of his coming victory—"the crisis at the eastern capital," he writes, "will be resolved shortly"—was preparing for peace, in which context he could not tolerate the unauthorized military activities of Buddhist clerics. Thus the future emperor's letter served a dual purpose, simultaneously praising and restraining the Shaolin monks.

Text 3: The Prince's Donation of 625

In his letter of May 26, 621, Li Shimin vowed to reward the Shaolin clerics. "Regardless of changing circumstances," he noted, "the monastery should be provided with fixed income." Four years later, on March 28, 625, the Prince of Qin fulfilled his promise and endowed the monastery with the Cypress Valley Estate. Previously, under the Sui regime, this same estate had already been bestowed upon the monastery. However, following the Sui disintegration and the war against Wang Shichong, its lands were confiscated by the Tang regime. In order for the Shaolin monks to enjoy it, the estate had to be conferred upon them anew.

The prince's donation should be evaluated in the context of his hostility to the Buddhist faith. On June 5, 621, a day after he captured Luoyang, Li Shimin decreed the closure of all the Buddhist monasteries in the eastern capital and the dispersal of the city's entire clergy, with the exception of sixty eminent monks and nuns.[34] There is some evidence that this blow to the church was also felt outside of Luoyang, where the administration proceeded to confiscate monastic property and defrock the clergy.[35] In 622, the Shaolin Monastery itself was closed and its monks sent home under the pretext that its lands had been illegally acquired. The monastery was allowed to reopen two years later only because of the military service it had rendered the dynasty.[36]

After he became emperor, Li Shimin's antipathy to the church did not abate. Even though he was careful not to stir opposition by an outright suppres-

sion of the religion, Li Shimin did issue a series of unprecedented anti-Buddhist
laws. In 629 he ordered the execution of illegally ordained monks, in 631 he forbade monks and nuns from receiving the homage of their parents, and in 637
he decreed that Daoist priests be given precedence over Buddhist monks in all
state ceremonies.[37] In his later years, the emperor did befriend one Buddhist
monk, the renowned pilgrim Xuanzang (596–664). However, he sought Xuanzang's counsel primarily on foreign affairs rather than on spiritual matters.
During his celebrated journey to India, Xuanzang gained an in-depth knowledge of western lands, for which reason the emperor implored him (unsuccess-
fully) to join his administration.[38]

Li Shimin's patronage of the Shaolin Monastery therefore was the exception rather than the rule. It resulted not from pious sentiments, which
the emperor had rarely harbored, but from his obligation to reward the
Shaolin monks for their military support. The emperor's disdain of the Buddhist faith underscores the significance of Shaolin's military activities as the
key to the monastery's prosperity. In a climate of hostility toward the church,
the military assistance the monastery had rendered the emperor was the
only assurance of its welfare.

Li Shimin's donation to the monastery took the form of an order, which
has attracted the attention of legal historians. As Niida Noboru has shown,
Tang period legal vocabulary distinguished between orders according to
which person issued them. An emperor's order was termed *ling* ("command"), an imperial prince's *jiao* ("instruction"), and so forth.[39] Since Li Shimin's donation was issued when he was still a prince, it was titled "instruction."
As inscribed on the "Shaolin Monastery Stele," this "instruction" includes
not only Li Shimin's original command, but also the communication of the
officials who carried it out.[40]

The monks' decision to engrave in stone the prince's donation was not
unique. During the Tang, as well as in later periods, it was common practice
to inscribe letters of patronage on steles. Such inscriptions, often specifying
the exact location and size of the bequeathed land, were intended to protect
the donation from infringement.[41] Occasionally, the inscription included
curses on any future violators. In Shaolin's case the inscription specified that
in addition to forty *qing* (approximately 560 acres) of land, the monastery
was granted a water mill (*shuinian*), which must have contributed to its income. During the medieval period, monasteries charged rent fees (usually
in flour) on the usage of their mills.[42]

Text 4: The Official Letter of 632

The legal woes surrounding Shaolin's Cypress Valley Estate did not end
with Li Shimin's donation of 625. As early as 626, Shaolin's property became
the subject of a lawsuit which concerned its size (forty *qing* or one hundred
qing) and legal status (should it be classified as "personal share land" (*koufen
tian*) or as "permanent monastic property" (*changzhu sengtian*)).[43] The case is

summarized in an official letter (*die*), signed by the Dengfeng County vice magistrate, and dated July 21, 632.

The official letter of 632 enriches our understanding of the war that preceded it by eleven years. In order to assess the monastery's property rights, Dengfeng County officials examined its military record. As conscientious judges (and historians), they gathered all the documents pertaining to the monks' participation in Li Shimin's campaign. Thus, they ascertained the date (May 23, 621) of the monks' Cypress Valley victory, they verified that one monk (Tanzong) was rewarded by appointment as a general-in-chief (*Da Jiangjun*) in Li's army, and they collected testimonies of the monks' military action:

> Following this testimony, we contacted Yanshi [County] by dispatch, asking them to cross-question [Liu] Wengchong and received a report from there to the effect that they had followed up Liu [Weng] chong for questioning. We received a report to the effect that: "The fact that previously, in the fourth month of Wude 4 (May 621), the monks of Shaolin Monastery turned Huanzhou over to legitimate rule is verified . . ."
>
> We went on to find Li Changyun and the other man concerned and questioned them. We are in receipt of a document to the effect that their testimony corroborated that of [Liu] Wengchong.
>
> We further questioned Sengyan and his fellow monks if as they say the monks of Shaolin [Monastery] received awards for the merit they showed in their action of returning [the fortress] to legitimate rule, why nothing was known of the monks receiving offices. In the testimony [regarding this matter] they stated:
>
> "We monks, previously on the twenty-seventh day of the fourth month of Wude 4 (May 23, 621) overtook the fortress and submitted it to the state. On the thirtieth day of the same month (May 26), we were honored to receive a letter containing a decree thanking us for our efforts. The letter containing this decree is still extant. Furthermore, in the second month of Wude 8 (625), we received a decree returning forty *qing* of monastic lands. The letter containing this decree is also extant. At that time, awards of offices were conferred on some monks, but the monks only wanted to pursue the religious life, to follow the [Buddhist] way and hold religious services to recompense the favor accorded by the state, so they did not presume to take up those official posts."
>
> The [Shaolin] Monastery monk, Tanzong, was awarded the title general-in-chief (Da Jiangjun); Zhao Xiaozai was awarded the title upper prefecture officer [dignified-as-general-in-chief]; and Li Changyun was awarded the title dignified-as [general-in-chief].[44] Moreover he is still here today.
>
> Furthermore, we have obtained the imperial decree, the [prince's] instruction, the certificates of land-return to the monks, etc. We have examined and verified them.[45]

Texts 5 and 6: The Emperor's Gift of 724

The Shaolin monks' assistance to Li Shimin guaranteed them the support of his successors. A hundred years after the Cypress Valley victory, the Tang emperor Xuanzong (r. 712–755) bestowed upon the Shaolin Monastery a caption in his own calligraphy for the "Shaolin Monastery Stele" (figure 4). This symbolic act of patronage created a link between Xuanzong and his venerable ancestor Li Shimin, whose letter to the Shaolin monks was to be engraved on the same stele.

Two brief official letters (*die*), which were themselves to be inscribed on the Shaolin stele, announced the bestowal upon the monastery of Emperor Xuanzong's handwritten caption, along with Li Shimin's autographed letter, a copy of which had been kept in the imperial archives.[46] The second letter, dated Kaiyuan, eleventh year, twelfth month, twenty-first day (January 21, 724), is noteworthy for the high-ranking official who signed it: Zhang Yue (667–730), who served as president of the secretariat (*zhongshu ling*).[47] Zhang issued his letter to the Shaolin Monastery in his additional capacity as director of the Academy in the Hall of Elegance and Rectitude (*Lizhengdian xiushuyuan*). His letter attests that the caption of the "Shaolin Monastery Stele" was handwritten by Emperor Xuanzong.[48] Furthermore, it verifies the authenticity of Li Shimin's letter, which was examined by a team of experts working under his supervision.[49]

It is noteworthy that Xuanzong's patronage of Shaolin, like his ancestor's benefaction, did not result from Buddhist piety. Xuanzong "acted with greater determination than any of his predecessors to curtail the power of the Buddhist clergy."[50] In 714, for example, he issued a ban on the construction of all new

FIG. 4. Xuanzong's imperial calligraphy on the 728 Shaolin stele. His caption reads: "Taizong Wen Huangdi's [Li Shimin] Imperial Letter [to the Shaolin monks].

monasteries, and in 727 he ordered the dismantling of all village chapels. Evidently, his support of the Shaolin Monastery was due solely to the monks' military assistance to his predecessor.

The emperor's benefaction of Shaolin was not merely symbolic. In addition to his imperial calligraphy, Xuanzong granted it property rights. In 722 he exempted the Shaolin Monastery from the confiscation order that was applied to all other monastic estates.[51] As Tonami Mamoru has suggested, it was probably this confiscation order—which they so narrowly escaped—that convinced the Shaolin monks of the necessity to engrave in stone their military exploits. The "Shaolin Monastery Stele" was erected to ensure that future rulers would be as mindful as Xuanzong had been of the monastery's contribution to the dynasty's founding.[52]

The construction of the "Shaolin Monastery Stele" safeguarded the monastery's fortunes, as its monks had hoped. In 798, seven decades after its dedication, the monastery was granted an official letter that reiterated the stele's import. A senior government official named Gu Shaolian (fl. 800), who began his career as assistant magistrate of Dengfeng County and concluded it as regent of the eastern capital, consented to the monks' request and, in celebration of the monastery's renovation, compiled a brief history. Shaolin monks, wrote Gu Shaolian, "capture bandits and succor the faithful. They suppress evil troops everywhere; they protect the Pure Land in times of adversity. This adds glory to our Tang dynasty."[53]

Even during the darkest moment in Tang Buddhist history, the memory of the monks' heroism guaranteed their safety. On April 6, 845, during the height of Emperor Wuzong's persecution of the Buddhist faith, the governor of Henan, Lu Zhen, graced the Shaolin Monastery with a visit, which was recorded on a Shaolin stele.[54] The governor's visit attests that the monastery had been spared at least the brunt of the government's Buddhist purge. Even as hundreds of other monasteries were being destroyed, the Shaolin Monastery enjoyed the patronage of high-ranking officials.

Text 7: The List of Thirteen Heroic Monks

The last text on the "Shaolin Monastery Stele" is a list of thirteen monks whose distinguished service in battle had been recognized by Li Shimin (figure 5). One monk, Tanzong, is already mentioned as a general-in-chief in the official letter of 632. This monk-cum-general is also cited, along with monks Zhicao and Huiyang, in Pei Cui's history of the monastery. Here is the complete list of his companions:

List of Shaolin Monastery Cypress Valley Estate monks who, during the Tang, Wude reign period, 4th year (621), were cited by Emperor Taizong Wenhuang for meritorious service:

Dean (*shangzuo*), monk Shanhu.
Abbot (*sizhu*), monk Zhicao.

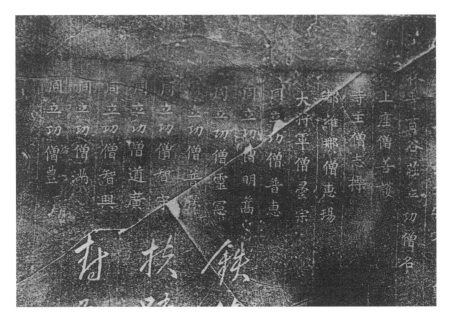

FIG. 5. List of the thirteen heroic monks on the 728 Shaolin stele.

Overseer (*duweina*), monk Huiyang.
General-in-chief (*da jiangjun*), monk Tanzong.

With them, were noted for meritorious service: monk Puhui, monk Mingsong, monk Lingxian, monk Pusheng, monk Zhishou, monk Daoguang, monk Zhixing, monk Man, monk Feng.[55]

The official letter of 632 noted that following their Cypress Valley victory, several Shaolin monks had been offered official posts, which, with the exception of Tanzong, they politely declined. It is conceivable that the monks in question are the thirteen listed in Text 7. However, it needs to be emphasized that the text itself does not date from Li Shimin's time.[56] Neither signed nor dated, the list of thirteen heroic monks was probably compiled when the "Shaolin Monastery Stele" was erected (728), if not later.[57] Thus even though some names in it are doubtless accurate (notably General Tanzong's), others may reflect the growth of popular lore surrounding the monks' victory.

Military Engagements or Military Training?

The legal vocabulary that enwraps the Shaolin inscriptions provides precise information: In 621, Shaolin monks went to war for Li Shimin, the future Tang emperor. The circumstances of their monastery being rewarded by state property permitted no error. Officials at all government levels—from the vice magistrate of Dengfeng County to the president of the secretariat—examined the details of the monks' military victory and affixed their signatures to legal documents confirming it. There can be no doubt, then, that as early as the Tang period, Shaolin monks fought.

Whereas the Shaolin monks' participation in warfare cannot be questioned, we may still ask whether, during the medieval period, they trained for it. Even though, at first glance, going to battle appears indistinguishable from practicing for it, the two are quite different. Shaolin monks might or might not have been trained for battle at their temple. For example, those monks that fought might have received martial training outside the monastery, or else they might have been trained *ad hoc* for the military engagements in which they participated (rather than being regularly instructed in fighting as part of their monastic regimen). It is even possible that Tang period Shaolin monks fought despite receiving no military training.

A comparison of the available Tang and Ming evidence may clarify the question. A wealth of sixteenth- and seventeenth-century sources attest not only that Shaolin monks participated in given battles, but also that they regularly practiced fighting. Late Ming visitors to the temple invariably allude to the sight of military exercises and the sound of clanking weaponry. By that period, Shaolin monks had developed their own fighting techniques, which had attracted renowned military experts to their monastery. The Shaolin method of staff fighting (*gun fa*) is abundantly praised in late Ming military literature. By contrast, the Tang inscriptions do not allude to a fighting technique developed by the Shaolin monks. Indeed they do not mention *how* Shaolin monks fought, or which weapons they employed in battle. Furthermore, in the poems and travelogues of renowned Tang literati that visited Shaolin, no allusion is made to military training at the temple.

Let us review what the "Shaolin Monastery Stele" does tell us. It alludes to *two* instances in which Shaolin monks resorted to arms—the first around 610 when they warded off an attack by bandits, and the second in 621 when they lent military support to the future Tang emperor, Li Shimin. That they participated, within a relatively short period of time, in *two* armed conflicts could indicate that some Shaolin monks did receive regular military training. In addition, the Shaolin inscriptions leave no doubt that one Shaolin monk (Tanzong) *was* appointed a general in Li's army. Presumably he was thus honored because of his outstanding fighting skills, strengthening the case for regular martial practice at the temple. Nevertheless, in order to conclude that Tang Shaolin monks practiced fighting, more evidence of their military training—or at least a hint of it—is necessary.

Such a hint may be provided by a short story included in a Tang anthology attributed to Zhang Zhuo (ca. 660–741). Its protagonist is a historical Shaolin monk named Sengchou (480–560), whom Buddhist historiography extolled as a master of meditation (*dhyāna*). Sengchou studied under Shaolin's Indian founder, Batuo, who reportedly exclaimed to him, "East of the Congling Mountains (in central Asia), the person who has attained the highest understanding of meditation is you."[58] However, Zhang Zhuo's anecdote concerns not Sengchou's profundity of meditation, but his fighting skills:

> The Northern Qi (550–577) monk Chou (Sengchou) came from Ye (today's Anyang, Henan). In his childhood he shaved his head and became a novice. His classmates were numerous. Whenever they had free time they would practice wrestling and pouncing for entertainment. Because the Dhyāna Master (Sengchou) was weak they bullied him. One after another they abused him and beat him up.
>
> The Dhyāna Master was ashamed of this. He entered the hall and shut its gate behind him. Clinging to Vajrapāṇi's feet, he addressed the god with the following vow: "Because I am frail, my fellow novices despise me. My humiliation is too great. It would be better to die. You are famous for your strength, so you are the one to help me. I will hang on to your feet for seven days. If you do not endow me with strength, I am sure to die right here rather than renounce my pledge."
>
> Having pronounced this vow, he proceeded to beseech the god most earnestly. During the first two nights his dedication to his purpose grew stronger. During the sixth night, just before dawn, Vajrapāṇi was revealed to him. In his hands the god held a large bowl, full to the brim with sinews-flesh.
>
> "Boy!" he said to Chou. "Do you wish to become strong?"
> "I do."
> "Are you determined?"
> "I am."
> Can you eat sinews-flesh?"
> "I cannot."
> "Why?" inquired the deity.
> "Monks are supposed to renounce meat."
>
> In response, the god lifted his bowl, and with his knife proceeded to force the sinews-flesh upon Sengchou. At first the Dhyāna Master refused to accept, but when the god threatened him with his *vajra* club (*jin'gang chu*), he was so terrified that he did eat. In a short while he finished his meal, whereupon the god said to him: "Now, you are already extremely strong. However, you should fully uphold the [Buddhist] teachings, Beware!"
>
> Since it was already daylight, Sengchou returned to his room. His fellow novices all interrogated him: "Scumbag! Where have you been just now?!" Chou did not answer. In a short while they all went to the hall for their common meal. After eating, they again entertained themselves with fighting. The Dhyāna Master said: "I have strength now. I suspect not the same kind as yours." Then he flexed his arms, revealing his powerful sinews and bones. He looked practically like a god.

Before they recovered their senses, the Dhyāna Master said, "I will give you a demonstration," whereupon he entered the hall and started walking horizontally on the walls. He advanced first from the east, then from west, a total of several hundred feet. Then he leaped upwards, his head hitting the ceiling-beams several times. Finally he lifted several thousand pounds.[59] His fighting was swift and powerful.

Those who belittled him prostrated themselves on the ground, their sweat trickling. No one dared face up to him.[60]

The violence and abuse recorded by Zhang Zhuo seem hardly fit for a Buddhist temple. Neither are the martial exercises he describes appropriate for Buddhist monks. Still, if his story reflects historical circumstances, then fighting was practiced in some Tang period Buddhist monasteries. It is possible, therefore, that medieval Chinese monks—either at Shaolin or in other temples—not only participated in war, but also trained for it.

Martial Deities and Martial Monks

Zhang Zhuo's story of monk Sengchou could have been rejected as pure fiction—neither related to Buddhist practice nor to Shaolin lore—if it were not for an intriguing motif it shared with both. Vajrapāṇi, whose divine help Sengchou sought, figured in Buddhist mythology as a military god who bestows strength. Moreover, we know that at least in later periods he had been worshipped in that very capacity at the Shaolin Monastery.

It is striking that a religion as intent on peace as Buddhism would arrive in China equipped with an entire gallery of martial gods. Buddhist iconography reveals to us an unexpectedly violent aspect of the faith. The Buddha is usually flanked by heavily armed, ferocious-looking deities who trample demons underfoot.[61] Vajrapāṇi (Chinese: Jin'gang (shen)) belongs to this category of divine warriors. As indicated by his name, his weapon is the mythic *vajra*, or thunderbolt (*jin'gang* in Chinese). By the time it was incorporated into the Buddhist arsenal, the magic instrument had enjoyed a venerable history. The Hindu god Indra had employed the *vajra* to vanquish the cosmic dragon Vṛtra.[62] The god's armament had assumed diverse shapes in visual art: the sword, the spear, the staff, the discus, and two transverse bolts that cross each other. Most commonly, however, the *vajra* was imagined as an ornamented short scepter, sometimes resembling a flower (figure 6).[63]

Vajrapāṇi, the *vajra* wielder, has been worshipped in China either as one deity or as two fearsome spirits—the so-called "Two Venerable Kings" (Erwangzun)—that stand guard on each side of temple gates. His iconography highlights his bodily strength. Unlike other tutelary divinities, Vajrapāṇi is not clad in armor. He wears light clothes, revealing his sinewy physique. His sturdy chest is exposed, and his muscular arms embrace his iconic

FIG. 6. Vajrapāṇi wielding a flower-like *vajra* in a ninth-century painting from Dunhuang. (© Copyright the Trustees of the British Museum).

FIG. 7. Vajrapāṇi's muscular physique in a Tang statue.

weapon (figure 7).[64] "Vajrapāṇi's images," notes an art historian, "carry but scanty dress, no doubt in order to permit full exhibition of the extravagantly exaggerated muscles."[65] His naked strength has likely been one reason for Vajrapāṇi's appeal to martial artists—whether the fictional monk Sengchou or the historical Shaolin warriors.

Chinese literature highlighted the raw strength that emanated from the divine warrior's icon. Here is a sixteenth-century author describing a pair of Vajrapāṇi's molten statues:

One has an iron face and steel whiskers as if alive;
One has bushy brows and round eyes that seem real.
On the left, the fist bones like raw iron jut out;
On the right, the palms are cragged like crude bronze.

Golden chain armor of splendid luster;
Bright helmets and wind-blown sashes of silk.[66]

Guardian deities such as Vajrapāṇi have won their tutelary posts due to their familiarity with the enemies of the faith. All too often they began their careers as lowly demons who had been converted to Buddhism to fight their own kind. As experts on evil, they were considered its most effective antidotes. "Figures originally functioning as disease-demons," writes Michel Strickmann, "have by the early medieval period become homeopathic protectors against the very ailments which previously, in their old, unenlightened, pre-Buddhist days, they had themselves provoked."[67] Vajrapāṇi's murky origins of a fiend are betrayed by his title of *vajra-yakṣa* (*jin'gang yecha*), identifying him as a Hindu *yakṣa* spirit. His contradictory traits of a demon *and* a demon queller are suggested by the ferociousness of his visual representations, the fire halo surrounding his head, the wide-opened jaws, and the protruding fangs (compare figures 6, 7, and 8).

The notion that Vajrapāṇi's vigor could be bestowed upon his devotees was not the product of Zhang Zhuo's literary imagination. Buddhist scriptures attest that the god had been worshipped as a provider of strength, even though they refer to him by one of his other names: Nārāyaṇa (Chinese: Naluoyantian, or Naluoyan). The latter had been used as an honorific of several Indian deities, (including Vishnu). In Chinese Buddhist texts it was commonly applied to Vajrapāṇi, denoting either the single warrior, or, when he assumed his dual form, the one standing guard on the right.[68]

Originally, Nārāyaṇa's powers were sought by magic means. The *Sutra of the Assembled Charms* (*Tuoluoni ji jing*), which was compiled in China on the basis of largely Indian materials in 654, includes two of his magic formulas, complete with verbal spells (Sanskrit: *mantra*; Chinese: *zhou*) and hand symbolisms (Sanskrit: *mudrā*; Chinese: *yinxiang*). These charms guarantee the practitioner the "boundless powers" (*wubian li*) of Nārāyaṇa, so much so that he will be able to "move mountains and churn oceans."[69]

Magic gave way to supplication in at least some Chinese Buddhist texts. In his *Dictionary of the Buddhist Canon* (*Yiqie jing yinyi*), Huilin (737–820) explains that Nārāyaṇa's powers could be elicited through prayer. Much like Zhang Zhuo, the Buddhist author emphasizes that earnestness is the key to the god's grace. "Those who wish to obtain great strength apply themselves to the nourishment of all living beings. If they earnestly beseech [Nārāyaṇa], they all obtain divine strength" (*Ruo jingcheng qidao, duo huo shen li ye*).[70]

The Buddhist conception of Nārāyaṇa as provider of strength influenced Shaolin religious practice. Archaeology proves that this deity had been worshipped at the monastery for his might. A twelfth-century stele, still extant at the monastery, depicts the powerful divinity brandishing his *vajra* (figure 8). Commissioned by Shaolin's abbot Zuduan (1115–1167), the stele features one of Nārāyaṇa's magic formulas, as copied from the *Sutra of the Assembled Charms*. A brief explanation follows:

Fig. 8. Twelfth-century Shaolin stele of Nārāyaṇa (Vajrapāṇi).

According to the scripture, this deity (Nārāyaṇa) is a manifestation of Avalokiteśvara (Guanyin). If a person who compassionately nourishes all living beings employs this [deity's] charm, it will increase his body's strength (*zengzhang shen li*). It fulfills all vows, being most efficacious. . . . Therefore those who study Nārāyaṇa's hand-symbolism (*mudrā*), those who seek his spell (*mantra*), and those who search for his image are numerous. Thus we have erected this stele to spread this transmission.

    Stele re-erected (*chong shang*) by Shaolin's abbot Zuduan.[71]

Even though Zuduan's stele quotes from the *Sutra of the Assembled Charms*, its understanding of the powers bestowed by Nārāyaṇa differs. The *Sutra* promises the possessor of Nārāyaṇa's charm that he will be endowed with "boundless powers" that are *not* embodied in his person. They are abstract magic influences to which presumably he has access. By contrast, the Shaolin stele—like Zhang Zhuo's story of the Shaolin cleric Sengchou—localizes Nārāyaṇa's strength within the practitioner's physique. Zuduan promises his Shaolin readers not intangible magic abilities but "an increase of [their] body's strength" (*zengzhang shen li*). He vouches that their sinews and bones would grow stronger.

The Shaolin stele reveals, therefore, how martial monks transformed a magic formula to suit their physical training agenda. Fighting monks such as Sengchou in Zhang Zhuo's anecdote were not interested in ethereal magic abilities. Their objective was more concrete: They required tougher muscles that would enable them to better perform their military exercises. Zuduan's Shaolin stele attests that they sought this physical goal with the ancient provider of Buddhist magic power, Nārāyaṇa.

Even though it dates from the Jin, Zuduan's stele shows that the Shaolin cult of Nārāyaṇa originated prior to that period. The stele is presented as "re-erected by Zuduan," suggesting that the monastery had featured a similar icon of this martial deity in earlier times. How much earlier it is impossible to say. However, considering the evidence of Zhang Zhuo's story, it is conceivable that during the Tang period, Shaolin monks worshiped Nārāyaṇa. If so, martial mythology had been related to monastic martial practice as early as medieval times.

Meat, Wine, and Fighting Monks

One element in Zhang Zhuo's story remains to be noted: the connection between fighting and the consumption of meat. As a prerequisite for strengthening Sengchou, Vajrapāṇi demands that his devotee violate a primary article of his faith by consuming animal flesh. When the monk refuses, the Buddhist god himself shoves the forbidden food down his throat. The association of martial monks with meat was to remain a permanent feature of martial arts literature. Novels, plays, and more recently films and television serials have invariably portrayed fighting monks as meat gobblers (and usually wine guzzlers as well). From the Tang period all through the twentieth century, fictional martial monks have delighted in nothing better than alcohol and animal flesh. The significance of meat in the fighting monk's ethos has been such that we will briefly stray from our chronological frame to discuss it synchronically—in sources ranging from medieval times to the present.

Vegetarianism, we should hasten to note, is not universally observed by Buddhist monks. Early Buddhist scriptures are not unanimous on the monastic diet: Whereas some Mahāyāna sutras do advocate abstention from animal flesh, compilations of monastic law for the most part do not prohibit meat per se. They only instruct monks to refrain from eating animals that have been slaughtered expressly for them. (As long as the animal has been butchered for others it is permitted for the clerics as well.) The inconsistency of the literature has been reflected in the divergence of practice. In most Theravāda countries, monks do eat meat. By contrast, Chinese Buddhism has been closely linked to vegetarianism. Beginning in medieval times, the abstention from meat has formed an important aspect of the identity of Chinese Buddhists, being observed not only by monks but often by lay believers.[72] Tang readers of Zhang Zhuo's story would have been startled therefore by the Buddhist god's insistence that his devotee transgress a defining tenet of their religion.

Why then were Chinese fighting monks imagined to relish animal flesh? One reason has been the assumption that meat is indispensable for physical strength. To this day there are those who, believing that athletic achievements require a meat-based diet, surmise that Shaolin monks consume it. However, the literary motif of the carnivorous fighting monk also mirrors another supposition, that those who violate one monastic prohibition (of war) are likely to transgress another (of meat). Occasionally, the two vices are metaphorically combined, as the savage monk is imagined feasting on the flesh of his fallen enemies. Before he heads for battle, the monkish protagonist of Dong Jieyuan's (fl. 1200) medley-play, *Story of the Western Wing*, exclaims, "Today I'll have meat to eat. . . . I'll mow down the thieves with my sword. Let them be pastry fillings for our meal!"[73] In the popular imagination, the cruelty of fighting has become indistinguishable from the brutality of a carnivorous diet.

One of the most memorable fighting monks in Chinese literature is Lu Zhishen, protagonist of the early Ming novel *Water Margin* (*Shuihu zhuan*) (ca. 1400). Also known as the "Tattooed Monk" (Hua Heshang), Lu is ordained at a Shanxi province monastery, where historical fighting monks practiced the martial arts. This is the Mt. Wutai monastic complex, the bravery of whose fighting monks—as we will see below—had been celebrated from the northern Song (960–1127). The novel has Lu Zhishen consume meat and wine inside the temple. When he goes so far as to force animal flesh into the mouths of his scandalized fellow monks, he is thrown out of the monastery and assumes the career of an itinerant martial artist. The fighting monk's adventures lead

him eventually to the heroic band of rebels who live by the "Water Margin" at
the Liangshan Marsh.

The novel highlights Lu's dietary transgressions, having him devour dog
meat, which, though consumed in parts of China, is shunned by many Chinese. The popular Chinese religion regards dogs as ritually polluting, for
which reason it also considers them magically potent. In Taiwan, for example, canine deities are the subject of nightly worship, and dog flesh is
sometimes utilized in black magic.[74] This does not deter the carnivorous Lu
Zhishen, who eagerly consumes *all* meat. The narrator exploits the literary
topos of the meat-eating monk for all its worth, savoring each detail as the
dog-hungry Lu thrusts both hands into the animal's carcass. It is no accident
that he has his savage protagonist garnish his meal with garlic, which, like
meat, is shunned by Chinese Buddhists:[75]

> Lu consumed ten big bowls of wine. "Have you any meat?" he asked. "I
> want a platter."
>
> "I had some beef earlier in the day," replied the proprietor, "but it's
> all sold out."
>
> Lu Zhishen caught a whiff of the fragrance of cooking meat. He
> went into the yard and found a dog boiling in an earthenware pot by the
> compound wall.
>
> "You've got dog meat," he said. "Why don't you sell me any?"
>
> "I thought as a monk you wouldn't eat it, so I didn't ask."
>
> "I've plenty of money here." Lu pulled out some silver and handed it
> over. "Bring me half."
>
> The proprietor cut off half the dog carcass and placed it on the
> table with a small dish of garlic sauce. Lu tore into it delightedly with
> both hands. At the same time he consumed another ten bowls of wine.
> He found the wine very agreeable and kept calling for more.[76]

Lu's dietary misdemeanor was taken up, six hundred years after the novel's
composition, by a movie that portrays Shaolin monks as dog eaters. Produced
in 1982, the film *Shaolin Temple* (*Shaolin si*) has played a significant role in the
monastery's modern history. Among the biggest blockbusters in mainland cinema history, it featured some of the greatest Chinese martial artists, most notably the legendary Li Lianjie (Jet Li) (b. 1963), who by the age of eighteen had
five times earned the title of All-Round National Champion. At the tender age
of eleven, Li had performed at the White House as part of a Chinese martial
arts tour, which figured in the hesitant beginnings of diplomatic relations between China and the United States. Eight years later, he was cast in the movie
Shaolin Temple as a monk, appearing side by side with some of the monastery's
own martial artists. The movie, which was filmed on location, aroused tremendous interest in the Shaolin Monastery. Following its screening, thousands of
aspiring martial artists flocked to the temple, initiating the construction of

dozens of fighting schools around it. Thus, reality imitated fiction, as the success of a movie on Shaolin contributed to the monastery's revival.[77]

Playing a major role in the monastery's modern history, *Shaolin Temple* furnishes a striking example of historical continuity. The film's subject matter is the monks' historical assistance to Li Shimin, which took place thirteen hundred years earlier. Indeed, the movie features the authentic Shaolin Monastery stele of 728, with which we have been concerned in preceding pages. This is not to say that history is not fictionally embellished. In the movie, the monks do not merely fight for Li Shimin, but they also save his life. In gratitude the emperor travels to Shaolin, where he himself exempts the monks from their faith's dietary rules, permitting them to consume meat. The political sanction is joined by a theological one; after they feast on dog meat, the monks pronounce, "When the Buddha is in your heart, meat and wine are nothing."

The stubborn recurrence of meat eating in fighting monks' fiction—from Zhang Zhuo's Tang period story of monk Sengchou to the 1980s movie *Shaolin Temple*—suggests that it might not be historically unfounded. Perhaps literary carnivorous monks had been fashioned after *real* Shaolin warriors. If so, at least some Shaolin monks disregarded not only their faith's prohibition of war, but also its proscription of meat. In his *Historian's Craft*, Marc Bloch notes that it is sometimes useful to conduct historical investigations "backwards"—from the present to the past—"for the natural progression of all research is from the best (or least badly) understood to the most obscure."[78] We may therefore follow his clue and begin our inquiry into Shaolin dietary history by an examination of the monastery's current conditions.

In a series of essays published in the California-based magazine *Kung Fu Tai Chi*, Gene Ching has unraveled the complexities of the Shaolin community. The title "Shaolin Monk" has been assumed by practitioners so diverse that it stretches our very understanding of Buddhist monasticism. The Shaolin fraternity includes at least four disciple types. At the core stand Buddhist-ordained clerics who reside inside the historical monastery itself. Then there is the much larger category of Shaolin-ordained monks, who, having graduated from the monastery's martial program, left it to pursue an itinerant military career, often opening up their own Shaolin martial schools. A third "Shaolin monk" group is made of professional martial artists, who have never been ordained as Buddhist clerics, but nevertheless—since they belong to the monastery's performing company—don monastic robes. Sometimes dubbed "fake monks" or "performance monks," they appear either in local shows for tourists or in international tours. Finally, there is the vast category of lay disciples (*sujia dizi*), accomplished martial artists who have been trained at the monastery but have never been ordained as Buddhist clerics (which they do not presume to be). Many of the latter were born in the monastery's Dengfeng County vicinity, and their families have been practicing Shaolin fighting for generations. Indeed, some of the greatest masters of the Shaolin fighting style are lay practitioners such as Liang Yiquan (b. 1931) and Liu Baoshan (b. 1931).[79]

As to Buddhist dietary laws, they are kept by the first type of Shaolin-residing clerics only. Meat is *not* provided in today's Shaolin Temple, and Buddhist monks who live inside the monastery adhere to a vegetarian diet. By contrast, most other Shaolin disciples are openly carnivorous. Lay practitioners of the Shaolin martial arts for the most part consume meat. Even more striking, Shaolin-ordained monks do so as well. Among the fighting monks who have left the monastery to open private schools, many—though not all—*do* eat meat. These tough martial artists continue to present themselves as monks, donning Buddhist uniforms, all the while consuming animal flesh. Indeed they give the impression that carnivorousness is an integral element of the martial monk's (*wu seng*) ethos. When interviewed about their dietary habits, they explain that Shaolin fighting monks have always consumed meat, sometimes citing the legend celebrated in the film *Shaolin Temple*, according to which it was Emperor Li Shimin who absolved the monks from the rule of vegetarianism. Indeed, it is hard to know whether this novel apology for carnivorousness preceded the movie or originated with it.

As the Shaolin community internationalized, its dietary customs spread overseas. In recent years several Shaolin fighting monks emigrated to the United States, where they opened martial arts schools. Nowadays, "Shaolin Temples" can be found in places as diverse as Cupertino, California; Houston, Texas; and New York. At least some are headed by Shaolin-ordained fighting monks who are openly carnivorous. Yanming, founder of the Manhattan Shaolin Temple, for example, eats meat, drinks wine, and is married to boot, all the while presenting himself as a Buddhist monk and donning monastic robes. Indeed, Yanming's Shaolin identity is important not only for religious reasons but also for business ones. It is by virtue of his being an authentic "Shaolin monk" that Yanming has been able to attract martial students, among them such celebrities as the rap music superstar RZA of the band "Wu-Tang Clan," named after the Chinese Wudang martial arts school.[80]

Living as he does in the remote United States, Yanming's dietary transgressions do not threaten his fellow monks who stayed at the monastery. However, other carnivorous "Shaolin monks" reside in the monastery's vicinity, where they come into daily contact with its vegetarian inhabitants. The majority of ordained monks who have left the monastery are making a living in Dengfeng County. Their martial schools are situated around the temple, where they regularly compete with resident monks. Similarly, when they are not touring faraway countries, Shaolin "performing monks" reside at the temple, from which they sneak out for meat snacks in nearby restaurants. Finally, lay disciples come and go to the temple to meet and train with their old masters. Thus, Shaolin-residing vegetarian monks come into close contact with other types of Shaolin practitioners who do eat meat.

The proximity of Shaolin Buddhist monks to what could be described as "semi-monks," "half monks," or "fake monks" has been one reason for Abbot Yongxin's (b. 1965) decision to physically remove the latter's residences from the monastery's vicinity. When he assumed his leadership position in 1999, Yongxin expelled from the monastery several high-profile carnivorous fighting monks. Backed by the Henan provincial authorities, he proceeded in the following year with an ambitious plan of dismantling hundreds of schools, restaurants, gift shops, and residential shacks from the temple's surroundings. The controversial project, which was critically reviewed in the foreign press, was motivated in part by aesthetic considerations. Like fellow-minded government officials, Yongxin wished to restore Shaolin to its pristine beauty, valued not only in its own right but also as a means of securing the temple's bid to become a UNESCO-recognized World Heritage Site.[81] However, religious concerns contributed to the relocation project as well. Apparently, Yongxin was attempting to create a physical boundary between his Buddhist sanctuary and the larger Shaolin community, which does not necessarily adhere to monastic laws.

Equipped with the example of Yongxin's purge, we may begin our "backwards" journey in time with a similar attempt to purify the Shaolin Monastery that was ordered by an emperor two and a half centuries earlier. In 1735, the governor-general of Henan and Shandong, Wang Shijun (?–1756), reported to the throne his plan to renovate the Shaolin Temple. The governor-general included in his memorial detailed drawings of the planned reconstruction. It was perhaps typical of the reigning emperor, who prided himself on reading government documents late into the night, that he did not perfunctorily approve the plan. Instead, the diligent Yongzheng emperor (reigned 1723–1735) carefully reviewed the sketches with an eye not to their architectural elegance, but to their implications for the monastery's supervision. The temple's reconstruction, the sovereign ordered, should be executed so as to get rid of fake monks, who violate monastic regulations:

> We have inspected the drawings and noticed that there are twenty-five gate-houses, which are located at some distance from the monastery proper. Like stars scattered far apart, none is situated within the temple. Throughout our empire, it has always been the case that most subsidiary shrine monk-types do not observe monastic regulations. Doing evil and creating disturbances, they are Buddhism's inferior sorts. Today, as the Shaolin Monastery is undergoing renovation, and it is becoming one temple, these subsidiary shrine monks should not be allowed to stay outside of it, where they are hard to supervise and control.[82]

According to the eighteenth-century emperor, corrupt monks did not reside inside Shaolin proper, but in scattered residences in its vicinity. This is not unlike the modern situation where most carnivorous practitioners—ordained and lay alike—live in private Shaolin martial schools, which are spread throughout Dengfeng County. The monarch alluded to these unscrupulous disciples as *fangtou seng* ("subsidiary shrine monks"). In the Buddhist idiom of late imperial times, the term *fangtou* designated either a monastic building or—as the emperor had in mind—a semi-independent shrine, located in the periphery of a large temple. Such subsidiary hermitages were established to en-hance the wealth and prestige of the parent temple, or, in case it was over-crowded, to provide it with additional housing space. As early as the seventeenth century, some monastic leaders were apprehensive of religious transgressions committed in subsidiary shrines. Monks in branch temples were more difficult to supervise than those residing in large monasteries, for which reason some clerics objected to the establishment of *fangtou*. The Vinaya Master Duti (1601–1679), who served as abbot of the Longchang Temple on Mt. Baohua, Jiangsu, lamented, "I have observed that, everywhere, ancient monasteries are estab-lishing subsidiary shrines (*fangtou*), dividing the monastery's operations, and initiating new enterprises. As a result, self-cultivation is no longer pure, and the monks cease to observe monastic regulations, so much so that the temples' bells and drums are silenced, and the monasteries degenerate."[83]

It is possible that the Yongzheng emperor's order to remove the scattered hermitages from Shaolin's periphery was due to a principled objection—simi-lar to abbot Duti's—to the "subsidiary shrine" (*fangtou*) institution. However, it is more likely that in addition to a general concern with the behavior of subsid-iary shrine monks, the emperor was informed of specific transgressions com-mitted by Shaolin-ordained clerics. As early as the sixteenth century, a high-ranking official named Wang Shixing (1547–1598) accused Shaolin monks of eating meat and drinking wine.[84] In the ensuing Qing period (1644–1911), the monastery was regularly blamed for religious violations, which were sometimes attributed to its own monks and sometimes to those occupying its periphery. In 1832, for example, a Dengfeng County magistrate issued a strict warning to the Shaolin Monastery concerning the behavior of its subsidiary shrine monks, whom he accused not only of dietary transgressions, but also of sexual offenses. Shaolin-affiliated monks, magistrate He Wei (fl. 1830) charged, engage in drinking, gambling, and whoring:

> Since ancient times, the Shaolin Monastery has been a famous temple. Everywhere, there is not a monk who does not look up to it. Its resident clerics should strictly adhere to the Buddhist code and carefully follow the Pure Regulations, thereby displaying their respect to the monastic community, and their reverence to its laws.
>
> Now, we have been hearing recently that [Shaolin's] various subsidiary shrine monks (*fangtou seng*) have been regularly interacting with the laity, and have been sheltering criminals. Some invite friends to drunken parties. Others gamble in groups, or even gang together to bring over prostitutes. They collude secretly and collaborate in all sorts of evil. This is extremely hateful.[85]

Even though he politely refrained from condemning the Shaolin monks themselves—reserving his criticism for their subsidiary shrine colleagues—one gets the impression that the magistrate had the former in mind as well. After all, He Wei addressed his admonition to the Shaolin monks, not to their affiliates. It appears, therefore, that his opening allusion to "subsidiary shrine monks" was meant to save face for the Shaolin monks. Indeed, as the letter unfolds, the distinction between "monastery monks" and "subsidiary shrine monks" blurs. The magistrate forewarns *all* Shaolin monks—residents and affiliates alike—that they would be severely punished for their religious transgressions:

> After the monks . . . read our order and are informed of its contents, they should all purify their hearts and cleanse their minds. Each one should burn incense, cultivate the way, and chant the sutras, as well as plough and weed the land. As to the various types of lay people, the monks are forbidden to collude with them in secret. Nor are the monks allowed to interfere in outside matters, harboring criminals, and instigating trouble. If they dare purposely disobey, and [their crimes] happen to be exposed, we are sure to consider them more serious and punish them accordingly.
>
> As to the lay people, they should not be permitted into the monastery. . . . Tenant farmers should reside elsewhere. They should not be allowed to live near the monks.[86]

The magistrate's warning suggests that he was primarily concerned with public order, not monastic law. His edict is replete with references to hidden criminals, which he claimed were sheltered at the Shaolin Monastery. In this respect, He Wei resembled other officials who were concerned with violations of Buddhist law only so far as they proved that their perpetrators were fake monks and as such prone to sedition and crime. We will see below that throughout the Qing period the government was apprehensive—with some reason—that graduates of Shaolin's military program would join sectarian rebels. In 1739, for example, the high-ranking Mongolian official Yaertu (?–1767) memorialized the Qianlong emperor (r. 1736–1795) that "the sturdy youths of Henan are accustomed to violence, many studying the martial arts. For example, under the pretext of teaching the martial arts, the monks of the Shaolin Temple have been gathering worthless dregs. Violent criminal types willfully study evil customs which become a fashion. Heterodox sectarians target such criminals, tempting them to join their sects, thereby increasing their numbers."[87]

The political concerns of government bureaucrats such as He Wei and Yaertu could cast doubt on the objectivity of their religious allegations. It could be argued that officials accused Shaolin monks of violating Buddhist law only because they wished to convince the throne that Shaolin was not a genuine monastery and hence that it posed a political threat. It is significant, therefore, that information on Shaolin religious transgressions is provided not only by outsiders (government officials) but also by insiders (monastic office holders). As early as the Ming period (1368–1644), Shaolin monastic authorities were struggling to stem breaches of Buddhist law among their congregation, weeding out monks who violated the monastic code. In 1595 the monastery's superintendents (*jiansi*)—who were responsible for monastic discipline—engraved in stone a warning to their fellow clerics not to transgress Buddhist law. The inscription they authored implies that disrespect for the monastic code was related to Shaolin's unique position as a military temple; because the martial arts were practiced at the monastery, it attracted monks who disregarded Buddhist law:

> Since ancient times, the Shaolin Chan Monastery has been an ancestral Buddhist temple. It ranks first among the world's famous monasteries. However, culture (*wen*) and warfare (*wu*) are cultivated there together, and crowds of monks flock to it. Thus, there are some among them who pay no respect to monastic regulations. . . . From now onwards, whenever cases occur where the code is breached and the regulations are violated: If the transgression is small, the offender will be forthwith punished by the abbot; if the transgression is serious, it will be reported by the monks who hold office at the time to the county authorities, and the offender will be punished in accordance with the law.[88]

We are now in a position to evaluate the evidence—literary, ethnographic, and historical—of Shaolin dietary practices. Beginning in the Tang period and all through the twentieth century, fiction and drama associated fighting monks with the consumption of animal flesh. In novels, short stories, plays, and more recently movies, martial monks are invariably depicted as meat gobblers. Fieldwork conducted at the Shaolin Temple and its vicinity corroborates the testimony of fiction, revealing that even as they present themselves as Buddhist clerics and don monastic robes, most monks who have left the monastery to pursue a martial career *do* eat meat. Finally, government documents and monastic correspondence—from the Ming and Qing periods alike—attest that some Shaolin or Shaolin-affiliated monks transgressed Buddhist dietary regulations. We may conclude, therefore, that throughout most, if not all, of Shaolin's history meat eating has been closely related to the fighting monk's ethos.

This is not to say that meat has been often consumed *inside* the temple. Throughout most of Shaolin's history, carnivorous monks have resided around the monastery in traditional subsidiary shrines or in modern martial arts schools, and their religious transgressions have taken place *outside* the temple proper. Admittedly, there were also times—such as after the Cultural Revolution—when discipline was lax and meat was eaten inside the monastery. However, for the most part it was enjoyed by wandering fighting monks who had left the monastery to pursue independent martial careers. In this respect the fictional figure of Lu Zhishen is particularly illuminating of historical conditions. The carnivorous "Tattooed Monk" of the early Ming novel *Water Margin* is ordained at a Mt. Wutai monastery, but abandons it for the freedom of itinerant military adventures. He is no different, therefore, from countless Shaolin-ordained fighting monks who have been earning a living outside the temple, consuming forbidden foods in taverns from Dengfeng County to New York City.

Whether they have received martial training or not, wandering monks have often transgressed monastic regulations. Chinese Buddhist history has known a special type of cleric occupying the fringes of the monastic community, who leads an itinerant life. Often venerated by the laity as miracle workers, such wandering monks engaged in healing, fortune-telling, and the like. Their extraordinary powers were believed to be intimately related to extraordinary behavior, for which reason perhaps they often breached monastic law, especially the dietary regulations forbidding meat and wine. Therefore, such folk thaumaturges were sometimes referred to as "crazy monks" (*dian seng*), "mad monks" (*feng heshang*), or "wild monks" (*ye heshang*). Beginning in the early medieval period, their hagiographies were included in such collections as Huijiao's (497–554) *Biographies of Eminent Monks* (*Gaoseng zhuan*), and they continued to figure in Chinese religious life all through the modern period, when they were referred to as "meat and wine monks" (*jiurou heshang*). One of the most famous of these eccentric saints was the Song period Daoji (?–1209), also known as Crazy Ji (Jidian), who has been celebrated posthumously in an enormous body of fiction and drama, becoming one of the most beloved deities in the pantheon of Chinese popular religion.[89]

We may note in conclusion that the connection between fighting monks and the consumption of meat extended to their heavenly patrons. Medieval sources indicate that unlike most Buddhist divinities, guardian deities were occasionally proffered animal flesh. In an edict dated 513, the piously vegetarian emperor Liang Wudi (r. 502–549) forbade animal sacrifices in all temples, whether administered by the state or by the people. One clause alluded to those Buddhist monasteries and nunneries where deer's heads, mutton, and the like were offered to such fighting deities as the Four Lokapālas (Hushi Si Tianwang), guardian monarchs of the Four Quarters. The decree suggests that such blood sacrifices were not uncommon. Evidently, heavenly warriors were imagined to relish animal flesh no less than their earthly counterparts.[90]

Conclusion

The Shaolin Monastery military activities can be traced back to the seventh century. Around 610, Shaolin monks warded off an attack by bandits, and in 621 they participated in the future emperor Li Shimin's campaign against Wang Shichong, who had occupied their Cypress Valley Estate. The two battles share a common connection to property: In the former, the monks protected their temple and in the latter they fought for control of their agricultural wealth. This common feature offers a clue for understanding the Shaolin martial tradition. As affluent landowners, Shaolin monks fought to protect their capital. Buddhist military strength was in Shaolin's case an extension of economic power.

Had the Shaolin Monastery been situated in a remote corner of the empire, its military activities would have remained unnoticed. It was the proximity of the temple to the imperial capital of Luoyang that transformed its local battle into a campaign of national significance. Shaolin's strategic location on a mountain road leading to the eastern capital embroiled its monks in a political struggle of far-reaching consequences. Geography played an important role in the fortunes of the Shaolin military tradition.

The monks' military services to the Tang secured their monastery's wealth under its regime. Their astute choice of Li Shimin over Wang Shichong earned them the gratitude of an emperor and his mighty dynasty. Most Tang emperors were not enthusiastic about the Buddhist faith. Their generous patronage of the monastery resulted from Shaolin's support of the dynasty's founder rather than from religious piety. The monks' disregard for the Buddhist prohibition of violence was therefore the very source of their monastery's prosperity.

Certain traits that were to characterize the entire history of Shaolin fighting are perceptible already in Tang sources. First is the association of the fighting monk's ethos with the consumption of meat. During the medieval period, some Shaolin-affiliated monks probably violated Buddhist dietary law by eating animal flesh, even though their transgressions likely took place outside the temple proper. Second, the connection between monastic martial practice and the veneration of Buddhist military deities can be traced back to medieval times. It is likely that as early as the Tang period Shaolin monks beseeched the divine warrior Vajrapāṇi to supply them with physical strength. More pertinently, the Buddhist guardian provided the monks with religious sanction for violence. If the Buddha himself required the protection of fighting deities, his monastic community certainly needed the protection of fighting monks.

These similarities notwithstanding, Tang Shaolin monks did not invent the fighting *techniques* for which their monastery was to become famous centuries later. We will see in the following chapter that by the mid-Ming period (1368–1644), the Shaolin martial arts were lauded throughout China. However, medieval sources do not allude to specific Shaolin fighting methods. Indeed they neither mention how Shaolin monks fought, nor which weapons they employed in battle. Attributing their descendants' martial arts to Tang Shaolin monks would be anachronistic.

PART II

Systemizing
Martial Practice
(900–1600)

CHAPTER 3

Defending the Nation

BY THE SECOND HALF of the Ming period (1368–1644), Shaolin's military reputation had been firmly established. A flood of sixteenth- and seventeenth-century sources attests the fame of the Shaolin martial arts. Late Ming authors leave no doubt that martial training had been fully integrated into the monastery's regimen, and that its monks had created their own quintessential fighting techniques.

The late Ming period witnessed a tremendous growth in commercial publishing. The burgeoning consumer economy required new types of printed literature: travel guides and encyclopedias, memoirs and local histories, military treatises and martial arts manuals, no less than a great variety of fiction—novels and short stories alike. The Shaolin martial arts figure in each and every one of these literary genres. They are celebrated in the writings of generals and martial arts experts, scholars and statesmen, monks and poets. By the sixteenth century, Shaolin fighting techniques were recorded in every corner of the empire, from Yunnan in the remote southwest to Zhejiang on the eastern seaboard.

Just how famous the Shaolin martial arts had become is indicated by proverbial references. Casual allusions to Shaolin fighting appear in every type of late Ming fiction, from tales in the classical language to short stories and novels in the vernacular.[1] When fictional tough guys brag that their techniques are superior to Shaolin, they reveal how well-known the latter had been. "The Shaolin staff is only good for beating up frogs," proclaims a protagonist of the *Plum in the Golden Vase* (*Jin Ping Mei*) (ca. 1600), proving that the monastery's martial arts had become a household name.[2]

The Ming evidence differs from the preceding Tang sources not only in scope but also in the precise information it provides on the Shaolin fighting techniques. We cannot properly speak of "Tang-period Shaolin martial arts," since we do not know *how* seventh-century Shaolin monks fought. By contrast, we can describe the late Ming Shaolin combat methods, which attracted to the monastery military experts from across the empire. By the sixteenth century,

Shaolin monks had developed quintessential fighting techniques that warrant the term "Shaolin martial arts."

What had happened between the Tang and the Ming? Did Shaolin monks practice fighting during the lengthy period that separated their military assistance to Li Shimin from the sixteenth-century flowering of their martial arts? The available sources do not permit us to answer this question with certainty. Nevertheless, they do indicate the possibility of a continuous military tradition. It appears likely that Shaolin monks did engage in martial training—at least intermittently—during the Northern Song (960–1126), the Jin (1115–1234), and the Yuan (1271–1368). We have mentioned in the previous chapter a twelfth-century stele dedicated to Vajrapāṇi evincing that the monks had been worshipping the tutelary divinity in the context of military training, and we will see below that in the fourteenth century they resorted to arms, defending their temple against the Red Turbans (Hongjin) that pillaged Henan. In addition, there is the circumstantial evidence of fiction; we will see in chapter 4 that fictional fighting monks had been celebrated in popular lore as early as the twelfth century. Assuming that they had been fashioned after *real* warriors, the martial arts figured—either at the Shaolin Temple or in other Buddhist monasteries—centuries before the burst of the Ming interest in them.

It is impossible to ascertain whether, prior to the Ming period, the martial arts had been as fully integrated into the monastery's regimen. However, it is probable that they figured there, at least sporadically. This is suggested not only by the available twelfth- through fourteenth-century sources but also by the very complexity and richness of the Ming evidence itself. The sixteenth-century Shaolin military system was so elaborate that it was likely the product of a lengthy evolution. Contemporary military experts, at any rate, were convinced that the Shaolin monks had been polishing their art for centuries. Ming literature abounds with such statements as "the Shaolin fighting techniques have enjoyed fame from ancient times to the present." Some authors even argued that Shaolin's renown was no longer justified, since its fighting monks were no match for their illustrious ancestors. The renowned general Yu Dayou (1503–1579), for example, believed that Shaolin clerics "have lost the ancient secrets of their [martial] art."[3]

Late Ming Shaolin monks practiced various fighting methods. They trained in the diverse techniques of spear fighting and unarmed hand combat (*quan*), and they carried to battle a variety of weapons including steel tridents (*gangcha*) and hooked spears (*gouqiang*). However, Ming sources leave no doubt that the weapon in which they specialized—indeed the one that made their monastery famous—was the staff.

Cheng Zongyou's *Exposition of the Original Shaolin Staff Method*

The earliest extant manual of the Shaolin martial arts was dedicated to staff fighting. Titled *Exposition of the Original Shaolin Staff Method* (*Shaolin gunfa chan zong*) (hereafter *Shaolin Staff Method*), it was compiled around 1610 by a military expert named Cheng Zongyou (Style: Chongdou) from Xiuning, Huizhou Prefecture, in the southern part of today's Anhui. The Cheng family belonged to the local gentry, and its late Ming members included several noted scholars and degree holders. However, Zongyou's interests, like those of several brothers and nephews of his, were not in classical learning but in the military arts. We possess a description of the entire Cheng household—Zongyou and his brothers—demonstrating martial techniques at the local yamen, as well as an account of an eighty-man military force, trained by Zongyou and made up entirely of members of his estate.[4]

Cheng Zongyou was neither a bandit nor a member of the Ming hereditary military, two groups we might expect to have mastered the martial arts. Rather he was of literati background, and his acquaintances included renowned scholars.[5] Still, martial arts were his passion, which was shared by some other members of his class. The earliest extant manual of the "internal school" (*neijia*) of fighting, for example, was compiled by Huang Baijia (1643–?), son of the renowned scholar Huang Zongxi (1610–1695), and seventeenth-century methods of spear fighting were recorded by Wu Shu (1611–1695), who was also a poet and a literary critic. These literati were often trained in fighting by instructors of lower social status. Their contribution to martial arts history lies in recording techniques that, having originated among the unlettered classes, would otherwise have been lost.[6]

In addition to his *Shaolin Staff Method*, Cheng Zongyou compiled an archery manual titled *History of Archery* (*She shi*) (preface 1629), as well as treatises on the techniques of the spear, the broadsword, and the crossbow. In 1621 he issued the latter three, together with his manual of the Shaolin staff, in a combined edition titled *Techniques for After-Farming Pastime* (*Geng yu sheng ji*).[7] The relative length of the manuals included in this handsomely illustrated book leaves no doubt that, as Cheng himself acknowledges, the staff was his weapon of choice. Indeed, the *Shaolin Staff Method* is as long as the other three manuals combined.

Cheng's familiarity with staff fighting was due to the lengthy period he spent at the Shaolin Monastery. According to his own testimony, his apprenticeship there lasted no less then ten years. His description of the training he received reveals that the monastery rendered late Ming society the unique service of martial education. The Shaolin establishment emerges from his writings as a military academy, where clergy and laity were trained together in staff fighting. Just how big this academy was we gather from General Yu Dayou, who was given a demonstration there by a thousand fighting monks.[8] Cheng writes:

> The Shaolin Monastery is nestled between two mountains: that of culture
> (*wen*) and that of fighting (*wu*). Indeed this monastery has transmitted
> the method of staff fighting and the doctrines of the Chan sect alike, for
> which reason gentlemen throughout the land have always admired it.

Since my youth I was determined to learn the martial arts. Whenever I heard of a famous teacher I wouldn't hesitate to travel far to gain his instruction. Therefore I gathered the necessary travel expenses, and journeyed to the Shaolin Monastery where I spent, all in all, more than ten years. At first I served Master Hongji, who was tolerant enough to admit me into his class. Even though I gained a sketchy understanding of the technique's broad outlines, I didn't master it.

At the time Master Hongzhuan was already an old man in his eighties.[9] Nevertheless his staff method was superb, and the monks venerated him the most. Therefore I turned to him as my next teacher, and each day I learned new things I had never heard of before. In addition, I befriended the two Masters Zongxiang and Zongdai, and I gained enormously from practicing with them. Later I met Master Guang'an, one of the best experts in the Buddhist technique. He had inherited Hongzhuan's technique in its entirety, and had even improved upon it. Guang'an tutored me personally, and revealed to me wonderful subtleties. Later I followed him out of the monastery and we traveled together for several years. The marvelous intricacy of the staff's transformations, the wonderful swiftness of its manipulations—I gradually became familiar with them, and I attained sudden enlightenment (*dun*). I chose this field as my specialty, and I believe I did have some achievements.

As for archery, riding, and the arts of sword and spear, I paid quite some attention to their investigation as well, however by that time my energy of half-a-lifetime had already been spent. My great uncle, the military student Yunshui and my nephews Junxin and the National University student Hanchu had studied with me once at Shaolin. They pointed out that so far the Shaolin staff method had been transmitted only orally, from one Buddhist master to the next. Since I was the first to draw illustrations and compile written formulas for it, they suggested I publish these for the benefit of like-minded friends. At first I declined, saying I was not equal to the task. But then illustrious gentlemen from all over the land started commending the supposed merits of my work. They even blamed me for keeping it secret, thereby depriving them. So finally I found some free time, gathered the doctrines handed down to me by teachers and friends, and combined these with what I had learned from my own experience. I commissioned an artisan to execute the drawings, and, even though my writing is somewhat vulgar, I added to the left of each drawing a rhyming formula (*gejue*).

Together these drawings and formulas constitute a volume, which I titled: *Exposition of the Original Shaolin Staff Method.* Just casting a glance at one of the drawings would probably suffice to figure the position depicted therein. Thus the reader will be able to study this method without the aid of a teacher. Despite an apparent simplicity, each sentence captures the secret of victory and defeat, each drawing harbors the essence of movement. Even though staff fighting is called a trivial art, its explication in this book is the result of a strenuous effort.

If this book serves like-minded friends as a raft leading them to the other shore [of enlightenment], if they rely upon it to strengthen the state and pacify its borders, thereby spreading my teachers' method and enhancing its glory, yet another of my goals would be accomplished.[10]

Cheng's hope that his *Shaolin Staff Method* would enhance the fame of his monastic instructors was not frustrated. Shortly after the manual's publication, the renowned Mao Yuanyi (1549–ca. 1641) commented, "All fighting techniques derive from staff methods, and all staff methods derive from Shaolin. As for the Shaolin method no description of it is as detailed as . . . Cheng Zongyou's *Exposition of the Original Shaolin Staff Method*."[11] Mao was so impressed with Cheng's manual that he incorporated it almost in full into his encyclopedic *Treatise of Military Preparations* (*Wubei zhi*).[12]

Cheng's exhaustive presentation of the Shaolin staff method begins with a description of the weapon. He provides specifications for the length, weight, and materials to be used in the preparation of the staff, to which, like most late Ming military experts, he refers as *gun*. According to Cheng, the staff can be made either of wood or of iron. In the former case its recommended length is 8 to 8.5 *chi* (which in the Ming would mean approximately 8.2 feet to 8.7 feet), and its weight 2.5 to 3 *jin* (approximately 3.2 pounds to 3.9 pounds). The iron staff is slightly shorter (7.5 *chi*, or approximately, 7.7 feet), and its suggested weight between 15 and 16 *jin* (approximately 19.5 to 20.8 pounds).[13] Cheng also discusses the type of timber to be used in the preparation of the wooden staff:

As the regions of the country vary, so do the types of wood. As long as the wood is solid and dense, as long as it is both hard and pliant, growing thinner and thinner from the base to the treetop like a mouse's tail, it will do nicely. A straight pole that is naturally free of scars and nodes would be preferable. By contrast, if the staff is produced by cleaving or sawing, it will easily break along the veins.[14]

Cheng distinguishes between fifty-three individual staff positions (*shi*), each of which he represents by a drawing, accompanied by an explanatory "rhyming formula" (figure 9). Individual positions are strung together into practice sequences called *lushi* (sequence of positions). Intricate diagrams guide the practitioner in the performance of these sequences, which simulate the kind of motions that characterize a real battle (figure 10). Finally, several practice sequences combine into what Cheng calls a "method" (*fa*). All in all, he lists five different methods of the Shaolin staff: Little Yakṣa Spirit (*yecha*), Big Yakṣa Spirit, Hidden Hands (Yinshou), Pushing Staff (Pai gun), and Shuttling [Staff] (Chuansuo). The Pushing Staff differs from the other four methods in being a technique of dual rather than solitary practice, and both the

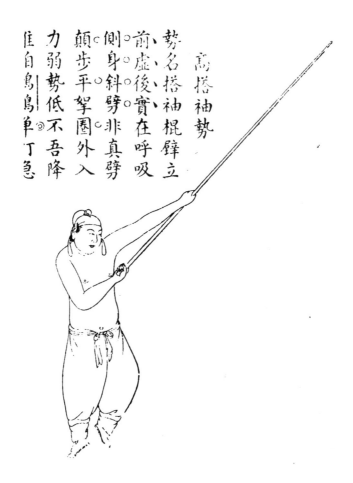

力弱勢低不吾降　顛步平拏圈外入　側身斜劈非真劈　前虛後實在呼吸　勢名搭袖棍竮立　高搭袖勢

住自鳥鳥單丁急

Fɪɢ. 9. The "Lifting-Sleeve Position" from Cheng Zongyou's 1621 *Shaolin Staff Method*.

Pushing Staff and the Shuttling [Staff] differ from the remaining three in being "free methods without fixed positions" (*huo fa wu ding shi*).[15]

According to Cheng, the five methods all originated at the monastery. In this respect, it is no accident that the word "original" (*zong*) figures in the title of his manual: *Exposition of the Original Shaolin Staff Method*. Cheng's goal was to expound what he argued were the authentic Shaolin techniques, as distinct from the numerous methods that—even as they carried the monastery's name—were far removed from its original teaching. His agenda mirrors the fame the Shaolin Monastery had acquired by the early seventeenth century. If it were not for the monastery's renown, practitioners of other techniques would not have capitalized on its name, and Cheng would not have been prompted to present the *original* Shaolin method.

Thus, Cheng's *Shaolin Staff Method* reveals a landscape familiar in today's

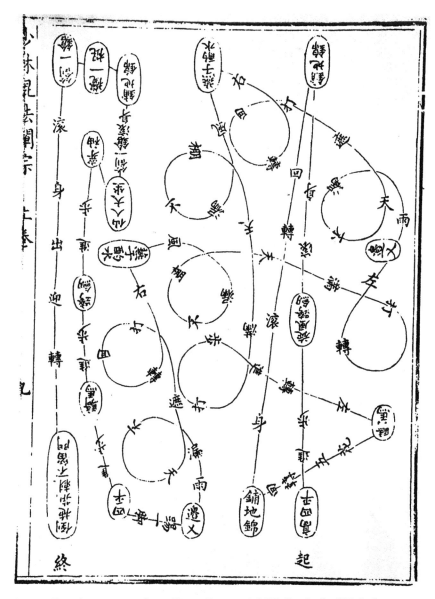

FIG. 10. Practice sequence from Cheng Zongyou's 1621 *Shaolin Staff Method*.

world of martial arts: one of competing schools, each professing to be the sole inheritor of the same original teaching. The rivalry between martial experts all claiming possession of *the* authentic Shaolin teaching is most apparent in the "Questions and Answers" section of the *Shaolin Staff Method*, where Cheng addresses the following query, posed by a hypothetical questioner:

"Today, there is no shortage of Shaolin staff experts. And yet their methods all differ. How could it be that by choosing a different teacher, a practitioner ends up being taught a different technique?"

I replied: "The teachings all derive from the same source. However, with the passage of time people turn their backs on it. Teachers esteem unusual methods, and prefer strange techniques. Some take the opening section of *this* practice sequence (*lu*) and mix it with the closing section of *that* sequence. Others take the closing section of *that* sequence and mingle it with the middle section of *this* sequence. So much so, that what was originally one sequence is transformed into two. Thus teachers confuse the world, and lead the practitioners astray, all for the sake of fame and profit. I am much grieved by this situation, and it is exactly for this reason that I strive to set things right."[16]

Throughout his manual, Cheng Zongyou weaves together the language of martial perfection and the idiom of spiritual attainment. He refers to the Shaolin staff method as the "unsurpassed Buddhist wisdom (Bodhi)" (*wushang puti*), and he describes his own mastery of it as "sudden enlightenment" (*dun*). He notes that Shaolin monks consider martial training a tool for reaching the "other shore" of liberation, and he expresses the hope that his own manual would serve as the "Buddhist raft" that would carry his readers to Nirvāṇa.[17] We need not necessarily doubt the sincerity of his Buddhist sentiments. Having spent more than ten years at the Shaolin Monastery, Cheng probably *did* associate martial training with religious self-cultivation. In this respect, his Buddhist vocabulary was more than a mere ornament to the core of his military theory. Cheng Zongyou hardly distinguished the mastery of his martial art from the mastery of the mind that led to liberation. The discipline and dedication that were necessary for the one were equally conducive to the other.

Monks and Generals

Although his was the most detailed exposition of the Shaolin staff, Cheng Zongyou was not the only expert to discuss it. On the contrary, references to the Shaolin techniques of staff fighting appear regularly in late Ming military encyclopedias, beginning with Tang Shunzhi's (1507–1560) *Treatise on Military Affairs* (*Wu bian*), written some seventy years prior to the publication of Cheng's manual.[18] Other military compilations that feature the Shaolin staff include *New Treatise on Military Efficiency* (*Jixiao xinshu*) (ca. 1562), by the renowned general Qi Jiguang (1528–1588); *Treatise of Military Preparations,* by the above-mentioned Mao Yuanyi; and *Records of Military Tactics* (*Zhenji*), by the military commander He Liangchen (fl. 1565). The latter composition indicates a spread of the Shaolin martial arts within monastic circles. It notes that the monastery's staff method has been transmitted to the monks at

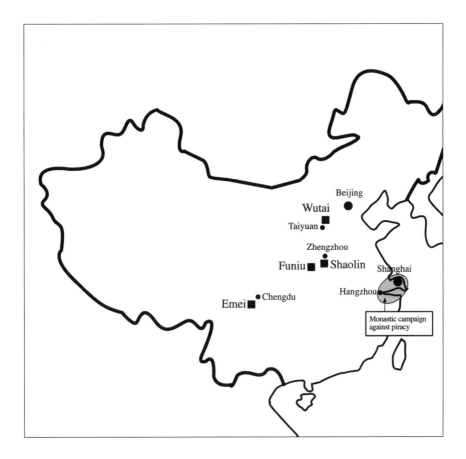

MAP 3. Ming centers of monastic fighting.

Mount Niu, by which it probably refers to the monastic center on Mount Funiu, Henan (map 3).[19]

Late Ming military experts usually heap praises on the Shaolin staff method. Qi Jiguang, for instance, lists it among the famous fighting techniques of his time, and Mao Yuanyi concludes that it has served as the source for all other staff styles. However, the information to be gathered from critical voices is no less significant. Martial artists who disapproved of the Shaolin method provide us with detailed information on it. This is especially true of those military experts that found fault with the Shaolin emphasis on the staff, for they offer the strongest testimony of its centrality in the monastery's regimen.

One expert who objected to the Shaolin concentration on staff fighting, arguing that it resulted in neglect and even distortion of training in other weapons, was Wu Shu. Wu was born on the banks of the Lou River (now called Liuhe), in the subprefecture of Taiqiang, some thirty miles northeast of Suzhou in today's Jiangsu. Like Cheng Zongyou, he was of literati background, and under his other name, Wu Qiao, he is known to us as author of the *Poetic Conversations Around the Fireplace* (*Weilu shihua*).[20] As a young man, Wu studied spear fighting with other gentry friends, one of whom, Lu Shiyi (1611–1672), was to become a renowned Confucian thinker. Their instructor was the itinerant martial artist Shi Dian (*hao*: Jingyan) (ca. 1572–1635).[21]

Wu practiced the spear throughout his adult life. In 1678 he summarized his studies in an anthology titled *Arm Exercises* (*Shoubi lu*), which includes seven different spear manuals. One of these, titled *Spear Method from the Dreaming-of-Foliage Hall* (*Menglü tang qiangfa*), is attributed to the Shaolin monk Hong-zhuan, whom Cheng Zongyou mentioned as his staff teacher. Even as he incorporated Hongzhuan's manual into his anthology, Wu was highly critical of the Shaolin method it represented. "Shaolin [monks] do not understand spear fighting at all," he exclaimed. "In fact, they employ their staff techniques for the spear."[22] In other words, because they overemphasize staff training, Shaolin monks fail to take advantage of the spear's unique features, as Wu further explains:

> The Shaolin staff method has divine origins, and it has enjoyed fame from ancient times to the present. I myself have been quite involved in it. Indeed, it is as high as the mountains and as deep as the seas. It can truly be called a "supreme technique." . . . Still as a weapon the spear is entirely different from the staff. The ancient proverb says: "The spear is the lord of all weapons, the staff is an attendant in its estate." Indeed, this is so. . . . The Shaolin monks have never been aware of this. They treat the spear and the staff as if they were similar weapons.[23]

Whereas Wu Shu disapproved of the monks' disregard for weapons *other* than the staff, another military expert, Yu Dayou, was critical of their staff method itself. Yu is known to us as a successful general who served as regional commander on five of China's frontiers. He was born into a military family in Jinjiang, Fujian, and his brilliant military career was due in large measure to his contribution to the suppression of piracy along China's southeastern coast.[24] Yu distinguished himself not only as a strategist but also as an accomplished martial artist. He specialized in a staff method called "Jingchu Long Sword" (Jingchu changjian), and he compiled a manual of staff fighting, titled *Sword Classic* (*Jian jing*), which won praise from contemporary military experts.[25]

Intrigued by Shaolin's renown, Yu traveled there around 1560 to observe the monastic fighting technique, but he was, according to his account, deeply disappointed. The monastic art had declined so much, he claimed, that he ended up teaching the monks his own martial techniques. In the following account of his visit to the monastery, Yu uses the word "sword" (*jian*) for the staff, as he does in the title of his staff manual:[26]

I had heard that the Shaolin Monastery in Henan possesses a divinely transmitted method of fencing (*jijian*) [staff fighting]. Later, when I was on my way back from Yunzhong (in Shanxi), I followed the path to the monastery. More than a thousand [Shaolin] monks considered themselves experts in this [staff] method, and they all came out to demonstrate it. I realized that the monastery had already lost the ancient secrets of the art, and I openly told them so. The monks immediately expressed their desire to be instructed, to which I responded: "One must dedicate years upon years to master this technique." So they chose from amongst them two young and courageous monks, one named Zongqing, the other Pucong, who followed me to the South, and took up residence inside my military barracks. I taught them the True Formula of the Yin and Yang Transformations,[27] as well as the profound and illuminating imperatives.

After more than three years had elapsed, the two said: "We have been here long enough. We beg permission to return in order that we may teach our fellow monks what we have learned. This way [your] method will be transmitted for ever and ever." And so I let them go. Thirteen years swiftly passed, and suddenly one day my gatekeeper announced that a monk was wishing to see me. He was allowed in, and lo and behold he was Zongqing! He told me that Pucong had already joined the ranks of divine beings, and that only he, Zongqing, had returned to the Shaolin Monastery, where he taught the Sword Formulas (staff formulas) and Chan Regulations. Amongst the monks, almost a hundred achieved a profound knowledge of the technique. Thus it can be transmitted for ever and ever![28]

General Yu was under the impression that his staff method would be transmitted for generations at the Shaolin Monastery. Did he overestimate his impact on the Shaolin tradition? An examination of Cheng Zongyou's manual reveals that the staff technique he learned at Shaolin, some fifty years after Yu's visit to the monastery, was entirely different from the one outlined in Yu's *Sword Classic*. The two staff styles—that taught by the general and that studied by Cheng—vary in everything from the names of methods (*fa*) and positions (*shi*) to the rhyming formulas and illustrations.[29] Furthermore, we can trace at least some of the nomenclature in Cheng's *Shaolin Staff Method* to a military encyclopedia that antecedes Yu's encounter with the Shaolin monks.[30] Clearly, an indigenous tradition of Shaolin staff fighting, which predated the general's visit to the monastery, continued to thrive there long afterwards.

General Yu misjudged his influence on Shaolin fighting, but it is not impossible that he left some mark on it. A hint is provided by the following passage from Wu Shu's *Arm Exercises*, which was compiled approximately a hundred years after the general's visit to the Shaolin monastery:

The Shaolin Monastery has a staff fighting method called "Five Tigers Interception" (Wuhu lan). "One strike down, one strike up" (*yi da yi jie*) is all there is to it. Striking down, the staff should reach the ground; striking up it should pass one's head. It is a simple method, and there is nothing spectacular about it, almost like a farmer hoeing the soil. Still, by practicing it long enough one attains refinement. "Striking down and up," one obtains strength. Even the other Shaolin techniques are all in awe of this method. It cannot be taken lightly just because it is so simple.[31]

Wu Shu highlights the formula "one strike down, one strike up" as characteristic of the "Five Tigers Interception." The same formula figures prominently in Yu Dayou's *Sword Classic*, for which reason it is likely that the method the general taught is none other than the one Wu Shu describes. If Tang Hao, who formulated this hypothesis, is correct, then by the late seventeenth century the Shaolin monks had been engaged in two systems of staff training, one recorded in Cheng's *Shaolin Staff Method*, which predated Yu's visit to their monastery, and the other called by Wu Shu "Five Tigers Interception," which they learned from the Ming general.[32]

Leaving aside the question of Yu Dayou's precise influence on the Shaolin martial arts, his association with the monastery reveals a connection between two segments of late Ming society, which scholarship tends to regard as quite distinct: the Buddhist *sangha* and the military. General Yu treated Shaolin monks as fellow professionals, with whom he conferred on the technicalities of his field. His conception of their monastery as a military institution enriches our understanding of the multifarious roles that Buddhism played in late Ming society.[33]

According to Yu's account, *he* instructed the Shaolin monks. In other instances Shaolin monks shared *their* martial expertise with members of the military. The clearest example is that of the mid-sixteenth-century campaign against piracy, during which military officials in the Jiangnan region called on the Shaolin monks for help. The monks who responded and joined the war did not forsake their religious identity. Rather than blending in with the other soldiers, they formed their own monastic units. However, at least one cleric was offered a position in the military and consequently returned to the laity. This is the seventeenth-century Shaolin monk Liu Dechang, who was appointed mobile corps commander (*youji jiangjun*) in the army. Even after he abandoned the monastic order in favor of the officer corps, Liu maintained contact with his Buddhist alma mater, accepting as students Shaolin monks who sought his instruction in spear fighting.[34]

If Shaolin monks conferred with generals, they also associated with the emerging community of martial artists that did not belong to the military. We met two literati members of that community, Cheng Zongyou and Wu Shu. A third one, Cheng Zhenru (fl. ca. 1620), received his military education not at the Shaolin Monastery but at another Buddhist center, Mount Emei in Sichuan. Cheng traveled there to gain the instruction of monk Pu'en (fl. ca. 1600), whose spear techniques he later recorded in his *Emei Spear Method* (*Emei qiangfa*).[35] He notes that Pu'en received this technique from a divine being, for which reason, perhaps, the monk was reluctant to part with it. Cheng was obliged to spend two years gathering firewood before Pu'en was convinced of his sincerity and revealed to him the mysteries of the spear.[36]

Cheng Zhenru voyaged far to be tutored by the best spear master. In this he resembled other late Ming martial artists—monks and laypersons alike—who led an itinerant life. "Liu Dechang . . . was unhappy with his [spear] technique, which he considered far from perfect. Therefore, he traveled all over the land until he obtained his goal." Pu'en "journeyed all over the land, but could find no rival"; Shi Dian traveled from village to village in search of students; Cheng Zongyou spent several years on the road with his Shaolin mentor Guang'an; and the Shaolin monk Sanqi Yougong (?–1548) is said to have acquired more than a thousand students in his extensive wanderings through Henan, Hebei, Shandong, and Jiangsu.[37]

Thus, late Ming martial artists were often on the road, or as the Chinese would have it, "on the water." Sixteenth- and seventeenth-century authors allude to martial artists in the context of the "rivers and lakes" (*jianghu*),[38] which term designated all those who earn a transient livelihood: actors, storytellers, fortune-tellers, and the like. Did martial artists, like other "rivers and lakes" itinerants, travel for economic reasons? At first glance it would appear that military experts journeyed for educational goals, to study, teach, or test their strength against worthy rivals. However, the cultivation of professional skills is hard to separate from financial considerations. Presumably, teachers were remunerated by students, and competitions could take the form of public performances paid for by spectators. In this respect, sources on the nineteenth-century martial community could shed light on its sixteenth-century antecedent. In his *Collected Talks on the Rivers and Lakes* (*Jianghu congtan*), Yun Youke (fl. 1900) describes in vivid detail the vagrant livelihood of martial artists. Some serve as armed escorts (*baobiao*), who accompany goods in transit; others journey to towns and villages, where on the local market day they "sell their art" (*maiyi*) in public displays of martial dexterity.[39]

Itinerancy creates a link between late Ming martial artists and their late Qing successors. It also associates both groups with their fictional representations. For as early as Tang period fiction, the itinerant realm of the "rivers and lakes" has been the inevitable environment for the heroic deeds of the knight-errant (*xiake*). Indeed, in "martial arts fiction" (*wuxia xiaoshuo*), the "rivers and lakes" no longer signify a manner of livelihood, much less a mode of transportation. Instead, they symbolize a realm of freedom, where the laws of family, society, and state no longer apply. Situated beyond everyday life, it is in the "rivers and lakes" that the dreams of knight-errantry are fulfilled.[40]

The Piracy Crisis

Late Ming military experts were convinced that Shaolin monks had been practicing the staff for centuries. Cheng Zongyou, Wu Shu, Yu Dayou, and Qi Jiguang concurred that "the Shaolin staff method has enjoyed fame from ancient
times to the present." Why, then, were they the first to record it? What happened in the sixteenth century that explains the sudden interest in the Shaolin
fighting techniques?

The late Ming growth of the publishing industry could provide a partial
explanation for the Shaolin martial arts being recorded at that time. Those
printed genres that documented fighting techniques—martial arts manuals
and vernacular fiction, for example—came into their own during the sixteenth and seventeenth centuries. This is especially true of a genre that is
critically important for the study of martial arts history: military encyclopedias. The late Ming witnessed the publication of large-scale military com-
pendiums, in which a wide variety of martial topics—from cannons and
warships to fencing and sparring—were discussed.[41] These printed compen-
diums provided the stage for the discussion of the Shaolin staff.

Another, more significant, reason for the growing interest in Shaolin fighting was the decline of the regular Ming army. By the mid-sixteenth century, the
army was in such dire straits that "the defense installations of the empire, along
with their logistical framework, had largely vanished."[42] The situation was so
grave that in 1550, the Mongol prince Altan was able to loot the Beijing suburbs
freely. The deterioration of the hereditary Ming army was reflected in the attention paid to a large variety of local troops (*xiang bing*) that could be recruited to
supplement it. Military analysts commented on the fighting skills of such diverse groups as mountaineers (from Henan), stone throwers (from Hebei), sail-
ors (from Fujian), and salt workers (from several provinces).[43] As for the Shaolin
monks, particular attention was given to *their* military capabilities following the
mid-sixteenth-century campaign—in which they took part—against piracy.

The 1540s and 1550s witnessed pirate raids on an unprecedented scale
along China's eastern and southeastern coasts. The pirates, known as *wokou* (literally "Japanese bandits"), included, in addition to Japanese and other foreigners, large numbers of Chinese, who were involved in illegal overseas trade. Their
attacks were especially severe along the Jiangnan coast, where they pillaged not
only the countryside but even walled cities. In 1554, for example, the city of
Songjiang was captured and its magistrate put to death. The government encountered tremendous difficulties in its attempts to control the situation, partly
because the local authorities were themselves involved in trade with the bandits
and partly because of the decline of the regular military. It was not before the
1560s when order was restored to Jiangnan, partially through the efforts of the
above-mentioned generals Yu Dayou and Qi Jiguang.[44]

Several sixteenth-century sources attest that in 1553, during the height
of the pirates' raids, military officials in Jiangnan resolved to mobilize Shao-

lin and other monastic troops. The most detailed account is Zheng Ruoceng's (fl. 1505–1580) "The Monastic Armies' First Victory" ("Seng bing shou jie ji"), included in his *The Strategic Defense of the Jiangnan Region* (*Jiangnan jing lüe*) (preface 1568).[45] Even though he never passed the examinations, Zheng gained the esteem of his contemporaries as an expert geographer of China's coastal regions. For this reason, he was selected in 1560 as advisor by Hu Zongxian (1511–1565), who was then the supreme commander of the armies in Fujian, Zhejiang, and the Southern Metropolitan Region (today's Jiangsu). Zheng's tenure in Hu's headquarters must have contributed to his familiarity with the campaign against piracy, of which Hu was in charge.[46]

Collating Zheng's and other late Ming accounts, we can ascertain which official initiated the mobilization of fighting monks: Wan Biao (*hao*: Luyuan) (1498–1556), who served as vice commissioner in chief in the Nanjing Chief Military Commission.[47] We can also pinpoint at least four battles in which monastic troops participated. The first took place in the spring of 1553 on Mount Zhe, which controls the entrance from the Hangzhou Gulf, through the Qiantang River, to Hangzhou City.[48] The remaining three were waged in the canal-strewn Huangpu River delta (which during the Ming belonged to Songjiang Prefecture): at Wengjiagang (July 1553), at Majiabang (spring of 1554), and at Taozhai (autumn of 1555).[49] The incompetence of an army general led to a monastic defeat in the fourth battle, following which the remains of four fallen monks were enshrined underneath the "Stupa of the Four Heroic Monks" on Mt. She, some twenty miles southwest of today's Shanghai (map 3).[50]

The monks scored their biggest victory in the Wengjiagang battle. On July 21, 1553, 120 fighting monks defeated a group of pirates, chasing the survivors for ten days along the twenty-mile route southward to Wangjiazhuang (on the Jiaxing Prefecture coast). There, on July 31, the very last bandit was disposed of. All in all, more than a hundred pirates perished, whereas the monks suffered four casualties only. Indeed, the monks took pity on no one in this battle, one employing his iron staff to kill an escaping pirate's wife. (Zheng Ruoceng does not comment on the monks' disregard for the Buddhist prohibition on killing, even in this instance when the murdered woman presumably was unarmed.)[51]

Not all the monks who participated in the Wengjiagang victory came from the Shaolin Monastery, and whereas some had previous military experience, others presumably were trained *ad hoc* for this battle. However, the cleric who led them to victory did receive his military education at Shaolin. This is Tianyuan, whom Zheng extols both for his martial arts skills and for his strategic genius. He elaborates, for instance, upon the ease with which the Shaolin friar defeated eighteen Hangzhou monks, who challenged his command of the monastic troops:

> Tianyuan said: "I am *real* Shaolin. Is there any martial art in which you are good enough to justify your claim for superiority over me?" The

eighteen [Hangzhou] monks chose from amongst them eight men to challenge him. The eight immediately attacked Tianyuan using their hand combat techniques. Tianyuan was standing at that moment atop the open terrace in front of the hall. His eight assailants tried to climb the stairs leading to it from the courtyard underneath. However, he saw them coming, and struck with his fists, blocking them from climbing.

The eight monks ran around to the hall's back entrance. Then, armed with swords, they charged through the hall to the terrace in front. They slashed their weapons at Tianyuan who, hurriedly grabbing the long bar that fastened the hall's gate, struck horizontally. Try as they did, they could not get into the terrace. They were, on the contrary, overcome by Tianyuan.

Yuekong (the challengers' leader) surrendered and begged forgiveness. Then, the eighteen monks prostrated themselves in front of Tianyuan, and offered their submission.[52]

The description of Tianyuan's martial skills would probably ring familiar to readers of martial arts fiction. Several motifs in Zheng Ruoceng's narrative became standard features of this late imperial, and modern, literary genre. Martial arts novels (and more recently films) commonly celebrate empty-handed, and single-handed, victories.[53] However, from Zheng Ruoceng's perspective, Tianyuan's martial skills were no fiction. The sixteenth-century military analyst was so impressed with the Shaolin monks' fighting abilities that he urged the government to make regular use of monastic armies:

In today's martial arts, there is no one in the land who does not yield to Shaolin. Funiu [in Henan] should be ranked as second. The main reason [for Funiu's excellence] is that its monks, seeking to protect themselves against the miners, studied at Shaolin. Third comes Wutai [in Shanxi]. The source of the Wutai tradition is the method of the "Yang Family Spear" (Yangjia qiang), which has been transmitted for generations in the Yang family. Together, these three [Buddhist centers] comprise hundreds of monasteries and countless monks. Our land is beset by bandits inside and barbarians outside. If the government issues an order for [these monks'] recruitment it will win every battle.[54]

Zheng's call for the recruitment of Shaolin monks illustrates the impact that the piracy campaign had had on their monastery's fame. The pirates' attacks on China's coasts constituted a national crisis, which was discussed on all levels of government, from local authorities in the numerous affected counties to the highest echelons of imperial bureaucracy. Shaolin's contribution to this campaign reverberated through Ming officialdom. The monastery's victories were recorded in numerous documents ranging from local gazetteers and standard histories to works of fiction. If Shaolin's assistance to Li Shimin was the source of its Tang period fame, then the piracy campaign secured its Ming period renown.

The Shaolin's piracy war was to inspire Chinese monks for centuries to come. Faced with Japanese aggression in the 1930s, Chinese Buddhists recalled the monastery's victory over the so-called "Japanese bandits" (*wokou*). In 1933, the enthusiastically patriotic monk Zhenhua authored a *History of Monastic National Defense* (*Sengjia huguo shi*), rallying his fellow Buddhists to fight the Japanese invaders. Arguing that in times of national crisis it was permissible for monks to fight, Zhenhua cited Shaolin's heroic contribution to the sixteenth-century piracy campaign.[55] By the twentieth century, the monastery's military legacy provided a precedent for Buddhist warfare.

Patronage

Even though the piracy war was their most famous, it was not the only campaign in which Shaolin monks took part. Beginning in the first decade of the sixteenth century, Shaolin warriors were regularly drafted to quell local unrest in north China. In 1511, seventy monks lost their lives fighting Liu the Sixth and Liu the Seventh, whose bandit armies swept through Hebei and Henan. In 1522–1523, Shaolin fighters battled the miner turned bandit Wang Tang, who pillaged Shandong and Henan, and in 1552 they participated in the government offensive against the Henan outlaw Shi Shangzhao.[56]

The monastery's military support of the Ming continued into the dynasty's turbulent last years. During the 1630s, Shaolin monks were repeatedly enlisted to the doomed campaigns against the swelling rebel armies that by 1644 were to topple the dynasty. We will see in chapter 7 that the monks' loyalty to the regime led to their monastery's destruction by its adversaries. In 1641 the bandit leader Li Zicheng (1605?–1645) marched his rebel army into Henan, where together with the local warlords he annihilated the Shaolin fighting force. Shaolin's fortunes were intimately related to those of the dynasty it had steadfastly served.

Epitaphs of Shaolin fighting monks provide us with important information on their military service to the Ming. Shaolin's Stupa Forest contains at least four stupa inscriptions dedicated to fighting monks. The memorials of two monks, Wan'an Shungong (1545–1619) and Benda (1542–1625), note that they "gained merit in battle," without specifying in which. Another inscription reveals that monk Zhufang Cangong (1516–1574) commanded the fifty Shaolin warriors that participated in the government offensive against Shi Shangzhao. A fourth attests that monk Sanqi Yougong (?–1548) was sent as far as Yunnan in the remote southwest to quell tribal unrest. His martial exploits had earned this Shaolin warrior the military position of chief supervising regional commander.[57]

Shaolin's military assistance to the state won praise from its highest-ranking officials. During the 1620s, the vice censor in chief, grand coordinator for Henan, Cheng Shao (*jinshi* 1589), visited the monastery and dedicated a poem to its fighting monks. Weaving together Buddhist and military imagery, the vice censor in chief argued that war on behalf of the state does not contradict the Buddhist prohibition of violence. On the contrary, Shaolin monks attain the "fruits of enlightenment" by their military protection of the people. They are able to "transmit the lamp"—that is, propagate the Buddhist message—by their heroic contribution to national defense:

> Imperial decorations for banditry suppression *are* the true fruits of
>   attainment,
> National defense and world pacification *are* the lamp-transmission.
> Under a prosperous reign, emergencies we need not fear,
> By loyalty and heroism Vairocana spreads the Mahāyāna.[58]

The Shaolin monks' support of the regime earned them not only words of praise but also material benefits. In 1581 and again in 1595, Dengfeng County officials issued formal letters, exempting Shaolin's lands from taxation. Both letters were engraved in stone at the monastery to ensure its tax-free standing under future bureaucrats. Interestingly, the two documents specifically warn low-ranking clerks not to exact money from the monastery for their own pockets.

Dengfeng County officials granted Shaolin tax breaks on the basis of the monastery's military record. Their letters provide important information on the monastery's involvement in warfare, for they list one by one the campaigns in which its monks took part:

> During the Jiajing (1522–1566) reign, the Liu bandits, Wang Tang, and
> the pirates, as well as Shi Shangzhao and others created violent distur-
> bances. This monastery's fighting monks (*wu seng*) were repeatedly
> called upon to suppress them. They courageously killed the bandits,
> many earning the merit of putting their lives on the line. Thus this
> monastery's monks have relied upon culture (*wen*) and warfare (*wu*)
> alike to protect the state and strengthen its army. They are not like
> monks in other monasteries throughout the land, who merely conduct
> rituals, read the Sutras, and pray for the emperor's long life."[59]

Word of the Shaolin's meritorious services had reached the imperial palace itself. Emperors, empresses, and eunuchs vied with each other in patronizing the monastery. In 1587, for example, the Empress Dowager Zisheng commissioned a special woodblock edition of Buddhist scriptures in 637 cases, to be kept at the Shaolin Monastery. The empress dowager's gift was announced in an imperial edict by her son, the reigning emperor Zhu Yijun (r. 1573–1620). In his edict, the emperor alluded to the Shaolin monks' military service to the state. "Buddhist scriptures," the emperor wrote, "are not without merit for the defense of the state and the protection of the people."[60]

Several decades earlier, the most powerful eunuch in Emperor Zhu Houzhao's (r. 1506–1521) court, Zhang Yong (1465–1529), lavishly supported the
monastery. Zhang might have become acquainted with Shaolin through his diverse military responsibilities—chief of the capital garrison and director of the
imperial military training corps, among others. Around 1519, he donated to
Shaolin a gilded statue of the monastery's patron saint Bodhidharma. His gift
may be admired to this day inside Shaolin's Standing-in-the-Snow Pavilion (Lixue
ting), which name recalls the trials undergone by Bodhidharma's disciple; Huike
was guided to enlightenment when standing motionless in the snow.[61]

It might have been Zhang Yong who suggested to the emperor that Shaolin
monks be invited to the palace. We know that Zhu Houzhao employed Shaolin
monks at the Leopard Quarter (Baofang)—the pleasure grounds he built
himself within the forbidden city. It is unclear what the monks' role within this
private palace was, whether they served as bodyguards, or whether the emperor was fascinated with their religious powers, as he was with Tibetan Lamas.
At any rate, that they served the emperor in his private chambers indicates that
Shaolin monks enjoyed unprecedented access to the imperial throne, maintaining an intimate connection with the reigning emperor himself. [62]

The Ming dynasty's patronage of Shaolin is apparent to this day in the
monastery's splendor. The court's financial support ushered in a period of
spectacular growth at the monastery. Many of Shaolin's most impressive monuments were built during the sixteenth and early seventeenth centuries. The
largest number of stupas (more than 130) in Shaolin's Stupa Forest date from
the Ming, as do the largest number of inscribed steles (more than thirty). Shaolin's biggest structure, the "Thousand Buddhas' Hall" (Qianfo dian) was constructed in 1588 to house the empress dowager's gift of Buddhist scriptures. Its
magnificent fresco of the "Five Hundred Arhats" (Wubai luohan) was likely
drawn by court painters.[63] Thus, Shaolin's grand architecture was largely the
product of Ming benefaction, itself due to the monastery's military support of
the dynasty.

Other Monastic Troops

In the spring of 1512, the government investigated accusations of brutality leveled against an imperial army deployed in Huguang (today's Hunan and
Hubei). It was alleged that the imperial forces—made of regular army units as
well as monastic troops—looted the civilian population. The soldiers, lay and
clerics alike, were so rapacious that they were "worse than roving bandits."[64]

It is not surprising that we do not know to which monastery the rapacious
fighting monks belonged. During the late Ming, the term "monastic troops"
(sengbing) was widely applied to martial monks all over the empire, from Fujian
in the southeast to Shanxi in the northwest, from Yunnan to Henan. Recall that
in his "Monastic Armies' First Victory," Zheng Ruoceng alluded to various Bud-

dhist units that contributed to the piracy campaign, including eighteen Hang-zhou clerics who challenged the leadership of the Shaolin monk Tianyuan.

Perhaps the distant memory of a monk turned emperor contributed to the late Ming vogue of fighting monks. Zhu Yuanzhang (1328–1398), founder of the Ming dynasty, began his career as a novice at the Huangjue Monastery, in Fengyang, Anhui. There is no evidence that Zhu, who entered the monastery when he was sixteen, practiced the martial arts there. Still, we do know that after leaving the monastery at twenty-three, he became the commander of an army that took over the Chinese empire.[65] Zhu's example might have inspired other monks, or at least facilitated government tolerance of them.

Be that as it may, late Ming fighting monks were so common that they aroused criticism within monastic circles. The renowned Buddhist thinker from Fujian, Yuanxian (1578–1657) condemned their disregard for the religion's prohibition of killing. "During the Yuan period upheaval in Quanzhou [Fujian]," the eminent monk wrote, "the officials were corrupt. They forced monks to become soldiers. . . . Alas! Among today's monks there are many who do not wait to be coerced, but become soldiers of their own accord. This is a sign that the Buddhist Dharma is being extinguished!"[66] Yuanxian proceeded to vent his frustration in a dramatic verse titled "Lament on Monastic Troops" ("Sengbing tan"):

> The Sentient Sovereign's [the Buddha] first rule prohibits killing,
> Animal slaughter is also reprimanded.

> The ancients warned us not to uproot living grass,
> How much more so join armies for mass slaughter.

> Heads uplifted, shoulders flexed, they emerge from their monasteries
> Only longing for battle, like the Asura Devils.

> Their monastic robes they easily discard forever,
> Clad in armor, they wield battle-axes.

> .....

> Loyalty and courage, they have none whatsoever,
> Out of obsessive craving only they bring disaster.

> Sword-mountains, dagger-trees, spread before their eyes,
> White bones strewn over shriveled-grass slopes.

> Even worse, the acute pains of the three torture realms,[67]
> Lasting for a thousand lives, a hundred eons.

> Alas! Alas! Why aren't they enlightened,
> Destroying themselves, like moths flying into fire.

> At Morning, when you wake and scratch your head, examine yourself,
> The Sentient Ruler may sermon forever, yet he alone can't save you.[68]

Ming authors considered Shaolin monastic troops the best; Funiu fighting monks ranked second, and the Wutai ones third. To these centers of Buddhist fighting could be added the monastic complex on Mt. Emei, Sichuan (map 3). However, fighting on a smaller scale was practiced in numerous other temples as well. Individual monks practiced the martial arts in various shrines, which were not necessarily militarily renowned. Huang Zongxi recalled accompanying the Internal School martial artist Wang Zhengnan (1617–1669) to the Tiantong Monastery, in Ningbo, Zhejiang. One monk there was famed for his martial skills, and Wang Zhengnan proceeded to test his strength and defeat him.[69]

Itinerancy created a link between various centers of monastic fighting. The martial arts did not emerge independently in each monastery. Rather, traveling monks spread their fighting techniques from one temple to another. Zheng Ruoceng noted that the Funiu monks excelled in fighting because they had been trained at the Shaolin Monastery. He Liangchen further specified that they had been instructed there in staff fighting. However, influence between the two monasteries did not go one way only: Shaolin's abbot Huanxiu Changrun (?–1585) had studied under the Funiu master Tanran Pinggong (?–1579).[70]

The Shaolin staff expert Biandun (?–1563) exemplifies itinerant monks' role in spreading monastic fighting. The martial monk studied staff fighting and hand combat at Shaolin under a Tibetan master, who was noted in the monastery's records not only for his fighting techniques but also for his effective fund-raising skills.[71] After graduating from the monastery's military program, Biandun traveled between his alma mater and the Sichuan center of Buddhist fighting on Mt. Emei, where likely he taught Shaolin fighting techniques. (He passed away in Sichuan and was brought back for interment at Shaolin by his disciples.)[72]

Biandun arrived in Yunnan as well. Cheng Zongyou notes that the martial monk saved a Miao person there, whereupon the Miao people venerated him as a god.[73] The Yunnan *Jizu Mountain History* (*Jizu shan zhi*) includes a biography of Biandun, which narrates how he employed Vajrapāṇi's "divine spell" to subdue local bandits (and ghosts). We have seen above that Vajrapāṇi had been worshipped at Shaolin in the context of martial training. The fearsome deity was believed to endow his martial devotees with extraordinary physical strength. It is likely therefore that, along with Vajrapāṇi's spell, Biandun had transmitted Shaolin fighting techniques to the Jizu Mountain monks.[74]

When they would hit the road, lay martial artists also sojourned in temples. Throughout Chinese history, temples functioned as inns. Buddhist and Daoist monasteries as well as temples of the popular religion offered shelter to the floating members of the "rivers and lakes"—lay and clerical alike. In 1663, when he arrived to Kunshan, Jiangsu, the itinerant martial artist Shi Dian, who was not a monk, stayed for two years at the local Returning Kindness Temple (Baoben si), where he taught his enthusiastic gentry students Wu Shu and Lu Shiyi spear fighting.[75]

Temples offered martial artists not only shelter, but also space to demonstrate their art. "Temples," writes Susan Naquin, "were overwhelmingly the most important component of public space in Chinese cities in the late-imperial era."[76] Martial artists often made a living by giving public performances on temple grounds. Like other "rivers and lakes" artists—actors, singers, and storytellers—they traveled from one shrine to another, performing on such holidays as the local god's birthday. A seventeenth-century pilgrim discovered at the Shandong Temple of the Eastern Peak "some ten wrestling platforms and theatrical stages, each attracting hundreds of spectators who clustered like bees or ants."[77] "In every city temple fair," observed the late Qing Yun Youke, "there are martial artists demonstrating their art."[78]

Martial artists performed in temples on holidays and temple fairs. After their show they would collect money from the audience or sell pills and ointments, which were supposed to make their clients as strong as they, the seller's physique proving the efficacy of his medicine. In addition, some military experts offered classes in temples on a regular basis. To this day, Taiwanese martial artists teach in neighborhood and village temples. Likewise, the seventeenth-century Wang Zhengnan taught his internal martial arts at the Ningbo Iron Buddha (Tiefo) Temple because, we are told, "his own house was too small."[79] This rare glimpse into an unlettered martial artist's life is given us by his literati student, Huang Baijia.

As distinct from local temples where martial arts were performed, the big centers of monastic fighting each merits a study in its own right. Here are only a few comments on some of them:

Mount Wutai

The "Four Great Mountains" (Sida ming shan) occupy a central place in Chinese Buddhist sacred geography. Each is associated with the cult of a Bodhisattva, who is supposed to be manifested there. Mount Wutai, in Shanxi Province, is considered the abode of the Bodhisattva of wisdom, Mañjuśrī (Wenshu). As early as the first centuries CE it had attracted pilgrims who sought the deity's epiphany. The mountain houses dozens of monasteries, some of which date back to the early medieval period.

The military activities of Wutai monks resulted in part from its strategic location on China's northwestern border. The mountain rises over nine thousand feet above the city of Taiyuan, in an area which has seen constant fighting between Han Chinese and nomadic central Asian people. Indeed, the earliest recorded instance of Wutai involvement in warfare dates from the twelfth-century Jurchen invasion, when its monks participated in the unsuccessful campaign to salvage the Northern Song dynasty (960–1127).[80]

In 1126, during the eight-month Jurchen siege of Taiyuan, two generals, Wu Hanying and Yang Kefa, sought Wutai military support. Their requests were granted by the mountain's abbots, and Wutai fighting monks participated in the doomed campaign to save the city. Two clerics, Li Shan-

nuo and Du Taishi, were even appointed "vanguard generals" in the imperial army.[81]

The courage of one Wutai fighting monk earned him a biography in the
"loyal heroes" section of the official *Song History*. The monk, Zhenbao, held the
government-appointed position of "chief monk" (*sengzheng*) for Mt. Wutai. During the dynasty's desperate last months he was summoned to the capital Bian-
liang (Kaifeng) for military consultation. Emperor Qinzong (reigned 1126–1127)
beseeched his help, and Zhenbao promised to do his best. He returned to the
mountain, gathered his monastic troops, and went to war, only to be defeated
and taken captive. Zhenbao's Jurchen captors were willing to spare him, but he
refused to collaborate. "My religion prohibits lying," the courageous monk said.
"I had already promised the Song emperor that I will fight for him to the death.
Was it merely a boastful lie?" Only then was he executed.[82]

As Ma Mingda has shown, Wutai's military fame is mirrored in popular literature. Ming fiction extols several fighting monks who are associated with the
mountain. The *Water Margin*'s (ca. 1400) heroic Lu Zhishen resides at the Mt.
Wutai's Mañjuśrī Temple, and the *Yang Family Generals* (ca. 1550) Yang the Fifth
(Yang Wulang) leads his five-thousand-strong monkish army from there in
support of his brothers.[83] We will return below to these fictional warrior monks.
Here suffice it to note that their legends can be traced back through drama
and oral literature to the twelfth century. Evidently, shortly after their 1120s assistance to the Northern Song, Wutai monks had been celebrated in Southern
Song (1127–1279) lore.[84]

Mount Emei

Originally one of Daoism's earthly paradises that were known as the "cave
heavens" (*dongtian*), Mt. Emei was sanctioned by the Buddhist tradition during
the Ming period, when it was chosen as one of the religion's "Four Great Mountains." It is dedicated to the cult of Samantabhadra (Puxian), and it houses
dozens of temples in honor of the Bodhisattva.

During the late Ming, both spear and empty-handed fighting were practiced at Emei. Information on the former is provided by the *Emei Spear Method*
(*Emei qiangfa*), which the spear expert Wu Shu considered worthy of inclusion
in his *Arm Exercises* (1678). The manual expounds the techniques of the Emei
Master Pu'en (fl. ca. 1600), as recorded by his lay student Cheng Zhenru (fl. ca.
1620).[85] As for Emei hand combat, it is celebrated in Tang Shunzhi's (1507–
1560) "Song of the Emei Monk's Fist" ("Emei daoren quan ge"), which alludes
to Shaolin's military renown as well:

> The Buddha is an expert magician; master of many techniques,
> Shaolin hand combat in the entire world is hardly equaled.
>
> This monk demonstrates even greater new marvels,
> For in the mountains' depth, the white monkey had instructed him.

That day, at the thatched cottage, crisp autumn sky,
Thin frost, light breeze, on the tranquil withered willow.

Suddenly his hair on end, a foot strike,
Rock cliffs splinter, causing pebbles to fly.

Speeding like the divine woman's magic shuttle,
He coils like the Deva dancers flapping their kingfisher sleeves.

Horrendous and sand spitting, a ghost mocks men,
Bearded and teeth grinding, a Xuan Monster catches beasts.

Embodied we ask: Is he formless?
As he turns heels over head, revealing his elbows.

. . .

His marvels not yet exhausted, the performance is over,
His breathing imperceptible, guarding his primordial *qi*.

The monk's transformations are unfathomable,
Back on his meditation mat, like a wooden statue.[86]

Tang's poem is replete with Buddhist allusions, from the Deva dancers who flap their kingfisher sleeves to the Buddha who is an expert magician. Moreover, it creates a link between military training and religious discipline, associating the monk's martial performance with meditation. The Emei warrior's "unfathomable transformations" lead him from the smashing of rock cliffs to the quiet sitting "like a wooden statue." Tang implies therefore that the monk's fighting techniques were intimately related to his religious practice. In this respect the poem evinces a perception of martial training as a form of Buddhist self-cultivation.

That martial practice could be related to a spiritual quest is hinted by other poems as well. In his "Song of the Sha Fist" ("Shaquan Ge"), Zhang Yongquan (1619–ca. 1700) extolled the bare-handed techniques of the Jiangsu martial artist Li Lantian. Borrowing from Tang's verse of the Emei monk, Zhang was more explicit in associating Buddhism and fighting. He tells us that Li "discoursed upon hand combat as if discussing Chan." Indeed his martial art is squarely equated with Buddhist meditation (*samādhi*; *sanmei*):

The old man of Mt. Yu[87] Li Lantian,
At seventy, dwindling tangles of white hair.
In a faltering step he becomes a nobleman's retainer,[88]
Discoursing upon hand combat, as if discussing Chan.
At the Artemisia-Wilds Hall he displays his dexterity,
Crags about to splinter, sand about to fly.
Soaring, he is like a falcon reaching the heavens,
Crouching, he resembles a Xuan Monster catching beasts.

I hear that this is the Sha Family Method,
Disdaining the "rivers and lakes," alone worthy of praise.
His clumsiness conceals an art—deep meditation,
His adroit turns joined together—six-flowers formation.[89]
The movements are no different from the divine shuttle,
The coiling is identical to fluttering silk brocade.
His four limbs made boneless supple,
His empty fist hardened into a battleaxe.[90]

Li Lantian was not a monk, and his bare-handed style did not originate at a Buddhist temple.[91] That Zhang Yongquan chose to describe his Sha Family Fist in religious terms indicates that the association of Buddhism and the martial arts was not limited to monastic circles. Whether they belonged to the clergy or to the laity, some practitioners invested the martial arts with a spiritual significance, which was expressed in Buddhist terms.

Mount Funiu

In the popular imagination, mining has often been associated with crime. From California gold mines to Guangxi coal pits (where the Taiping rebellion began), miners have been portrayed as an unruly bunch, at best adventurers in search of easy money, at worst ruthless gangsters.[92] Such perceptions have also been applied to Henan miners, for whom—a Ming author tells us—"mining was a vocation, and killing people was a means of livelihood."[93] Perhaps for this reason, Zheng Ruoceng attributed the Funiu monks' military activities to the dangers posed by gold hunters. In order to protect themselves against the latter, he explained, Funiu monks had sought Shaolin martial training.[94]

To this day, gold is still excavated from the slopes of Mt. Funiu, in remote southwestern Song County, Henan. During the Ming period the mountain featured several Buddhist monasteries, the most famous of which was the Clouds Cliff (Yunyan) Temple. Founded during the Tang period by monk Zizai (fl. 627), the Yunyan Monastery flourished under Ming rule. It was destroyed during the dynasty's turbulent last years, when Li Zicheng's rebel army advanced through Henan.[95] The bandit leader likely detested its monks because of their steadfast support of the dynasty.

In September 2001, I joined a small Shaolin expedition to Mount Funiu. Shaolin monks were curious about their old brethren, and the local authorities wished to develop the mountain's tourist industry after the successful Shaolin model. The renowned Buddhist archaeologist Wen Yucheng also joined the trip.[96]

The remains of the Yunyan Monastery are situated just under Mount Funiu's six-thousand-foot Longchiman Peak. The temple was originally made of two sections: Lower Monastery and Upper Monastery. The former still features a Ming period hall, now serving as a village shrine. Of the latter nothing is left, with the exception of a six-foot-tall Ming stele situated at the edge of a corn-field. Dated 1518, it narrates the monastery's history from its Tang founding through the fifteenth century.[97]

A small hamlet is situated at the site of the Upper Yunyan Monastery. Its people, who welcomed us with hot water and sugar, showed us a pressed-earth terrace, where, they said, the monks had practiced fighting. During the Qing period some monks returned to the monastery, where martial training apparently lasted through the 1950s.

Conclusion

The late Ming was the heyday of Chinese monastic armies. Fighting monks could be found in every corner of the empire, from Shanxi to Fujian, from Zhe-jiang to Yunnan. The state's tolerance of them was due in part to the decline of the professional Ming army, which compelled the government to employ other military forces, including monastic troops.

Of all monastic armies, Shaolin's was considered the best. Beginning in the first decades of the sixteenth century and all through the dynasty's last years, Shaolin monks rendered dependable military service to the state. They participated in local campaigns against Henan outlaws and bandits and fought marauding pirates along China's southeastern coast. Their contribution to na-tional defense earned Shaolin monks not only resounding applause but also state patronage. The late Ming witnessed spectacular growth at the monastery, as high-ranking officials and members of the imperial family vied with each other in supporting its renowned fighting monks.

If their relations with the state resembled those of their Tang ancestors in that in both instances military service resulted in state patronage, the differ-ence between Ming and Tang Shaolin monks concerned fighting technique. There is no evidence that seventh-century Shaolin monks—who presumably carried to battle common Tang weaponry—had created their own combat method. By contrast, Ming period Shaolin monks developed a quintessential staff technique, which is described in detail in contemporary literature. This fighting method did not emerge at the monastery in one day. It was the prod-uct of a lengthy evolution, which culminated in the sixteenth century, when it was abundantly praised by military experts.

The techniques of the Shaolin staff were invested in some cases with spiritual significance. Cheng Zongyou expressed the hope that his manual would lead his readers to the shore of enlightenment. For him, the arduous process of martial self-cultivation was indistinguishable from the quest for religious liberation. Evidently, the Shaolin martial arts served as a tool for Buddhist self-realization.

The Ming period saw the emergence not only of a unique Shaolin martial art, but also of a martial arts community to which Shaolin monks belonged.

This floating community of "rivers and lakes" was made of itinerant martial artists who traveled in search of teachers, students, and spectators. Whether they belonged to the clergy or the laity, members of this community often resided, performed, and taught in temples—Buddhist, Daoist, and those of the popular religion. Considerations of time and space created an inextricable link between temples and the martial arts. Whatever his beliefs, whichever the temple, the martial artist found there the festival occasion and the public space necessary for the performance of his art.

CHAPTER 4

Staff Legends

THE STAFF WAS NOT the only weapon Ming period Shaolin monks used. Contemporary literature alludes to other Shaolin arms and fighting methods. Wu Shu's *Arm Exercises* includes a spear manual attributed to the Shaolin monk Hongzhuan, Tang Shunzhi alludes to Shaolin unarmed hand combat (*quan*), and Zheng Ruoceng notes that in addition to staffs, Shaolin monks carried to battle steel tridents and hooked spears. Even the greatest advocate of the Shaolin staff, Cheng Zongyou, acknowledges that by the early seventeenth century, Shaolin monks began practicing empty-handed combat.[1]

Still, even authors who attribute weapons other than the staff to Shaolin leave no doubt that the monks specialized in it. Wu Shu criticizes Shaolin clerics for applying the techniques of the staff to spear fighting, and Zheng Ruoceng's illustrations of their deftness invariably concern staffs or stafflike weapons. In one anecdote, he celebrates the skills of Tianyuan, who employed a door bar as an improvised staff, and in another, he tells of monk Guzhou, who used a *real* staff to beat up eight assailants. The second story features the military official Wan Biao, who initiated the mobilization of Shaolin monks against the pirates:

> The three provincial officers (*sansi*) mocked Luyuan [Wan Biao]:
> "Monks are useless," they said. "Why do you honor them so?" Luyuan
> told them of the cultural and military accomplishments of some monks.
> The three provincial officers suggested they bet wine on it, so Luyuan
> arranged a banquet at the Yongjin Gate [in Hangzhou]. The three
> provincial officers came, and secretly ordered eight military instructors
> to lie in ambush. They urged Luyuan to invite an eminent monk to fight
> them. Luyuan invited Guzhou, who didn't know what it was all about
> and happily came.
>   When Guzhou arrived, the eight military instructors, each armed

with a staff, pounced on him and started hitting him from all sides. Guzhou was completely unarmed and he employed the sleeves of his monastic robe to evade the blows. One of the staffs got caught in his sleeve. Guzhou effortlessly snatched it, and started hitting back his assailants. Employing his staff, he instantly threw all eight of them to the ground. The three provincial officers burst into applause.[2]

Vajrapāṇi's Legend

Religious lore, no less than military and historical writings, attests to the staff's importance in the monastery's regimen. During the Ming period, Shaolin monks changed the image of their tutelary deity Vajrapāṇi, arming him with a staff. Visual representations of Vajrapāṇi, also known as Nārāyaṇa, show that all through the twelfth century Shaolin monks envisioned him holding the *vajra* (see figure 8 in chapter 2). However, a Ming period legend replaced his iconic weapon with Shaolin's quintessential one. According to the legend, Vajrapāṇi was incarnated at Shaolin as a lowly scullion. When the monastery was attacked by bandits, he emerged from the kitchen and, wielding a divine staff, repelled the aggressors. The Indian *vajra*-holder, Vajrapāṇi, was thus transformed into a staff expert, progenitor of the monastery's renowned staff techniques.

Shaolin's legend of Vajrapāṇi the staff wielder survives in several versions: Cheng Zongyou's *Shaolin Staff Method*, Fu Mei's *Song Mountain Book* (preface 1612), and two seventeenth-century gazetteers.[3] However, the earliest evidence is epigraphic. A 1517 stele contains a version of the legend authored by the Shaolin abbot Wenzai (1454–1524). Titled "The Deity Nārāyaṇa Protects the Law and Displays His Divinity" ("Naluoyan shen hufa shiji"), the stele is engraved with the divine warrior's image, replacing his short *vajra* with a long staff (figure 11):

> On the twenty-sixth day of the third month of the Zhizheng period's eleventh, *xinmao*, year (April 22, 1351), at the *si* hour (between 9 A.M. and 11 A.M.), when the Red Turbans (Hongjin) uprising in Yingzhou [in modern western Anhui] had just begun, a crowd of bandits arrived at the monastery. There was a saint (*shengxian*) at Shaolin, who up until then had been working in the monastery's kitchen. Several years he diligently carried firewood and tended the stove. His hair was disheveled, and he went barefoot. Wearing only thin trousers, his upper body was exposed. From morning till night he hardly uttered a word, arousing no interest among his fellow monks. His surname, native place, and first name, were unknown. He constantly cultivated all the deeds of enlightenment (*wan xing*).
>
> That day, when the Red Turbans approached the monastery, the Bodhisattva wielded a stove poker (*huogun*), and he stood mightily alone

FIG. 11. Abbot Wenzai's 1517 Vajrapāṇi's (Nārāyaṇa) stele. Note that the divine warrior's *vajra* has been replaced by the staff.

atop the lofty peak. The Red Turbans were terrified of him and escaped, whereupon he disappeared. People looked for him, but he was seen no more. Only then did they realize that he was a Bodhisattva displaying his divinity. Thereafter, he became Shaolin's protector of the law (*hufa*),[4] and occupied the seat of the monastery's "guardian spirit" (*qielan shen*).[5]

The legend is not unrelated to historical events. The Shaolin Monastery was attacked by bandits during the 1350s Red Turbans' uprising.[6] As Tang Hao has demonstrated, the attack on the monastery probably took place not in 1351 (as the 1517 inscription has it), but rather in or around 1356, during the Red Turbans' northern offensive, in the course of which the rebels captured most of Henan, including Kaifeng city.[7] That the monastery was plundered and even partially destroyed by the Red Turbans (or by other bandits who took advantage of the rebellion) is attested by two fourteenth-century inscriptions (one dated probably 1371), which celebrate its restoration during the first years of Ming rule, as well as by two epitaphs, dated 1373, for Shaolin monks who lived through the revolt.[8]

Even as fourteenth-century sources confirm that the Shaolin Monastery was attacked during the 1350s, their version of events differs from that of the sixteenth-century legend. Whereas the latter has a staff-wielding deity leading the monks to victory, the former depicts a monastic defeat. According to the early Ming sources, the bandits captured the monastery and wreaked havoc upon it, peeling off the gold coating the Buddha images and breaking the statues in search of hidden treasures. The destruction was so thorough that the monks were forced to abandon the monastery. Tang Hao concludes that they could not have returned to Shaolin prior to 1359, when the government's counteroffensive, led by Chaghan Temür, forced the Red Turbans out of Henan.[9]

The legend elaborates the divine standing of its staff-wielding protagonist, as Vajrapāṇi (alias Nārāyaṇa) is elevated to the position of a Bodhisattva. Some versions specify that he is an incarnation of the Bodhisattva Avalokiteśvara (Guanyin), who is shown in a bubble above her fearsome avatar in Shaolin works of art (figures 11 and 12). Even before they equipped the god with their weapon, Shaolin monks had stressed the identity of Vajrapāṇi and Avalokiteśvara. Shaolin's twelfth-century abbot, Zuduan, noted, "According to the scripture, this deity (Vajrapāṇi) is a manifestation of Avalokiteśvara."[10] As A'de points out, the scripture in question is the influential *Lotus Sutra*, which teaches that the Bodhisattva assumes whichever form would be conducive to spreading the dharma. For example: "To those who can be conveyed to deliverance by the body of the spirit who grasps the *vajra* (Vajrapāṇi) he preaches Dharma by displaying the body of the spirit who grasps the *vajra*."[11]

Vajrapāṇi is not only elevated to a Bodhisattva rank, he is also given a specific post: the monastery's "guardian spirit" (*qielan shen*). Ming authors note that this office distinguished Shaolin from other Buddhist temples, where another valiant deity—Guangong—held it.[12] Unlike Vajrapāṇi, Guangong is not a deity of Buddhist origins. He is a third-century general whose veneration originated in the popular religion and evolved in a Daoist ritual context. The heroic general was probably incorporated into the Buddhist pantheon of divinities no earlier than the Song period, when a legend emerged of his posthumous enlightenment. According to the legend, Guangong's departed spirit was led to salvation by the historical monk Zhiyi (538–597), whereupon in gratitude it volunteered to officiate as the guardian deity in the latter's monastery.[13] To this day Guangong occupies the post of tute-

大聖緊那羅王顯神像

FIG. 12. The staff-wielding Vajrapāṇi (referred to as Kiṃnara) atop Mt. Song. Note the Bodhisattva Avalokiteśvara of whom he is considered to be an avatar.

lary deity in most Chinese Buddhist temples, whereas Vajrapāṇi holds this office at the Shaolin Monastery.[14]

Even as Vajrapāṇi's divinity is magnified, it is hidden behind the façade of a lowly menial. The staff-wielding hero begins his career as a kitchen hand, clad in rags. Unnoticed by his fellow monks, he is a saint in disguise. Walking barefoot and wearing thin trousers, his appearance is not merely humble, it also contradicts monastic regulations. The future guardian spirit disregards Buddhist tonsure, flaunting "disheveled hair." As such, the tutelary god of the Shaolin martial arts resembles other Chinese holy fools, whose divinity is masked behind shabby clothes and eccentric behavior. Hidden saints such as Daoji, nicknamed Crazy Ji (Jidian), disregard appearances and accepted norms of behavior.[15]

Vajrapāṇi's myth is particularly reminiscent of Huineng's (638–713). According to the ninth-century *Platform Sutra of the Sixth Patriarch*, the great Chan master began his illustrious career as a scullion treading the pestle in the monastery's kitchen.[16] His hagiography might therefore have influenced the Shaolin myth, whose protagonist carries a souvenir from his kitchen days, a stove poker (*huogun*). In the muscular saint's hands the kitchen utensil is transformed into a fighting staff, whereby his menial origins are skillfully associated with Shaolin's quintessential weapon.

Vajrapāṇi's transformation from a *vajra*-holding deity into a staff-wielding one was accompanied by an accidental yet far-reaching change in his identity. All through the 1520s Shaolin monks referred to their tutelary deity as Vajrapāṇi or, using his other name, Nārāyaṇa. However, several decades later, they started calling him Kiṃnara (Jinnaluo), which name originally designated semidivine/semihuman heavenly musicians.[17] In Hindu and Buddhist literature alike, the Kiṃnaras have nothing to do with warfare, and the only reason for their association with the Shaolin martial arts was the similarity of their Chinese name, Jinnaluo, with Nārāyaṇa's, Naluoyan. As A'de suggests, Shaolin monks confused the two deities, transforming Vajrapāṇi (Jingang shen), through his other name Nārāyaṇa (Naluoyan), into Kiṃnara (Jinnaluo).[18]

The earliest evidence of a change in Vajrapāṇi's identity dates from 1575, when a Shaolin inscription alluded to the monastery's staff-wielding hero as Kiṃnara. In accordance with the *Lotus Sutra*, which mentions four Kiṃnara kings, the stele depicts four tutelary divinities, each armed with a staff.[19] In 1610, Cheng Zongyou continued the new tradition, alluding to the progenitor of Shaolin fighting as Kiṃnara. Cheng's narrative makes an explicit connection between the god's and the monks' fighting technique:

> During the Zhizheng period (1341–1367) of the Yuan Dynasty the Red Troops (Hongjun) revolted. The monastery was badly ravaged by this sect. Luckily, just then somebody came out of the monastery's kitchen and reassured the monks saying: "You should all be calm. I will ward them off myself." Wielding a divine staff (*shen gun*), he threw himself into the stove. Then, breaking out, he emerged from [the stove], and

stood astride Song Mountain and the "Imperial Fort" (Yuzhai). The Red Troops disintegrated and withdrew.

The monastery's residents marveled at this event. A monk addressed the crowd saying: "Do you know who drove away the Red Troops? He is the Mahāsattva Avalokiteśvara (Guanyin dashi), incarnated as the Kiṃnara King (Jinnaluo wang)." Therefore they wove a wickerwork statue of him, and to this day they continue to practice his [fighting] technique."[20]

Cheng Zongyou's version of the legend contains a curious element: Kiṃnara, he tells us, threw himself into the stove from which he emerged to stand astride Mt. Song and the "Imperial Fort." Situated atop the Shaoshi mountain peak, the "Imperial Fort" is five miles away from Mt. Song.[21] Only a giant of supernormal dimensions could have stood astride both, indicating that inside the blazing stove Kiṃnara underwent a process of magic transformation. That this is what Cheng Zongyou had in mind is confirmed both by the woodblock illustration that accompanies his text (figure 12), and by Fu Mei's version of the legend, which specifies that Kiṃnara's "figure was transformed (bianxing) and he grew several hundred feet tall."[22] Kiṃnara's gigantic proportions explain why the terrorized bandits dispersed upon seeing him. He was revealed to them not as a mortal but as a deity.

The significance of Vajrapāṇi, now called Kiṃnara, in Shaolin's pantheon of divinities is attested by numerous icons, which are still extant at the monastery. Shaolin's Standing-in-the-Snow Pavilion contains a (seventeenth-century?) statue of the staff-brandishing deity, and the monastery's White-Attired-Mahāsattva Hall (Baiyi dashi dian) is decorated with a nineteenth-century mural of the gigantic Kiṃnara treading Mt. Song and the "Imperial Fort." Furthermore, by the eighteenth century at the latest, Kiṃnara was accorded his own ritual space when a chapel was erected in his honor. A wickerwork statue of the deity occupied the center of a "Kiṃnara Hall," which also contained bronze and iron icons of the deity (figure 13).[23] The wickerwork sculpture is mentioned already in Cheng Zongyou's seventeenth-century *Shaolin Staff Method*, which specifies that it was woven by the monks. However, a century later the common view was that the god himself sculpted it, for which reason the likeness was accurate.[24] This addition to the Kiṃnara legend mirrors an anxiety, not uncommon in Chinese religion, concerning the truthfulness of a deity's image. The myths of several Chinese deities have their protagonists create their own icons, probably to relieve the believers' concern lest they pay homage to a wrong one.[25] Kiṃnara's self-made wickerwork statue no longer survives. In 1928, the entire Kiṃnara Hall burnt down when Warlord Shi Yousan set fire to the monastery. The shrine was reconstructed in 1984 and again in 2004, and it houses three new statues of the deity, who is the object of a rejuvenated religious cult.[26]

Shaolin's legend of its tutelary deity penetrated the local culture of surrounding villages. A late eighteenth-century manuscript discovered in Changzi County, southeastern Shanxi, near the Henan border, reveals that Kiṃnara's

紧那罗像在殿内

FIG. 13. Vajrapāṇi's (Kiṃnara) Qing Shaolin statue; woodblock illustration from the 1748 *Shaolin si zhi* (History of the Shaolin Monastery).

heroic defense of the monastery was staged there as part of the three-day *sai* ritual operas. In the village drama version, the monastery's guardian spirit appears in the abbot's dream warning him of the approaching bandits' attack and urging him to seek help with his lowly kitchen menial. The latter was enacted by a youth masked with four heads, six arms, and protruding tusks. One difference between the play and its Shaolin source concerned the god's weapon. Kiṃnara was armed with a battleaxe instead of a staff.[27]

Vajrapāṇi/Kiṃnara was not the only Buddhist deity whom Shaolin monks armed with their own weapon. The Shaolin monastery's "Thousand Buddhas Hall" (Qianfo dian) contains an enormous wall painting of the "Five Hundred Arhats" (Wubai luohan), dozens of whom are equipped with staffs. In this magnificent painting, which dates from the early seventeenth century,[28] staffs appear in numerous shapes and fulfill diverse functions. Some are adorned with metal rings, identifying them as the Buddhist ring staff, the *xizhang* (Sanskrit:

FIG. 14. Staff-wielding arhat in a seventeenth-century Shaolin fresco.

khakkhara). Others serve as walking sticks or carrying poles. However, in the hands of many arhats, the staff assumes the aspect of a weapon. Consider, for example, the one wielded by an awe-inspiring arhat whose protruding nose, large eyes, and bushy eyebrows exemplify the tendency of Chinese artists to exaggerate the foreign features of the Mahāyāna saints (figure 14).[29] The staff's motion, no less than its proprietor's muscular arms, suggest that it is used for combat, and the fearsome tiger contributes to the martial atmosphere. Evidently, Shaolin monks projected their martial art into the realm of the Mahāyāna divinities.

Why did Shaolin monks ascribe their fighting techniques to Buddhist deities? On one level their attribution to the gods enhanced the prestige of the Shaolin combat methods. Declaring that a technique originated in heaven is equivalent to praising it. Presumably for this reason, military experts such as Yu Dayou and Wu Shu noted that the Shaolin staff has divine origins, thus revealing their familiarity with its etiological myth. On another level, martial deities such as Vajrapāṇi exonerated the monks from their responsibility for the creation of military techniques. In this respect their legends could be read as Buddhist apologies for the monastic exercise of violence.

As Paul Demiéville has shown, Buddhists, like other people, have found ways to justify violating their own principles.[30] Even though the religion upholds peace, its vast literature contains an entire arsenal of justifications for war. One sutra tells how the Buddha in a previous life killed several Brahmins who were slandering Mahāyāna teachings. The text explains that in any case they were each an *icchāntika*—one incapable of salvation.[31] Another sutra has the Bodhisattva Mañjuśrī lift his spear against the Buddha to demonstrate the illusory nature of all things. Since everything is emptiness, Mañjuśrī and the Buddha are equally unreal, and neither crime, nor perpetrator, nor victim could exist.[32] Another ingenious excuse is "compassionate killing." When no other way to prevent a crime is available, it is permissible to kill the would-be criminal, relieving him of bad karma and punishment in the afterlife. Two sutras have the Buddha in a previous life kill a bandit who is about to commit murder. Instead of enduring tortures in hell, the bandit is then reborn in heaven. Such "compassionate killing" is acceptable only when it is motivated by pure intentions, namely when one knowingly shoulders upon himself the future punishment that awaited the would-be sinner, as Asaṅga (fourth or fifth century) emphasizes in his *Bodhisattva-bhūmi*:

> "If I take the life of this sentient being, I myself may be reborn as one of
> the creatures of hell. Better that I be reborn a creature of hell than that
> this living being having committed a deed of immediate retribution,
> should go straight to hell." With such an attitude, the Bodhisattva
> ascertains that the thought is virtuous or indeterminate and then,
> feeling constrained, with only a thought of mercy for the consequence,
> he takes the life of that living being. There is no fault, but a spread of
> much merit.[33]

These excuses for violence did not emerge in the ephemeral world of Buddhist ethical discourse, but in response to historical conditions of warfare that embroiled the monastic community. When pacifism was deemed impractical, Buddhist authors found ways to condone war. Medieval Indian Buddhists responded to interstate violence by endorsing the king's duty to wage war in defense of his subjects,[34] and as recently as World War II, "compassionate killing" was invoked by the rival Asian powers. The Japanese employed the Buddhist concept to justify their invasion of China, and the Chinese used it to sanction their resistance. Chinese monks who had been trained as martial artists even joined the guerrillas that fought the Japanese aggressors.[35]

Drawing on mythology rather than philosophy, Shaolin's justification of violence is different. Instead of hair-splitting arguments, it is a martial god's personal example that vindicates Buddhist military action. If Vajrapāṇi can descend from heaven to defend a Buddhist temple, then by implication his Shaolin devotees can resort to arms as well. That his legend *was* read in this way is indicated by several hymns (*zan*) in honor of the staff-wielding deity. The hymns seek moral grounds for the god's military action in the Buddhist virtue of loving kindness (*ci*; Sanskrit: *maitreya*). They suggest that the protection of the Buddhist faith—even if it involves violence—is an act of compassion. Cheng Zongyou's brother, Yinwan, who authored one hymn, summarizes the argument: "Loving-kindness," he writes, "is cultivated through heroism" (*ci yi yong yang*).[36]

Fictional Staff-Wielding Monks

Staff fighting occupied a central place at the Shaolin Monastery, both in the lives of its resident monks and in the myths of its tutelary deities. However, it was not limited to that monastic circle. Late Ming military experts were intrigued by Shaolin staff techniques, precisely because of the weapon's prominence in common military training. Government troops, such as Yu Dayou's and Qi Jiguang's, were regularly instructed in the art of the staff, which was considered useful not only in its own right but as an introduction to other fighting methods. Yu Dayou expressed the common view when he wrote that "staff training is comparable to the study of the four books. The hooked sword, the broadsword, the spear and the rake resemble each one of the six classics. When the four books are understood, the underlying principle of the six classics becomes clear. If one can handle the staff, he will achieve proficiency in the methods of all other sharp weapons."[37]

Widely used in the late Ming military, the staff was far from being the monopoly of Shaolin monks. Still, popular perception associated the weapon with the Buddhist clergy. This does not mean that all staff experts were believed to be monks, but that fighting monks were usually imagined as staff experts. Evidence of this common perception in Ming society is provided by fiction and drama. Novels and plays that were written during the Ming—and even during the preceding Yuan and Southern Song—periods depict fighting monks as staff experts. Four well-known examples come to mind: Huiming of the romantic comedy *The Western Wing* (*Xixiang ji*), Lu Zhishen of the martial arts novel *Water Margin*, Yang the Fifth (Yang Wulang) of the military saga *Yang Family Generals*, and, most beloved of all, Sun Wukong of the mythological epic *The Journey to the West* (*Xiyou ji*).

Sun Wukong

Probably the most famous Buddhist warrior in Chinese literature, Sun Wukong figures in a body of legends surrounding Xuanzang's (596–664) historical journey from China to India in search of Buddhist scriptures. The legends, which can be traced back to the Song period, evolved through a series of prose narratives and plays, culminating in the sixteenth century in one of the masterpieces of Chinese fiction, *The Journey to the West*. Generally believed to have been authored by Wu Cheng'en (ca. 1506–ca. 1582), the novel served as a source for an enormous body of oral literature and drama, securing Sun Wukong's position as a popular literary and dramatic hero, as well as the object of a religious cult, for centuries to come.[38]

Sun Wukong's role in the *Journey to the West* cycle is that of protector to his master Xuanzang. Throughout their pilgrimage, the two are attacked by countless monsters, whom Xuanzang is unable to counter, both because he is physically feeble and because he is morally committed to the Buddhist prohibition of violence. It is therefore his "Monkey Novice Monk" (Hou Xingzhe), as Sun Wukong is titled, who shoulders the responsibility for their defense, which he admirably performs through the use of a magic weapon. The fearless monkey is armed with a divine staff (*bang*),[39] which he obtained at the Water Crystal Palace of the Dragon King of the Eastern Ocean (figure 15). As indicated by its name, "As You Wish, Golden Rings Clasped Staff" (Ruyi jingu bang), the weapon complies with its proprietor's wishes, changing its size at will. Its regular operational length is two *zhang* (approximately twenty feet), but it can be as tiny as a needle, hidden inside Sun Wukong's ear, or as tall as the heavens.

Sun Wukong can change not only his staff's dimensions, but also his own. Mastering transformation magic (*bian*), the heroic monkey is capable of assuming at will any shape or size:

> [Sun Wukong] held the treasure [the staff] in his hands and called out, "Smaller, smaller, smaller!" and at once it shrank to the size of a tiny embroidery needle, small enough to be hidden inside the ear. Awestruck, the monkeys cried, "Great King! Take it out and play with it some more." The Monkey King took it out from his ear and placed it on his palm. "Bigger, bigger, bigger!" he shouted, and again it grew to the thickness of a barrel and more than twenty feet long. He became so delighted playing with it that he jumped onto the bridge and walked out of the cave. Grasping the treasure in his hands, he began to perform the magic of cosmic imitation. He bent over and cried, "Grow!" and at once grew to be ten thousand feet tall, with a head like the Tai Mountain and a chest like a rugged peak, eyes like lightning and a mouth like a blood bowl, and teeth like swords and halberds. The staff in his hands was of such a size that its top reached the thirty-third Heaven and its bottom the eighteenth layer of Hell. Tigers, leopards, wolves, and crawling creatures, all the monsters of the mountain and the demon kings of the seventy-two caves, were so terrified that they kowtowed and paid homage to the Monkey King in fear and trembling. Presently he revoked his magical appearance and changed the treasure back into a tiny embroidery needle stored in his ear.[40]

FIG. 15. Sun Wukong's staff; late Ming (ca. 1625) woodblock illustration

The superhuman dimensions of the staff-wielding monkey remind us of another staff expert, who likewise could change his size at will. This is, of course, Shaolin's guardian spirit, Vajrapāṇi (alias Kiṃnara), who emerged from the monastery's stove as a giant, standing astride the Mt. Song peaks. Sun Wukong similarly changed his appearance, in one instance after being smelted in a stove (belonging to Laozi's alchemical laboratory).[41] Which of these staff-brandishing deities inspired the other's myth? Did the *Journey to the West* story cycle serve as a source for the hagiographic literature of the Shaolin Monastery, or, conversely, did Shaolin monastic legends influence novels and plays celebrating Sun Wukong?

If the Sun Wukong and Vajrapāṇi legends *are* related, it is likely that the former influenced the latter. Whereas Vajrapāṇi was armed with the Shaolin staff in the sixteenth century, the divine monkey wielded the weapon as early as the thirteenth. The earliest extant version of his adventures, *Master of the Law, Tripitaka of the Great Tang, Procures the Scriptures* (*Da Tang Sanzang fashi qu jing ji*), is believed by most scholars to have been authored during the Southern Song,[42] approximately three hundred years before the appearance of Vajrapāṇi's Shaolin legend. The hagiographic literature of a Buddhist military temple was influenced then by popular literature.

Huiming

If Sun Wukong is a supernatural being whose "As You Wish, Golden Rings Clasped Staff" yields to his wishes, Huiming is an ordinary cleric, whose iron staff (*tiebang*) is no magic weapon. Still, Huiming's mastery of staff fighting is such that he employs it to save two of the most beloved figures in the history of Chinese literature: Zhang Gong and Cui Yingying, romantic protagonists of Wang Shifu's (ca. 1250–1300) *zaju* play *Story of the Western Wing* (*Xixiang ji*). Wang elaborates on his protagonist's addiction to meat no less than on his fighting skills, combining the two vices in zestful parody. In order to spice his vegetarian fare with flesh, he tells us, the monk goes to battle.[43]

In Wang's play, the romantic Zhang and Cui are stranded in a monastery that is besieged by bandits. The staff-wielding Huiming saves the day by breaking the blockade and calling army units to the rescue. However, Wang was not the first to assign the monk this role. Wang's *Story of the Western Wing* derives from an earlier version of the tale written in the *zhugongdiao* (all-keys-and-modes) genre by Dong Jieyuan (Master Dong) (fl. 1190–1208). Sometimes known as *Dong Jieyuan's Story of the Western Wing*, this early version already features a staff-wielding cleric named Facong, whose role is that of savior to the romantic couple. Moreover, the *zhugongdiao* version elaborates on his mastery of the weapon more than the *zaju* version does. Dong Jieyuan dedicates an entire song suite to Facong's virtuosity in staff fighting. In the following poem, for instance, the monk relies on his staff—which he manipulates from horseback—to defeat the bandit leader, Flying Tiger (figure 16):

> Facong uses an iron staff,
> Flying Tiger uses a steel axe.
> One smites the monk with his axe,
> One attacks the tiger with his staff.
> Flying Tiger excels in offensive jabs,
> Facong's superb with defensive parries.
> Facong has the upper hand,
> Flying Tiger tries to escape.[44]

Fig. 16. Huiming manipulating the staff from horseback; woodblock illustration dated 1498.

Even as he leaves no doubt that his protagonist specializes in staff fighting, Dong Jieyuan supplies him with other weapons as well. In addition to the staff, Facong is armed with a whip and a "prohibitions' knife" (*jiedao*; Sanskrit: *śastraka*). Mentioned also in Wang Shifu's *zaju* version, the latter has a Buddhist provenance. Monastic regulations list the "prohibitions' knife" among the monk's "eighteen belongings" (*shiba wu*), which include such items as soap, water bottle, mat, begging bowl, and the Buddhist ring staff (*xizhang*). Originally intended for such tasks as shaving the head, cutting the fingernails, and mending clothes, the "prohibitions' knife" was only a few inches long. However, Dong Jieyuan's literary fancy has enlarged it to the size of a three-foot dragon-slaying sword.[45]

Lu Zhishen

This fighting monk has been mentioned twice before, first as an example of the literary topos of the meat-eating fighting-monk—like Huiming, Lu delights in nothing better than animal flesh, especially dog meat—and second because of his affiliation with the Mt. Wutai monasteries, which probably reflects their military renown. We have seen that historical Wutai monks did go to war, and their heroism was mirrored in popular literature. We turn now to the valiant monk's typical weapon: the staff.

Lu Zhishen, also known as the "Tattooed Monk" (Hua Heshang), figures in the enormously popular novel of physical heroism, *Water Margin* (*Shuihu zhuan*). This early Ming novel derives from dramatic and oral antecedents, which can be traced back to the Southern Song. It is noteworthy that even in the earliest versions of the story cycle, Lu is armed with the staff. A Southern Song list of topics popular among storytellers classifies the "Tattooed Monk" story in the category of "staff" (*ganbang*) tales.[46]

Like Huiming, Lu Zhishen is equipped with a "prohibitions' knife" in addition to his weapon of choice, the staff. In the Ming period novel, the latter is cast iron and weighs sixty-two *jin* (approximately eighty pounds), or four times the weight recommended by Cheng Zongyou in his *Shaolin Staff Method*. The staff's improbable weight likely is meant to highlight its proprietor's extraordinary strength. Indeed, the tattooed monk is so strong that he wishes his staff would be even heavier, as he explains to the blacksmith:

> "I need a 'Chan staff' (*chan zhang*) and a 'prohibitions' knife' (*jiedao*)," said Lu Zhishen. "Do you have any first-rate metal?"
>
> "I do indeed. How heavy a staff and knife do you want? We'll make them according to your requirements."
>
> "The staff should be a hundred *jin*."
>
> "Much too heavy," the smith laughed. "I could make it for you, but you'd never be able to wield it. Even Guangong's broadsword (*dao*) wasn't more than eighty-one *jin*!"
>
> "I'm every bit as good as Guangong," Lu Zhishen burst out impatiently. "He was only a man, too."
>
> "I mean well, Reverend. Even forty-five *jin* would be very heavy."
>
> "You say Guangong's broadsword was eighty-one *jin*? Make me a staff of that weight, then."
>
> "Too thick, Master. It would look ugly, and be clumsy to use. Take my advice, let me make you a sixty-two *jin* Chan staff of burnished metal. Of course, if it's too heavy, don't blame me."[47]

Ming visual representations of Lu Zhishen reveal a tiny crescent at one end of his weapon (figure 17). A similar design is discernible in a few of Huiming's images (figure 18), as well as in those of another fictional staff-wielding cleric: "Sha Monk" (Sha Heshang), who figures as a secondary character in the *Journey to the West* (figure 19). So far we have not mentioned "Sha Monk," whose name—literally "Sand Monk"—derives from the Buddhist "God of the Deep Sands" (Shensha shen). In the sixteenth-century novel, the weapon of the "Sand Monk" is referred to as "Precious Staff" (*baozhang*) as well as "Demon-Felling Staff" (*xiangyao zhang*).[48] Interestingly, in all three cases—Lu Zhishen, Huiming, and "Sha Monk"—the crescent is perceptible in some of the fighting monks' visual representations, but it is not mentioned in the written narratives celebrating them.

Future research may determine the origins of the crescent shape, which is visible in some Ming period illustrations of the staff. Here I will mention only that an identical design is common in a wide variety of twentieth-century martial arts weapons, whether or not they are wielded by Buddhist clerics. The

FIG. 17. Late Ming
woodblock illustra-
tion of Lu Zhishen
manipulating the
staff.

crescent's significance in contemporary weaponry can be gauged by its appear-
ance in the names of such instruments as the "Crescent-Shaped (*yueya*) Spade,"
"Crescent-Shaped Spear," "Crescent-Shaped Battle-ax," and "Crescent-Shaped
Rake."[49]

Yang the Fifth

Protagonist of the late Ming novel *Yang Family Generals*, Yang the Fifth
(Yang Wulang) shares with Lu Zhishen a Wutai connection, and with Sun Wukong a magic weapon. Joining the Buddhist order on Mt. Wutai, Yang the Fifth
leads a monastic army from there in support of his heroic Yang family brothers
and sisters. In the two slightly different versions of the novel, he is armed with
a battleaxe as well as a "Dragon-Felling Staff" (*xianglong bang*), which, as its
name suggests, subdues the mythic creatures.[50]

FIG. 18. Huiming brandishing the staff; woodblock illustration
dated 1614.

The *Yang Family* story cycle evolved around the historical figure of the
Northern Song general Yang Ye (?–986), who was followed by his son and grand-
son in serving the dynasty's cause. It developed through Southern Song oral literature and Yuan drama, culminating in the two versions of the Ming novel. It
is noteworthy that the cycle's monkish protagonist is armed with a staff already
in its earliest versions. Along with Lu Zhishen's story "The Tattooed Monk,"
"[Yang] the Fifth Becomes a Monk" is classified in a Southern Song list of oral
tales in the category of "staff" (*ganbang*) tales.[51]

FIG. 19. Late Ming woodblock illustration of Sha Monk wielding the staff.

The Origins of Monastic Staff Fighting

Ming period popular lore extends the connection between fighting monks and the staff beyond Shaolin's walls. Even though Sun Wukong, Huiming, Lu Zhishen, and Yang Wulang are not affiliated with the monastery, all four wield the weapon. Two of these fictional staff-wielding monks are associated with the Wutai monasteries, and two others are not connected to a historical center of monastic fighting. Taken together, they indicate that novelists and playwrights conceived of the staff as the quintessential Buddhist weapon, regardless of monastic affiliation.

The narratives of the four fictional monks can be traced back to the Southern Song, strengthening the impression gained from military literature that monastic staff fighting originated earlier than the Ming. Sixteenth-century generals such as Yu Dayou and Qi Jiguang insisted that Shaolin monks had been practicing the staff for centuries. Sun Wukong, Huiming, Lu Zhishen, and Yang Wulang employ the weapon in their story cycles' earliest extant versions, which date from the thirteenth century. Assuming that these characters have been fashioned after *real* monks, staff fighting had been practiced either at Shaolin, or in other Buddhist monasteries, as early as the Southern Song.

Why did Shaolin monks, or other Buddhist monks, choose the staff as their weapon? Some scholars sought an answer in what they construed as the weapon's defensive quality, which supposedly accords with the Buddhist prohibition of violence. The staff cannot injure or kill, they claim, and it is used for self-defense only. Cheng Dali illustrates the argument: "the staff is a blunt instrument, which, moreover, is made of wood. Its power to kill and injure is far inferior to those of the broadsword, the sword, and other metal sharp weapons. Evidently, using the wooden staff is relatively appropriate to the position of Buddhist disciples, who are permitted to employ the martial arts for limited purposes only."[52]

Cheng's argument cannot be dismissed as irrelevant for the monastic choice of the weapon. When it is made of wood the staff is indeed less dangerous than other weapons, and for this reason perhaps some monks preferred to use it. The problem is, as Cheng acknowledges, that the Shaolin weapon was often forged of iron, just like the heavy rods wielded by the fictional monks Sun Wukong, Huiming, Lu Zhishen, and Yang Wulang. It was therefore a lethal instrument, with a capacity to kill that is attested by military literature no less than by fiction and drama. Moreover, we need not assume that fighting monks were concerned with the Buddhist prohibition of violence, which they disavowed by going to battle. Recall for example the sixteenth-century Shaolin monk who employed a metal staff to annihilate an unarmed pirate's wife.

The staff's presumed defensive quality provides therefore no more than a partial explanation for its use by Buddhist monks. It might be more useful to examine the staff's place in Buddhist history, for its military role might have derived from earlier functions the tradition assigned it.

The Ring Staff

Long before it was relied upon for fighting, the staff served as the emblem of the monk. Monastic regulations, which were translated into Chinese during the early medieval period, prescribe a staff as among the "eighteen belongings" that a monk should carry in the performance of his duties. They also ordain its exact shape, which differed from that of the fighting staff, Instead of an unadorned pole of equal thickness throughout its length, the staff decreed by monastic law was decorated at one end with two to four metal loops, from which hung between six to twelve metal rings (figure 20). Named in Sanskrit *khakkhara*, this ring staff was called in Chinese transliteration *xiqiluo* and *qihelan*. More commonly, however, it was known in China as *xizhang* (*xi* staff). The word *xi*, meaning tin or pewter, may allude to the metal of which the rings were made, or onomatopoeically to the sound they emitted. In his *Translated Buddhist Terminology* (*Fanyi mingyi ji*), Fayun (1088–1158) explains that "the *xiqiluo* is called *xizhang*, because when rattled it emits a *xixi* sound. For this reason the *Sarvāstivāda-vinaya* names it 'Sounding Staff' (*shengzhang*)."[53]

Fayun's etymological analysis of the *xizhang* shows the significance that Buddhist scriptures accord its ringing. Monastic regulations provide three raisons d'être for the ring staff, two of which depend on the chiming of its rings. First, the ringing produced by shaking the staff can scare away snakes, scorpions, and other dangerous beasts. Second, it can alert a donor to the presence of an alms-begging monk at his door. The third function is not related to the staff's acoustics: like any walking stick, the ring staff can offer support for old and sick monks. These practical functions are accompanied by the symbolic significance that Buddhist monks attached to the staff's varying number of loops and rings. One scripture recommends, for example, four loops, symbolizing "the severance from the four types of birth, meditation on the four truths, cultivation of the four forms of equanimity, entrance into the four *dhyānas*, the purification of the four empty [regions], the clarification of the four areas of thought, the fortification of the four proper forms of diligence, and attainment of the four divine powers."[54]

Numerous references to the ring staff in medieval literature attest that at least some monks followed monastic regulations and carried it. As John Kieschnick has pointed out, biographies of eminent monks use such expressions as "picked up his ring staff" to signify that a monk set on a journey, and Tang poetry alludes to the "crisp sound of the ring staff on a snow-covered path."[55] Occasionally, the ring staff signified by metonymy its clerical owner, as when Bai Juyi (772–846) wrote of the "ring staff climbing to the monastery on high."[56] Similarly, visual works of art reveal that the ring staff, like the alms bowl, became a

FIG. 20. The ring staff as the emblem of the monk; detail of a Xixia period (1038–1227) wall painting from the Yulin Caves, Gansu.

monk's symbol. Paintings of Buddhas and Bodhisattvas often have the deity's monkish attendant carry one or both of these monastic insignia. The Bodhisattva of Medicine (Bhaiṣajyaguru; Yaoshi), for instance, is flanked in an enormous fourteenth-century wall painting by two monks, one carrying the bowl, the other displaying the ring staff.[57] An earlier, Xixia period (1038–1227) composition of the Bodhisattva Mañjuśrī (Wenshu) has one monk carrying both emblems (figure 20). The ring staff was even incorporated into the iconography of deities. The Bodhisattva Kṣitigarbha (Dizang pusa) is usually depicted as brandishing it.

The emblematic Buddhist staff was not always fashioned in accordance with monastic regulations. Some clerics retained it as a symbol of religious authority, even as they dispensed—for practical or financial reasons—with its rings. An impressive seventeenth-century portrait of the monk Yinyuan (1592–1673) shows him holding an enormous wooden staff that is not adorned with the prescribed rings (figure 21). Yinyuan's seated posture, like his serene expression and grand monastic robes, suggest that the staff serves him not as a weapon, but as a symbol of religious authority. However, devoid of its rings, his emblematic staff is identical in shape to the one fighting monks employed in

FIG. 21. The staff as the emblem of the monk; Japanese
portrait of the Chinese monk Yinyuan (1592–1673).

combat. Here, then, we perceive a connection between the ring staff and the fighting staff. Slightly altered, the Buddhist symbol is indistinguishable from the monastic weapon.

The Magic Weapon

The similarity of the ring staff and the fighting staff extends beyond their shape. Occasionally the two poles have been used for the same purpose. To this day, Shaolin monks sometimes employ the ring staff in martial demonstrations. Even more intriguing, the Buddhist emblem has been used as a *magic* weapon. Beginning in the medieval period, the ring staff figured in ritual warfare. In this respect the monastic symbol is not unique. The staff has been accorded magic qualities in numerous cultures, where it has served as a symbol of religious and political authority. Comparative analysis could therefore shed light on its Buddhist significance.

The staff has been used as an insignia of office across religious and political boundaries. Egyptian priests and Roman augurs wielded it, just as today it serves as an emblem of Catholic bishops (whose crosier is crook-shaped).[58] In these clerical instances the staff signifies religious authority, but in a political context it symbolizes sovereignty. In Western kingship the scepter is borne by the sovereign in his coronation ceremony, and in ancient Israel it was carried by the chiefs of the nation's twelve tribes (for which reason the Hebrew word *ma'teh* has two meanings: staff and tribe). Other rulers in the ancient Near East likewise bore the staff: Hittite, Phoenician, Babylonian, and Assyrian kings wielded it, as did the pharaohs of ancient Egypt.[59] Precisely because its purport has not been limited to a given cultural context, it is tempting to interpret the staff psychoanalytically as a phallic symbol.

In the ancient Near East, the king's staff was believed to have been bestowed upon him by a god, who thereby imparted to him some of his divine strength. Traces of this Mesopotamian and Egyptian belief are visible in the Hebrew bible, where Moses' staff is alluded to twice as "God's staff." Because of its divine provenance, the prophet's emblem is endowed with supernatural powers. Moses relies on it to bring the plagues upon the Egyptians and to transform the sea into dry land, releasing his people from Egypt.[60]

If God bestowed his staff on his chosen prophet, the Buddha equipped his favorite disciple with his. According to a legend that enjoyed tremendous popularity in China, he lent his emblem to monk Mulian (Sanskrit: Maudgalyā-yana), who employed it to break through the infernal regions. Combining the virtues of filial piety and Buddhist celibacy, the legend has its monkish protagonist descend to the netherworld to rescue his mother, who is being punished there for her sinful life. Armed with the Buddha's magic weapon, the monk defeats the demonic wardens of the underworld, smashing open the gates of the

Avīci Hell. His staff enables him to rescue his mother, just as Moses' permitted the prophet to deliver his people.

One of the earliest performance versions of Mulian's journey is the Tang period alternating prose and verse narrative *Transformation Text on Mahāmaudgalyāyana Rescuing His Mother from the Underworld* (*Damuqianlianmingjian jiumu bianwen*). Originally performed by storytellers, the narrative explained how to activate the staff's magic. To release his emblem's formidable force, Mulian "rattled" (*yao*) or "shook" (*zhen*) its rings. When the monk "rattled the ring staff, ghosts and spirits were mowed down on the spot like stalks of hemp." Similarly:

> With one shake of [Mulian's] staff, the bars and locks fell from [hell's]
> black walls, On the second shake, the double leaves of the main gate
> flew open.[61]

Mulian's legend has enjoyed tremendous popularity in Chinese drama, where its performance has been invariably embedded in a ritual complex. Mulian plays are usually performed on the occasion of the Ghost Festival (Guijie), also known by its Buddhist name Yulanpen, where they are intended for the salvation of community members who died prematurely. Otherwise they are staged as part of an individual's funerary rites, for the redemption of his soul.[62] Sometimes the mortuary play is performed by ritual specialists, Buddhist or Taoist, instead of professional actors. The priest dons Mulian's robe and, wielding his divine staff, smashes a sand or paper replica of hell, thereby delivering the deceased.[63] Thus, the ring staff still figures as a magic weapon in Chinese religion today.

Whereas Mulian wielded the ring staff in his harrowing journey to hell, others flew on it to heaven. Like European witches who were believed to ride on sticks and brooms, Chinese monks were imagined soaring on the ring staff. As early as the fourth century, Sun Chuo (ca. 310–397) compared the Taoist mode of flying on a crane to the Buddhist style of riding the staff:

> Wang Qiao drove a crane and soared to the heaven,
> The Arhats flung their staffs and trod the air.[64]

In medieval poetry the flying staff became a symbol of liberation from earthly toils. Du Fu (712–770) dreamed of "flying the ring staff away from the world of dust," and in Liu Zongyuan's (773–819) vision:

> The Immortals' Mountain isn't subject to the appointed officials,
> There you can freely soar to the sky, flying the ring staff.[65]

The term "flying staff" (*feixi*) figured so prominently in medieval literature that it was eventually applied to itinerant monks. In his encyclopedic *Buddhist Essentials* (*Shishi yaolan*) (preface 1020), the Buddhist lexicographer

Daocheng explained that "the elegant term for Buddhist itinerancy is 'flying staff.' This is because when the eminent monk Yinfeng traveled to Mt. Wutai, his route passed through Huaixi Province (in the upper Huai river valley), [where war raged]. He hurled his staff, rose into the air, and flew [above the war zone]."[66] According to the Buddhist historian Zanning (919–1001), the monk soared above the opposing armies to convince them to lay down their arms. His aerial journey was therefore a fine example of Buddhist "expedient means" (Sanskrit: *upāya*; Chinese: *fangbian*), which were meant to inculcate the virtue of peace:

> During the Yuanhe reign period (806–820) Yinfeng announced he would journey to Mt. Wutai. His route passed through Huaixi Province, which was then under the control of Wu Yuanji (fl. 815). Relying on the strength of his army, the latter defied the emperor's orders. Government troops were sent to counter the rebel. The two sides engaged in battle, but none could prevail over the other. "I will put an end to this mutual slaughter," Yinfeng said, whereupon he hurled his staff into the air, soared upwards, and gracefully floated behind [his staff]. When he flew above the opposing armies' formations, and all the soldiers saw a monk soaring to heaven, they instantly drew their weapons back into their scabbards.[67]

Sun Wukong's Ring Staff

The magic attributes of the ring staff are not necessarily relevant for the staff's choice as weapon. Monastic warriors were probably concerned with the effectiveness of the unadorned fighting staff more than with the supernormal qualities of its ring-ornate predecessor. However, ring staff legends did influence the depiction of fighting staffs in novels and plays. The magic aura that enwraps Sun Wukong's "As You Wish Staff," Sha Monk's "Demon-Felling Staff," and Yang Wulang's "Dragon-Felling Staff" derives from the divine powers that the Buddhist tradition accorded the ring staff.

The clearest indication of a literary connection between the ring staff and the fighting staff is provided by the evolution of Sun Wukong's armament within the *Journey to the West* cycle. In the journey's earliest extant version, the monkey's weapon *is* the ring staff. The Southern Song *Master of the Law, Tripitaka of the Great Tang, Procures the Scriptures* describes it as a "golden rings staff" (*jinhuan zhang*) or "golden rings ring staff" (*jinhuan xizhang*).[68] Only in later renditions did the rings disappear, giving way to the unadorned and efficient fighting staff, referred to as *gun* or *bang*.[69] However, even as depicted in the cycle's latest versions, Sun Wukong's "As You Wish, Golden Rings Clasped, Staff" (Ruyi jingu bang) betrays its Buddhist ancestry, for it is bound at each end by a golden ring.[70] It might not be too fanciful to see in these binding rings (*gu*) a relic of the ring staff's original loose ones (*huan*). If so, the resonance between the names "Jinhuan zhang" ("Golden Rings Staff") and "Jingu bang" ("Golden Rings *Clasped* Staff") is not incidental.

In its divine provenance, Sun Wukong's original ring staff resembled the magic weapons wielded by Mulian and Moses. According to the Southern Song *Master of the Law*, it was bestowed upon him by Vaśravaṇa of the North, Mahā-brahmā Devarāja (Beifang Pishamen Dafan Tianwang).[71] The staff is impregnated with such extraordinary powers that it can be brought to life. In two instances the monkey transforms it into supernatural creatures that fight on his behalf, once into an iron dragon and, on another occasion, into a *yakṣa* spirit, "its head touching the sky and its feet the earth, and brandishing in its hands a Demon-Felling Club."[72] This magic, not uncommon in Chinese Buddhist lore,[73] is reminiscent of the biblical miracle, in which the prophet transformed his staff into a mythic snake:

> And the Lord said to Moses and Aaron, "When Pharaoh says to you, 'Prove yourselves by working a miracle,' then you shall say to Aaron, 'Take your staff and cast it down before Pharaoh, that it may become a serpent (*ta'nin*)." So Moses and Aaron went to Pharaoh and did as the Lord commanded; Aaron cast down his staff before Pharaoh and his servants, and it became a serpent. Then Pharaoh summoned the wise men and the sorcerers; and they also, the magicians of Egypt, did the same by their secret arts. For every man cast down his staff, and they became serpents. But Aaron's staff swallowed up their staffs.[74]

Conclusion

We may not be able to ascertain why Chinese monks chose the staff as their weapon. However, it is likely their preference was due to its Buddhist significance. Monastic regulations instructed monks to carry a staff, which gradually became a symbol of their religious authority. Buddhist literature and popular lore accorded magic powers to the emblem, which was originally adorned with rings, but sometimes fashioned without them. Perhaps because they regularly carried it, fighting monks who went to battle transformed the staff into a weapon.

Whichever its origins, the staff became so prominent in the Shaolin's military regimen that it influenced the monastery's lore. According to a Ming Shaolin legend, the god Vajrapāṇi was incarnated at the monastery as a lowly menial equipped with a divine staff. When the monastery was attacked by bandits, he repelled them with his emblematic weapon. The legend illustrates the reciprocal relations between martial mythology and martial practice in the Buddhist tradition. On the one hand, violent deities such as Vajrapāṇi inspired Buddhist military training, providing physical strength to martial monks and religious sanction to monastic violence; on the other, fighting monks changed the image of their tutelary divinities to fit their own martial training. In this instance, the ancient *vajra* holder, Vajrapāṇi, was transformed into a staff expert, progenitor of the renowned Shaolin fighting technique.

His transformation into a staff expert would not be the last in Vajrapāṇi's Shaolin career. Twentieth-century images of the tutelary divinity reveal a clenched fist, attesting to his mastery of empty-handed fighting. As we will see in the next chapter, by the eighteenth century hand combat (*quan*) gradually eclipsed the staff as the dominant form of Shaolin fighting.

PART III

Fist Fighting and
Self-Cultivation
(1600–1900)

CHAPTER 5

Hand Combat

MARTIAL TECHNIQUES MAY require centuries to evolve. Shaolin monks had been practicing the staff for several hundred years before it was lauded in late Ming literature as an outstanding fighting method. Similarly, their bare-handed techniques—now famous the world over—have been unfolding for some four hundred years. As early as the sixteenth century, some Shaolin monks practiced unarmed fighting; in the course of the seventeenth, they developed sophisticated empty-handed techniques, and by the mid-Qing period (the eighteenth and early nineteenth centuries), hand combat (*quan*) had eclipsed the staff as the dominant form of Shaolin martial training.

The term *quan*, which I render "hand combat," means literally "fist." During the late imperial period it designated unarmed fighting techniques, all of which made use of legs in addition to arms; kicking figures prominently in all *quan* styles, in which sense "hand combat" is misleading. "Boxing," which has also been used as a rendition of *quan*, suffers from the added disadvantage that it connotes a specific Western sport. I have opted therefore for "hand combat," but where it sounds too awkward—especially in the names of individual styles —I have resorted to the literal "fist."

The earliest reference I am aware of to Shaolin hand combat occurs in Tang Shunzhi's (1507–1560) poem "Song of the Emei Monk's Fist," which extols not only the Emei monasteries' empty-handed fighting, but also the Shaolin's.[1] However, in his comprehensive *Treatise on Military Affairs* (*Wu bian*), where he lists contemporary bare-handed styles such as "[Song Emperor] Zhao Taizu's Long-Range Fist" (Zhao Taizu changquan) and "Wen Family Fist" (Wenjia quan), the same author does not allude to Shaolin, indicating that the monastery had not developed as yet a recognized empty-handed style. In the military encyclopedia, Tang, like other sixteenth-century military experts, alludes to the Shaolin staff instead.[2]

Several decades later, allusions to hand combat began to appear in the travelogues and poems of late Ming visitors to Shaolin such as Wang Shixing (who explored it in 1581), Gong Nai (*jinshi* 1601), Wen Xiangfeng (*jinshi* 1610), and Yuan Hongdao (who visited the monastery in 1609). However, it is hard to gauge the importance of unarmed fighting in Shaolin's regimen from their poetic compositions, which were meant to convey the monastery's ambiance, not to analyze its military techniques.[3]

Curiously, the clearest indication that late Ming Shaolin monks *were* turning their attention to hand combat is provided by the most vocal exponent of their staff method, Cheng Zongyou. In his *Shaolin Staff Method* (ca. 1610), the staff expert has a hypothetical interlocutor ask: Why do Shaolin monks practice bare-handed fighting? Cheng's answer acknowledges that some monks were seriously engaged in hand combat, even as it leaves no doubt that, for them, it was a newly acquired fighting style. Furthermore, Cheng explains that throughout China, empty-handed techniques are not yet widely practiced, which is precisely why Shaolin monks explore them— they wish to develop hand combat to the same level of perfection as their ancient staff method. Cheng's reply associates the Shaolin investigation of the novel martial art with Buddhist self-cultivation:

> Someone may ask: "As to the staff, the Shaolin [method] is admired. Today there are many Shaolin monks who practice hand combat (*quan*), and do not practice staff. Why is that?
> I answer: The Shaolin staff is called the Yakṣa (Yecha) [method]. It is a sacred transmission from the Kiṃnara King (Jinnaluo wang) (Shaolin's tutelary deity, Vajrapāṇi). To this day it is known as "unsurpassed wisdom (Bodhi)" (*wushang puti*). By contrast, hand combat is not yet popular in the land (*quan you wei shengxing hainei*). Those [Shaolin monks] who specialize in it, do so in order to transform it, like the staff, [into a vehicle] for reaching the other shore [of enlightenment]."[4]

The *Hand Combat Classic* and *Xuanji's Acupuncture Points*

Which shape did seventeenth-century Shaolin hand combat take? A possible answer is provided by two Qing period (1644–1911) manuals, which purport to record it. The two treatises, which share similarities so striking that they have been treated by scholars as two versions of one work, circulated in Qing manuscript editions before being published in Shanghai during the Republican era (1912–1949). They are: *Hand Combat Classic, Collection of Hand Combat Methods* (*Quan jing, Quan fa beiyao*), with a preface of 1784 by Cao Huandou (style: Zaidong), and *Xuanji's Secret Transmission of Acupuncture Points' Hand Combat Formulas* (*Xuanji mishou xuedao quan jue*), which carries an undated preface by one Zhang Ming'e.

The *Hand Combat Classic* and *Xuanji's Acupuncture Points* trace their military

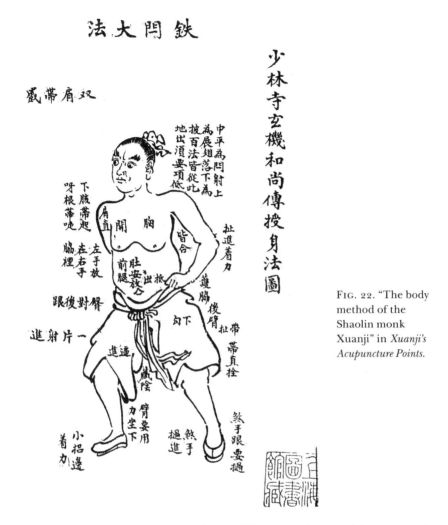

法大門鉄

雙肩帶戲

少林寺玄機和尚傳授身法圖

FIG. 22. "The body
method of the
Shaolin monk
Xuanji" in *Xuanji's
Acupuncture Points.*

techniques—through an almost identical lineage of lay practitioners—to the
Shaolin Monastery. In his 1784 preface to *Hand Combat Classic,* Cao Huandou
explains that the manual he annotated had been authored more than a century earlier by one Zhang Kongzhao (style: Hengqiu). He further notes that
Zhang Kongzhao studied his Shaolin method with Zhang Ming'e, who is given
as author of the preface to *Xuanji's Acupuncture Points.* The latter manual also
mentions Zhang Kongzhao's name.[5] Finally, preceding these lay disciples, the
two manuals identify the same Shaolin cleric as the source of their teachings.
This is the monk Xuanji, whose name appears in the title *Xuanji's Acupuncture
Points* (figure 22).[6]

The *Hand Combat Classic*'s and *Xuanji's Acupuncture Points'* claims of common origins are borne out by their teachings. The two manuals expound the

same fighting principles and employ an identical martial vocabulary. There is also textual convergence—almost half the text, as well as some illustrations, are identical. There is no doubt, then, that the two books do not merely reflect the same *oral* tradition, but also derive from the same *written* text.[7] Judging by Cao Huandou's dating of Zhang Kongzhao, this original manual of the Shaolin style must have been authored in the seventeenth century.

The Republican period witnessed the publication of numerous treatises that, just like *Hand Combat Classic* and *Xuanji's Acupuncture Points,* claim to record the original Shaolin Fist. The most famous is *Secret Formulas of the Shaolin Hand Combat Method* (*Shaolin quanshu mijue*) (1915), which is still regarded by some as an authentic composition. However, scholars have shown that most of these publications have nothing to do with the monastery. *Secret Formulas,* for example, expounds a southern Chinese style known as the Hong Fist (Hongquan), which is related to Shaolin by legend only. According to late Qing lore, the Hong Fist was created by Shaolin monks who fought the Manchu invaders. The latter supposedly burnt the monastery, whereupon the monks escaped to the south, where they established the Hong Fist lineage. We will return to this legend, which was celebrated in nineteenth-century fiction, Triads' literature, and manuals of southern style fighting. Here, suffice it to note that its influence on *Secret Formulas* belies the latter's authenticity.[8]

Whereas most Republican Shaolin manuals derive from late Qing lore, *Hand Combat Classic* and *Xuanji's Acupuncture Points* share a seventeenth-century frame of reference. The martial techniques they mention were practiced during the late Ming, and even the legends they paraphrase date from that period. Consider, for example, the opening paragraph of *Hand Combat Classic*:

> The history of hand combat originated at the Shaolin Monastery. Ever since the Song emperor [Zhao] Taizu studied there, the monastery's fame spread throughout the land. Thereafter, there have been "Wen Family Seventy-two Posture Moving Form," "Thirty-six Posture Locking Form," "Twenty-four Throws Pat on Horse," "Eight Evasive Maneuvers," and "Twelve Postures Close-Range Fist," Lu Hong's hard "Eight Throws," Shandong Li Bantian's leg technique, Eagle Claw Wang's grappling technique, and Zhang Jingbai's striking technique. These techniques are all famous throughout the land, each having its own wonderful aspects. However, they are all guilty of either emphasizing the top to the neglect of the bottom, or the bottom to the neglect of the top. Even if one successfully relies on them to overcome an opponent, they cannot be considered perfect in every respect.[9]

The entire paragraph has been borrowed from the sixteenth-century general Qi Jiguang's *Essentials of the Hand Combat Classic* (*Quan jing jieyao*) (ca. 1562).[10] The only difference concerns the Shaolin's role in the evolution of bare-handed fighting. The late Ming general did not associate the monastery with empty-handed techniques, mentioning their staff method instead. Furthermore, Qi Jiguang did not relate the Song dynasty founder, Emperor Zhao Taizu (reigned 960–975) to the monastery. Ming period lore attributed to the emperor a popular bare-handed technique known as "Zhao Taizu's Long-Range Fist" (Zhao Taizu changquan). As befitting a Shaolin manual, *Hand Combat Classic* twisted the legend, having the emperor study his method at the monastery.[11]

The late Ming context of *Hand Combat Classic* and *Xuanji's Acupuncture Points* supports Cao Huandou's 1784 claim that the manual he annotated had been authored more than a century earlier. It would seem that the two manuals derived from an earlier text that had been authored around the Ming-Qing transition. Further support for this time frame, as well as for the manual's Shaolin provenance, is provided by the name "Xuanji," to which both manuals attribute their teachings. A 1631 Shaolin stele inscription alludes to a monk named Xuanji as a *dutidian* (superintendent), which term was commonly applied to military appointees in the monastery's internal administration. It is likely, therefore, that Xuanji *was* a seventeenth-century Shaolin fighting monk, as asserted by the treatises that purport to record his teachings.[12]

If the Shaolin method recorded in both manuals dates from as early as the seventeenth century, we are struck by its complexity. *Hand Combat Classic* and *Xuanji's Acupuncture Points* depict a sophisticated fighting system. They expound underlying principles such as "the weak defeating the strong" (*ruo di qiang*) and "the soft subduing the hard" (*rou sheng gang*); they analyze fundamental techniques such as stepping (*bu*), throwing (*die*), seizing (*na*), and throwing off balance by hooking the opponent's legs (*guan*); and they provide detailed instructions for the proper maneuvering of each body part: the head, eyes, neck, shoulders, arms, hands, chest, waist, buttocks, legs, knees, and feet.

The two manuals concur that in certain instances "close-range hand combat can overcome long-range hand combat" (*duanda sheng changquan*), for "short-range makes it easier to reach the adversary's body."[13] The *Hand Combat Classic* includes an entire text—missing from the other manual—titled "Comprehensive and Original Treatise of the Shaolin Monastery's *Close-Range Fist* Body Method" ("Shaolin si duanda shen fa tong zong quan pu").[14] For its part, *Xuanji's Acupuncture Points* elaborates on another short-range style called "Yue Family Close-Range Fist" (Yuejia duanda).[15] The emphasis both manuals place on "close-range hand combat" is typical of late Ming and early Qing military literature, which usually distinguished between two types of hand combat: "long-range" (*changquan*) and "close-range" (*duanda*). Sixteenth- and seventeenth-century military experts allude to various short-range styles including "Cotton Zhang's Close-Range Fist" (Mian Zhang duanda), "Ren Family Close-Range Fist" (Renjia duanda), and "Liu [Family] Close-Range Fist" (Liu duanda).[16]

As suggested by its title, *Xuanji's Acupuncture Points*, the second manual also expounds the techniques, attributed to the Shaolin monk, of striking the opponent's cavities, or acupuncture points (*xuedao*). The concept was borrowed from traditional medicine, where it described sensitive spots along the body's internal circuits of energy (*qi*). Acupuncture treatment is applied to these points, which are not only receptive to treatment but also susceptible to injury. It is to them, the manual explains, that the accomplished Shaolin warrior directs his blows. The author employs the *Zhuangzi* metaphor of Cook Ding to explain the technique. The legendary cook's knife remained as good as new, even after nineteen years of butchering, for it had always followed the natural cavities in the oxen's body. Hand combat should similarly target acupuncture points:

> The book [*Zhuangzi*] says: "strike in the big hollows, guide the knife through the big openings." Why does it say so? Because when Cook Ding cut up oxen "he no longer saw the whole ox."[17] I say it is the same with hand combat. Why? Because I am looking for my opponent's soft points, acupuncture points, and those forbidden to strike and I engrave them in my mind's eye. For this reason, the moment I lift my hand, I am able to target my opponent's empty points, and strike at his acupuncture points, "no longer seeing the whole person."[18]

The manual identifies acupuncture points the striking of which will cause immediate or postponed death, as well as those leading to temporary or permanent paralysis. There is even a point that causes the adversary to "cry to death," and another that makes him "laugh to death." (Twentieth-century manuals of the Emei style similarly recognize a "laughing-waist acupuncture point" (*xiaoyao xue*), which, when struck, causes "serious injury and/or uncontrollable laughter."[19]) Their exact locations are marked in illustrations, which the *Xuanji's Acupuncture Points*' reader is advised not to divulge "lest wicked people intentionally use them to injure people" (figure 23).

Expounding as they do an entire fighting philosophy as well as its diverse applications, *Hand Combat Classic* and *Xuanji's Acupuncture Points* feature a rich technical vocabulary, as the latter's preface demonstrates:

> There are various hand combat styles, each with its own strength:
>   Some excel in palm method (*zhang*): The "According Palm," "Flipping Palm," "Offering Palm," "Saluting Palm," "Obstructing Palm," "Sweeping Palm," "Single Palm," "Double Palm," and "Mandarin-Duck Palm" all differ.
>   Some excel in fist method (*quan*): The "According Fist," "Flipping Fist," "Supporting Fist," "Inserting Fist," "Pulling Fist," "Shearing Fist," "Accompanied Fist," and "Reversing Fist" all differ.
>   Some excel in elbow method (*zhou*): The "Flipping Elbow," "According Elbow," "Horizontal Elbow," "Straight Elbow," "Angled Elbow," "Dashing Elbow," and "Back Elbow" all vary.
>   Some excel in body method (*shen*): The "Advancing Body," "Retreating Body," "Stretching Body," "Contracting Body," "Leisured Body,"

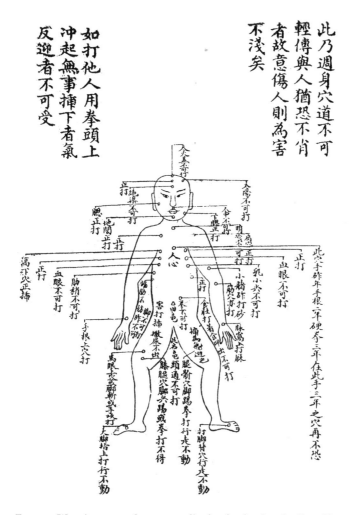

F<small>IG</small>. 23. Warning to readers not to divulge fatal points in *Xuanji's Acupuncture Points*.

"Dodging Body," "Growing Body," and "Leaping Body" are all dissimilar.

Some excel in knee method (*xi*): The "Left-Thrusting Knee," "Right-Thrusting Knee," "Kneeling Knee," "Back Knee," "Contracting Knee," and "Receiving Knee" are all distinct.

Some excel in leg method (*tui*): The "Single Leg," "Two Legs," "Changing Legs," "Spinning Leg," "Drilling Leg," "Thrusting Leg," "Following Leg," "Facing Leg," and "Upside-Down Leg" are all different.

Some excel in step method (*bu*): The "Long Step," "Short Step," "Angled Step," "Straight Step," "Dodge-Lean-Back Step," "Reverse Step,"

"According Step," "Exchanging Step," "Tracing Step," "Full Step," "Empty Step," "Curved Step," "Direct Step," and "Cylindrical Step" are all distinguishable.[20]

The *Xuanji's Acupuncture Points'* discussion of various palm postures is accompanied by an illustration that betrays Buddhist influence (compare figures 24 and 25). At least in its graphic design, if not in its specific finger positions, the various palm stances resemble the depiction of symbolic hand gestures (Sanskrit: *mudrā*; Chinese: *yinxiang*) in Buddhist scriptures. The pattern of a hand emerging from a cloud, or a lotus, is shared by both. We know of course that hand gestures *were* practiced at the Shaolin Monastery, not only because, as Michel Strickmann has shown, they were an integral element of Tantric rituals (which had a pervasive influence on Chinese Buddhism),[21] but more specifically because they figured in the Shaolin's Vajrapāṇi cult. Recall that in his twelfth-century Vajrapāṇi stele, Shaolin's abbot Zuduan noted that the martial deity's powers were invoked through palm signs and oral spells.

Following their exposition of hand combat principles, the two manuals detail specific fighting styles, first of which is the "Drunken Eight-Immortals Fist" (Zui baxian quan) (figure 26).[22] The eight Daoist immortals have been borrowed from late Ming lore, in which they were depicted as carefree, often

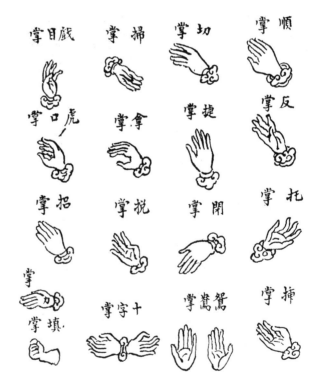

FIG. 24. Palm postures betraying the influence of Buddhist *mudrās* (from *Xuanji's Acupuncture Points*).

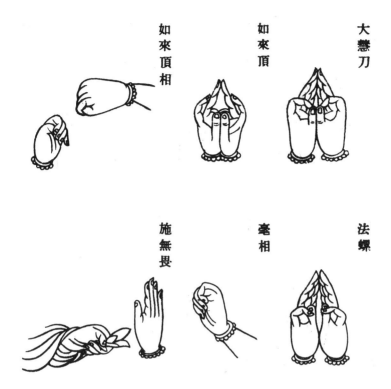

如來頂相   如來頂   大慧刀

施無畏   毫相   法螺

Fɪɢ. 25. Buddhist hand symbolism (*mudrās*).

lascivious, drunks. Novels and plays usually associate each of the insouciant saints with a given emblem: a flute, a flower basket, a gourd, a whisk, etc. The martial artist mimics wielding the icon in his training routine, which, even as it appears intoxicated, is perfectly sober. The "Drunken Eight-Immortals Fist," sometimes referred to as the "Drunken Fist," is still practiced today. In recent decades it has become internationally renowned through Jackie Chan's (Cheng Long) (b. 1954) theatrical rendition in his blockbuster movie *Drunken Master* (*Zui quan*) (1978).[23] The style's occurrence in *Hand Combat Classic* and *Xuanji's Acupuncture Points* might indicate that it has been practiced at the Shaolin Monastery since as early as the seventeenth century.

Another style depicted in the two manuals is the "Confounding Fist" (Mi-quan), so named because its quick and unexpected moves "are impossible for the eyes to follow."[24] "Confounding Fist" is the likely ancestor of the modern style known as "Confounding-*Track* Fist" (Mizong quan), which similar name is matched by an identical etymology. According to one twentieth-century expert, the "Confounding-Track Fist" is so called "because its unique footwork deceives the adversary's eyes."[25] In recent decades the modern style has become internationally famous because of a series of movies celebrating its legendary practitioner Huo Yuanjia (1869–1909). Bruce Lee's *Fists of Fury* (1972) and Li Lianjie's

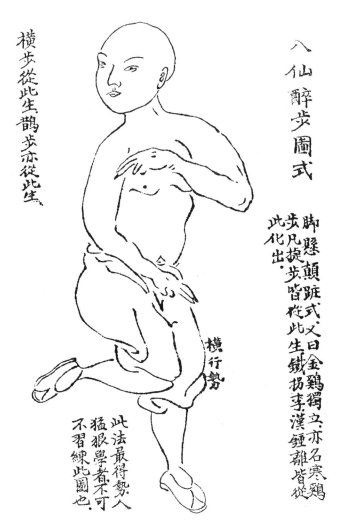

FIG. 26. The "Eight-Immortals Drunken Step" in *Hand Combat Classic.*

(Jet Li) *Fearless* (2005) have familiarized Western audiences with Huo's "Confounding-Track Fist."

The modern style is also referred to by various other names, some of which are homophonous with Mizong quan (Confounding-Track Fist) but differ from it semantically, being written in other characters. It is known as the "Tantric Fist" (Mizong quan) and the "Wild-Beast Fist" (Nizong quan), as well as "Yan-Qing Fist" (Yanqing quan). These diverse titles suggest that the technique has evolved, at least partially, within an illiterate environment. By the time its practitioners sought to write it down, they variously interpreted its phonetic pronunciation: Mizong.[26]

From another angle, the technique's diverse appellations reflect the large body of lore that grew around it. Mizong quan is surrounded by legends, many of which associate it with the Shaolin Monastery. According to one, the technique was created by a Tang period Shaolin monk—in some versions he is the monastery's tutelary deity Vajrapāṇi (Jinnaluo) himself—who was so impressed with the agility of an ape-like creature that he named his fighting technique after him: "Wild-Beast Fist" (Nizong quan). Another tradition associates the historical monastery with the fictional protagonists of the Ming novel *Water Margin*. The heroic Lu Junyi is said to have developed this deceptive method at the Shaolin Monastery and later transmitted it to his disciple Yan Qing. When the outlaw was escaping from government troops to the bandits' haven at Liangshan, he relied on it to hide his footprints in the snow, calling it the "Confounding-Track Fist" (Mizong quan). Yan Qing's disciples named the technique in honor of their master, "Yan Qing Fist," but in deference to its Buddhist provenance referred to it also as the "Tantric Fist" (Mizong quan).

The repeated allusions to Shaolin in the legends surrounding Mizong quan (Confounding-Track Fist) suggest that the monastery might have played some role in its evolution. Further support for this hypothesis is found in the little we know about the modern style's historical lineage: Scholars usually trace the technique to an eighteenth-century Shandong martial artist named Sun Tong (style: Li Kuan) who might have studied at the Shaolin Monastery.[27] It is possible, therefore, that the Mizong quan (Confounding-Track Fist), with which we are familiar today, derives—at least partially—from the Miquan (Confounding Fist) recorded in *Hand Combat Classic* and *Xuanji's Acupuncture Points*.

A third fighting style, described in *Hand Combat Classic* but missing from *Xuanji's Acupuncture Points*, is the Plum Flower Fist (Meihua quan), which is characterized by a five-positions feet routine, named after the flower's five petals.[28] Even though it figures prominently in today's Shaolin regimen, the Plum Flower Fist probably did not originate at the monastery. That it is mentioned in *Hand Combat Classic* only (and not in *Xuanji's Acupuncture Points*) might indicate that it was not part of the original seventeenth-century Shaolin text, which had served as the manuals' source. Furthermore, studies of other Qing period manuals—as well as the Plum Flower practitioners' family genealogies—suggest that the technique was originally developed in Xuzhou, Jiangsu, by members of the Zou family, who transmitted it to Henan, on their way to Hebei, around 1700.[29] It is likely, therefore, that the Plum Flower Fist was incorporated into the Shaolin martial arts—and into Cao Huandou's *Hand Combat Classic*—no earlier than the eighteenth century.

Whether or not Shaolin monks practiced it in earlier times, the Plum Flower Fist was firmly entrenched in their monastery's vicinity by the mid-eighteenth century. Titled *Introduction to Martial Practice* (*Xiwu xu*), one of the style's earliest manuals was authored by a Henan military expert named Yang Bing (b. 1672) who had ranked third on the government's highest military examination and had served in the metropolitan garrison. Yang compiled his Plum Fist

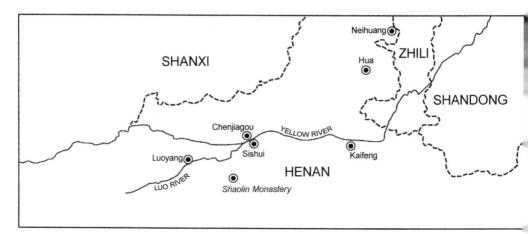

MAP 4. Some Henan sites associated with the Qing martial arts: Taiji Quan originated at Chenjiagou; Wang Zongyue, author of Taiji Quan classics, taught at Luoyang and Kaifeng; Chang Naizhou composed his martial arts treatises at Sishui; Yang Bing compiled his Plum Flower manuals at Neihuang County; and Bagua Palm figured in the Bagua Uprising at Hua.

treatise in 1742 after he had retired to his native Balizhuang village, in Neihuang County, northern Henan (map 4).[30] Several decades later, the technique was mentioned in official reports of rebellious activities in the province: Members of the failed 1813 Eight Trigrams uprising in Hua County, northern Henan, studied the Plum Flower Fist.[31]

One reason for the relative wealth of information on Plum Flower history is the method's association with the late nineteenth-century Boxer uprising (Yihe quan). By that time, the term "Plum Fist" designated not only a technique, but also an organization. The north China plains witnessed the spread of military brotherhoods with religious overtones, which were sometimes referred to as "Plum Flower Fist Associations (quanhui)" and sometimes as "Plum Flower Fist Religion (quanjiao)." Members of these groups—which combined martial practice with religious veneration of valiant deities such as the Journey to the West's heroic Sun Wukong (Monkey)—played an important role in the early stages of the anti-Christian Boxer revolt, arousing the attention of scholars, whose fieldwork has unearthed Qing period sources on the Plum Flower Fist.[32]

We may conclude our brief comments on Hand Combat Classic and Xuanji's Acupuncture Points with Cao Huandou's 1784 introduction to the latter. Cao's autobiographical preface sheds light on his social background, which was probably shared by other literate martial artists. The Shaolin practitioner was born into a family of small landowners belonging to the lower echelons of the local gentry. The clan was prominent enough to have its own school, which Cao attended, and the immediate family was sufficiently affluent for his father to hire him a private martial arts instructor, with whom the boy practiced after school. Nevertheless, Cao repeatedly failed the licentiate exams, and hence he could not aspire to an educational, let alone a government, career. He chose, therefore, the martial arts as his vocation:

> Hand combat is an excellent method for protecting one's body and preventing humiliation. It originated at the Shaolin Monastery. My fellow townsman Zhang Kongzhao once met a mysterious person (*yiren*) who transmitted it to him. This technique alone reaches divine subtlety.
>
> At the time there were many who studied it, but only three who received [Master Zhang's] authentic transmission: Cheng Jingtao, Hu Wojiang, and Zhang Zhonglue. Afterward it branched into numerous substyles, gradually losing the original method. Sometimes, gifted practitioners rise to prominence, and, for a while, become famous. However, for the most part, they strain their muscles and expose their bones, waste their energy (*qi*) and use force. None of them has heard of Master Zhang's technique's ingenious applications, of the subtlety of its limitless transformations.
>
> Practicing the Master's hand combat method, one guards his spirit between the eyebrows, and directs his *qi* to the lower belly. Fighting, it is like a beautiful woman plucking flowers. Resting, it resembles a literatus laying down his brush. It could be compared to Zhuge Liang's (181–234) scholarly cap and feathered fan, to Yang You's (221–278) elegant sash and dignified robes. How could it possibly have sharp edges?
>
> We are four brothers in my family, me being third. My eldest brother is Yanchun, style Peiyu. In our native village the weak were insulted and the few bullied. I was always afraid of being abused, and therefore I was devoted to the martial arts. My father did not object to my training. On the contrary, he invited from afar an outstanding martial artist to teach me. At the time I was thirteen, and I was studying the classics in our clan school. When I would return from school I would practice with him.
>
> When I was eighteen I obtained Master Zhang Kongzhao's *Hand Combat Classic* (*Quan jing*), which he compiled while serving under my clan's remote great-uncle in Huguan County (in Southeastern Shanxi, near Henan's border). I took it with me to school and investigated it day and night, treating it as if I had obtained a rare treasure. When I arrived at the "[Shaolin Close-Range Hand Combat] Ten Principles of Striking,"[33] my resolution was firm and my spirit concentrated. I pondered it strenuously, until suddenly I dreamt that two old men explained it to me. Thereafter I dreamt about them several times. My body grew suppler and my hands became livelier. My mind grasped the subtlety of "cultivating *qi*" (*lianqi*).
>
> When I reached twenty-eight, because I had repeatedly taken the licentiate exams and failed, I left home and looked for success else-

where. However, on several occasions I suffered illness and was obliged
to return. Thereafter I dedicated myself to the practice of the martial
arts. I wandered all over the Yangtze and Huai river basins, the coastal
regions, and the South. I encountered numerous people. I cannot even
count all the formidable adversaries I fought. Luckily I was never
defeated. Now I have retired to my native home. As I think of things
past, I still feel that my disquiet has not dissipated, for which reason I
deeply conceal myself.

Since my friends all wished for me to disseminate this teaching, I
could not possibly keep it a secret to myself. Therefore, using what I had
obtained by daily practice, I copiously annotated the *Hand Combat
Classic*. Moreover I illustrated each position with a drawing. . . . By
merely casting a glance the reader can understand it, making it most
suitable for practice.

However, the subtlety of the method's application depends entirely
on "internal strength" (*neili*). It cannot be exhausted by words. Like an
old hunchback who catches cicadas,[34] like archer Yang Youji who shot
lice.[35] When one's resolution is not distracted, when his spirit is concen-
trated, he will begin to acquire the agility of "mind conceiving, hands
responding" (*dexin yingshou*). At this point there is sure to be no straining
of muscles nor exposure of bones. Would not this be almost like tracing
Master [Zhang] Kongzhao's authentic transmission to its source?

I have respectfully prefaced the manual's origins; the time: Qianlong's reign's forty-ninth, *jiachen* year (1784), auspicious mid-tenth
month. Cao Huandou, style: Zaidong.[36]

Cao Huandou's preface reveals the multifarious roles the martial arts have
played in his life. His initial interest was due to the violent atmosphere in his
native village, where the weak were bullied and humiliated, but he also practiced for medical reasons (he had suffered repeatedly from illness) and as a
form of self-cultivation. In addition, Cao aspired in his martial practice for
what could be described as artistic perfection. He does not hide his contempt
for crude techniques that rely on force only and involve "straining muscles and
exposing bones." These are far inferior to his own sophisticated fighting system, which resembles a "beautiful woman plucking flowers . . . a literatus laying
down his brush." Finally, religious overtones are not lacking either. Zhang
Kongzhao receives his teachings from a "mysterious person" (*yiren*), and Cao
Huandou is instructed in the art of the Shaolin Close-Range Fist by divine
epiphany—venerable teachers appear in his dream, following which "his body
grows suppler and his hands become livelier, as his mind grasps the subtlety of
qi-training (*lianqi*)."

Cao Huandou authored his preface to *Hand Combat Classic* in 1784. Four
decades later, in 1828, a prominent Manchu official named Lin Qing (1791–
1846) visited the Shaolin Temple. By then, bare-handed techniques had com-

pletely eclipsed the monastery's ancient staff methods, and instead of an armed display, the distinguished guest was entertained by a sparring demonstration:

> In the evening we returned to the Shaolin Monastery, and paid our respects at the Jinnaluo Hall. The deity's image is most awesome. He wears thin garments, and wields a stove poker (*huo gun*). Tradition has it that once he displayed his divinity and warded off bandits. Today he is the monastery's guardian spirit (*qielan*). Praying to him is invariably efficacious.
>
> I proceeded to ask the monks about their hand combat method (*quan fa*), but they refused to utter a word about it. I made it clear that I had heard about the Shaolin Fist long ago, and I knew it had been relied upon solely for guarding monastic regulations and protecting the famous temple. Therefore they need not make pretence.
>
> The abbot laughed and assented. He selected several sturdy monks to perform in front of the hall. Their "bear-hangings and bird stretchings"[37] were indeed artful. After the performance the monks retreated. I sat facing Mt. Shaoshi's three peaks, which resembled a sapphire tripod. Watching the shaded forests, misty mountains, and emerald green thickets, my body and spirit were equally at peace. I resolved to stay overnight.[38]

Published in 1849, Lin Qing's account of his visit was accompanied by a woodblock illustration of Shaolin monks practicing hand combat. The martial artists were shown under the gigantic shadow of their tutelary deity, Vajrapāṇi (Kiṃnara), who still wielded his staff of old. The Manchu official, in ceremonial cap and robes and surrounded by his entourage, appeared in the picture as well. Apparently he was fascinated by the performance. Whereas the elderly abbot remained sitting under the hall's eaves, Lin Qing rose from his seat to watch the martial artists up close (figure 27).

Lin Qing's woodblock illustration leads us to another, more elaborate, artwork, which depicts a similar scene: Shaolin's White-Attired Mahāsattva Hall (Baiyi dashi dian) is decorated with an early nineteenth-century mural of fighting monks, who are demonstrating their bare-handed skills to visiting dignitaries, probably government officials. The guests, identified by their queues, are entertained by the abbot in a central pavilion, which is surrounded by the performing artists (figures 28 and 29). The gorgeous fresco was executed with such attention to detail that some modern practitioners are able to identify in it the bare-handed postures they practice today.[39]

Ming Foundations

By the time seventeenth-century Shaolin monks were turning their attention to it, hand combat had already been highly developed. The Ming period witnessed the emergence of individual bare-handed styles, which were identified

拳校林少

FIG. 27. Shaolin monks demonstrating their fist techniques to the Manchu official Lin
Qing; woodblock illustration dated 1849.

by their own training routine of fixed positions (*shi*). Late Ming military
encyclopedias—the very same compilations that lauded the Shaolin staff—
enumerate over a dozen *quan* styles, including "[Song] Emperor Zhao Taizu's
Long-Range Fist," "Cotton Zhang's Close-Range Fist," "Acolyte Worshiping
Guanyin Miraculous Fist" (Tongzi bai guanyin shen quan), "Zhang Fei Miraculous Fist" (Zhang Fei shen quan), "Sun Family Armored Fist" (Sunjia pigua
quan), "Ruler's Fist" (Bawang quan), "Six-Step Fist" (Liubu quan), "Decoy Fist"
(E quan), and "Monkey Fist" (Hou quan).[40] By the early sixteenth century, at
least some fighting schools already had handwritten, if not published, manuals. In his *Treatise on Military Affairs*, Tang Shunzhi (1507–1560) quotes from a
handbook of the "Wen Family Fist."[41]

The most comprehensive account of Ming period unarmed fighting is
Qi Jiguang's (1528–1588) *Essentials of the Hand Combat Classic* (*Quan jing
jieyao*), included in his *New Treatise of Military Efficiency* (*Jixiao xinshu*). Qi was
among the most successful and innovative generals of sixteenth-century
China. He played a major role in the suppression of piracy along China's
southeastern coasts and in the pacification of its northern borders. In his

FIG. 28. Shaolin monks performing for visiting dignitaries; early nineteenth-century
Shaolin fresco.

FIG. 29. Shaolin monks performing for visiting dignitaries (detail).

New Treatise of Military Efficiency, the renowned general covered every aspect of mass warfare, from the selection and training of troops to discipline, command, tactics, logistics, and weaponry. The book did not regurgitate earlier military compilations—it was based upon the commander's hard-won experiences in the battlefield. Completed in late 1561 or early 1562, *New Treatise* alludes to campaigns won by Qi only a few months earlier.[42]

Qi's *Essentials of the Hand Combat Classic* is not only a survey of contemporary bare-handed techniques, but also the earliest extant manual of a given style. The general surveyed sixteen sparring methods, all of which, he concluded, were "guilty of either emphasizing the top to the neglect of the bottom, or the bottom to the neglect of the top."[43] To amend the deficiencies of individual styles, Qi created a synthesis. He chose what he considered the thirty-two best postures of all styles, explicating each with an illustration and a rhyming formula. His treatise is therefore a handbook of his own standardized hand combat technique.

Hand combat, Qi Jiguang argued, could be used for troops' training. The experienced general was well aware that bare-handed methods were useless in the battlefield. He suggested, however, that they were not without merit in instilling courage. Moreover, bare-handed practice was a good starting point for armed training: "In general," Qi writes, "the hand, staff, broadsword, spear, fork, claw, two-edged sword, two-pronged spear, bow and arrow, hooked sword, sickle, and shield all proceed from bare-handed techniques to train the body and hands. Bare-handed techniques are the foundation of the martial arts."[44] A similar argument is echoed by Qi Jiguang's contemporary He Liangchen (fl. 1565), who held that "in practicing the martial arts one should begin with hand combat and proceed to staff training. When the methods of fist and staff are understood, the sword, spear and all other techniques would be especially easy to acquire."[45]

Qi was critical of flowery postures that were aesthetically pleasing but had no combat implications. Efficiency in battle was more significant than beauty of performance. Furthermore, in actual confrontation it was necessary to go beyond the fixed training forms. The general quoted a common martial arts saying: "Without obvious postures or techniques, you will be effective with one move; if you do make the mistake of posturing and posing, you will be ineffective with ten moves."[46] Douglas Wile has demonstrated that this view was shared by another sixteenth-century military expert, Tang Shunzhi (1507–1560): "The reason for postures in the martial arts," writes Tang, "is to facilitate transformations. . . . Forms contain fixed postures, but in actual practice there are no fixed postures. When applied they become fluid, but still maintain their structural characteristics."[47]

Even though martial arts historians unanimously praise it, Qi was ambiguous about his *Essentials of the Hand Combat Classic.* As the commander of regular armies, Qi's main interest lay in weapons instruction for mass troops. The bare-handed skills of individual artists were not as significant, and might even have been suspect for their association with the lower classes. Qi's apprehension of sparring is obvious from the reluctance with which he included it in his *New Treatise on Military Efficiency*. His hand combat manual was inserted into the book's last chapter, preceded by a disclaimer: "Bare-handed techniques seem irrelevant to the art of mass warfare. However, exercising the limbs and habituating the body to effort are the foundation of primary military studies. Therefore we keep [this manual] at the book's end, to round off our military method."[48] Twenty years later, when the bitter general, who had been relieved from office, sat down to revise his writings, he decided to excise hand combat from them altogether. In 1584, he deleted the *Essentials of the Hand Combat Classic* from the—nowadays rarely read—fourteen-chapter version of the *New Treatise on Military Efficiency*.[49]

As Ma Mingda has suggested, the distinction between the early version of the *New Treatise* (which includes hand combat) and the later one (from which it is omitted) might be related to the disparity in their author's age. When he compiled his original book, Qi was a young man of thirty-four. He was surrounded by martial artists, whose bare-handed techniques intrigued him. At the time, the energetic commander probably practiced himself and achieved some proficiency in *quan* fighting. By contrast, the fifty-five-year-old general who revised his writings was already contemplating his legacy, in which there was no place for dubious popular arts.[50]

Information on Ming hand combat is also provided by genres other than military encyclopedias. The proliferation of sixteenth-century bare-handed techniques is attested to by popular fiction: *The Plum in the Golden Vase* (*Jin Ping Mei*) (ca. 1600) alludes to a style of hand combat called "Dong Family Fist" (Dongjia quan),[51] and the hundred-chapter *Journey to the West* (1592) has even the quintessential staff warrior Sun Wukong fight with his fists. When he is deprived of his weapon, the valiant monkey resorts to hand combat, giving the author an opportunity to display his familiarity with the contemporary jargon of "postures" (*shi* and *jiazi*), "Long-Range Fist" (*changquan*), and "Close-Range Fist" (*duanquan*):

> Opening wide the "Four Levels Posture";[52]
> The double-kicking feet fly up.
> They pound the ribs and chests;
> They stab at galls and hearts.
> "The Immortal pointing the Way";
> "Lao Zi Riding the Crane";
> "A Hungry Tiger Pouncing on the Prey" is most hurtful;
> "A Dragon Playing with Water" is quite vicious.
> The demon king uses a "Serpent Turning Around";
> The Great Sage employs a "Deer Letting Loose its Horns."
> The dragon plunges to Earth with heels upturned;
> The wrist twists around to seize Heaven's bag.

A green lion's open-mouthed lunge;
A carp's snapped-back flip.
Sprinkling flowers over the head;
Tying a rope around the waist;
A fan moving with the wind;
The rain driving down the flowers.
The monster-spirit then uses the "Guanyin Palm,"
And pilgrim counters with the "Arhat Feet."
The "Long-Range Fist," stretching, is more slack, of course.
How could it compare with the "Close-Range Fist's" sharp jabs?
The two of them fought for many rounds—
None was the stronger, for they are evenly matched.[53]

Possibly the clearest indication that bare-handed techniques became an integral element of late Ming culture is provided by encyclopedias for daily use. The sixteenth century witnessed the emergence of a new genre of household manuals, which were intended not only for the male bureaucratic elite, but also for other segments of society that had received a modicum of education: women, merchants, artisans, and the like. Sometimes referred to as *Complete Books of Myriad Treasures* (*Wanbao quanshu*), they covered every aspect of knowledge necessary for maintaining a household, from practical advice on making a living to education, ritual, and entertainment. Generously illustrated and often published in simplified or shorthand characters, the encyclopedias featured entries on such diverse topics as farming, livestock breeding, trade, arithmetic, divination, nutrition, health, calligraphy, music, jokes, and even romance.[54]

Household encyclopedias also devoted space to hand combat, which was considered useful for health and self-defense. The 1599 and 1607 editions of the *All-Purpose Correct Way* (*Wanyong zhengzong*), for example, lists one by one the famous bare-handed techniques of the day such as "[Zhao] Taizu's Long-Range Fist," "Wen Family Moving Fist," "Sand-Washing-Waves Fist" (Langlitaosha quan), and "Spear-Seizing Fist" (Qingqiang quan). For their readers' benefit, the editors selected choice positions from these varying styles, explicating each with a rhyming formula and an illustration.[55] Evidently, such manuals as *All-Purpose Correct Way* mirror the growing popularity of bare-handed fighting, even as they contributed to its dissemination.

Ming period unarmed techniques, which are recorded in sixteenth-century literature, served as the foundation for new bare-handed styles that emerged in the ensuing century. Some of the most important martial systems with which we are familiar today—Taiji Quan (Supreme Ultimate Fist), Xingyi Quan (Form-and-Intent Fist), and, of course, Shaolin Quan—originated in the seventeenth-century Ming-Qing transition period. For our purpose, it is significant that much of this development took place within range of the Shaolin Monastery.

Other Fighting Styles

In the winter of 1930, pioneering martial arts historian Tang Hao (1897–1959) traveled to Chen Family Village (Chenjiagou) in Wen County of northern Henan. Tang, whose research combined textual scholarship with fieldwork, was searching for materials on the origins of Taiji Quan, which was known to have been developed at the village. He unearthed there two Qing documents suggesting that the foundations of the world-renowned technique had been laid in the seventeenth century: a family history that attributed the Chen bare-handed style to the clan's ninth-generation ancestor, Chen Wangting (ca. 1580–ca. 1660), and a poem by the latter describing his invention of a *quan* technique. Most scholars have accepted Tang Hao's view that Chen Wangting's martial art was either the same as—or the immediate ancestor of—the Taiji Quan with which we are familiar today, even though in Chen's surviving writings the term *taiji* does not appear.[56]

Chen Wangting had served as an official in the Ming dynasty. During the 1610s and 1620s he had been appointed regional inspector for Shandong, Zhili, and Liaodong. He also had firsthand battle experience, having participated in several military confrontations with the Manchus along the northern borders. By the Qing invasion of 1644, however, he was living in retirement at his native village, where he dedicated himself to the perfection of his bare-handed technique. Musing on his experiences, he versified, "I sigh, as I think of those years; when, clad in armor and wielding a spear, I swept away the bandits' hordes, repeatedly putting myself in danger. . . . Now, old and withered, I have nothing left but the [Daoist] book *Yellow Court*[57] to keep me company. When bored, I invent techniques of hand combat (*quan*); during the busy season, I till the land; taking advantage of my leisure, I instruct a few disciples and descendants, enabling them to become easily as strong as dragons and tigers."[58]

Chen Wangting created his bare-handed style in the vicinity of the Shaolin Monastery; his native Chenjiagou village was located approximately thirty-five miles north of the temple (see map 4). Moreover he laid the foundations of Taiji Quan during the very same period, the seventeenth century, when the Shaolin monks were turning their attention to hand combat. It should not come as a surprise, therefore, that his Taiji Quan shared common traits—such as an emphasis upon "close-range hand combat" (*duanda*)—with Shaolin Quan. The term *taiji* (supreme ultimate) figures in Shaolin's *Hand Combat Classic* (figure 30), just as the monastery's legend of the staff-wielding Vajrapāṇi found its way into the Chen family's military writings.[59] "Most people," writes Matsuda Ryūchi, "believe that Taiji Quan and Shaolin Quan are completely different forms of hand combat. Actually, in their basic postures, hand methods, leg methods, and other fighting aspects, the two styles are entirely alike."[60]

Taiji Quan was not the only bare-handed style that emerged at the Shao-

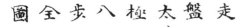

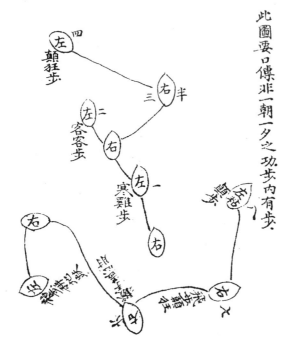

FIG. 30. The "Supreme
Ultimate Eight Steps" in
Hand Combat Classic.

lin Monastery's vicinity. Beginning in the seventeenth century, and all
through the Qing period, Henan was a hotbed of martial arts. Along the Yellow River basin (from Shanxi through Henan to Shandong), numerous fighting styles emerged, many of them in the context of sectarian rebellion. The
intimate connection between martial art and religious sectarianism in the
north China plains is attested by common nomenclature. We have seen above
that Plum Flower was the name of a bare-handed style (*quan*) as well as a religion (*jiao*), and our earliest evidence of Eight-Trigrams Palm (Bagua Zhang)
comes from the religious uprising of that name. In 1786 and again in 1813,
the Eight-Trigrams sect rebelled in Hebei and Northern Henan. The confes-
sions of its captured members, many of whom came from Hua County,
Henan, provide us with the earliest accounts of the bare-handed style of that
name.[61]

Another unarmed style that figured in Qing period Henan is Xingyi
Quan (Form-and-Intent Fist), also known as Xinyi Liuhe Quan (Mind-and-
Intent Six-Harmonies Fist). Qing period manuals and family histories suggest that it was created by Ji Jike (fl. 1650), who was a native of Henan's
neighboring Shanxi province. Ji is said to have created his empty-handed
style on the basis of a spear method, in which he had excelled. Following the

Manchu conquest, he was reported to have said that bare-handed fighting was more appropriate than armed combat for peaceful times. By the eighteenth century, at any rate, Ji's Xingyi Quan had been transmitted to Henan, where a local substyle emerged. One of the earliest extant Xingyi treatises, *Mind-and-Intent Six-Harmonies Fist's Manual* (*Xinyi Liuhe Quan pu*), was likely authored in Henan, where it was discovered by Tang Hao in the early twentieth century. The manual carries four prefaces—dated 1733, 1735, 1754, and 1779—all by Henan authors.[62]

According to some Xingyi manuals, Ji Jike had spent more than ten years at the Shaolin Monastery, where he studied—and even taught—fighting.[63] However, this claim should be treated cautiously. Whereas the fighting style's Henan connection is certain, its founder's personal affiliation with the monastery should be questioned, if for no other reason than because it is a suspiciously recurring motif in the hagiographies of numerous martial artists. During the Qing period, a Shaolin connection appears to have become a prerequisite in the mythology of the martial arts, as the inventors of new fighting styles were supposed to have traveled to the monastery and mastered its techniques before creating their own superior ones. The legendary founder of the Internal School (Neijia), Zhang Sanfeng (fl. 1400?), is said to have thoroughly studied the Shaolin style before "reversing" its principles.[64] Similarly, Wang Lang (fl. seventeenth century), presumed creator of the Praying Mantis Fist (Tanglang Quan), is believed to have resided at the Shaolin Monastery, where he was repeatedly defeated by its outstanding martial artists. Leaving the monastery in despair, Wang spent several years on the road, until he happened one day upon a praying mantis catching a cicada. Imitating the insect's forelimbs, he invented his unique style, whereupon he returned to Shaolin and finally overcame his monastic rivals of old.[65]

If we turn our attention from the consideration of individual styles to the examination of literature, we are again struck by Henan's significance. Even though, as we will see below, important bare-handed treatises were composed elsewhere, some of the most influential ones were authored within a day or two's mule ride from the Shaolin Monastery. Chang Naizhou (fl. 1740) penned his martial arts treatises at Sishui, some thirty miles north of the monastery, and Wang Zongyue (fl. 1780), albeit a Shanxi native, probably authored his theoretical Taiji Quan essays either in Luoyang or in Kaifeng, where he resided in the 1790s.[66] Likewise, Chen Changxing (1771–1853) and Chen Xin (1849–1929) compiled their Taiji manuals in Henan,[67] and, as we have seen, Yang Bing (b. 1672) authored his Plum Flower one in the province's Neihuang County (see map 4). The Xingyi manual *Mind-and-Intent Six-Harmonies Fist* was probably written in the province as well. We may conclude, therefore, that Shaolin hand combat prospered in a region that had played a major role in the evolution of Chinese bare-handed fighting.

The late Ming and the early Qing were pivotal periods in the history of Chinese hand combat. Drawing on earlier, Ming period *quan* techniques, the seventeenth century witnessed the emergence of new bare-handed styles, which, three hundred years later, were to spread all over the world. The origins of Taiji Quan, Xingyi Quan, and Shaolin Quan—the earliest vestiges of which are recorded in *Hand Combat Classic* and *Xuanji's Acupuncture Points*—can be traced equally to the Ming-Qing transition era. Their emergence was accompanied by the articulation of a new martial arts philosophy and mythology, to which we should now turn.

CHAPTER 6

Gymnastics

LATE MING Shaolin monks did not turn their attention to hand combat because it was militarily effective. In real combat, bare-handed fighting was not as useful as the staff that the monks had been practicing for centuries, not nearly as lethal as swords and spears that they had always employed in battle, and certainly not as dangerous as firearms that, having been invented in China several centuries earlier, were being reintroduced to it by the Portuguese in the sixteenth century.[1] Rather, Shaolin monks were intrigued by the philosophical and medical dimensions of the new bare-handed styles. The late Ming and early Qing techniques of Shaolin Quan, Taiji Quan, and Xingyi Quan were couched in a rich vocabulary of physiological and spiritual self-cultivation. They were marked by a unique synthesis of martial, therapeutic, and religious goals. Practitioners were no longer interested in fighting only. They were motivated instead by considerations of health, at the same time that they sought spiritual realization.

In this chapter we examine the late Ming and early Qing synthesis of fighting, healing, and religious self-cultivation. We begin with a Qing aficionado of Shaolin fighting whose passion for the art had been spurred by therapeutic concerns, and we proceed to examine the origins of the exercises he had studied at the monastery. Our investigation leads us backward in time to an ancient gymnastic tradition called *daoyin*, which during the late Ming had been integrated into hand combat. *Daoyin* calisthenics had largely evolved within a Daoist context, and they served as a vehicle for the religion's impact on the martial arts. Unlike the techniques of the Shaolin staff, which were enwrapped in a Buddhist mythological framework, hand combat drew on Daoist self-cultivation. During the late imperial period, Buddhist monks at the Shaolin Monastery were trained in empty-handed styles that harked back to Daoist physiological and meditative methods.

An Official–Cum–Martial Artist

Wang Zuyuan (ca. 1820–after 1882) might illustrate the interest of some Qing officials in martial practice. A scholar of some reputation and the holder of a minor bureaucratic post, Wang was an amateur martial artist who had been practicing since his early teens. His devotion to his hobby was such that in his thirties he traveled to the Shaolin Temple, where he studied for several months. The training Wang received at the monastery stood him in good stead in his later years. Still a low-ranking bureaucrat in his sixties, he noted, "Whenever I chase my superiors, rushing behind them, I am as light-footed as a young man. Hastening to kneel down for sacrifice, I have never failed in propriety. This may demonstrate the strength I have gained [by my martial practice]."[2] The Shaolin martial arts provided at least one Confucian official with the stamina necessary for the performance of his ritual duties.

Which martial arts did Wang study at Shaolin? A likely answer is provided by a manual he published in 1882, which he titled *Illustrated Exposition of Internal Techniques* (*Neigong tushuo*). The treatise was not authored by Wang. It had been issued as early as 1858 by one Pan Weiru under another name: *Essential Techniques of Guarding Life* (*Weisheng yaoshu*). However, when Wang happened upon it, he realized it was identical to a manuscript he had obtained at the Shaolin Monastery in 1854 or 1855. He therefore published Pan's manual anew, restoring its original Shaolin title: *Illustrated Exposition of Internal Techniques*.[3]

Wang's manual outlined several sets of gymnastic exercises that integrated limb movements, breathing, massage, and meditation. One training program, "Formulas of the Divided External Technique" ("Fenxing waigong jue") included seventeen exercises, which were assigned each to a different body part: the mind, body frame, head, face, ears, eyes, mouth, tongue, teeth, nose, hands, feet, shoulders, back, abdomen, loins, and kidneys. Here are a few examples in a translation that was made by the Western physician John Dudgeon as early as 1895. At the time Dudgeon was teaching anatomy and physiology at the Tongwen Academy in Beijing. Apparently he practiced the exercises with a local instructor:

> THE HEAD: 1. – Close the ears with the hands, let the index finger fold itself on the middle one and thrum the two bones at the back of the skull with the index finger to make them sound. This is called sounding the "heavenly drum." *Note*: This is to remove the harmful air from the "wind pool" acupuncture opening in the region of the mastoid. 2. – Twist the neck with the hands and glance back to the right and left and at the same time rotate the shoulders and arms twenty-four times each—to remove the obstructed air in the stomach and spleen. 3. – Interlock the hands and grasp the back of the neck, then look upwards and let the hands wrestle with the neck—to remove pain of the shoulders and indistinctness of vision.

THE FACE: Rub the hands until hot, then rub the face with them, high and low, all over, no spot to be left un-rubbed; then spit on the palms and rub them warm and apply them several times to the face. While rubbing, the breath, by the mouth and nose, is to be closed. The aim of this exercise is to brighten the countenance. The more you rub the better the color. This is the cure for wrinkles; with this action you will have none.

THE EAR: 1. – Place the hands over the ears, then rub them right and left and up and down several times. This is to hear distinctly and prevent deafness. 2. – Sit level on the ground with one leg bent and the other extended. Stretch forth the arms horizontally with the hands perpendicularly towards the front as if pushing a door, and twist the head 7 times to each side, to cure ringing in the ears.[4]

The exercises are not directly related to fighting. Apparently, while at the Shaolin Temple, Wang studied methods that were primarily therapeutic rather than martial. Instead of hand combat, the *Illustrated Exposition of Internal Techniques* teaches the prevention and cure of disease. Occasionally, the text goes as far as intimating the possibility of immortality. The connection to fighting is implicit only; to the degree that the exercises contribute to one's health, they will also provide a foundation for his martial training. It is instructive therefore that according to his own testimony Wang's martial practice was motivated by therapeutic considerations:

As a child I was weak and was always fed medicines. My late father was constantly worried about my health. During the Daoguang *jiawu* year (1834), when I was thirteen years old, I accompanied him to Jiangxi, where he assumed the post of tax circuit intendant. At the time a guard commander named Zhou Jiafu, from Laiyang [in Shandong] was stationed there. He excelled in fighting and was practicing the *Sinews Transformation Classic* (*Yijin jing*).

My late father had him teach me, and within less than a year I significantly regained my strength and was able to lift ten *jun* (approximately 300 pounds). During the *xinchou* year (1841) I returned to my native town [Fushan, Shandong] to prepare for the examinations. I traveled together with the Laiyang [martial artist] Xu Quanlai, and I thoroughly studied his technique.

During the Xianfeng *jiayin* (1854) year, I stayed with my late elder brother in Guanzhong (Shaanxi), where I met the Lintong native Zhou Bin. Zhou was the most famous martial artist in Guanzhong. I frequently traveled with him, and we also journeyed together to Henan, where we visited the Shaolin Temple. We stayed there for over three months, and obtained the monastery's *Illustrated [Exposition] of Internal Techniques* (*Neigong tu*) as well as spear and staff manuals before heading back.[5]

What was the source of the gymnastic exercises Wang studied at the Shaolin Temple? Did they originate at the monastery or were they adopted from elsewhere? To answer this question we must journey two thousand years back to the origins of the Chinese gymnastic tradition.

Ancient Foundations

Chinese gymnastics has been intimately related to medical practice. As early as the first centuries BCE, physicians recommended calisthenic exercises called *daoyin* (guiding and pulling) as a tool for the prevention and cure of disease. *Daoyin* gymnastics combined limb movements with breathing techniques. The exercises were considered beneficial for "nourishing life" (*yangsheng*), and they were practiced in conjunction with other methods —dietary, pharmacological, hygienic, and sexual—that were intended to protect and increase vitality. A brief *Zhuangzi* passage dating from ca. 200 BCE illustrates the tradition's goal of longevity:

> To pant, to puff, to hail, to sip, to spit out the old breath and draw in the new, practicing bear-hangings and bird-stretchings, longevity his only concern—such is the life favored by the scholar who practices gymnastics (*daoyin*), the man who nourishes his body, who hopes to live to be as old as Pengzu, for more than eight hundred years.[6]

What is merely paraphrased in the *Zhuangzi* is elaborated upon in recently discovered manuscripts. Archaeological excavations in tombs dating from the mid-second century BCE have unearthed two manuals of calisthenics: the *Pulling Book* (*Yinshu*) and the handsomely drawn *Illustrations of Guiding and Pulling* (*Daoyin tu*), showing that as early as the Western Han (206 BCE–8 CE), therapeutic gymnastics had been highly developed. The two handbooks outline dozens of *daoyin* stretching and bending exercises, which were recommended for men and women alike. Most exercises were practiced from a standing posture, but some were conducted sitting. The majority were bare-handed, but others made use of a pole and possibly a ball. One feature *daoyin* gymnastics shared with late imperial hand combat was the naming of individual training routines after the animals they purportedly imitated. In addition to the bear that is mentioned in the *Zhuangzi*, the *Illustrations of Guiding and Pulling* describes crane, monkey, gibbon, merlin, dragon, and possibly turtle postures.[7]

The Western Han manuals assign specific exercises for the cure and prevention of given illnesses. They allude to the treatment of such pathological conditions as "deafness," "feverishness," "upper-side accumulation," "internal hotness," and "knee pain."[8] The *Pulling Book* recommends the following cure for stiff shoulders: "If the pain is located in the upper part [of the shoulder] one should rotate it carefully 300 times. Should it be found toward the back, then one should pull the shoulder to the front 300 times."[9] A similar association of specific calisthenics with particular health disorders lasted into the Eastern Han (25–220) when the renowned physician Hua Tuo (ca. 190–265) created "five-animals" exercises, each intended for the relief of a different set of symptoms:

> Wu Pu of Guangling and Fa A of Pengcheng were both pupils of Hua Tuo. Wu Pu followed exactly the arts of Hua so that his patients generally got well. Hua Tuo taught him that the body should be exercised in every part but that this should not be overdone in any way. "Exercise," he said, "brings about good digestion, and a free flow of the blood. It is like a door pivot never rotting. Therefore the ancient sages engaged in *daoyin* exercises, [for example] by moving the head in the manner of a bear, and looking back without turning the neck. By stretching at the waist and moving the different joints to left and right one can make it difficult for people [to grow] old. I have a method," said Hua Tuo, "known as the 'play of the five animals,' the tiger, the deer, the bear, the ape and the bird. It can be used to get rid of diseases, and it is beneficial for all stiffness of the joints or ankles. When the body feels ill, one should do *one* of the exercises. After perspiring, one will sense the body grow light and the stomach will manifest hunger." Wu Pu followed this advice himself and attained an age greater than ninety yet with excellent hearing, vision, and teeth.[10]

Breathing techniques were an integral element of *daoyin* gymnastics. Since external air (*qi*) was considered vital for the body's proper functioning, it was believed that the more a person obtained of it the better. Practitioners usually inhaled through the nose and then shut their mouths, trying to hold the air inside their bodies for as long as possible. Various methods were devised for calculating the time a person should hold his breath. Sometimes it was measured against a fellow practitioner's normal breathing, it being recommended that it be held for as many as twelve or more regular breathing cycles. The air was to be exhaled slowly and gently through the mouth, the amount going out being smaller than that which came in. In addition to these techniques of *breathing* air, some practitioners apparently *ate* air. Medieval texts describe the immortals as feeding on pure breaths rather than on coarse foodstuffs such as grains. As Henri Maspero and Joseph Needham have shown, some adepts probably learned to push air into their intestinal tract. This was perhaps one reason why swallowing saliva figures in *daoyin* gymnastics—it made it easier to gulp down air.[11]

Whether it was pumped into the respiratory canal or digested into the intestinal tract, the external air had to be circulated inside the body, nourishing its various parts. The breath was guided therefore by meditation in prescribed internal routes. One of its destinations was the so-called "lower cinnabar field" (*dantian*) under the navel, which was chosen in part because of its Daoist significance. Reversing the natural process of aging was the goal of Daoist adepts, who attempted to regain their vitality by returning to their embryonic origins. By subverting biological time it was possible to regain the fetus's limitless potential for growth. Since the embryo was fed through the umbilical cord, it was necessary to emulate him, breathing through the navel.[12] Titled "embryonic respiration" (taixi), this physiological practice harked back to the fecund imagery of the infant in the Daoist Way and its Power (Daode jing) (ca. fourth century BCE):

> One who possesses virtue in abundance is comparable to a new born
>   babe;
> Poisonous insects will not sting it;
> Ferocious animals will not pounce on it;
> Predatory birds will not swoop down on it.
> Its bones are weak and its sinews supple yet its hold is firm.
> It does not know of the union of male and female yet its male member
>   will stir:
> This is because its virility is at its height.
> It howls all day yet does not become hoarse:
> This is because its harmony is at its height.
> To know harmony is called the constant;
> To know the constant is called discernment.[13]

More than a millennium after its formulation, "embryonic respiration" was to influence the late imperial martial arts. The term "lower cinnabar field" figures in late Ming and early Qing bare-handed fighting styles such as Shaolin Quan, Taiji Quan, and Xingyi Quan. There, however, the navel's significance is explained not only in terms of breathing but also in terms of mechanical balance. Quan practitioners consider the navel as the body's center of gravity, and they recommend turning from it, rather than from the chest or shoulders. This emphasis upon the lower abdomen is related to the significance of the legs in Chinese fighting. Unlike Western boxing, which makes use of the arms only (and in which the chest is often the center of attention,) quan techniques make abundant use of kicking.

Daoyin breathing techniques underwent a significant transformation during the medieval period, when the emphasis shifted from the manipulation of external qi (air) to the circulation of internal qi (the body's inborn vitality or energy). Perhaps because holding the breath for prolonged periods led to accidents, practitioners turned their attention to the flow of one's own "primary vitality" (yuanqi), which was bestowed upon each person at birth and was considered identical to the primordial energy of heaven and earth. One could either follow by meditation the natural flow of energy within the body, or one could actively alter its course, directing it to specific locations. The internal qi could be guided, for example, to an ailing area, thereby curing it.[14] These techniques were to exert a profound influence on the later evolution of unarmed fighting. In late imperial hand combat, the martial artist concentrates his internal energy for defensive and offensive purposes alike. He may muster his qi

功翻江攪海運氣六口
治五穀不消仰面直臥兩
手在胃并肚腹上往來行
宋玄白臥雪

FIG. 31. Massaging and
qi circulation in the
treatment of indiges-
tion, from the 1578 *Red
Phoenix's Marrow*
(*Chifeng sui*).

to receive a blow, thereby lessening the pain and possibly preventing injury, or
he may direct his internal power to augment the strength of an attack. For example, a performer who smashes stones with his bare hands is said to have circulated his *qi* into his palms.

The internal circulation of *qi* was facilitated by massaging—either self-ap-
plied or performed by others. Massage was relied upon to cure a variety of
health disorders from obstructions to the internal flow of breath to injured
tendons and dislocated bones. It was also used to warm up the body, spreading
energy to its outer layers, so that the skin would retain its youth.[15] Usually,
kneading was combined with *qi* circulation as in the following remedy for indi-
gestion, from the sixteenth-century *Red Phoenix's Marrow* (*Chifeng sui*) (preface
1578): "One should lie straight, facing upwards. He should apply massage with
both hands to his upper and lower abdomen. He should circulate his *qi* (*yunqi*)
thereby capsizing the river and churning the ocean six times"[16] (figure 31).

The *Zhuangzi*'s reference to the Chinese Methuselah Pengzu (who supposedly lived eight hundred years) indicates that as early as the first centuries BCE,
gymnastics were considered useful not only for safeguarding one's natural life
span but also for ushering divine longevity. Some pre-Qin authors explicitly associated *qi* circulation with the quest for transcendence.[17] During the ensuing

medieval period, the supernormal efficacy of physiological exercises was further elaborated, as *daoyin* gymnastics were harnessed to the search for immortality. This evolution took place largely within the context of the emerging Daoist faith, which incorporated the ancient gymnastic tradition into its religious regimen. Daoism integrated calisthenics with other disciplines—ethical, ritual, meditative, and alchemical—that led to transcendence. Even as they retained their therapeutic importance of old, *daoyin* exercises were now part of a religious system that was directed toward eternal life.

The significance of physiological cultivation in Daoism ultimately derives from the centrality of the body in the religion's conception of immortality. As Joseph Needham has emphasized, the Chinese did not conceive the possibility of eternal life enjoyed by a disembodied soul. For them, liberation took the form of "material immortality"—eternal life of a biological entity.[18] Daoist immortals (*xian*) were not spiritual beings. They possessed physical bodies, albeit more refined than those of ordinary creatures. By an arduous process of self-cultivation, the immortals transformed their perishable and heavy bodily building blocks into durable and light substances—so light they could fly. It is exactly because Daoist eternal life was not merely spiritual that spiritual self-cultivation did not suffice. In order to enjoy liberation, it was necessary to create within the mortal bodily frame a new physiological entity that would ascend into immortality. Hence the Daoist significance of physiological exercise—gymnastic, sexual, dietary, and alchemical.[19]

Why did Chinese conceptions of immortality differ from Western ones? Why did the former envision "material immortality" whereas the latter imagined "spiritual eternity"? The answer is related to fundamentally diverse conceptions of nature. The Chinese did not establish a dichotomy of spirit and matter, of god creator and created world. For them, there were only gradations of spirituality, which separated refined beings such as the immortals from gross matter. From another perspective, the body contained numerous spirits that were believed to disperse upon death. To preserve a post-mortem personal identity, it was necessary to sustain the physical body that held them together, as Henri Maspero has noted:

> If the Daoists in their search for longevity, conceived it not as a spiritual but as a material immortality, it was not as a deliberate choice between different possible solutions but because for them it was the only possible solution. The Graeco-Roman world early adopted the habit of setting Spirit and Matter in opposition to one another, and the religious form of this was the conception of a spiritual soul attached to a material body. But the Chinese never separated Spirit and Matter, and for them the world was a continuum passing from the void at the one end to the grossest matter at the other; hence "soul" never took up this antithetical character in relation to matter. Moreover, there were too many souls in a man for any one of them to counter-balance, as it were, the body; there

were two groups of souls, three upper ones (*hun*) and seven lower ones
(*po*), and if there were differences of opinion about what became of
them in the other world, it was agreed that they separated at death. In
life as in death, these multiple souls were rather ill-defined and vague;
after death, when the dim little troop of spirits had dispersed, how
could they possibly be re-assembled into a unity? The body, on the
contrary, was a unity, and served as a home for these as well as other
spirits. Thus, it was only by the perpetuation of the body, in some form
or other, that one could conceive of a continuation of the living personality as a whole.[20]

This is not to say that the body that was to enjoy eternal bliss was the one with
which we were endowed at birth. Instead, practitioners endeavored to create
a new body within the body. They fashioned an internal luminous embryo
that was to be liberated from the confinements of the external body like a cicada breaking out of its cocoon. The immortal inner body was much more
refined than the external one. It was, as it were, a purified version of the latter. Still, as "spiritual" as it might have been, the immortal embryo was largely
constructed from the physiological building blocks of the external body. Biological rejuvenation was therefore a precondition for Daoist self-cultivation:
"For most medieval Daoists aspiring to immortality," writes Anna Seidel,
"there was no mystical way around some kind of physical preservation or restoration of the body."[21]

Diverse methods existed for the preservation of the body. The Daoists
pioneered alchemical laboratory research on substances that might increase
vitality. Ge Hong (283–343) considered calisthenics an inferior method, believing that cinnabar (*dan*) could be manipulated into an elixir. *Daoyin* could
prolong one's years, he noted, but unlike the elixir it could not prevent death.
Most Daoist mystics, however, did recommend calisthenic training at the
very least as a preparatory stage for more elaborate alchemical and meditative methods.[22] In many Daoist schools the typical practice consisted of "dual
cultivation," combining physiological exercises with techniques of mental
concentration. In Daoist "inner alchemy" (*neidan*) the adept joins elaborate
meditations with methods of controlling the internal flow of bodily substances: breath, saliva, and semen, concocting within his own body an inner
elixir. As Joseph Needham has noted, the process was not purely mental, for
it had a concrete physiological aspect. "It was born upon us," he writes, "that
we were face to face with a physiological (indeed at bottom a biochemical)
elixir, to be prepared by physiological, not chemical, methods, out of physiological constituents already in the body."[23]

One of the earliest texts to combine physiological training with meditation was the *Scripture of the Yellow Court* (*Huangting jing*) (ca. third century CE),
which, thirteen hundred years after its compilation, influenced the late imperial martial arts. (Recall that the probable founder of Taiji Quan, Chen

Wangting, alluded to it as a source of inspiration.) The *Scripture of the Yellow Court* outlines techniques of breath circulation that are coupled with visualization of the body's interior divinities. By nourishing his corporal deities the adept is able to produce within himself a divine embryo that ascends into immortality. The scripture's language is esoteric, describing the physiological circulation of bodily fluids as a celestial journey through the heavenly palaces of the body's internal divinities. The following brief excerpts (in Paul Kroll's translation) describe the swallowing of saliva ("numinous liquor") followed by meditation on a spleen goddess ("the person within the yellow court"):

> The mouth is the Jade Pool, the Officer of Greatest Accord.
> Rinse with and gulp down the numinous liquor—calamities will not
>   encroach;
> One's body will engender a lighted florescence, breath redolent as orchid;
> One turns back, extinguishes the hundred malignities—one's features
>   refined in jade.
> With practice and attention, cultivate this, climbing to the Palace of
>   Ample Cold [where the moon is bathed].
> …
> The person within the yellow court wears a polychrome-damask jacket.
> A volant skirt of purple flowering, in gossamer of cloudy vapors.
> Vermilion and azure, with green withes, numinous boughs of halcyon
>   blue.[24]

Even as they suffused *daoyin* gymnastics with a rich mystical language, Daoist practitioners continued to stress the exercises' therapeutic value. Clapping the teeth (*kouchi*), for example, figures in Daoist meditation as a method for summoning the body's interior divinities. The practice can be traced back to Western Han medical literature, which considered it useful for the prevention of tooth decay. Daoist authors did not doubt the method's hygienic efficacy, they merely supplemented it with a spiritual one—religion joined medicine rather than replacing it.[25]

In addition to refining their individual *qi*, some Daoists sought to increase their vitality by absorbing cosmic *qi*. Chinese cosmology recognized several manifestations of the primordial *qi*: A female form (*yin*) and a male form (*yang*), as well as five energetic configurations that were known as the "five elements" (*wuxing*): water, fire, wood, metal, and earth. In order to inhale the female and male energy one faced the moon and the sun respectively. Gazing at the five directions, he or she was similarly blessed with the power of wood (east), metal (west), fire (south), water (north), and earth (center). Irradiation by the heavenly bodies combined physiological, meditative, and ritual procedures. Controlling their breathing and swallowing their saliva, practitioners exposed their bodies to the sun's rays. They meditated on the colors produced on their closed retinas, and they directed the absorbed energies into their internal organs. They also wrote the character "sun" on a piece of paper, which they burnt and mixed in water. By drinking the potion it was possible to assimilate the luminary's energy. Evidently, the process of absorbing cosmic qi was not devoid of magic overtones.[26]

Methods of qi circulation are enjoying renewed popularity in contemporary China, where they are commonly referred to as Qigong (which could be rendered as Qi technique, Qi efficacy, or Qi skill). The ancient Chinese techniques are also becoming increasingly popular in the West. Even though the Chinese state has attempted to couch Qigong in scientific terms, endowing it with an aura of secular modernity, its practice is not devoid of religious hues. David Palmer has argued that despite the party's express aims, "Qigong became a conduit for the transmission, modernization and legitimization of religious concepts and practices within the Communist regime."[27] The latent religiosity of Qigong could even burst forth in a messianic zeal. Emerging from Qigong circles, the renowned Falungong sect has pronounced the imminent arrival of the apocalypse.[28]

The religious aspect of Qigong is likely due, at least partially, to the historical impact of Daoism on *daoyin* gymnastics. Daoism embedded the ancient exercises of qi circulation in a rich vocabulary of religious transcendence. As we will see, the religion was to exercise a similar influence on the late imperial martial arts. When, during the late Ming and the early Qing, *daoyin* calisthenics were integrated into martial training, they colored it with the spiritual hues of Daoist self-cultivation. Even though the Daoist language did not shape the aspirations of all martial artists, it did influence at least some late imperial styles of hand combat.

The Late Ming Synthesis

All through the medieval period, *daoyin* literature had not been related to fighting. Whether they are preserved in the Daoist canon or have been discovered in archaeological excavations, the available manuals of gymnastics and breathing do not presume to enhance military skills. Their avowed goals are two only: health and spiritual liberation. When *daoyin* was integrated into the newly emerging methods of hand combat, during the late Ming and early Qing, it was thoroughly transformed. The ancient gymnastic tradition acquired a martial dimension, and *quan* fighting techniques were enriched with a therapeutic and a religious significance. A synthesis was created of fighting, healing, and self-cultivation.

Tang Hao was the first scholar to note the contribution of gymnastics and breathing techniques for the evolution of the late imperial martial arts. The seventeenth-century Taiji Quan, he pointed out, was created by combining the Ming styles of bare-handed fighting with the ancient *daoyin* methods of gymnastics and breathing:

Taiji Quan is a product of the Ming-Qing transition period. It inherited, developed, and created a synthesis of the various Ming bare-handed styles that were practiced by the people and the military, combining them with the ancient methods of gymnastics (*daoyin*) and breathing (*tuna*). It absorbed the ancient material philosophy of *yin* and *yang* as well as the Chinese fundamental medical concept of meridians (*jingluo*) [in which the *qi* flows], creating a bare-handed technique that equally cultivates the internal and the external. . . . After it integrated the methods of gymnastics and breathing, Taiji Quan was not merely able to advance the motion of joints and muscles, but it was also capable of coordinating movement and breathing, enhancing the performance of the internal organs. . . . In Taiji Quan training the three aspects of consciousness, movement, and breathing are harmoniously integrated. The holistic approach to training and the emphasis upon the unity of the internal and the external are the hallmarks of Taiji Quan practice.[29]

Lin Boyuan has argued similarly that *daoyin* gymnastics transformed the late imperial martial arts. Unlike Ming hand combat that was intended for fighting only, Qing bare-handed styles were also meant to cure and prevent illness. The very adjective "martial" is misleading, or limiting, when applied to the new synthesis. Fighting is only one aspect of the bare-handed styles that emerged during the seventeenth-century Ming-Qing transition:

During the Ming period, the various hand combat styles were all one-sided, specializing in actual fighting only. By contrast, Qing *quan* styles emphasized diverse training, creating a particularly thorough synthesis with the methods of *daoyin* and *yangsheng* ("nourishing the vital principle"). This integration was motivated by a double-purpose: Firstly, it added efficacy to the bare-handed fighting methods; secondly, it strengthened the body, preventing and curing disease. . . . The Qing widespread integration of *daoyin* training and martial practice demonstrates that the recognition of *daoyin*'s efficacy became more common. *Daoyin* transformed the popular martial arts in terms of contents, methods of training, and goals. The martial arts were no longer fighting methods only. They were transformed, rather, into a physical activity that is variously practiced, that enhances both skill and strength, and that is efficacious in curing and preventing illness. Evidently, by Qing times the martial arts evolved into a completely unique method of physical education.[30]

Even though the seventeenth century was pivotal in the integration of hand combat and gymnastics, the synthesis was not born overnight. The process of combining gymnastics, breathing, and fighting probably spanned several centuries. It is likely that as early as the mid-Ming (the fifteenth and sixteenth centuries), some *quan* styles incorporated aspects of *daoyin*. The integration was accelerated with the appearance of Shaolin Quan and Taiji Quan in the last decades of the Ming and the early Qing (the seventeenth century), and it reached maturity in the eighteenth and nineteenth centuries, by which time most bare-handed styles were colored by therapeutic and religious hues. One indication is the prevalence in Qing literature of the term "internal strength" (*neili*), which was sought by the "internal techniques" (*neigong*) of breathing, meditation, and energy circulation. Wang Zuyuan's handbook, for example, is titled *Illustrated Exposition of Internal Techniques,* and in his preface to the Shaolin manual *Hand Combat Classic* (1784), Cao Huandou explains that "the subtlety of the method's application depends entirely on *internal strength.*"[31]

A triple synthesis of religion, healing, and fighting is first attested in late Ming sources. The earliest extant handbook that integrates *daoyin* and *quan* is the *Sinews Transformation Classic (Yijin jing)*, which as we will see below likely dates from 1624. The manual advocates the dual goal of martial excellence and religious transcendence, which it articulates mostly in terms of Daoist immortality. The treatises that followed it were not necessarily as explicit in their Daoist orientation. Nevertheless, most did incorporate at least some aspects of *daoyin*. We may mention Huang Baijia's *Internal School Fist Method* (1676); the two Qing manuals of the Shaolin style *Hand Combat Classic* and *Xuanji's Acupuncture Points* (which probably derive from a common seventeenth-century source); Chang Naizhou's (fl. 1740) military writings; the eighteenth-century Xingyi Quan handbook *Mind-and-Intent Six-Harmonies Fist*; and the various Qing classics of Taiji Quan.

Breathing and *qi*-circulation techniques figure in most manuals. This aspect of the *daoyin* tradition was probably integrated with some bare-handed fighting styles as early as the Ming. A hint is provided by Tang Shunzhi's (1507–1560) "Song of the Emei Monk's Fist." "His breathing imperceptible, guarding his primordial *qi*" (*bixi wusheng shenqi shou*).[32] In the ensuing martial literature of the Qing period "*qi* cultivation" (*lianqi*) became a key term. The eighteenth-century Cao Huandou claimed to have mastered it following a dream revelation: "I pondered it strenuously, until suddenly I dreamt that two old men explained it to me. . . . My body grew suppler and my hands became livelier. My mind grasped the subtlety of '*qi* cultivation'"[33] Chang Naizhou (fl. 1740) described the sensation of the flowing *qi* as an epiphany: "It is like being startled in a dream, suddenly realizing the Dao, experiencing an unexpected burning sensation on the skin, cold creeping up and causing a shiver, or suddenly thinking of a certain scene. The true *qi*, so turbulent and dense, is like thunder and lightning suddenly striking or smoke and flames from a fire. . . . The *qi* issues like the discharge of a cannon or a bolt from a crossbow, striking with a sudden impact."[34]

Qing manuals of fighting were steeped in the vocabulary of *qi* circulation. Successful masters were those who mustered their internal energy and channeled it to the proper action. "Making strong contact and being a fierce fighter depends on the *qi* of the whole body concentrating on one point," writes Chang Naizhou.[35] The manipulation of *qi* implied a harmony of mind and body, intent and movement. Qi cultivation was a form of mental concentration, subduing the body to the performer's will. The idea was expressed poetically in the late Qing Taiji Quan classic "Song of the Circulation of the Primordial *Qi*," here in Douglas Wile's translation:

> The mind (*yi*) and *qi* are rulers,
> And the bones and flesh are ministers,
> The waist and legs are commanders;
> The hands are vanguards,
> And the eyes and skin are spies.
> The ruler gives orders and the ministers act;
> The commanders give orders and the ruler acts.
> The spies must immediately report to the commander,
> And the commander issues orders to the troops.
> Ruler and follower work together;
> Above and below act in harmony,
> And the whole body is one flow of *qi*.[36]

Fiction mirrored the belief that effective fighting depended upon *qi* circulation. The *Classified Anthology of Qing Anecdotes* (*Qing bai lei chao*) tells of one Iron-Fist Bian, who "chose a large stone slab, positioned himself, circulated his *qi* (*yunqi*) and struck. A deafening crack was heard, as the stone slab split in the middle."[37] Memoirs of the Tianqiao entertainment district in Beijing similarly attributed the fits of performing artists to internal energy. The following description of a martial artist nicknamed "Stupid Chang" is noteworthy for the light it throws on the performer's livelihood (he sold his clientele "Power-Increasing Pills") no less than for the narrator's skeptical tone:

> The secret art of Stupid Chang was stone smashing. The stones were large, round, and smooth. Prior to the performance, his younger brother, Old Chang the Second, took two stones and hit them against each other, letting the audience here the clacking sound. He then allowed the spectators to feel them. Meanwhile, Chang circulated his *qi* at his side. The circulation being over, Chang took the stone, placed it on the edge of a stool, and searched for the exact spot to be hit. Two large cries Ah! Ah! were heard, and his hand struck. As if responding to his cries the stone broke. Stupid Chang could also drill with his fingers into stones, smashing them.
>
> Once the performance was over, Chang sold his spectators his "All-Nourishing Power-Increasing Pill." According to him it was miraculously effective—not only could it strengthen the tendons and build one's bones, it could also cure all other internal and external injuries,

including those resulting from falling, fighting, a sprained waist or a choked chest. Indeed, he himself became so powerful only because he took it. Truth is, his "All Nourishing Power-Increasing Pill" had no miraculous effects whatsoever, but swallowing it did not cause much damage either."[38]

Internal energy could be channeled not only for offensive but also for defensive purposes. The ability to withstand a blow is often analyzed in Qing manuals in terms of *qi* circulation. The early seventeenth century *Sinews Transformation Classic* teaches a systematic method of *qi* cultivation that results in a body resilient to injury. Training proceeds from *qi* circulation and massaging to pounding of the body with increasingly harder objects from a wooden pestle and a wooden mallet to a pebble bag. The practice is expected to forge a body "as hard as iron and stone," so much so that one would be able to "smash a tiger's brain with his fist" and "cut an ox's neck with his palm."[39] By the mid-eighteenth century such methods were commonly practiced, as is attested by vernacular fiction. Wu Jingzi's (1701–1754) *Unofficial History of the Scholars* (*Rulin waishi*) celebrates a valiant hero who relies on *qi* circulation to withstand court torture.[40]

Qing methods of hardening the body were known by the generic labels of Golden Bell Armor (Jinzhong zhao) and Iron Cloth Shirt (Tiebu shan), implying that the practitioner manipulated his *qi* into an impenetrable shield.[41] There were some, even among the bureaucratic elite, who believed that such techniques could avert injury not only from bare-handed blows but also from sharp weapons. A government official named Ruan Zutang (fl. 1890), who served as circuit attendant of Xuzhou, Jiangsu, commented on the Golden Bell Armor: "where the *qi* moves, even a fierce chop cannot penetrate. But if one loses concentration, then the blade will enter."[42] The physical exercises of hardening were sometimes joined by ritual procedures. Some martial artists enhanced the efficacy of *qi* circulation with charms, spells, and prayer to valiant deities. A Daoist priest who became entangled in the 1813 Eight Trigrams uprising was said to have practiced the Golden Bell Armor by "swallowing charms and circulating his *qi*" (*chifu yunqi*).[43] Late nineteenth-century members of the Big Swords militia likewise practiced breathing techniques and pounded their bodies with bricks, while at the same time swallowing charms that were burnt and mixed in water.[44] Hardening the body was simultaneously a martial technique and an invulnerability ritual.

The association of some *qi*-circulation techniques with ritual procedures might suggest that the concept of *qi* was occasionally colored with a supernormal aura. We have seen that the *qi* implied diverse things to different martial artists. It was a method of breathing and a technique of mental concentration, and it suggested a harmony of intent and action as well as an unhindered delivery of force. It is possible, however, that some practitioners—especially those involved in sectarian activities—attributed to their hidden *qi* miraculous powers as well.

An early Boxer leader, a Buddhist monk named Xincheng, reportedly boasted in 1899 that "my whole body has Qigong (Qi efficacy); I can resist spears and guns. When the hard and precious [Buddhist guardians] possess my body, the foreigners cannot oppose me."[45] It appears that for monk Xincheng, the term Qigong implied divine powers similar to those of the guardian deities that possessed him. If it could only be tapped, the *qi* could make one invulnerable to bullets.

If the example of monk Xincheng is indicative of others, then the integration of martial training and invulnerability rituals might have been facilitated by the extraordinary powers that were sometimes attributed to the *qi*. From this perspective, the religiously impregnated vocabulary of *daoyin* might have given some fighting techniques a magic twist.[46] Qing fiction, at any rate, is replete with tales of supernormal fits that were accomplished by the hidden powers of *qi*. Consider, for example, the following story of a martial artist who relies on his *qi* to levitate:

> Lian Fangjun possessed divine strength (*shenli*). Often, during the afternoon siesta, he would retire to a secluded room, where he would sit cross-legged on an iron chair. After approximately half an hour he would stretch his arms, gradually lifting the chair upwards. The chair would float a long time high above ground, and Lian's body would not stir. This was due to the concentration, and the circulation, of *qi* (*qianqi neiyun*).[47]

Chinese medical theory had the *qi* flow in prescribed channels called *jingluo* (meridians). The channels were dotted with cavities (*xuedao*), which were points sensitive to acupuncture treatment. The concept was adopted by late imperial martial artists who held that the points responsive to therapy were equally susceptible to injury. The significance of acupuncture points in Shaolin hand combat has been noted earlier. The term "cavities" figured in the very title of the Shaolin handbook *Xuanji's Secret Transmission of Acupuncture Points' Hand Combat Formulas*. However, the concept was equally important in other barehanded styles. It figured prominently in the late Ming method of the Internal School Fist (Neijia Quan), the foremost exponent of which was Wang Zhengnan (1617–1669). The two surviving accounts of the Internal School—Huang Zongxi's epitaph for Wang Zhengnan and Huang Baijia's *The Internal School Fist Method (Neijia quanfa)* (1676)—detail some of the cavities it targeted. According to Huang Zongxi, "in striking opponents, Wang Zhengnan made use of acupuncture points—death points, mute points, and vertigo points—just as illustrated on the bronze models of the channels."[48]

The importance of acupuncture points in empty-handed fighting is one indication of the integration of medical theory into the late imperial martial arts. In some empty-handed styles, the martial goal of toning the body for battle is indistinguishable from the medical objective of preventing illness. The

Sinews Transformation Classic, for instance, outlines a method of hardening the body that is supposed to be equally effective against martial adversaries and disease. By a combination of *qi* circulation, massage, and self-pounding, the practitioner is expected to gain "internal robustness" (*neizhuang*) that would eliminate all illness. Medication figures in this training regimen. The *Sinews Transformation Classic* provides specific recipes for "internal robustness medicines" to be consumed in conjunction with physical exercises.[49] Other military treatises likewise delve into medical theory and drug production. The second fascicle of *Xuanji's Secret Transmission of Acupuncture Points' Hand Combat Formulas* is titled "The Secret Volume of Treating Weapon Cuts, Fighting Injuries, and Broken Bones." In addition to outlining emergency treatments for a variety of wounds, it also discusses moxibustion and pulse taking.[50]

The handbooks' medical orientations were matched by the practitioners' therapeutic expectations. We have opened this chapter with the nineteenth-century Wang Zuyuan, whose martial journey to the Shaolin Temple originated in his father's concern for his health. A century earlier, Cao Huandou's practice of Shaolin fighting was motivated at least partially by medical considerations. In his preface to the *Hand Combat Classic* (1784), Cao alludes to repeated illness.[51] If, however, Cao's martial training provided him with a self-cure, then he could just as easily treat others. The seventeenth century witnessed the appearance of the martial artist–cum–physician. He who could take the body apart could presumably put it back together. In some instances only the martial artist could restore his victims to their health, for he alone possessed the antidote to their injury. We are told that one of Wang Zhengnan's adversaries regained the ability to urinate only after he apologized to the master, who cured him.[52] Biographies of other martial artists similarly allude to therapeutic activities. Gan Fengchi (fl. 1730) was a famous Nanjing martial artist who was believed to be capable of squeezing lead into liquid with his bare hands. According to the *Draft Qing History*, Gan cured patients by sitting with them back to back and emitting his internal energy into their bodies. A few decades later, the leader of the 1774 White Lotus uprising, Wang Lun, earned an itinerant livelihood by teaching the martial arts and healing.[53] The Qing martial artist was an expert on the human body, which he could equally injure and cure.

The formulation of fighting techniques in terms borrowed from Chinese medicine was one aspect of the theorization impulse that characterized the late imperial martial arts. Beginning in the late Ming, many authors were no longer satisfied to describe limb movements only. Instead, they embedded fighting postures in the rich vocabularies of medicine, religion, and philosophy. Martial artists identified within their own bodies the universal forces of *yin* and *yang*, the five elements, and eight trigrams, investing the martial arts with a cosmological dimension. The intricate interplay of *yin* and *yang* serves in all *quan* styles to illuminate the twin concepts of defense and offense, contract and expand, close and open, soft and hard. Xingyi Quan identifies the five striking techniques of Splitting Fist (Piquan), Drilling Fist (Zuanquan), Crashing Fist

(Bengquan), Exploding Fist (Paoquan), and Shearing Fist (Hengquan) with the five elements of metal, water, wood, fire, and earth respectively; and, as indicated by its name, the Eight Trigrams Palm (Bagua zhang) revolves in a concentric movement around the eight configurations that are described in the *Classic of Changes* (*Yijing*).[54]

The identity of microcosm and macrocosm that characterizes much of Chinese thought permitted martial artists to re-enact within their own bodies the process of cosmic evolution. Beginning with the first centuries BCE *Classic of Changes* and culminating with Zhou Dunyi's (1017–1073) *Diagram of the Supreme Ultimate* (*Taiji tu*), Chinese philosophy usually described the history of the universe in terms of differentiation from a primordial unity called *taiji* (supreme ultimate). In this creation process, several stages, or forces, were discernible, including the *yin* and the *yang*, the five elements, and the eight trigrams. In such Qing fighting styles as Taiji Quan—which is consciously named after the cosmology—the practitioner repeats the process of universal evolution by a prescribed set of movements. The training routine opens in the quiescence of the primordial *taiji* and proceeds through the interplay of *yin* and *yang*, five elements, and eight trigrams, to the profusion of the myriad phenomena. Rather than ending in this state of multiplicity, the martial artist then heads back in time to the origins of the universe, receding from the myriad things to the eight trigrams, contracting further to the two cosmic principles *yin* and *yang*, and culminating in the tranquility of *taiji*.

As early as the Ming period, the concept of five elements was incorporated into martial arts literature. It appeared, for example, in Tang Shunzhi's (1507–1560) discussion of spear fighting.[55] However, the complete re-enactment of cosmic evolution within the martial arts likely appeared no earlier than the Qing. Among its earliest textual records is Yang Bing's Plum Fist manual *Introduction to Martial Practice* (1742), in which he quotes verbatim from the *Classic of Changes*: "In the *Changes* there is the supreme ultimate (*taiji*), which produced the two forms. These two forms produced the four emblems, and these four emblems produced the eight trigrams."[56] Several decades later Wang Zongyue (fl. 1780) repeated in his Taiji Quan essays the fuller version of cosmic creation as it had been formulated by the Song thinker Zhou Dunyi. Wang identifies specific Taiji Quan postures with the evolutionary stages the *yin* and the *yang*, the five elements, and the eight trigrams.[57]

Thus, Chinese cosmology enriched the martial arts with the vocabulary of a mystical union. Practitioners re-enacted the process of cosmic differentiation, then reversed it to achieve oneness with the primordial unity of *taiji*. Their spiritual goal was explicitly stated in late Qing manuals, such as the following Taiji Quan classic in Douglas Wile's translation:

> The ears and eyes, hands and feet, being divided into pairs are like *yin* and *yang*, and their uniting into one is like *taiji*. Thus the external becomes concentrated in the internal, and the internal expresses itself

externally. In this way we develop within and without, the fine and the gross, and with penetrating understanding, we realize the work of the wise men and sages. Wisdom and knowledge, sagehood and immortality, these are what we mean by fulfilling our intrinsic nature and establishing life. Herein lies the perfection of spirit and divine transformation. The way of heaven and the way of humanity is simple sincerity.[58]

The cosmological vocabulary of mystical union was joined by the Daoist language of immortality. At least some Qing martial artists employed the terminology of Daoist "inner alchemy" (*neidan*) in their military treatises. They described martial strength as the by-product of an inner elixir leading to eternal life. Chang Naizhou went as far as claiming that "inner alchemy" was the foundation of martial training, following the Daoist scheme of three stages in the smelting of the inner elixir: the first stage of refining essence (*jing*) and transmuting it into breath (*qi*), the second stage of refining breath and transmuting it into spirit (*shen*), and the third stage of refining spirit and returning it to the primordial void (*xu*). The same stages are outlined in at least some manuals of Xingyi Quan.[59]

Before we examine two texts that illustrate the impact of gymnastics on the late imperial martial arts, a qualifying comment is in order. I have argued that the foundations of late imperial bare-handed styles such as Shaolin Quan, Taiji Quan, and Xingyi Quan were laid during the late Ming and the early Qing by the integration of Ming hand combat with an ancient gymnastic tradition that had largely evolved within a Daoist context. This is not to say, however, that aspects either of *daoyin* gymnastics or of cosmological thought did not figure in some fighting techniques as early as ancient times. A survey of classical Chinese warfare goes beyond the scope of this study. Fencing, however, merits a brief mention.

Scholars have pointed out the significance of the sword in Daoist ritual. As early as the first centuries CE, Daoist priests ascribed magic powers to the blades they employed as liturgical implements. Considered the incarnations of dragons, swords could fly, and they were believed to be efficacious against water creatures; Ge Hong (282–343) recommended the dagger as a talisman against dragons, crocodiles, and the like.[60] The sword's role in exorcistic rituals was matched by the elaborate ceremonies that accompanied its production. The forging of a divine blade was conducted according to intricate ritual rules resembling those that surrounded the concoction of the elixir. Precious swords, in addition, figured in the relations between priest and ruler. The Shangqing patriarch Sima Chengzhen (647–735) presented his patron, the Tang emperor Xuanzong, with thirteen divine swords, each engraved with the name of a different deity.[61]

To this day, sword dances are an integral element of Daoist ritual. Their primary goal is exorcistic. Demon-expelling swordplay purifies the altar in the fundamental Daoist rite of offering (*jiao*). The sword dance follows a minutely prescribed choreography, which correlates the priest's steps with cosmic powers. Wielding his magic weapon, the priest pronounces:

I hold my precious sword, whose name is Dragon Source;
Flashing as I unsheathe it, it illumines the Nine Heavens.
With the roar of a tiger, it comes through space;
It mounts on high to the Great Void.
Sun and moon, wind and clouds emerge on either side;
Auspicious clouds of energy carry the Eight Immortals.
When ordinary mortals see it, calamities disappear;
When perverse demons hear it, they go down to the Nine Springs.
The Most High gave me these secret instructions:
Walking the constellation, I circumambulate the altar.
Heavenly Worthy Who Responds as Shadow to Light.[62]

That the sword can substitute for the priest in his grave is the clearest indication of their intimate relationship. The seeker of eternal life may feign death
by transforming his sword into a replica of his body. Whereas the weapon remains entombed, he is liberated to immortality. Detailed guidelines for the
performance of the metamorphosis are provided by Daoist scriptures, in which
the adept addresses his sword: "with you I replace my person so that my body
may be invisible; I am going to hide myself, you will enter my tomb."[63] Hence, if
the staff was the symbol of the Buddhist priest, the sword was the emblem of
his Daoist counterpart. (In Japan, however, the situation was different, for
swordsmanship did flourish there in a Buddhist (Zen) ideological context).[64]
    The centrality of the sword in Daoist religious practice might have con-
tributed to the incorporation of *daoyin* gymnastics into fencing. It is likely
that as early as the first centuries CE, breathing methods, and possibly even
qi-circulation techniques, figured in sword training. A hint is provided by a
short story that is anthologized in *The Annals of Wu and Yue* (*Wu Yue chunqiu*)
(ca. second century). Its protagonist is an outstanding swordswoman who is
invited by the king of Yue to instruct him in fencing. The swordswoman's exposition of the art is replete with the *daoyin* vocabulary of breathing, *qi*, and
spirit (*shen*), as well as the cosmological terminology of *yin* and *yang*:

    The art of swordsmanship is extremely subtle and elusive; its principles
    are most secret and profound. The Dao has its gate and door, its *yin* and
    yang. Open the gate and close the door; *yin* declines and *yang* rises.
    When practicing the art of face-to-face combat, concentrate your spirit
    internally and give the impression of relaxation externally. You should
    look like a modest woman and strike like a ferocious tiger. As you
    assume various postures, regulate your *qi*, moving always with the spirit
    (*shen*). Your skill should be as obvious as the sun and as startling as a
    bolting hare. Your opponent endeavors to pursue your form and chase
    your shadow, yet your image hovers between existence and nonexis-
    tence. The breath moves in and out and should never be held. Whether
    you close with the opponent vertically or horizontally, with or against

the flow, never attack frontally. Mastery of this art allows one to match a hundred, and a hundred to match a thousand. If your Highness would like to test it, I can demonstrate for your edification.[65]

The story of the Yue swordswoman suggests that fencers espoused breathing techniques. It might indicate, furthermore, that sword training was considered by some a method of spiritual cultivation. Just as the concepts of *yin* and *yang* could facilitate the study of swordplay, the practice of fencing could illuminate cosmological principles. It is instructive, therefore, that medieval fiction associated swordsmanship with the Daoist immortality techniques. The Tang story "The Old Man of Lanling" ("Lanling laoren") celebrates a sword master whose demonstration of the art is preceded by a penetrating discourse of "nourishing life" (*yangsheng*). The swordsman—the narrator hints that he is a Daoist priest—performs a sword dance with seven blades which he effortlessly throws and catches in mid-air. He concludes the demonstration by throwing the swords down, planting them in the ground in the position of the seven stars of the big dipper.[66]

When we turn our attention from fencing to bare-handed fighting, our investigation is hampered by the dearth of evidence. Warring States and Han literature allude, for example, to an unarmed technique called *shoubo* (literally: hand combat), which is regarded by some scholars as the predecessor of *quan* fighting. *Shoubo* evolved partially in the context of a daring sport of empty-handed wrestling with wild animals. Athletes vied bare-handed with tigers and bears, whose teeth and claws were said to have been removed prior to the contest. By the first century CE, *shoubo* was likely highly developed, for it figured as the subject of what must have been an elaborate book. In his *History of the [Former] Han* (*Hanshu*), Ban Gu (32–92) mentions a work titled *Shoubo*, in no less than six chapters.[67]

Unfortunately, the *Shoubo* book listed by Ban Gu is no longer extant, and in its absence the available information on the art is meager indeed. To the best of my knowledge, the existing references to the empty-handed style do not associate it with *daoyin* gymnastics. However, had we possessed the now-lost manual the picture might have been different. We have seen that recently discovered Han manuscripts have shed invaluable light on ancient gymnastics. It is not impossible that future archaeological or textual research will likewise unravel new information on hand combat. We may still learn that the connection between bare-handed fighting and therapeutic and religious gymnastics extended further back in time than we are currently able to establish.

The *Illustrated Exposition of Internal Techniques*

Equipped with information on *daoyin* gymnastics, we may return to Wang Zuyuan's *Illustrated Exposition of Internal Techniques* (1882), which demonstrates the tradition's influence on the Shaolin martial arts. Even though Wang was under the impression that the Shaolin methods he studied originated at the monastery, they can all be traced to earlier manuals of gymnastics and breathing. The various training routines in the *Illustrated Exposition*—like its immediate source, *Essential Techniques of Guarding Life*—derive from *daoyin* treatises that are permeated with a Daoist vocabulary. Following Tang Hao, I will illustrate the *daoyin* pedigree of Wang's techniques by his "Twelve-Section Brocade" (Shier duan jin), which, as suggested by its name, includes twelve exercises. The opening five read as follows:

(1) SIT DOWN, YOUR EYES SHUT AND YOUR MIND OBSCURE (*MINGXIN*). CLENCH YOUR FISTS (*WOGU*), CONTEMPLATING QUIETLY (*JINGSI*) THE DIVINITIES:[68]

> Sit cross-legged, shutting your eyes tightly and clearing your mind of all thoughts. When sitting straighten your spine: The waist should not be loose; the body should not bend. *Clenching fists*: By clenching firmly your fists you will be able to close the gate and expel the demons. *Contemplating quietly*: By stopping all thoughts you will visualize the divinities (*cunshen*).

(2) CLAP YOUR TEETH (*KOUCHI*) THIRTY-SIX TIMES. EMBRACE KUNLUN WITH BOTH HANDS:[69]

> Clap the upper teeth against the lower teeth, making a sound. It should ring thirty-six times. By clapping the teeth you will assemble the body's interior divinities, preventing them from being dispersed. Kunlun is the head. Embrace firmly your nape with both hands, the ten fingers crossed together. At once cover tightly your outer ears with both palms. Count silently nine nose breaths. Exhale and inhale gently, without emitting a sound.

(3) LEFT AND RIGHT, SOUND THE HEAVENLY DRUM (THE OCCIPUT) AUDIBLY TWENTY-FOUR TIMES:

> Remember to count nine inhalations and nine exhalations from the nose. These completed, release your crossed hands, and with both palms cover your ears. Fold your index finger on your middle finger and press it tightly. With your index finger tap repeatedly the back of the brain. It should sound like a drum. Repeat this in this same fashion with both hands, tapping on the left and on the right twenty-four times each for a total of forty-eight vibrations. Again, release your hands and clench your fists.

(4) LIGHTLY SHAKE THE HEAVENLY PILLAR:

> The Heavenly Pillar is the nape. Lower your head and turn your neck. Look sideways on your shoulder. Then, on left and right shake twenty-four times each.

(5) LET THE RED DRAGON (THE TONGUE) STIR THE SALIVA. GARGLE TWENTY-SIX TIMES. WHEN THE DIVINE WATER (THE SALIVA)

FILLS THE MOUTH, DIVIDE EACH MOUTHFUL INTO THREE, AND
SWALLOW. WHEN THE DRAGON (THE SALIVA) MOVES, THE TIGER
(THE *QI*) NATURALLY FLEES:

> The Red Dragon is the tongue. Press your palate with your tongue.
> Then stir your entire mouth—up, down, and on both sides—
> producing the saliva naturally. Gargle at the mouth thirty-six
> times. The Divine Water is the saliva. Divide it into three and
> swallow, making a gurgling sound. Quiet your mind and shut your
> eyes. Guide the swallowed saliva directly to the "Lower Cinnabar
> Field" below the navel. The dragon is the saliva. The Tiger is the
> *qi*. When the saliva goes down, the *qi* naturally follows.[70]

The shaven pates and monastic robes in the drawings that accompany Wang's
treatise (figure 32) suggest a Buddhist affiliation. Nevertheless, even a cursory
reading reveals the exercises' origins in a Daoist-related gymnastic tradition.
Staple *daoyin* routines are all included in the "Twelve-Section Brocade." Clapping

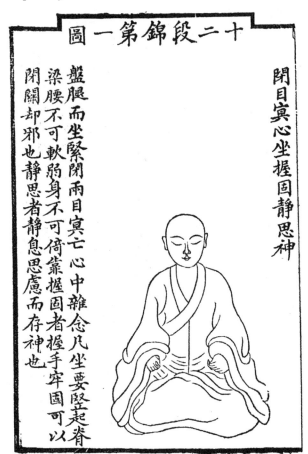

FIG. 32. The first
exercise of the
Twelve-Section
Brocade in Wang
Zuyuan's 1882
Illustrated Exposition.
The wrapped
thumbs—imitating a
newborn baby—
betray the exercise's
Daoist ancestry.

the teeth and swallowing the saliva, breathing and directing the *qi* to the "Lower Cinnabar Field." Furthermore, the manual Wang had obtained at the Shaolin Temple expounds Daoist meditation techniques: the "obscure mind" (*mingxin*) method of clearing the mind of all thoughts; the technique of clenching the fists, that is, unwrapping the thumbs in imitation of a newborn baby (thereby expelling the demons); and, most noticeably, the meditation of "actualizing the divinities" (*cunshen*), namely, visualizing the body's corporal deities.

It is not surprising therefore that the "Twelve-Section Brocade" can be traced back to earlier *daoyin* manuals. "The method's original name," the text notes, "was 'Eight-Section Brocade' (Baduan jin)."[71] The latter is familiar to us in Daoist literature dating all the way back to the Song period. A twelfth-century encyclopedia of inner alchemy, *The Pivot of the Way* (*Dao shu*) (ca. 1150), outlines an early version of the exercise.[72] That the technique was already ridiculed in Song times is likely the best indication of its popularity. Hong Mai's (1123–1202) collection of popular lore *Stories Heard by Yijian* (*Yijian zhi*) tells of an adept who learns to his dismay that the "Eight-Sections Brocade" may lead to premature death. The troubling news is brought to him by his servant, who turns out to be a Daoist sage in disguise.[73]

Despite Hong Mai's twelfth-century warning, in both China and in the West the "Eight-Section Brocade" is still widely practiced. The gymnastic set exists in several varieties, standing and sitting.[74] The seated version that Wang Zuyuan described in his nineteenth-century manual can be traced back through an earlier Qing manual, *Immortality Teachings to Benefit the World* (*Shou shi chuan zhen*) (1771), and two late Ming ones, *Eight Treatises on Guarding Life* (*Zunsheng bajian*) (1592) and *Red Phoenix's Marrow* (*Chifeng sui*) (1578), all the way to a twelfth-century Daoist encyclopedia, *Ten Compilations on Cultivating Perfection* (*Xiuzhen shishu*) (completed ca. 1300), in which the exercises are accompanied by drawings.[75] The Song encyclopedia attributed the "Eight-Section Brocade" to the semidivine pair of immortals Zhongli Quan and Lü Dongbin, whom Daoist mythology had credited with an entire corpus of alchemical and physiological writings.[76]

Thus, Wang Zuyuan's manual illustrates the depth of Daoist influence on the late imperial martial arts. By the nineteenth century, Buddhist monks at the Shaolin Temple were practicing gymnastic methods that had been recorded in Daoist scriptures, that had evolved in Daoist circles, and that had been attributed to Daoist immortals.

The *Sinews Transformation Classic*

One section of the *Illustrated Exposition of Internal Techniques* is titled "The *Sinews Transformation Classic*'s Twelve Illustrations."[77] It includes twelve exercises that are conducted in a standing posture. The first form, which is called "Weituo Offering his [Vajra]-Club" (Weituo xian chu), has been fashioned after the deity's iconography (compare figures 33 and 34). Weituo has been among the

FIG. 33. Shaolin statue of
Weituo (Skanda).

most popular tutelary divinities of Chinese Buddhism. Originally a Hindu
warrior—Weituo is a mistranscription of the Sanskrit Skanda—he has been incorporated into the Buddhist pantheon as the guardian of monasteries, where
his image is usually stationed opposite the Buddha Śākyamuni's. Facing his superior, Weituo presses his palms reverently, his club lying horizontally across
his elbows, just as in the exercise that bears his name.[78]

Despite their undeniable connection to Buddhist mythology, Weituo's exercises are also related to Daoist gymnastics. The twelve-form routine features
the common *daoyin* aspects of breathing, swallowing the saliva, circulating the
qi, and gathering the body's internal spirits. Indeed, like the entire text of the *Illustrated Exposition*, the twelve exercises did not originate at the Shaolin Temple.
As betrayed by their title, they derived from the late Ming manual *Sinews Transformation Classic*. The latter survives in quite a few editions (manuscript and

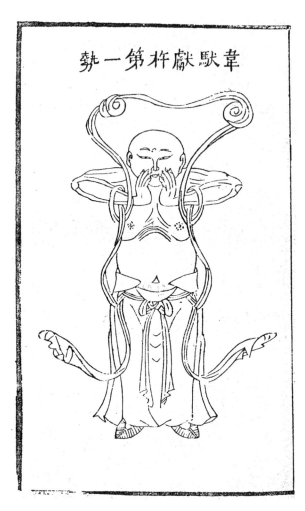

FIG. 34. "Weituo
offering his [demon-
felling] club"; Dao-
guang (1821–1850)
edition of the *Sinews
Transformation Classic*.

printed alike), which attest to its popularity in Qing times (see appendix).
Weituo's exercises were borrowed from an early nineteenth-century edition,
for they did not figure in earlier ones.[79]

The original version of the *Sinews Transformation Classic* was likely authored in the early seventeenth century. As Tang Hao has suggested, the key
to its dating is provided by a postscript dated 1624 that accompanies some
editions and is signed by the Purple Coagulation Man of the Way (Zi ning
daoren), Zongheng, from Mt. Tiantai, in Zhejiang.[80] Nothing is known of
Zongheng, and all we can infer about him is his self-perception as evinced by
his sobriquet. This is marked by a tantalizing ambiguity that is perhaps in-
tentional just as it is typical of Ming religious syncretism. The term "Man of
the Way" (*daoren*) was usually applied to Daoist priests, but it could also designate a Buddhist monk, and Mt. Tiantai held an equally eminent position in

the sacred geographies of both faiths. It was the site of dozens of Daoist and Buddhist shrines, the most famous of which were the Daoist Tongbai Temple and the Buddhist Guoqing Monastery.[81]

This ambiguity notwithstanding, "Purple Coagulation" does have a clear Daoist ring. Purple is the color par excellence of Daoist mythology. It is the elixir's hue, and by implication the color of everything from deities and divine palaces (many of which are located within the body) to sacred scriptures. Coagulation (*ning*) is a stage in the alchemical production of the elixir, and it also designates the meditative techniques of concocting the "inner elixir."[82] Hence, the "Purple Coagulation Man of the Way" could be rendered as the "Purple Elixir Daoist." This religious pen name is certainly justified by the manual's teachings. The *Sinews Transformation Classic* is premised upon the Daoist notion of an internal bodily transformation. Its goal is "internal robustness" (*neizhuang*) that will make the body resilient to injury, that will eliminate all illness, and that will ultimately lead to immortality:

> The contrast between internal and external is that between robustness and enfeeblement. The difference between robustness and enfeeblement is that robustness lasts. Comparing the internal and the external, the external might be dispensed with.
>
> Internal robustness is called firmness (*jian*); external robustness is called valor (*yong*). Firm, and simultaneously valiant, is truly valiant. Valiant, and simultaneously firm, is truly firm. Firmness and valor, valor and firmness—by these an imperishable body of ten thousand eons is obtained. It is the diamond (*jin'gang*; Sanskrit: *vajra*) body.
>
> Any practice of internal robustness involves three principles: The first is called "Guarding the Center" (*shouzhong*). "Guarding the Center" is nothing but the accumulation of *qi*. The *qi* is accumulated by the eyes, ears, nose, tongue, body, and mind (*yi*). The method's subtlety is apparent in the following massaging technique: During the massage one should loosen his garments and lie facing upward. He should place his palms between his chest and his abdomen. This is the so-called "center." The center is the only place where the *qi* is stored. It must be guarded. . .
>
> The second principle is called "Avoiding other thoughts." At the center of the body, the essence (*jing*), spirit (*shen*), vital energy (*qi*), and blood are incapable of controlling themselves. Rather, they fully adhere to the mind (*yi*): When the mind moves, they move; when the mind rests, they rest. When practicing "Guarding the Center" the mind should follow the palms downward [to the abdomen]. This is the appropriate form. . .
>
> The third principle is called "Keeping it Full." Massaging and storing it, the *qi* accumulates. When the *qi* accumulates, the essence (*jing*), spirit (*shen*), and blood vessels all follow it. Guarding the *qi*, it

does not escape. Massaging it, it lasts. When the *qi* is stored at the center it does not spill to the sides. When the *qi* accumulates, strength (*li*) naturally accumulates; when the *qi* is replete, strength naturally fills the entire body. This is what Mencius called: "[The *qi*] is in the highest degree, vast and unyielding, filling the space between Heaven and Earth. It is my flood-like *qi*."[83]

Despite some Buddhist and even Confucian allusions (the former's *vajra*; the latter's "flood-like *qi*"), the text's Daoist orientation is unmistakable. "Guarding the Center" (*shouzhong*) is a Daoist method of concentrative meditation,[84] which is accompanied here by the common *daoyin* techniques of *qi* circulation and massaging. Furthermore, the forging of "internal robustness" involves irradiation by the heavenly bodies, as the *Sinews Transformation Classic* resorts to the medieval Daoist methods of energy absorption:

> The sun's essence, the moon's spirit—these two cosmic energies (*qi*) mix together, giving birth to the myriad things. Among the ancients, those who excelled in absorbing these energies had all, after lengthy practice, attained immortality. The method is secret, and most people do not know it. Even if they do know it, lacking firm will and constant mind, they are wasting in vain their time. Therefore, those who have mastered it are few.
>
> All those who engage in internal training, from the early stages of training until they master the technique—indeed throughout their lives (and whether busy or not)—refrain from involvement in worldly matters. If one does not temporarily suspend his absorption practice, then it should not be difficult for him to obtain the immortals' way.
>
> Those who practice absorption, inhale the essence of *yin* and *yang* to increase their spiritual consciousness (*shenzhi*). Thus stagnant substances are gradually eliminated, and pure ones increase daily. The myriad diseases are prevented, and great benefit accrues.
>
> This is the absorption method: The sun's essence should be inhaled at the first of the lunar month, when the moon is in its earliest, and its *qi* has been renewed. It is possible then to inhale the sun's essence. The moon's spirit should be inhaled at the fifteenth of the lunar month, when the metal and water elements are at their fullest, and the moon's *qi* at its most prosperous. It is possible then to inhale the moon's spirit.[85]

Within a century of its compilation, the *Sinews Transformation Classic*'s method of forging an invulnerable body was already widely practiced, as attested by both martial arts literature and popular fiction. Chang Naizhou (fl. 1740) alluded to the late Ming manual in his own military writings, as did Wu Jingzi (1701–1754) in his novel *Unofficial History of the Scholars*. It is noteworthy that both authors apparently assumed their readers' familiarity with the teachings of the "Purple Coagulation Man of the Way." Chang Naizhou compared his own external method to the *Sinews Transformation Classic*'s internal technique, and Wu Jingzi attributed the strength of his knight errant protagonist Feng Mingqi to his reliance on it.[86] It is perhaps noteworthy that the latter has been modeled after the historical martial artist Gan Fengchi (fl. 1730) with whom the novelist might have been personally familiar (both were Nanjing natives). It has been pointed out that Wu tended to leave clues—in this instance the character "feng"—to his protagonists' identity.[87]

The *Sinews Transformation Classic* is the earliest extant manual that assigns *daoyin* gymnastics a martial role. Its likely author, the "Purple Coagulation Man of the Way," was the first to explicitly associate military, therapeutic, and religious goals in one training routine. As such, the manual holds an important position in the history of Chinese hand combat. From the perspective of Shaolin fighting, however, the *Sinews Transformation Classic* bears another significance. Even though it had been authored outside the monastery, the manual formulated a legend that was eventually adopted by the Shaolin monks themselves, namely that their martial arts were created by the Buddhist saint Bodhidharma.

The Bodhidharma Legend

It has been pointed out that forgery played a significant role in the siniciza-tion of Buddhism. Beginning in the early medieval period, Chinese authors did not shy from attributing their Buddhist writings to historical or fictional Indian monks, who supposedly penned them in Sanskrit. Presented as if they had been translated from the Buddha's native tongue, apocryphal scrip-tures contributed to the emergence of an indigenous Chinese Buddhism.[88] That the creator of the *Sinews Transformation Classic* ascribed his manual to an Indian author (and translator) is therefore not unprecedented. What is novel perhaps is the boldness of his fabrication. No less than a thousand years separate the "Purple Coagulation Man of the Way" from the person to whom he attributed his writings: Bodhidharma (fl. 500).

The claim that the Indian saint had authored the *Sinews Transformation Classic* is made in an elaborately forged preface, which is signed by the re-nowned general Li Jing (571–649), who had led the Tang army to numerous victories in China and central Asia. The general explains that the manual has been handed down to him from Bodhidharma through a chain of Buddhist saints and martial heroes, and that his own military achievements have been due to his reliance on it. The preface serves therefore to enhance the manual's prestige. The *Sinews Transformation Classic* was the source of a famous general's strategic genius:

> During the Northern Wei Emperor Xiaomingdi's Taihe reign period
> (477–499),[89] the Great Master Bodhidharma traveled from the Kingdom

of Liang [in south China] to the Kingdom of Wei [in the north]. He faced the wall [in meditation] at the Shaolin Monastery. One day he addressed his disciples saying: Why would not each of you tell us what he knows so that we can evaluate his level of self-cultivation. The monks then proceeded to expound each what he had attained. The master declared: "So and so will receive my skin; so and so will receive my flesh; so and so will receive my bones." Only to Huike he said: "You will receive my marrow (*sui*)." People of later generations arbitrarily explained this as a metaphor for the disciples' depth of spiritual attainment. They failed to realize that he meant what he said. The master's words were no metaphor.

After his nine years of meditation were completed, the master pointed the way to Nirvana. His remains were enshrined on Mt. Xionger [in Western Henan]. Then carrying one shoe he returned to the west. Later, the brick wall he faced in meditation was damaged by wind and rain. When the Shaolin monks repaired it, they discovered inside a metal case. . . . Hidden inside it were two scrolls, one titled *Marrow Cleansing Classic* (*Xisui jing*), the other titled *Sinews Transformation Classic*. . . .

The *Marrow Cleansing Classic* was handed over to Huike and along with his cassock and bowl became part of a secret transmission. In later generations it was rarely seen. Only the *Sinews Transformation Classic* remained as the cornerstone of the Shaolin Monastery, treasuring forever the master's virtue. However, because it was written entirely in the language of India, Shaolin monks could not fully understand it. Occasionally one or another would understand some twenty or thirty percent of it, or even forty or fifty percent. However the secrets they unraveled were not orally transmitted to future generations. Thus, each Shaolin monk interpreted and performed the classic as he pleased.

Eventually, the Shaolin monks strayed into side paths, and sank into trivialities. Therefore, they failed to enter the true Dharma Gate of Buddhism. To this day, if the Shaolin monks excel in martial competitions only this is because of their limited understanding of the *Sinews Transformation Classic*.

There was among the Shaolin crowd a monk of unsurpassed wisdom who reflected that if the Great Master Bodhidharma had left a sacred scripture it could not possibly contain trifle techniques only. Since the Shaolin monks could not read it, a translator had to be found. Therefore, he held the *Sinews Transformation Classic* to his bosom and traveled far to all the famous mountains. One day he arrived at the land of Shu [Sichuan] and climbed Mt. Emei, where he encountered the Indian holy monk Pramiti.[90] The [Shaolin] monk told Pramiti of the *Sinews Transformation Classic* and explained the purpose of his visit, whereupon the Indian holy monk said: "Indeed the Buddhist patriarch's mind transmission is contained in this scripture. However, the scripture's wording cannot be accurately translated for the language of the Buddha is esoteric. By contrast, the scripture's meaning can be rendered. It is intelligible to the common person, leading to sainthood. Thereupon, Pramiti explained point by point the *Sinews Transformation Classic*, and minutely rendered its meaning.

Pramiti convinced the Shaolin monk to stay on the mountain, where he guided him in self-cultivation. After a hundred days the monk's body coagulated into hardness (*ninggu*). After another hundred days it was replete [with strength]. After another hundred days it fully extended. He had obtained what is known as the "Sturdiness of the Diamond (*vajra*)." He had entered unobstructed the realm of Buddhist wisdom. Indeed the *Sinews Transformation Classic* provided him with a foundation.

The [Shaolin] monk was resolved to sink no more into worldly affairs. Therefore he followed the [Indian] holy monk on a pilgrimage to the sacred islands.[91] Nobody knows where he disappeared to. Xu Hongke met him across the seas, and received his secret doctrine. He handed it over to the Bushy-Bearded Hero, and the Bushy-Bearded Hero handed it over to me.[92]

When I put the *Sinews Transformation Classic* into practice, I obtained marvelous results. Only then did I realize that its words were authentic and not empty. It is a pity that I did not obtain the secrets of the *Marrow Cleansing Classic*, otherwise I would have been able to roam the Buddha realm. It is likewise regrettable that I was lacking in resolve, and so, unlike the [Shaolin] monk, I remained mired in worldly matters. I have merely relied on the Six-Flowers trifle technique to make a name for myself.[93] I will always be ashamed of this.

Nevertheless, since the world is hardly familiar with this classic's wonderful teachings, I respectfully submit this preface, explaining its derivation from beginning to end. I hope that the readers would strive after Buddhahood. I wish they would not limit themselves to the conventional pursuits of the human world. If they all attain Buddhahood then they would accomplish the purpose for which the Eminent Master Bodhidharma handed down this classic. If they hold that martial heroism suffices to make one famous, history furnishes many examples of such heroes. Is not this a good enough reason to keep this classic?

Third day of the third Spring month, Second year of the Tang Zhenguan reign (628). Preface compiled by Li Jing, Yaoshi.[94]

Qing bibliographers were quick to note the numerous errors and anachronisms that proved the preface was spurious. For example, the Taihe reign period was assigned to the wrong emperor, and the Indian translator Pramiti (fl. 705) was not yet born at the time he supposedly rendered the manual into Chinese. Most conspicuously, the creator of the *Sinews Transformation Classic* treated a fictional protagonist of a famous Tang story as if he had really existed. The Bushy-Bearded Hero (Qiuran ke) was not a historical figure, and there is no way he could have handed the manual to Li Jing. Evidently, the "Purple Co-agulation Man of the Way" did not get his history right. The Qing scholar Ling Tingkan (1757–1809) dismissed him as an "ignorant village master."[95]

Even though the compiler of the *Sinews Transformation Classic* evidently was not very learned, he did attempt some allusions to Buddhist hagiography. The legend of Bodhidharma's return to the West is mentioned, as is his farewell conference in which he metaphorically bestowed his marrow (*sui*) on his chosen disciple Huike. It is possible that the latter had attracted the author's attention because the term "marrow" had figured in the Daoist discourse of internal bodily transformation. An influential sixteenth-century manual of inner alchemy was titled, for example, the *Red Phoenix's Marrow* (*Chifeng sui*). Be that as it may, the "Purple Coagulation Man of the Way" had Bodhidharma bestow on his successor—along with the *Sinews Transformation Classic*—a *Marrow Cleansing Classic* (*Xisui jing*). A text bearing that title (and prefaced by Huike) was added to some editions of the *Sinews Transformation Classic* by the nineteenth century.[96] It likely contributed to the prevalence of the term "marrow" in the twentieth-century discourse of physical education and national rejuvenation. Republican reformers sought to revitalize the nation's "marrow" by a combination of traditional martial arts and Western sports.[97]

In case Li Jing's authority would not suffice, the "Purple Coagulation Man of the Way" manipulated another national hero to enhance his book's prestige. It turns out that the great Song general Yue Fei (1103–1142) had been initiated into the mysteries of the *Sinews Transformation Classic*. This is revealed in a second preface, which spurred a wave of allusions to the patriotic hero in later military literature. By the eighteenth century, Yue Fei had been credited with the invention of Xingyi Quan, and by the nineteenth century the "Eight-Section Brocade" and weapon techniques were attributed to him as well.[98] The *Sinews Transformation* preface is signed by Yue Fei's historical lieutenant, General Niu Gao (1087–1147):

> I am a military man. I cannot read as much as a single written character. I like handling the long spear and the broadsword. Maneuvering on horseback and drawing the bow make me happy.
>
> When the Central Plains were lost [to the Jurchens], emperors Huizong (r. 1101–1125) and Qinzong (r. 1126) were taken captive to the north. Prince Kang crossed the river [to the south] on a clay horse, and there were various disasters in Jiangnan. I responded to the call of my commander, the junior guardian, Field Marshal Yue Fei, and I was designated his second in command. I scored several victories, following which I was appointed general-in-chief.

I recall that several years ago, acting on the junior guardian's command, I went on the offensive, and then headed back to E [Hubei]. On my return route I suddenly noticed a wandering monk. His appearance was otherworldly, of the same type as the arhats (*luohan*). In his hands he held a letter. The monk entered the camp, and entrusted me with delivering it to the junior guardian. When I inquired for his reason, he retorted: "General! Do you know that the junior guardian possesses divine strength (*shenli*)?" I replied that I did not, but added that I did see my commander the junior guardian drawing a hundred stones bow, which is something an ordinary person cannot do.

The monk said: "Do you think that the junior guardian's divine strength was bestowed upon him by heaven?" I answered that it must be so, whereupon he retorted: "No, I gave it to him! In his youth the junior guardian studied with me. Once he had attained extraordinary powers, I exhorted him to join me in following the Way. He was not convinced however, and strove instead for achievements in the human world. Even though he will become famous, it will be hard for him to realize his goals. This is heaven's will. This is fate. Nothing can be done about it! Today, the general is in danger. May I trouble you to deliver him this letter. Perhaps it will prompt self-examination, thereby preventing him harm.

Hearing the monk's words, I was completely taken aback. I asked for his name, but he did not answer. I inquired where he was going to, and he said: "to the West, to look for Master Bodhidharma." I was awed by the monk's divine aura, and I did not presume to urge him to stay. Suddenly, he vanished like the wind.

The junior guardian received the letter. He had not finished reading it when he broke into tears. "My Master is a divine monk," he said to me. "If he does not wait for me, it means that my end is near." Then he took a volume from inside his gown, and handed it to me, exhorting me with the following words: "Treasure this book. Choose a worthy disciple and transmit it to him. Do not let the Dharma Gate of Entering the Way be closed. If the book's transmission ceases, this will amount to a betrayal of the divine monk."

Before several months had passed, the junior guardian fell prey as predicted to the evil prime minister's trumped-up charges. I am grieved that the injustice done to the junior guardian has not been redressed. Nowadays, fame means no more than dirt to me. Therefore I no longer wish to live in the human world. I cherish the junior guardian's command, and I do not wish to carelessly betray it. However, I regret that as a military man I lack perception. I do not know who in this world is capable of becoming a Buddha, and could therefore be entrusted with this volume. Since it is hard to identify such a person, there would be no benefit in random transmission. Today I will hide this volume inside a brick wall on Mt. Song [where the Shaolin Monastery is located], allowing a person destined to reach the Way to find it himself. That person will use it to open wide the Dharma Gate of Entering the Way. Thus, hopefully, I will be spared the guilt of random transmission, and I will be able to face the junior guardian in heaven.

The twelfth year of the Song Shaoxing reign (1142).

Preface compiled by the resolute general, Niu Gao Hejiu of Tangyin, serving under the command of the subduing grand field marshal, the junior guardian Yue [Fei].[99]

Niu Gao's preface is plagued with the same anachronisms that made scholars ridicule Li Jing's. The general could not have been familiar with the posthumous temple name Qinzong, which was bestowed upon Emperor Zhao Huan in 1161, some twenty years after it was supposedly written.[100] Some errors are due to the author's reliance on popular lore. His portrayal of Niu Gao as illiterate—an impossibility in the case of a Chinese general (certainly one who writes prefaces!)—derives from popular novels in which Yue Fei embodies culture whereas his uneducated lieutenant stands for the untrammeled powers of nature. This image reflected the influence of the early Ming *Water Margin* on the late Ming Yue Fei story cycle. The friendship between the civilized Song Jiang and the savage Li Kui inspired the relationship of Yue Fei and Niu Gao as portrayed in the popular narratives that had served as a source for the *Sinews Transformation Classic*.

The motif of Prince Kang's clay horse was likewise borrowed from popular literature. According to a legend frequently quoted in Ming fiction, the future Southern Song emperor happened to be sleeping in a Kaifeng temple when the Jurchen army invaded. The local god appeared in the prince's dream and urged him to escape: "A horse is waiting for you outside," he said. Prince Kang woke up, strode outside, and found the promised stallion. He rode seven hundred miles in one day and crossed the river to the south, whereupon the animal galloped no further. When he dismounted, the prince discovered it had been made of clay.[101]

Li Jing's preface similarly drew on contemporary fiction: His legendary Six-Flowers Formation (Liuhua zhen) was celebrated in martial novels such as *Water Margin*, and he himself figured in a large body of historical romances on the Sui-Tang transition, as well as in the widely influential mythological novel *Investiture of the Gods* (*Fengshen yanyi*).[102] Xu Hongke was described in Ming-Qing lore as a Daoist priest of miraculous fighting skills, and even the Indian patriarch was eulogized in contemporary literature. Bodhidharma's sanctity was the subject of at least two late Ming novels: The Wanli period (1573–1619) *Bodhidharma's Origins and Transmission of the Lamp* (*Damo chushen chuandeng zhuan*) and *The Conversion of the East* (*Dongdu ji*) (1635).[103]

The *Sinews Transformation Classic* betrays therefore an intimate connection between martial arts mythology and popular lore. Its invulnerability techniques are attributed to characters whose martial prowess—or in Bodhidharma's case sainthood—had been celebrated in contemporary fiction. In later periods, the martial arts remained similarly related to popular culture. We have seen above that the Qing technique of the "Confounding Fist" was associated with the *Water Margin*'s Yan Qing, and other protagonists of the same novel were likewise credited with fighting methods. Li Kui was celebrated as the creator of a battleaxe technique, and, as suggested by its name, the tied-wrists method of "Wu Song Breaks Manacles" (Wu Song tuo kao) was inspired by an episode in which the handcuffed hero overcame armed bodyguards who had been hired to assassinate him. In the modern technique, the martial artist's wrists are manacled, forcing him to rely on his legs, hips, shoulders and elbows.[104]

Even as he manipulates martial heroes such as Li Jing and Yue Fei to enhance his manual's prestige, the author criticizes their spiritual shortcomings, and his disappointment is voiced by the protagonists themselves. It's a pity, Li Jing exclaims, that he has remained mired in worldly affairs, making a name for himself by his military achievements only. Niu Gao similarly laments that Yue Fei has failed to follow his Buddhist master in search of religious salvation. Had he adhered to the monk's advice and abandoned his military career, his life might have been saved. The *Sinews Transformation Classic* is marked therefore by a tension between its dual goals of military perfection and spiritual liberation. Other manuals of fighting likewise belittled those who failed to realize their religious end. The sentiment is suggested, for example, by Cao Huandou's contempt for those who "strain their muscles and expose their bones, waste their energy and use force."[105] Evidently, some artists considered the martial aspect of their technique secondary to the spiritual one.

The author faults the Shaolin monks themselves for failing to realize the spiritual potential of the manual *he* had ascribed to them. "If the Shaolin monks excel in martial competitions only," Li Jing's preface reads, "it is because of their limited understanding of the *Sinews Transformation Classic*." Why then did the "Purple Coagulation Man of the Way" attribute his teachings to their monastery in the first place? The answer probably lies in the temple's military fame, such that new fighting techniques were often created in reference to it. We have seen in the previous chapter that martial arts inventors were often said to have received a Shaolin education prior to developing their own superior fighting techniques. The *Sinews Transformation Classic* followed a different strategy. Instead of claiming to have created a style better than Shaolin's, the author censured the monks for failing to fathom—as he did—the depths of *their* methods. From this perspective the manual's forgery is a measure of the monastery's seventeenth-century fame.

Why did the "Purple Coagulation Man of the Way" attribute the Shaolin Monastery techniques to Bodhidharma? It is possible that his myth of origins resulted from ignorance of Shaolin conditions. As an outsider to the monastery, the author of the *Sinews Transformation Classic* did not know that the monks considered Vajrapāṇi the progenitor of their martial arts. He had assumed that their fighting techniques had been credited to Bodhidharma, whom he knew to be the source of their Chan teachings. However, as much as confusion might have contributed to it, his legend was primarily due to his Daoist heritage. As early as the medieval period, Daoist authors attributed *daoyin* gymnastic techniques to the Buddhist saint. The eleventh-century Daoist encyclopedia *Seven Slips from a Cloudy Satchel* (*Yunji qiqian*) includes a treatise of embryonic respiration that is ascribed to Bodhidharma, and the *Song History* lists two breathing and gymnastic manuals (now lost) under his name: *Bodhidharma's Formula of Embryonic Respiration* (*Putidamo taixi jue*) and *Monk Bodhidharma's Visualization Method* (*Seng Putidamo cunxiang fa*).[106] The Indian saint's Daoist literature must have enjoyed considerable popularity, as is suggested by the criticism that had been leveled against it. The Yuan monk Pudu (1255–1330) warned his lay devotees not to consume the fake Bodhidharma scriptures.[107]

Daoist authors might have alluded to Bodhidharma because of his position as patriarch of a school that influenced their teachings. It has been pointed out that Chan contributed to the evolution of Daoist meditation, especially in inner alchemy circles. One stage of the inner alchemical process is known as the "Barrier of Nine Years," in reference to the legend of Bodhidharma meditating in front of a wall for that length of time.[108] However, in addition to being a Chan symbol, the foreign monk might have represented broader Indian influences. In that case, the attribution of *daoyin* exercises to Bodhidharma might mirror the authors' awareness of possible yogic contributions to Daoist gymnastics. Scholars have noted that mutual borrowings between *daoyin* calisthenics and Indian yoga are not implausible. Some Tang texts mention "Brahamanic gymnastics" (*Poluomen daoyin*) and "Indian massage" (*Tianzhu anmo*). However, which elements of the Indian tradition might have influenced Chinese gymnastics, and how extensive their contribution might have been, goes beyond the scope of this study.[109]

Whichever the reason for the Daoist interest in the Buddhist saint, the Shaolin monks had never associated him with their martial arts. All through the seventeenth century, they clearly distinguished between Bodhidharma, whom they venerated as the patriarch of the Chan school, and Vajrapāṇi, whom they worshiped as the divine progenitor of their fighting techniques. It was no earlier then the mid-Qing that Shaolin monks gradually absorbed the Daoist legend of the Chan master as the source of their martial tradition. As the *Sinews Transformation Classic* became widely popular in military circles, and as the monks themselves began to practice it, they started attributing their methods to the Indian saint. Weituo's twelve exercises were ascribed to Bodhidharma by the mid-1850s (when Wang Zuyuan obtained them at the temple), and several decades later another training routine, "The Eighteen Arhats Hand" (Shiba Luohan shou), was assigned to him as well.[110] Nowadays, the Shaolin arsenal features a weapon that bears the saint's name: The "Bodhidharma Cane" (Damo zhang) is a T-shaped instrument, the bottom point of which is often capped with a metal spike (figure 35).[111]

Beyond his association with specific techniques and weapons, Bodhidharma gradually emerged as the ultimate ancestor of the monastery's martial

FIG. 35. The Shaolin "Bodhidharma Cane" (courtesy *Kung Fu Tai Chi* magazine).

tradition. Even though they still credit Vajrapāṇi with their staff method, in the imagination of most Shaolin monks the Indian saint has overshadowed the Indian deity as the source of their military vocation. This perception was mirrored in popular fiction beginning with Liu Tieyun's (1857–1909) *Travels of Lao Can* (*Laocan youji*), which traced Shaolin hand combat through Huike to the Indian patriarch.[112] Shaolin monks eventually accepted the Daoist legend of Bodhidharma as the progenitor of their martial arts.

Religious Syncretism and the Martial Arts

That the Buddhist Shaolin Temple's martial arts should be attributed to a Buddhist saint by a Daoist is a measure of Ming syncretism. "The three religions unite into one" (Sanjiao heyi) was the slogan of the late Ming, which experienced tolerance and mutual borrowings between Confucianism, Buddhism, and Daoism. To be sure, the tendency to find common traits in the three faiths had existed in earlier times as well. However, during the sixteenth and the seventeenth centuries the syncretistic urge reached an unprecedented height, engulfing the entire society, from commoners who worshiped side by side the three religion's deities to leading intellectuals who argued that the three faiths were no more than different paths to the same ultimate truth. The Neo-Confucian Jiao Hong (1540–1620) advocated the study of Daoist and Buddhist scriptures, for they could elucidate the meaning of the Confucian classics, and Lin Zhaoen (1517–1598) advanced one step further, arguing that the three religions were equivalent and hence interchangeable.[113] The spirit of the age was certainly espoused by the "Purple Coagulation Man of the Way," whose spiritual goal was phrased in terms of immortality and Buddhahood alike. His postscript to the *Sinews Transformation Classic* is typical, addressing both Daoist and Buddhist readers:

> I have been studying the *Sinews Transformation Classic* because I realize that in the two schools of Buddhism and Daoism those who seek the Way are as numerous as cattle's hair, but those who obtain it are as few as the unicorn's horn. This is due not to the Way being hard to achieve, but to the adepts not recognizing its gate. Lacking a foundation, in Chan meditation there is the danger of insanity; in gymnastics there is the fear of exhaustion; in sexual practices there is the specter of premature death; and in drug taking there is the anxiety of being parched—all because people have not read the [*Sinews Transformation*] *Classic*. If they obtain it and practice it—if they take it and expand upon it—then on a large scale they will render the state meritorious service, and on a small scale they will protect self and family. The farmer will by it diligently till the land, and through its practice the merchant will carry heavy loads on long journeys. The sick will regain his health, and the weak will be strengthened. The childless will abundantly reproduce, and the old will revert to his youth. The human will progress into a Buddha, and the mortal will be transformed into an immortal. Little practice will bring modest results; thorough practice will lead to great accomplishments. The *Sinews Transformation Classic* is indeed the world's ultimate treasure.[114]

The *Sinews Transformation Classic* suggests that the emergence of the late imperial martial arts might have been related to Ming syncretism. Its author's fascination with the Shaolin fighting techniques was doubtless sustained by his tolerance of their religious practice. An atmosphere of spiritual inclusiveness might have contributed to the Buddhist monks' acceptance of Daoist teachings as well. If leading Buddhist thinkers such as Zhu Hong (1535–1615) could promote Confucian and Daoist values, then Shaolin monks could just as well practice the gymnastic exercises of the "Purple Coagulation Man of the Way."[115] Syncretism permitted self-styled Daoists to study Buddhist-related fighting, just as it encouraged monks to investigate Daoist-related gymnastics. A climate of religious exchange might have contributed therefore to the integration of *daoyin* and hand combat.

A fictional counterpart of the Shaolin fighting monks might illustrate their readiness to absorb Daoist-inspired techniques. We have seen in previous chapters that the literary evolution of the simian warrior Sun Wukong shared significant similarities with the development of the Shaolin martial arts. Throughout the early versions of his *Journey to the West*, the "Monkey Novice Monk" had been armed like the Shaolin monks with a staff. Then, in the 1592 novel, he tried his hand in fist fighting just when historical Shaolin monks were beginning to explore it. Significantly, in the Ming version, Monkey was initiated into Daoist immortality teachings as well. A Daoist master disclosed to him not only the magic techniques of transformation and cloud soaring, but also the mysteries of concocting the inner elixir. Evidently, the author perceived no contradiction between his simian protagonist's mastering Daoist immortality techniques and his ascending to the Western Paradise as a Buddha.[116] It is likely that Shaolin monks likewise felt no compunction in engaging in gymnastic exercises that bore a distinctive Daoist flavor. Syncretism might have provided, therefore, an intellectual foundation for the late Ming evolution of empty-handed fighting.

That Ming Shaolin monks cherished the syncretistic inclusiveness of their age is visually attested. Among the monastery's art treasures is a sixteenth-century stele titled "The Primordial Unity of the Three Religions and the Nine Schools [of pre-Qin thought]," which renders the contemporary religious trend by a fusion of headdresses. It features an adept who wears both a Confucian cap and a Daoist kerchief at the same time as he displays the Buddhist tonsure (figure 36). It has been pointed out that tolerance of other faiths does not preclude their being considered inferior to one's own.[117] This is certainly true of the Shaolin stele that reserves the pride of center to the Buddhist shaven pate, while relegating the other religions' emblematic headgears to the sides. Even as they accepted the validity of other spiritual paths, Shaolin monks probably regarded their own as superior.

Mythological Structure

The tendency to define novel fighting techniques in reference to Shaolin's established reputation is best exemplified by the seventeenth-century Internal School Fist (Neijia Quan), which was taught by Wang Zhengnan (1617–1669) in Zhejiang. Huang Zongxi (1610–1695) and his son Huang Baijia (1643–?)—who left us the earliest accounts of the school—contrasted it with the Shaolin method, which they designated "external." In his 1669 epitaph for Wang Zhengnan, Huang Zongxi wrote that "Shaolin is famous for its hand combat.

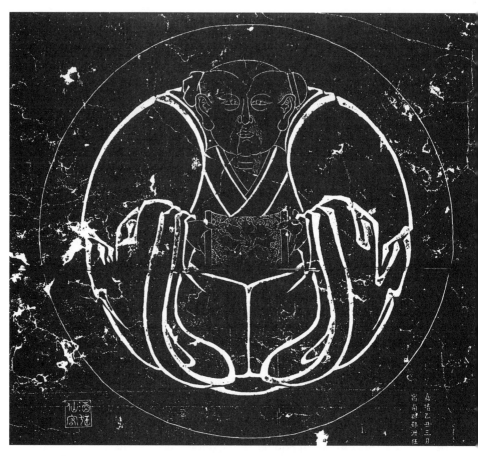

FIG. 36. "The Primordial Unity of the Three Religions and the Nine Schools" as depicted in a Shaolin stele dated 1565.

However, its techniques are chiefly offensive, which creates opportunities for an opponent to exploit. Now there is another school that is called 'internal,' which overcomes movement with stillness. Attackers are effortlessly repulsed. Thus we distinguish Shaolin as 'external.'"[118]

The Huangs attributed Wang Zhengnan's seventeenth-century Internal School to a mysterious Daoist immortal named Zhang Sanfeng (fl. 1380), who had lived two and a half centuries earlier. According to Huang *fils*, Zhang had studied the Shaolin style before creating his own more sophisticated method. "The External School flourished at Shaolin," wrote Huang Baijia. "Zhang Sanfeng, having mastered Shaolin, reversed its principles, and this is called the Internal School."[119] Very little is known of the historical Zhang Sanfeng (whose name was originally written with a different character for *feng*), except that he had been active during the early Ming in the Daoist monastic complex on

Mt. Wudang in Hubei. However, it is clear from the early records that he had nothing to do with the martial arts.[120] Why then did the Huangs, or Wang Zhengnan, attribute the Internal School to the obscure Daoist?

Zhang Sanfeng's association with a military god was likely one reason for his choice as creator of the Internal School. The saint had resided at the Wudang temple complex, which had been dedicated to the cult of a valiant deity, the Perfect Warrior (Zhenwu) (also known as the Dark Warrior (Xuanwu)). Beginning in the eleventh century, some Chinese emperors attributed their successes in battle to the martial god, who was extolled for warding off nomadic invasions. Moreover, the third Ming emperor Chengzu (r. 1403–1424) credited the martial deity with his successful usurpation of the throne, for which reason he embarked upon a massive temple construction on Mt. Wudang.[121] Huang Zongxi, at any rate, explicitly linked the Perfect Warrior's fighting techniques with the Daoist saint's Internal School. "That night," he wrote, "Zhang Sanfeng dreamt that the Primordial Emperor (The Perfect Warrior) transmitted the techniques of hand combat to him, and the following morning he single-handedly killed over a hundred bandits."[122]

Another, more significant, reason for crediting Zhang Sanfeng with seventeenth-century martial arts was his relation to the Ming royal family. The saint's hagiography had several Ming emperors seeking his blessing, and in the popular imagination his miracles were inextricably linked to the glory of the dynasty's early days.[123] His residence on Mt. Wudang was similarly tied to the Ming fortunes. As Yang Lizhi has shown, the Wudang monasteries functioned as a family shrine of the ruling house, being directly supervised by the imperial palace. Royal birthdays and other family events were celebrated at the Wudang temples, where the Daoist priests prayed for the dynasty's longevity.[124] Writing some twenty years after the Manchu conquest of 1644, the Huang's choice of Zhang Sanfeng as the founder of the Internal School— and of Mt. Wudang as the martial arts' birthplace—amounted to a political statement. Huang Zongxi employed the Daoist saint as a symbol of his Ming loyalism. Douglas Wile is likely right in his assertion that by combining the mythic figures of the Perfect Warrior and Zhang Sanfeng with the righteous martial artist Wang Zhengnan, "the Huangs attempted in an environment of strict censorship to issue a spiritual rallying cry against alien aggression."[125]

Huang Zongxi was among the leading intellectuals of the anti-Qing resistance movement. He served the Ming all through its disastrous retreat to the South, and throughout his life he remained steadfast in his refusal to join the new administration. Scholars have interpreted his epitaph for Wang Zhengnan as a political manifesto of his Ming loyalism. Huang expressly dispensed with Qing reign years in his dating of the martial artist, and he voiced admiration for the latter's vow of vegetarianism that followed the Ming's demise. Wang Zhengnan refused to prostitute his fighting skills, declining repeated invitations to serve in the local yamen. In his uncompromising defiance, the illiterate martial artist could serve as a model for the scholarly elite. "Zhengnan gave up his post and retired to his home," wrote Huang Zongxi. "Those who admired his skill thought that because he was poor he could easily be compromised. The high-ranking military officials all paid their respects, but he was completely unaffected and ignored them. He continued to dig in the fields and haul manure as if unaware that he possessed a skill that could gain him an easier living. . . . May those who read this inscription, learn from his life."[126]

Huang Zongxi's son, Baijia, had studied fighting with Wang Zhengnan, whose techniques he recorded in his *Internal School Fist Method* (*Neijia quanfa*) (1676). His interest in the Internal School was kindled, like his father's, by the Manchu conquest. In his adventurous youth, Huang *fils* sought to rely on Wang's military arts to defeat the invaders: "At the time I was hot-tempered and impetuous," he reminisced. "I believed that the affairs of the world could not be entrusted to those contemptible Confucian scholars, but required men who could jump on their horses and slay the enemy, jump off and capture the king. This is the only life worth living."[127] The fervent nationalism of father and son might suggest that by "internal" they were secretly alluding to their native land. As Douglas Wile has noted, the Internal School that was associated with the indigenous Daoist religion might have represented China, as opposed to the External School that was affiliated with the foreign Buddhist faith, and by implication might have stood for the Manchu invaders.[128]

Thus, if it were not for the Qing conquest, we might have known nothing of Wang Zhengnan's martial art. The Manchu invaders turned the attention of scholars such as the Huangs to fighting techniques that, having originated among the unlettered masses, had been previously considered unworthy of documentation. In this respect, the Ming's demise contributed inadvertently to martial arts historiography. As members of the elite lamented their fatal disdain for military training, they provided us for the first time with biographies of uneducated martial artists such as the Internal School's Wang. We will see below that the collapse of the Ming has enriched our knowledge of Shaolin fighting as well. Here, suffice it to note that as Qing scholars began to investigate folk fighting techniques, they invested them with medical, philosophical, and religious significance. The theorization impulse that characterized the late imperial martial arts was due at least partially to their practice by members of the elite. Even though the broadening of the martial arts into self-conscious systems of thought was well under way during the last decades of Ming rule—as evinced, for example, by the 1624 *Sinews Transformation Classic*—it was doubtless given a fresh impetus by the dynasty's fall.

There might have been yet another motivation for the Zhang Sanfeng legend. The Huangs might have attributed the Internal School to a Daoist immortal to counterbalance the External School's affiliation with a Buddhist saint. Zhejiang natives like the "Purple Coagulation Man of the Way," Huang Zongxi, and Huang Baijia might have been familiar with the legend he had created of Bodhidharma as the master of Shaolin fighting. The correlation between their myth and his legend is, at any rate, striking. Whether or not this had been the

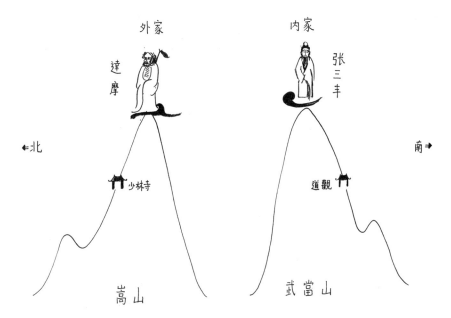

外家 内家

達摩 张三丰

←北 南→

少林寺 道觀

嵩山 武當山

FIG. 37. The structure of martial arts mythology (drawing by Noga Zhang-Hui Shahar).

Huangs' intention, the Zhang Sanfeng genealogy matched the Bodhidharma ancestry in a perfectly harmonious structure. On the one hand was an "External" school associated with Buddhism and attributed to an Indian patriarch who supposedly meditated on the sacred Mt. Song; on the other hand was an "Internal" school affiliated with Daoism and ascribed to an immortal who reputedly secluded himself on the holy Mt. Wudang. This flawless symmetry of directions (external and internal), religions (Buddhism and Daoism), saints (Bodhidharma and Zhang Sanfeng), and sacred peaks (Song and Wudang) was joined, on the geographical axis, by a correlation of north and south (figure 37). Because Mt. Song was the more northern of the two peaks, the "External" School was named the "Northern," whereas its "Internal" rival came to be known as the "Southern." Like Chan Buddhism a thousand years earlier, the martial arts were gradually imagined in terms of a "Northern School" and a "Southern School."[129]

Claude Lévi-Strauss has argued that the meaning of individual mythological motifs is determined by the structure into which they combine, just as in music the significance of particular tones is embedded in the melody they constitute.[130] The Bodhidharma legend and the Zhang Sanfeng myth matched in a perfectly harmonious melody, which was likely the source of their ongoing appeal, long after the fighting techniques themselves were forgotten. Huang Baijia lamented that with Wang Zhengnan's demise his fighting techniques would be lost, and it is clear that by the eighteenth century the Internal School no longer existed.[131] Nevertheless, the fascination of the Zhang Sanfeng myth was such that other martial styles have assumed his school's mantle. By the second half of the nineteenth century, Taiji Quan had been traced to the Daoist saint, only to be followed by other martial styles such as Xingyi Quan and Bagua Zhang.[132] The mythological structure that was created in the seventeenth century still captivates the imagination of martial artists, even though the term "Internal School" designates new fighting methods.

Conclusion

The foundations of the modern Chinese martial arts were laid during the late Ming and the early Qing by the integration of Ming bare-handed fighting techniques with an ancient gymnastic tradition that had largely evolved in a Daoist context. In varying degrees all of the bare-handed styles familiar today incorporate aspects of *daoyin* calisthenics, combining limb movement with breathing and the internal circulation of the vital energy *qi*. The absorption of *daoyin* gymnastics transformed not only the training routines but also the very purpose of the martial arts. Bare-handed styles such as Shaolin Quan, Taiji Quan, Xingyi Quan, and Bagua Zhang are not intended for combat only. Rather, they combine movement and mental concentration for fighting, healing, and religious self-cultivation. The very term "martial" is in this sense misleading. Chinese hand combat is a self-conscious system of mental and physical self-cultivation that has diverse applications of which fighting is but one.

It is likely that aspects of *daoyin* gymnastics were absorbed into armed or unarmed fighting prior to the sixteenth century. Future research may well reveal that breathing and *qi*-circulation methods figured in ancient hand combat, as they almost certainly did in medieval fencing. However, at present our evidence of the integration dates from the late Ming. The *Sinews Transformation Classic* of 1624 is currently the earliest available manual that self-consciously combines military, therapeutic, and religious goals in one training program. Compiled by the self-styled "Purple Coagulation Man of the Way," the treatise exemplifies the impact of Daoism on bare-handed fighting. Its goal is an internal bodily transformation that will make one invulnerable to injury, that will eliminate all illness, and that will ultimately lead to immortality. *Daoyin* gymnastics served as a vehicle for the Daoist influence on the late imperial martial arts. Whether it was practiced by the laity, by Daoist adepts, or by Buddhist monks, hand combat drew heavily on Daoist physiological and meditative techniques. Training routines such as the "Twelve-Section Brocade"—which were integrated into the Shaolin monastic regimen—can be traced back to canonical Daoist scriptures.

Investing the martial arts with therapeutic and religious significance, the creators of bare-handed techniques relied upon wide-ranging sources, from

Daoist encyclopedias and medical literature to the classics of Chinese philosophy that articulated the culture's traditional worldview. The very names of such fighting techniques as Taiji Quan and Bagua Zhang were borrowed from Chinese cosmology, betraying the styles' spiritual aspirations. In the two martial arts, the practitioner re-enacts the process of cosmic differentiation—from the primordial unity through the interplay of the *yin*, the *yang*, and the eight trigrams to the myriad phenomena—only to reverse the course of history, thereby achieving mystical union with the Supreme Ultimate (Taiji). To the degree that these fighting techniques self-consciously express philosophical tenets, their articulation belongs to the history of ideas. Even though the agent of the martial arts is the body, their evolution is in this respect the domain of intellectual history.

The late Ming broadening of empty-handed styles into self-conscious systems of thought was likely one reason for their growing popularity. Seventeenth-century Shaolin monks did not turn their attention to hand combat because it was militarily effective. In real battle, bare-handed fighting was not as useful as the staff fighting the monks had previously utilized, not to mention fighting with sharp weapons or firearms. Rather, Shaolin monks were probably fascinated by the medical, religious, and philosophical opportunities that were opened by the new empty-handed techniques. The synthesis of martial, therapeutic, and religious goals has been a primary reason for the popularity of hand combat both in its native land and in the modern West.

If modern hand combat is not only a fighting method but also a system of thought, then it is not surprising that its evolution was partially spurred by intellectual developments. Late Ming syncretism provided a philosophical foundation for the integration of bare-handed fighting and *daoyin* calisthenics, permitting Daoist mystics to explore Buddhist-related martial arts and allowing Shaolin monks to study Daoist gymnastics. Intellectual trends were joined by political upheavals that contributed to the transformation of the martial arts. The Manchu conquest turned the attention of the literati elite to the fighting techniques of the unlettered masses. As leading scholars began to practice folk martial arts, they rewrote them in a sophisticated language. The articulation of hand combat in therapeutic and religious terms was due in large measure to their espousal by members of the elite.

The seventeenth-century transformation of bare-handed fighting was accompanied by the emergence of a novel martial arts mythology. Shaolin monks gradually accepted a legend that had originated outside the monastery according to which their fighting techniques had been invented by the Chan patriarch Bodhidharma. The legend of the Buddhist saint evolved in conjunction with the myth of a Daoist immortal. As the "External" Shaolin martial arts were attributed to a Buddhist master who reputedly resided on the sacred Mt. Song, an "Internal" school of fighting was ascribed to a Daoist recluse who supposedly hid on the holy Mt. Wudang. The two legends matched each other in a perfectly harmonious mythological structure, the flawless symmetry of which has likely been the source of their ongoing appeal.

CHAPTER 7

Suspect Rebels

IN THE SPRING of 1679, Gu Yanwu (1613–1682) traveled to the Shaolin Temple. The renowned historian had turned his attention to military affairs following the Manchu conquest, which had demonstrated to the Chinese elite the fatal consequences of its disregard for warfare. The demise of the native Ming rule and the establishment of the alien Qing dynasty (1644–1911) created a surge of interest in military questions—from the strategic significance of diverse provinces to the popular martial arts. It kindled Huang Zongxi's curiosity about the "internal" fighting techniques of Wang Zhengnan, and it prompted Gu Yanwu's investigation of the Shaolin "external" martial arts. At the monastery, Gu carefully examined the historical records of the monks' military activities. He transcribed the Tang steles that recorded their heroic support of Li Shimin, relying on them as one source for an essay on Buddhist warfare.[1]

The scholarly satisfaction that accompanied Gu's visit was matched by a sense of moral purpose. His research trip was motivated by intellectual curiosity and sentiments of loyalty to the Ming alike. Shaolin monks had been famous for their unfailing support of the former regime, for which they fought through to its bitter end. During the first decades of the Qing dynasty, their monastery was regarded by many as a symbol of its predecessor. In this respect Gu's Shaolin trip resembled his repeated pilgrimages to the Ming royal tombs—he had paid his respects at the dynasty's burial grounds north of Beijing no fewer than six times, and at the Nanjing mausoleum of its founder no fewer than seven.[2]

Indeed, more than three decades after Beijing's fall, the monastery's desolation testified to the demise of its erstwhile patrons. Gone were the days when a Ming official complained that Shaolin's splendor was too extravagant for Buddhist meditation—the temple Gu visited was in ruins. The lofty halls once bedecked with precious gifts from imperial donors were overgrown with weeds, and the sounds of clanking weaponry had been silenced. Where hundreds of Ming soldiers had once trained, only a handful of old monks remained, complaining to their guest of harsh treatment by the new authorities. Gu vented his frustration in a poem that likened the nation's and the monastery's fate. If only a new Prince of Qin (Li Shimin) could be found, both would be succored. Assisted by the likes of the Tang monk Huiyang, he would overthrow the foreign aggressors and restore the monastery to its former glory:

Lofty rises the Wuru Peak,[3]
Majestic lies the Shaolin Monastery.
Once its warriors roamed the earth,
Famed for heroism since the Sui.
Grand buildings resembled an imperial palace,
Monastic robes reflected fairy garments.
Buddhist crisp chimes pierced the heavens,
Chan lamps shone on emerald peaks.
. . .
Today how desolate it appears,
Deserted and overgrown with weeds.
From broken walls wandering bees emerge,
In empty halls wild pheasants caw.
They tell me of harsh new orders,
Land allotments by corrupt officials.
Taxes increased even on a monastic estate,
Caring not which dynasty had bestowed it.
Short of rice gruel, the monks leave,
Not even one or two have remained.

All things undergo rise and decline,
Their fortunes depend on Heaven.
Could there be no hero,
Resolutely restoring the monastery from its ruins?
I am sending a note to the like of Huiyang:
Wait for the arrival of a Qin prince![4]

Did Gu really believe that after they had been consolidating their rule for decades, the Qing could be overthrown? Or is his poem a mere fantasy—a conscious expression of wishful thinking? It is hard to answer this question, which has been asked of the historian's other writings as well.[5] However, he clearly made no pretense that a Shaolin uprising did occur. The poem is not a description of what *had* happened, but of what *should* have. It cannot be taken as evidence that the monks had resisted the Manchus.

What Gu Yanwu had refrained from claiming, other, less educated authors had not. Qing period lore glorified the Shaolin warriors as fearless rebels. A widespread legend, which originated in South China, attributed the founding of the Heaven and Earth Society (Tiandihui) ("Triads" in Western literature) to the Shaolin monks who had escaped persecution by the Qing government. After imperial forces had burned down the Shaolin Temple, it went, a handful of martial monks managed to escape to the South, where they established the secret society for the purpose of "overthrowing the Qing and restoring the Ming" (*fan Qing fu Ming*).

During the Qing period, the Heaven and Earth Society was the largest and most powerful brotherhood in South China. Flaunting an overtly anti-Manchu ideology, the society was variously engaged in mutual aid and in criminal activities, which led to repeated armed clashes with the state.[6] Its foundation myth survives in diverse nineteenth-century versions, some of them in the interrogation records of captured members. Ignoring the inconsistencies between varying accounts, the legend may be briefly summarized as follows:

During the reign of the Kangxi emperor (r. 1662–1722), the historically unidentifiable Xi Lu barbarians defeated the Qing army. The courageous monks of the Shaolin Temple—wrongly located by some versions in Gansu Province—came to the emperor's rescue. After subduing the rebels, they were invited to the capital to be honored with imperial posts, which they declined, expressing their desire to resume their humble monkish lives. Once back at the temple, the heroic warriors fell prey to political intrigue. Government forces led by traitorous officials set the monastery on fire, killing most of the monks. A handful managed to escape to the South, finding (in some versions) refuge at a temple whose name resonates with Shaolin—Changlin. Swearing an oath of brotherhood with the local clerics, they established the Heaven and Earth Society. A magic incense burner emerged from the sea, providing divine sanction for their enterprise. It was inscribed "Overthrow the Qing, Restore the Ming."[7]

The legend has been variously approached by scholars. Some have searched in it for clues on the society's historical origins in South China (correlating verifiable names from its diverse versions with information culled from other sources); some have analyzed its mythic structure; some have highlighted its indebtedness to popular narratives such as *Water Margin*; some have emphasized its communality with the messianic lore of millenarian sects.[8] Whichever approach we assume, it is clear that the legend's immediate background—historical and folkloric alike—lies in South China. Two examples may suffice to make the point. The motif of the Shaolin Monastery's burning is likely related to Fujian lore concerning the conflagration of a local southern Shaolin Temple,[9] and the name Changlin, which is mentioned in several versions, has been shown to designate a historical monastery in that province. Some scholars consider it the source of the brotherhood's foundation myth.[10]

Bearing in mind its southern provenance, is the secret society's myth relevant to the history of the Shaolin Temple in Henan? On the most general level, the legend mirrors the monastery's fame. By the eighteenth century, the Shaolin Temple had acquired mythic proportions in the imagination of warriors nationwide. We have seen in previous chapters that a Shaolin connection became a prerequisite in the hagiographies of Qing martial artists. Creators of novel fighting techniques sought to enhance their prestige by associating them with the temple, and military authors went as far as forging their writings to provide them with a Shaolin pedigree. The temple's legendary military standing—coupled with its famed support of the Ming—made it a symbol of choice for anti-Qing brotherhoods such as the Heaven and Earth Society. The Shaolin ancestry enhanced the society's military standing at the same time as it colored it with an aura of fervent Ming loyalism.

Even as it attests to Shaolin's fame, the myth betrays the temple's precarious political conditions under the Qing. To be sure, as we have it, the story is spurious: Shaolin monks never fought on behalf of the dynasty, nor was their monastery ever destroyed by it. Nevertheless, wittingly or unwittingly, the legend mirrors the tensions that have characterized the temple's relations with the Qing regime. It would have been surprising if a legend of a Shaolin uprising would have circulated during a period in which the monastery was famed for its loyal service to, and generous benefaction by, the state. That such a myth was created during a time of mutual suspicion is less astonishing. The seventeenth century marked a sharp decline in the Shaolin Temple's fortunes, in which sense the brotherhood's foundation myth mirrors historical conditions.

The decline began prior to the Qing conquest. Like much of the Ming military, the Shaolin Temple had been destroyed by the rebel armies that had toppled the dynasty, paving the way for the foreign invasion. During the 1630s Shaolin monks were regularly drafted to the largely unsuccessful government campaigns against the marauding troops of Li Zicheng (1605?–1645) and Zhang Xianzhong (1606?–1647). By the early 1640s their defense of the Ming cause became a struggle for their monastery's survival. In 1641 Li marched his bandit army, swollen by hungry peasants to hundreds of thousands, into Henan. The government lost control of the province, which was sacked by his roving troops as well as by feuding local warlords.[11] Neither Li nor the local strongmen had any sympathy for the Shaolin monks, who had consistently supported the Ming. They razed much of the monastery and butchered most of its monks. By the time the Manchus had crossed the Great Wall in the spring of 1644, the Shaolin fighting force existed no more.

Late Ming destruction was followed by Qing suspicion. The new dynasty perceived in the Shaolin monks' behavior marks of lingering loyalty to the temple's erstwhile patrons. By the time the apprehension over Shaolin's devotion to their predecessors had subsided, new fears of the monks' collusion with sectarian rebels took hold. As peasant rebellions swept through the poverty-stricken north China plains, the Shaolin Temple became a prime target of investigation. The government scrutiny of its monks was probably not unwarranted. Shaolin's was a fluid community of which resident clerics occupied no more than a fraction. As members of the itinerant world of the "rivers and lakes," Shaolin warriors did come in touch with potential rebels. Even though the monastery itself was never involved in a rebellion, some of its alumni might have been.

Late Ming Destruction

The desolation that was revealed to Gu Yanwu at the Shaolin Monastery was also witnessed by other visitors during the first decades of Qing rule. "After the upheaval only a handful of monks have remained," lamented Ye Feng (1623–1687). "Who will preach here the Dharma?"[12] From the 1640s through the 1680s, the Shaolin Monastery had been largely deserted. Most of its monks had left, and the majority of the buildings had been falling apart, some of the most precious ones being past repair. Zhang Siming visited Shaolin in 1684:

> When I arrived at the temple, I discovered that long ago it had been consumed by the end-of-era's fires (*jiehuo; kalpāgni*). The Dharma Hall was overgrown with weeds, and the disciples had scattered. Sighing there for a long time, I let my legs carry me west of the Thousand Buddhas Hall. There I saw piles of dirt overgrown with thick bushes, scattered tiles and fallen beams that were exposed to the wind and the rain. Monk Yunshi pointed them out to me, lamenting: "This used to be the White-Attired Mahāsattva [Guanyin] Hall. It was built during the reign of the Northern Wei emperor Xiaowen (r. 471–499). It was a grand building. Being subject to the bandits' turmoil, it has been reduced to this state!"[13]

The Buddhist concept of the *kalpāgni*—the cosmic fire that will burn the world to ashes at the eon's end—was applied by Zhang Siming to the devastation of the monastery that had accompanied the Ming's demise. This same metaphor was also used by Shen Quan (1624–1684), who nonetheless remained hopeful that the monastery's heritage would not be extinguished:

> I have heard that the Shaolin Temple
> Several times has endured the end-of-era's ashes.
> Broken steles covered by moss,
> Shattered walls exposed to the blue sky.
> . . .
> Dense, the monastery's ancient cypresses,
> Forever protect its divine spirit.[14]

The Qing-appointed governor of Henan left us a similar record of the monastery's dismal conditions in mid-century, except that his tone was less sympathetic. Wang Jie (ca. 1620–ca. 1700) apparently disdained the miserable few monks who had remained amongst their monastery's ruins: "Today the monastery is falling apart. As I was visiting one or two of its dilapidated monks' rooms, I ordered the novices to demonstrate their martial skills. Their performance was no better than that of street beggars. It was not worth watching." The governor proceeded to detail the circumstances under which the monastery had been destroyed in the 1640s:

> During the Chongzhen reign (1628–1643) the traitor Chuang (Li Zicheng) plundered like a vicious tiger. Liang Song mountain bandits[15] rose in swarms, each sacking another region. At Songyang [on the southern slopes of Mt. Song][16] there was one Li Jiyu (?–1647), who agitated ten thousand men and stationed them atop the "Imperial Fort" Mountain [the Shaoshi Peak overlooking the Shaolin Monastery]. He burned and looted everywhere, but he particularly hated the Shaolin monks, whom he regarded as potential thorns in his side. He pretended, therefore, to befriend them, sending daily money to their abbot. The monks believed him and offered no resistance.
>
> One day Li sent a message to the monks that he would like to commission the ceremony of the Thousand Buddhas Supplication for his birthday. All the monks should prepare themselves for his arrival, purifying themselves, burning incense, and reciting the scriptures. Then, leading several hundred men clad in armor, Li entered the monastery and stole his way to the Sutra Hall. Just as the monks were beating the drums and prostrating themselves in prayer, the bandits drew their swords and butchered them. The monks were not prepared, and they were wiped out to a man.[17]

Wang's is the only account in Shaolin's history that suggests a tension between the monks' religious duties and their military vocation. According to him, Li Jiyu had been able to slaughter the clerics because they had been engaged in a Buddhist ceremony. Even though the monks made no conscious choice to favor their religious role over their military one—after all they had been deceived by the Henan warlord—in this instance their two functions clashed. The monks' performance of their ritual duties hampered their efficacy as warriors. Their identity of Buddhist priests collided with their role of soldiers.

Li Jiyu, who butchered the Shaolin monks, emerged in 1640 as one of the strongest warlords in northern Henan. Like other local bandits, he tried to maintain his independence, shifting his alliances in accordance with the rapidly changing military situation. He had allied himself with Li Zicheng (in 1641), submitted to the Ming but colluded again with Li (1643), clashed with Li (1643), yielded to the Nanjing regime of the Southern Ming (summer of 1644), and finally surrendered to the Qing (December 1644), who did not trust him and had him executed three years later.[18] (At one point, incidentally, Li had befriended the would-be founder of Taiji Quan, Chen Wangting).[19] The warlord's decision to eliminate the Shaolin monks was due to tactical considerations no less than to their famed support of the Ming. Li had established his base atop the Shaoshi Peak's "Imperial Fort," which towered over the temple. As Wang Jie noted, the bandit leader could not afford a "potential thorn" in such proximity to his side.

If it was Li Jiyu who dealt the Shaolin monks the final blow in the early 1640s, their ranks had by then already been decimated. All through the 1630s, Shaolin monks had been drafted for the largely unsuccessful government campaigns against the roving bandits. In 1635 they had been enlisted to train a local militia in Shanzhou County, western Henan. They were able to score at least one victory before being defeated by the vastly larger armies of the "Muslim Fellow" (Lao Huihui), Ma Shouying, who was one of Li Zicheng's closest allies.[20] At approximately the same time, the Shaolin staff expert Hongji—who had been Cheng Zongyou's instructor—was killed in battle. We are told that he "led his troops to a decisive victory over the bandits. Then, chasing them far away, he ran into fresh outlaw contingents. His support troops did not arrive, but to the end he was not willing to retreat. As the bandits swelled in numbers, he struggled with them to his death. Thus, he did not betray his [Shaolin] heritage."[21]

Shaolin's contribution to the late Ming banditry campaigns is attested by a stele erected some three decades later. Dating from 1677, the inscription evinces the monks' lingering sentiments of loyalty toward the Ming, for it was dedicated to the monastery's early Ming abbot, Ningran Liaogai (1335–1421).[22] On it were inscribed the names of some seventy martial monks (*wu seng*) who had fought under the command of the Ming minister of war, Yang Sichang (1588–1641). Most came from the Shaolin Monastery, but some came from its adjacent subsidiary, the Yongtai shrine. Yang had assumed personal field command of the banditry campaign in 1639, only to be routed by the rebel armies of Zhang Xianzhong and Li Zicheng in 1641, whereupon he committed suicide.[23] The monks must have fought for him around 1640.

The Shaolin inscription is moving. Unlike the grand stone monuments that had been built during the Tang and the Ming and had recorded the monks' support of those dynasties, this one could not have earned them imperial recognition. If anything, the Qing authorities would have been angered by a memorial to their predecessors' steadfast warriors. The humble epitaph was motivated, therefore, by a sincere wish to record the names of fallen comrades. Its author, himself likely a fighting monk, was not highly educated, as is evinced by an orthographic error in the minister's name, *si* 思 instead of *si* 嗣 (figure 38).

Even though the Shaolin Monastery had been destroyed prior to the 1644 invasion, it is not impossible that the advance of the Manchu army had caused it some further damage. A possible hint—it is no more than that—is provided by an inscription dating from 1653 that commemorates the reconstruction of the monastery's Universal Chan Courtyard (Shifang Chan Yuan). Situated outside the monastery proper, across from its main gate, the Chan Courtyard had served as a hostel for pilgrims. During the Ming pe-

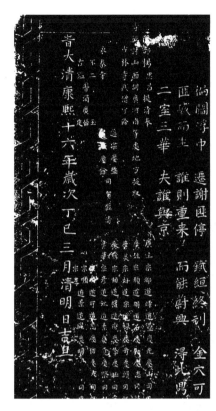

FIG. 38. Detail of a Shaolin stele dated 1677 commemorating the monks who had fought under Yang Sichang; note the orthographic error in the minister's name.

riod, it had been renovated by the staff expert general Yu Dayou.[24] Then, in the 1640s, it was burned down "by the army" (*bing*), as the inscription puts it. The choice of the term over the common derogatory appellations for rebels (*zei* or *kou*, both meaning bandits) might indicate that the troops in question were Manchus, which the author discreetly refrained from naming. If so, the Qing dynasty had some hand in the monastery's devastation.[25]

We may note, in conclusion, that the dismal fate of the Shaolin Temple was shared also by other Henan temples that had allied themselves with the Ming dynasty and were therefore targeted by its adversaries. The monastic complex atop Mt. Funiu in the province's southwest was destroyed by the roving bandit armies.[26] We have seen in chapter 3 that its monks had been famed for their fighting skills. Having been trained at the Shaolin Temple, they were ranked second only to it by Ming military experts.

Qing Suspicion

Qing authorities encountered difficulties in their attempts to appoint an abbot to the Shaolin Monastery. Their first choice had been monk Haikuan (1596–

1666), who had held the post during the last years of the Ming. In 1646 he was officially approached by the Ministry of Rites, but he declined the offer due to a "leg illness." This lame excuse most likely concealed the Shaolin monk's refusal to cooperate with the new regime. By 1657, however, Haikuan had changed his mind.[27] We are told that he had "completely recovered," whereupon he assumed the monastery's leadership, handing it to his disciple Yongyu in 1661. The latter filled the office for three years before departing abruptly to Hebei, leaving no heir behind him. The monastery was to remain without an officially appointed abbot all through 1999—three hundred years later—when Yongxin was assigned the post by the communist authorities.[28]

We do not know why Yongyu resigned his post, but we may conjecture that his decision was related to the monastery's uneasy relations with the Qing, of which there are other indications. Between 1652 and 1654 Shaolin monks conducted a series of elaborate requiems, which were supported by donors from three Henan counties: Dengfeng, Yanshi, and Gongxian. As Wen Yucheng has suggested, the masses were most likely directed to the salvation of the souls of the victims from the Ming-Qing cataclysm.[29] Two and a half decades later, the monks were still paying their respects to the previous regime, as evinced by the 1677 stele that honored the Shaolin warriors who had fought under the Ming minister of war, Yang Sichang.

Cherishing the memory of the Ming, Shaolin monks bitterly complained of its successor. Gu Yanwu recorded their grievances (which he might have exaggerated in accordance with his own political inclinations): "They tell me of harsh new orders, land allotments by corrupt officials. Taxes increased even on a monastic estate, caring not which dynasty had bestowed it." The complaints were likely not unfounded. Consider the indifference of the Qing governor who in the 1650s had compared the Shaolin monks to street beggars. That the monastery had remained for decades in ruins is an indication of the authorities' lingering suspicions. Had the Qing officials entertained any sympathy for the monastery, they would not have allowed it to disintegrate.

By the late seventeenth century, the mutual suspicion that had characterized the monastery's relations with the regime gradually abated. As the Ming dynasty faded from the memories of monks and officials, Qing authorities were willing to recognize the Shaolin Temple's religious significance. In 1704 the Kangxi emperor signaled the dynasty's changing attitude when he graced the temple with two specimens of his calligraphy, which were promptly engraved on the Heavenly Kings Hall (Tianwang Dian) and the Buddha Hall (Daxiong Dian).[30] In 1735 the Yongzheng emperor approved an ambitious restoration plan for the monastery, which amounted to nine thousand silver taels. Finally, in 1750, the Qianlong emperor (r. 1736–1795) capped the imperial honors, personally visiting the temple and staying there overnight. The sovereign penned four poems for the occasion, celebrating the monastery's scenery and the religious lore of its Indian patriarch Bodhidharma.[31]

The eighteenth century might have ushered in a new era in the monastery's relations with the regime, if it were not for the officials' apprehension of the monks' military activities. Even as it respected the Shaolin Temple's cultural legacy, the dynasty remained deeply suspicious of its military tradition. Unlike the Ming officials, who had employed fighting monks in the battlefield, Qing authorities never condoned the military activities of Buddhist clerics. The same Qing emperors who patronized the temple's restoration carefully curbed its military practice. We have seen in chapter 2 that the Yongzheng emperor took advantage of the temple's renovation to tighten government control. He ordered the destruction of Shaolin's subsidiary shrines, thereby weeding out fake monks who "do evil and create disturbances."[32] The demolition of the monastery's surrounding shrines was meant to separate the Shaolin monks from the unruly community of itinerant martial artists, who were deemed potentially dangerous.

Yongzheng's successor was equally wary of the Shaolin monks' military activities. The Qianlong emperor, who had been moved to poetry by the monastery's scenery, was outraged when he heard in 1775 that the newly installed governor of Henan, Xu Ji (1732–1811), had enlisted Shaolin monks to train his troops. The emperor promptly forbade the military deployment of Buddhist clerics. An imperial decree asserted that monks should dedicate their lives to religious ends. That an official should abet their violations of Buddhist law by having them instruct his soldiers was preposterous:

> As they have left their families, monks need strictly adhere to the monastic regulations, cultivating the virtues of harmony and forbearance. How could they possibly practice violent techniques, showing off fierceness and flaunting strength? There have been some officials in charge who have heard of [Shaolin's renown], and have devised ways to imperceptibly challenge our norms. How could they disrupt the monks' vocation, calling them to demonstrate and having them sell their military skills? Having monks train his soldiers is not only beyond one's authority, it also makes him into a laughing stock. How could Xu Ji be as ignorant as that?![33]

Itself unwilling to embrace the Shaolin monks, the dynasty was fearful they would join its enemies. Fighting clerics were suspected of colluding with bandits, and worse still of associating with sectarian rebels. The specter of religiously inspired uprisings loomed large in the minds of Qing officials, who relentlessly pursued the "heterodox" sects. Whether their fears of messianic revolts were invariably justified goes beyond the scope of this study. Recent scholarship has suggested that many of so-called "White Lotus Sects" that were targeted by the state had not been involved in rebellious activities. Those that were might have in some cases resorted to arms due to the government's persecution.[34] Be that as it may, for our purpose the *perception* of imminent danger was more significant than its uncertain basis, for it proved detrimental to the temple's relation with the regime. Here is Yaertu warning the Qianlong emperor in 1739 of the Shaolin monks' joining the "heterodox" sects. The temple, explains the vice minister of war, is a breeding ground for rebels:

> In the provinces under our supervision, such as Huguang, Shandong, Henan, and the like, the problem of the "heterodox sects" (*xiejiao*) is common. The people of Henan are particularly ignorant and easily swayed. The villagers are agitated whenever some good-for-nothings drift from somewhere. Daoist and Buddhist types make a name for themselves as healers, claiming to cure illness by casting spells and other evil magic. Otherwise they pretend to bring good fortune and avert disaster, as they burn incense and they sacrifice to the Big Dipper; they read Sutras and they supplicate the Buddha. Stupid men and foolish women are immediately incited by such people into joining the heterodox sects.
>
> The heterodox sects are gradually transmitted from a single locality to numerous others. Disseminated across diverse areas they attract disciples, eventually spreading in every direction. Once the sectarians are numerous enough, all types of evil issue. It is enough for someone to recklessly draw an illicit plan, for disaster to follow, as the criminals gang together. . . .
>
> Furthermore, the sturdy youths of Henan are accustomed to violence, many studying the martial arts. For example, under the pretext of teaching the martial arts, the monks of the Shaolin Temple have been gathering worthless dregs. Violent criminal types willfully study evil customs, which become a fashion. Heterodox sectarians target such criminals, tempting them to join their sects, thereby increasing their numbers."[35]

The authorities' wariness of the monastery is attested by the interrogation records of suspected rebels. In 1757 a Buddhist monk named Xu Ji'an had been arrested in Anyi County, southern Shanxi, after meeting with sectarians. The unfortunate cleric, who had been too poor to purchase an ordination certificate, had been itinerant for years. Yet of all the monasteries in which he had sojourned, it was his association with the Shaolin Temple— some twenty years earlier!—that aroused his interrogator's concern. All the more so, since the search of the monk's meager belongings yielded a Shaolin-related document that seemed suspiciously seditious. His notebook contained the militant couplet: "Incarnated at Shaolin his divine powers great; The benevolent one repelled the million-strong Hong army."[36]

Monk Xu told the story—with which the magistrate had not been familiar —of the Shaolin tutelary divinity Vajrapāṇi. We have seen in chapter 4 that the valiant god was believed to have defeated the Red Turbans (Hongjin), who threatened the monastery. The monk explained that he had copied the Shaolin couplet during his sojourn at the temple. That it had remained among his belongings for more than twenty years might have been purely accidental. However, it might have signified, as the magistrate suspected, that for monk Xu the legend of the Shaolin guardian spirit had acquired an eschatological significance. If this was the case—our evidence is not sufficient to ascertain whether it was or not—the myth that had provided Shaolin monks with a divine excuse for violence had similarly figured within a sectarian environment. Qing period millenarian groups might have incorporated the Buddhist guardian spirit into their pantheon, imagining him to lead his Shaolin troops in a war of redemption.

Was the Qing-fear justified? Did Shaolin monks or Shaolin affiliates join in rebellion? It is hard to answer this question, for the sources at our disposal are likely biased. The official accounts are tainted by prejudice (against the monastery), whereas its monks, if they had ever been involved in an insurgency, would not have recorded it. Bearing this methodological problem in mind, our ethnographic study of the monastery does lend at least some credence to the government's apprehension. We have seen in chapter 2 that Shaolin's is a fluid community, of which resident monks are a small minority. Most Shaolin graduates—lay and clerical alike—leave the temple to pursue itinerant military careers, at the same time as their monastic fellows regularly train with outsiders. As a renowned center of the martial arts, Shaolin attracts countless practitioners who go there to learn new techniques, test their skills, and meet old friends. It is thus extremely difficult to separate the monastery from the larger martial community. To the degree that Qing officials considered folk martial artists as dangerous, they could not but scrutinize the Shaolin Temple. Guarding against the society of the "rivers and lakes" required supervision of its monastic hub.

Qing officials were fully aware of the professional and the social networks that tied the monastery to the larger martial community. Following the failed Eight Trigrams uprising of 1813, some rebels apparently sought shelter in the Shaolin Temple's vicinity. Responding to the Jiaqing emperor's (r. 1796–1820) urgent query on the matter, Governor Fang Shouchou elaborated on the monks' association with suspected criminals: "The Shaolin Temple is situated in Henan's Dengfeng County, at the foot of Mt. Song. Remote and desolate, the area is suitable for hiding. *If persons similar to them with whom they have been previously familiar* arrive there, the monks are sure to welcome them, and offer them shelter."[37] Because they belonged to the same martial community, Shaolin monks were likely to harbor their fellows who had been implicated in rebellion.

The Qing government was not concerned, then, with the Shaolin Temple itself igniting a rebellion. The fear was rather of its association with rebels— either that its itinerant alumni would join in insurgencies or that its resident monks would give shelter to their former colleagues. Hence the government's repeated attempts to sever the ties between the monastery and the larger martial community. Here is the Dengfeng County magistrate He Wei (fl. 1830) warning the Shaolin monks not to collude with outsiders:

> After the monks . . . read our order and are informed of its contents, they should all purify their hearts and cleanse their minds. Each one should burn incense, cultivate the way, and chant the sutras, as well as plow and weed the land. As to the various types of lay people, the monks are forbidden to collude with them in secret. Nor are the monks allowed to interfere in outside matters, harboring criminals, and instigating trouble. If they dare purposely disobey, and [their crimes] happen to be exposed, we are sure to consider them more serious and punish them accordingly.
>
> As to the lay people, they should not be permitted into the monastery. . . . Tenant farmers should reside elsewhere. They should not be allowed to live near the monks.[38]

Far from being limited to official circles, the perception that Shaolin monks *were* related to the outlaw community was widespread in late Qing society. The iconoclast Liu Tieyun (1857–1909), himself a martial arts aficionado, declared in 1904 that the art of Shaolin fighting no longer existed at its birthplace. The author of *The Travels of Lao Can* attributed its monastic decline to the monks' association with bandits and criminals. "Hand combat is now a lost art at the Shaolin Temple" he wrote. "[The Shaolin styles] were originally developed for the use of the monks, who practiced the art in order to develop toughness and endurance. . . . Who could have known that afterwards the Shaolin Temple art would become famous? Outsiders came in increasing numbers to learn it, and one would often hear that among those who went out masters of the art, there were bandits and seducers of men's wives and daughters."[39]

The dynasty's suspicion of the monks' sedition did not prevent some officials from being intrigued by their art. In previous chapters we met two Qing administrators who traveled to Shaolin to behold its renowned fighting techniques: the low-ranking Wang Zuyuan (ca. 1820–after 1882), who had practiced the Shaolin martial arts, and the high-ranking Lin Qing (1791–1846), who included an account of them in his illustrated *Record of a Goose Life's Traces in the Snow*. However, the relations between the regime and the monastery were so strained that in order to be given a demonstration, they had to convince the monks of their sincerity. Unlike their Ming predecessors, who readily displayed the art to imperial patrons, Qing Shaolin monks were fearful that their performances would be used as evidence against them. Lin Qing labored to put them at ease. "I proceeded to ask the monks about their hand combat method, but they refused to utter a word about it. I made it clear that I have heard about the Shaolin Fist long ago, and I know it has been relied upon solely for guarding monastic regulations and protecting the famous temple. Therefore they need not make pretence. The abbot laughed and assented."[40]

Epilogue

Contemporary visitors would be hard-pressed to imagine Shaolin's dismal nineteenth-century conditions. Today's Shaolin Temple is as flourishing as it has ever been. Paved with marble and decorated with gold, each year it attracts more than a million tourists from around the globe. The monastery is surrounded by dozens of martial arts schools, where tens of thousands of aspiring athletes vie to become China's martial arts champions. The tourists and the students have transformed the Dengfeng County economy, establishing the temple as its most important financial asset.

The monastery's economic power is matched by its political clout. Contemporary Shaolin monks nestle as comfortably in the regime's embrace as did their Ming ancestors five centuries earlier. The monastery's abbot, Yongxin, is concurrently a member of China's People's Congress and the vice president of the Chinese Buddhist Association. His political influence may be gauged by his ability to forcibly remove (in 2000) some twenty thousand people from their residential shacks around the temple, thereby restoring Shaolin to what he—and fellow officials—regarded as its pristine beauty. The temple's links to the regime are also evinced by its place on dignitaries' tours. The likes of the Russian president Vladimir Putin and the former U.S. secretary of state Henry Kissinger are marched through the Shaolin Temple, where they are entertained with martial demonstrations and are ceremoniously offered antique swords.

How did the Shaolin Temple emerge from the ashes of civil war, Japanese occupation, and the Cultural Revolution to become an international sports center? The answer to this question goes beyond the scope of this book, which does not cover the temple's twentieth-century history. Nevertheless, a few preliminary observations may be made, if nothing else as suggestions for future research.

The National Arts (*guoshu*): Shaolin's revival has been related to a fundamental change in the state's attitude to the martial arts. Unlike the Qing dynasty, which suspected martial artists of collusion with rebels, twentieth-century governments—whether nationalist or communist—considered their art a national treasure. Beginning in the Republican period (1912–1948), the native fighting techniques were heralded as the means for rebuilding the bodies and the spirits of the Chinese citizens who were faced with the onslaught of Western athletics. Their very name—"National Arts" (*guoshu*)—attests to the incorporation of the martial arts into the realm of nationally sanctioned culture, as do the repeated attempts to include them in international sporting events.[41] The martial arts have evidently become a source of national pride. At the time of writing it is uncertain whether the Chinese martial arts will be featured in the 2008 Beijing Olympics (possibly as a demonstration sport). It is clear, though, that the games loom large in the minds of Shaolin officials, who plan to reopen in 2008 their Northern Shaolin Temple in the outskirts of Beijing.[42]

The Media: Reality has imitated fiction as the rise of the Shaolin Temple has followed close upon the growing popularity of the movies and the television series dedicated to it. The international success of the kung fu genre is among the most striking aspects of contemporary cinema. Hong Kong movies—which have exerted a significant influence on Hollywood filmmaking—have played an enormous role in spreading the martial arts' fame, both within China and around the globe. The modern media has thereby recreated the Shaolin legend for contemporary audiences. Particularly noteworthy in this respect has been Li Lianjie's (Jet Li's) 1982 blockbuster *Shaolin Temple*, which has been briefly mentioned in chapter 2. In the wake of the movie's success, thousands of aspiring athletes flocked to the monastery, laying the foundations for the martial arts schools that would mushroom around it. The temple's revival has been intimately linked, therefore, to the flowering of the kung fu genre.

Economic Reform: Whereas the Ming dynasty promoted Shaolin's military power, the Communist regime appreciates its economic significance. Even though some of its alumni *have* joined the PRC military, the monastery is valued primarily as a financial asset. The spectacular success of the Shaolin Temple as a tourist and as a sporting attraction has had far-reaching implications for the previously depressed Dengfeng County economy, resulting in enthusiastic government support. State-sponsored attempts to revive other martial arts centers—such as the Funiu Monasteries mentioned in chapter 3—have been modeled on the Shaolin example. The temple's revival needs to be interpreted, therefore, in terms of the economic reforms that have so dramatically changed contemporary Chinese lives.

CONCLUSION

History, Religion, and the Chinese Martial Arts

THE HISTORY OF the Shaolin Temple is not identical to the evolution of the Chinese martial arts. The monastery made important contributions to the development of late imperial fighting, armed and unarmed alike, and its military history mirrored trends that have transformed the martial arts in general. Nevertheless, the history of the martial arts is larger than the temple's. The fighting techniques with which we are familiar today—such as Taiji Quan, Xingyi Quan, *and* Shaolin Quan—emerged during the sixteenth and the seventeenth centuries by a combination of economic, religious, and political factors that far exceeded the monastery's reach. At the same time, these bare-handed styles drew on an ancient gymnastic tradition that had matured centuries before the monastery's founding. Hand combat is in some respects the remote descendant of *daoyin* calisthenics that had flourished prior to the arrival of Buddhism in China.

From another angle, the history of the Shaolin Monastery involves questions that, despite their interest for the Buddhologist, are not necessarily pertinent to the martial arts historian: How could Buddhist monks ignore a primary tenet of their faith that forbade violence? Did some aspects of the Buddhist religion of compassion lend themselves to a military interpretation? These questions are irrelevant to fighting techniques such as Taiji Quan, Xingyi Quan, and Bagua Zhang that evolved in a non-Buddhist environment. Even though these martial styles are intimately related to religion, *their* spiritual vocabulary largely derives from native traditions. Contemporary hand combat is couched in the rich terminologies of the Daoist religion and of Chinese philosophy. Bare-handed styles integrate the culture's conceptions of immortality with its cosmology of the Supreme Ultimate, the *yin* and the *yang*, and the eight trigrams.

It might be useful, therefore, to sort out our principal findings, those related to Buddhism and violence on the one hand, and those that concern martial arts history and its relation to native religion on the other.

Buddhism and Violence

"Throughout East Asia," wrote Frederick Mote, "the Buddhist religion of compassion that regards the taking of any life as a great evil has often appealed to warrior societies."[1] The circumstances under which the Indian-born faith had been involved in violence—across cultures, historical periods, and geographic regions—doubtless differed. Nevertheless, the Shaolin military tradition might shed light on other instances of Buddhist involvement in warfare. At least some of the elements that had fashioned the temple's martial history might have figured—in diverse combinations and varying degrees—in other cases of monastic violence.

Two factors stand out in the early history of Shaolin monastic warfare: economic power and strategic significance. The temple's vast holdings required military protection, and its commanding position on a road leading to the imperial capital embroiled its monks in a battle with nationwide consequences. The monastery's military history was thus a reflection of institutional wealth as well as geographic proximity to the nexus of political power.

These initial reasons for the monks' military activities were quickly joined by a third: sanction by the political authorities. Even though it likely had not been the Tang emperor's intention, Li Shimin's letter of thanks proved to be a momentous event in the history of the Shaolin Temple. His approbation protected the monks' military activity from the intervention of the political authorities, arguably even from the wrath of the Qing rulers a millennium later. For despite their stubborn suspicion of it, Qing officials refrained from annihilating the temple. The emperor's approval, moreover, licensed their military occupation to the monks themselves. In the Chinese cultural context, a political sanction could outweigh a religious prohibition. Even if they did not explicitly admit it, Shaolin warriors likely relied on the emperor's mandate in their violation of their faith's proscription of killing. In this respect Li Lianjie's (Jet Li) portrayal of the emperor as a religious authority was faithful to the monks' understanding of the Tang ruler. In his 1982 blockbuster *Shaolin Temple*, Li attributed the Shaolin transgressions of Buddhist dietary laws to the emperor's absolution.

Imperial authorization was joined by divine sanction. The history of the Shaolin Temple betrays an intimate connection between Buddhist violence and the veneration of Buddhist violent deities. In this respect, the Shaolin military tradition reflects the age-old contradiction between Buddhism as an ethical philosophy and Buddhism as a religion of salvation. It was in the latter—in the mythological realm of martial gods—that Shaolin monks sought an excuse for their military practice. They did not resort to the sophisticated arguments

of Buddhist thinkers who had explained that killing was in certain circumstances merciful. Rather, they found in Vajrapāṇi's muscular physique a self-
evident and tangible proof that the religion of compassion required military
protection. The iconography of the military gods left no doubt that the Buddha himself had sanctioned the armed defense of his faith.

Soliciting the military might of the Vajrapāṇi, Shaolin monks employed
spells (*mantras*) and hand symbolisms (*mudrās*). This leads us to an aspect of
Buddhist warfare that we have not touched upon: the role of Tantric ritual in
the protection of the state. Medieval Chinese rulers—like their counterparts
throughout Asia—commissioned Buddhist monks with the performance of
elaborate rites that were meant to assure their victory in battle. Tantric masters such as Amoghavajra (705–774) conjured an entire panoply of warrior
deities, who accompanied the Tang armies on their military campaigns. The
Heavenly King Vaiśravaṇa (Pishamen), for example, was repeatedly said to
have revealed his divine powers, subduing the dynasty's foes.[2]

In their fifteen-hundred-year evolution, the Shaolin martial arts gradually
absorbed other aspects of the Buddhist religion. By Ming times, Shaolin monks
had chosen as their quintessential weapon a Buddhist emblem: the staff. Their
choice of the instrument was probably related to its role in monastic life. Buddhist regulations instructed monks to carry the staff, which by metonymy came
to signify its clerical owner. The same weapon had also been wielded by fictional fighting monks such as the heroic simian Sun Wukong, protagonist of
Journey to the West. The legend of the divine monkey resembled that of the Shaolin tutelary god Vajrapāṇi. The two Buddhist warriors had been equipped with
the same magic staff that changes its dimensions at will.

Those who trained within a monastic environment came to regard their
martial practice as a religious discipline. By the sixteenth century, Shaolin disciples—lay and clerical alike—hardly distinguished the mastery of their fighting technique from the mastery of mind that led to liberation. Martial artists
such as Cheng Zongyou expressed both the exertion of physical practice and
the exhilaration that followed it in Buddhist terms. Significantly, the association of martial practice with spiritual liberation extended beyond the monastery's walls. Late Ming poetry suggests that practitioners of styles other than
Shaolin sometimes invested their techniques with a Buddhist meaning. At least
some martial artists employed the vocabulary of enlightenment to describe the
mastery of their art.

Religion and Martial Arts History

The martial arts historian is confronted by a methodological problem. To
the degree that the fighting techniques of individual warriors—as distinguished from the training methods of regular armies—had evolved among
the unlettered masses, their evolution might have escaped the writings of

the literary elite. Whereas the strategic maneuvering of armies—the so-called "art of war" (*bingfa*)—had been investigated by Chinese authors as early as the Zhou period, the humble techniques of the individual peasant had rarely been deemed worthy of documentation. Our history of the martial arts is strictly speaking a chronicle of the scattered literary references to them. New information, deriving from archaeological discoveries or textual revelations, may alter our understanding of martial arts evolution.

Bearing this reservation in mind, the available sources do indicate that the traditions of hand combat underwent a significant transformation during the late Ming and the early Qing. This development was twofold. First, during the sixteenth and the seventeenth centuries, the *quan* techniques of bare-handed fighting grew in popularity, becoming more prevalent than they had ever been. Shaolin monks, who had trained for generations in the arts of the staff, began turning their attention to hand combat in the sixteenth century. Secondly, those bare-handed styles with which we are familiar today—such as Taiji Quan, Xingyi Quan, *and* Shaolin Quan—can be traced back to the Ming-Qing transition period. We have seen that their emergence in the seventeenth century was accompanied by the creation of a novel martial arts mythology. The new bare-handed styles were attributed to obscure Buddhist and Daoist saints who had supposedly created them centuries earlier.

Thus, in the case of many late Ming martial artists—Shaolin monks included—specialization in unarmed fighting had followed the mastery of armed techniques. New bare-handed styles emerged during a period when the manipulation of weapons, including firearms, had already been highly developed. That bare-handed fighting should follow armed warfare contradicts not only the accepted mythology of the martial arts (itself a product of the seventeenth century) but also common sense. The natural progress of warfare, we would assume, would be from less dangerous to more dangerous, from bare-handed fighting to armed combat. Why did Shaolin monks, who had successfully tested their weapons in battle, turn their attention to bare-handed techniques, useless in battle?

The answer suggested by this book lies in this seeming contradiction itself. Late Ming hand combat was not created for fighting. The bare-handed styles with which we are familiar today had not been narrowly designed for warfare, but had been broadly conceived for healing and spiritual realization. They were created by integrating calisthenic and breathing techniques—originally intended for therapeutic and religious goals—into unarmed combat. The result was a synthesis of fighting, healing, and religious self-cultivation. Shaolin monks did not study hand combat because they considered it militarily effective. They were intrigued, rather, by the therapeutic benefits and religious horizons of the novel bare-handed styles.

Transforming hand combat into a self-conscious system of thought, late imperial martial artists drew on diverse sources: Daoist manuals of gymnastics, medical treatises of acupuncture, cosmological interpretations of the *Classic of*

Changes and, in some cases, Buddhist scriptures. The result was a unique amalgamation of physiological and spiritual vocabularies. Beginning with the seventeenth century *Sinews Transformation Classic*, fighting manuals simultaneously employed diverse religious terminologies to articulate their spiritual goals. The imagination of Daoist immortality, the cosmology of the Supreme Ultimate, and the vocabulary of Buddhist enlightenment were equally harnessed to describe the practitioner's mystical experience.

Why the late Ming? Why was a martial arts synthesis created at *that* period? The sixteenth century witnessed remarkable economic and cultural creativity, from the growth of domestic and international commerce to the spread of women's education, from the development of the publishing industry to the maturation of new forms of fiction and drama. Hand combat evolution could be seen as another indication of the vibrancy of late Ming society. More specifically, the integration of Daoist-related gymnastics into bare-handed fighting was related to the age's religious syncretism. A climate of mutual tolerance permitted Shaolin practitioners to explore calisthenic and breathing exercises that had been colored by Daoist hues, at the same time it allowed *daoyin* aficionados to study martial arts that had evolved within a Buddhist setting. Intellectual trends were joined by political traumas as the Manchu conquest of 1644 convinced literati of the necessity to explore the folk martial arts. As scholars trained in bare-handed techniques, they rewrote them in a philosophical parlance. The broadening of the martial arts into a self-conscious system of thought was largely due to their practice by members of the elite.

The spiritual aspect of martial arts theory was joined by the religious setting of martial arts practice. Temples offered martial artists the public space and the festival occasions that were necessary for the performance of their art. Itinerant martial artists resided in local shrines, where the peasant youths trained in fighting. The temple's role as a location for military practice leads us to a topic we had only briefly touched upon: the integration of the martial arts into the ritual life of the village. Future research, anthropological and historical alike, would doubtless shed much light on peasant associations that combined military, theatrical, and religious functions. Preliminary studies of such local organizations as lion-dance troops and Song Jiang militias (named after *Water Margin*'s bravo) reveal that their performances have been inextricably linked to the village liturgical calendar. The very names of some late imperial martial arts troops betray their self-perception as ritual entities; in the villages of north China, congregations of Plum Flower martial artists are called "Plum Flower Fist *Religion*" (Meihua quan *jiao*).[3]

This is not to say that all martial artists were equally keen on spiritual perfection. The traditions of hand combat are extremely versatile, allowing for diverse interpretations and emphases. Whereas some adepts seek religious salvation, others are primarily concerned with combat efficiency; whereas some are attracted to stage performance, others are intent on mental self-cultivation. Various practitioners describe the fruits of their labors in diverse terms.

What this book reveals, then, practitioners have already known: The Chinese martial art is a multifaceted system of physical and mental self-cultivation that has diverse applications, from health and well-being to theatrical performance, from competitive sport to religious self-cultivation, from self-defense to armed rebellion. It is this versatility that has accounted for the tradition's vitality in the face of dramatically changing social and political conditions. The martial arts' unique combination of military, therapeutic, and religious goals has made them attractive to the young and the old, women and men, rebels and scholars, the affluent and the needy, in diverse societies around the globe.

Appendix

Some Editions of the *Sinews Transformation Classic*

(The best modern edition is included in *Zhongguo chuantong yangsheng zhendian* 中國傳統養生珍典 (*Rare classics of Chinese traditional methods for nourishing life*), edited by Ding Jihua 丁繼華 et al., pp. 202–330. Beijing: Renmin tiyu, 1998.)

(1) Early Qing, possibly seventeenth-century, manuscript edition. The postscript by Zining daoren 紫凝道人 is undated. The comment "Stored at the Narrating-Antiquities Library of Qian Zunwang" might indicate that the manuscript belonged to the library of Qian Ceng 錢曾 (style: Zunwang 尊王) (1629–1701) (even though the book is not listed in his extant library catalogue). Copy at the National Central Library, Taipei.

(2) Qing manuscript edition. The postscript by Zining daoren is undated. Kangxi period (1662–1722) preface attributed to the Recluse from the Clouds Shrine (Yuntan yinshi 雲壇隱士) Wang Jingyang 汪景陽. Copy at the Shanghai Library.

(3) Early nineteenth-century printed edition. The observance (on p. 62a) of the taboo on Emperor Minning's 旻寧 name identifies it as belonging to his Daoguang (1821–1850) reign period. The twelve exercises of "Weituo Offering His Club" (which were later incorporated into the *Illustrated Exposition of Internal Techniques*) are included, as is the *Marrow-Cleansing Classic* (*Xisui jing* 洗髓經). Appendix by "Mr. Laizhang" (Laizhang shi 來章氏). Copy at the Shanghai Library.

(4) 1875 printed edition titled *Guarding Life and the Sinews Transformation Classic* (*Weisheng Yijin jing* 衛生易筋經). Pan Weiru's *Essential Techniques of Guarding Life* (*Weisheng yaoshu* 衛生要術) of 1858 is included. On this edition (which I have not seen), see Tang Hao, "Wo guo tiyu ziliao jieti," pp. 68–69; and Dudgeon, "Kung-fu or Medical Gymnastics," pp. 503–519.

(5) 1875 manuscript edition. Photographic reproduction titled *The Illustrated Sinews Transformation Classic* (*Huituben Yijin jing* 繪圖本易筋經), in the series Jingdian wuxue xilie 經典武學系列. Taipei: Yiwen, 2000. The postscript by Zining daoren is undated.

(6) 1884 printed edition titled *The Meaning of the Sinews Transformation Classic* (*Yijin jing yi* 易筋經義), included in vol. 34 of the *Collected Books from the Sweeping Leaves Mountain Residence* (*Saoye shan fang* 埽葉山房). The postscript by Zining daoren is dated Tianqi 天啟 4th year, *jiazi* 甲子 (1624). Judging by another postscript, this edition was based on an earlier 1825 edition collated by one Zhu Wenlan 祝文瀾. Copy at the Shanghai Library.

Notes

Introduction

1. The comparison has been made by Wile, *Lost T'ai-chi Classics*, pp. 25–30. On the Republican discourse of nation building and martial training, see also Morris, *Marrow of the Nation*, pp. 185–229; and *Zhongguo jindai tiyu shi*, pp. 127–145, 265–296.

2. Bloch, *Historian's Craft*, p. 45.

1. The Monastery

1. On the Shaolin Monastery, see Fu Mei, *Song shu* (preface 1612); Jing Rizhen, *Shuo Song* (preface 1721); and *Shaolin si zhi* (preface 1748), compiled by Ye Feng et al., revised by Shi Yizan et al. The above three are also available in a modern typeset edition in *Song yue wenxian congkan*.

The best modern history is Wen Yucheng, *Shaolin fanggu*. See also Xu Changqing, *Shaolin si yu Zhongguo wenhua*; *Shaolin si ziliao ji*, ed. Wu Gu and Liu Zhixue; *Shaolin si ziliao ji xu bian*, ed. Wu Gu and Yao Yuan; *Xin bian Shaolin si zhi*; and the entry "Shôrinji" in Mochizuki Shinkô, ed., *Bukkyō daijiten*, 3:2806–2807.

2. Henan ranks twenty-sixth in household consumption, twenty-eighth in per capita net income of rural households, and twenty-ninth in per capita annual income of urban residents (of China's thirty-two provinces and independent municipal regions). These 1999 figures are culled from the *China Statistical Yearbook 2000*, pp. 70, 332, and 319 respectively.

3. The price of an individual ticket is 40 yuan, or US $5. The income they provide is shared by the monastery and the provincial authorities (information gathered by the author during visits to the temple in the late 1990s).

4. See Ching's essays "United Nations, Divided Shaolin," "Battling to be Shaolin's Best," and "13,000 Warriors of Taguo"; see also Howard W. French, "So Many Paths. Which Shaolin Is Real?"

5. See Ching, "In the Dragon's Den."

6. See Ching, "United Nations, Divided Shaolin," p. 11.

7. Fu Mei, *Song shu*, 9.35a.

8. Fu's *Song shu* covers all the mountain's sacred sites (Buddhist and Daoist alike). However, its bulk is dedicated to Shaolin-related materials.

9. See *Shaolin si qianfodian bihua*; *Shaolin si shike yishu*, ed. Su Siyi et al.; and the three-volume *Zhongguo Shaolin si*, gen. ed. Yongxin.

10. Faru's (638–689) stupa, for example, sheds important light on the evolution of Chan genealogy; on this stupa (which is located outside the Stupa Forest proper), see Wen Yucheng, *Shaolin fanggu*, pp. 99–105; and Cole, "It's All in the Framing: Desire and Innocence in Early Chan Narratives—A Close-Reading of the Biography of Chan Master Fa Ru."

11. Chavannes (1865–1918), *Le T'ai chan*, p. 3.

12. See Naquin and Chün-fang Yü, *Pilgrims and Sacred Sites in China*, p. 11.

13. See Kroll, "Verses from on High," p. 225.

14. See Fu Mei, *Song shu*, 4.2b–3a.

15. As early as 676, Empress Wu convinced the then reigning Emperor Gaozong to perform the *fengshan* sacrifice on Mt. Song. However, because of the Tibetan incursion the plan was called off. Eventually, the empress performed the sacrifice there in 696 in the name of her own Zhou dynasty. See Fu Mei, *Song shu*, 4.5b. See also Wechsler, *Offerings of Jade and Silk*, pp. 188–189, 192, and Chavannes, *Le T'ai chan*, pp. 194–202.

16. See Wen Yucheng, *Shaolin fanggu*, pp. 5–7, and Faure, "Relics and Flesh Bodies," pp. 154–155.

17. The temple's dating is unclear. It could possibly be traced back to the second century CE. See Fu Mei, *Song shu*, 3.8a–b. See also the entry "Zhongyue miao" in *Zhonghua Daojiao da cidian*, p. 1667.

18. See Yang Xuanzhi, *Luoyang qielan ji* (ca. 547), 5.228. See also Yi-t'ung Wang's translation of Yang Hsüan-chih, *A Record of Buddhist Monasteries in Lo-yang*, p. 248. Yang Xuanzhi does not allude to the Shaolin Monastery. Wen Yucheng, *Shaolin fanggu*, pp. 14–16, speculates that Yang's Daochang Monastery is the Shaolin Monastery.

19. See Faure, "Relics and Flesh Bodies," pp. 155–165.

20. See Yampolsky, *The Platform Sutra of the Sixth Patriarch*, pp. 1–57.

21. For a summary of modern scholarship see McRae, *The Northern School and the Formation of Early Ch'an Buddhism*, pp. 15–19; and Faure, *Le traité de Bodhidharma*, pp. 13–22.

22. See Faure, "Relics and Flesh Bodies," pp. 156–157. On Faru and Huian (also known as Laoan) see McRae, *The Northern School and the Formation of Early Ch'an Buddhism*, pp. 43–44 and 56–59 respectively.

23. See respectively Yang Xuanzhi, *Luoyang qielan ji*, 1.26–28, and Yi-t'ung Wang's translation, *A Record of Buddhist Monasteries in Lo-yang*, pp. 20–21; Daoxuan, *Xu Gaoseng zhuan*, *Taishō shinshū daizōkyō* (hereafter "*T*"), no. 2060, 50:552a; and *Chuanfa baoji*, compiled by Du Fei, *T*, no. 2838, 85:1291c.

24. This is McRae's translation (*The Northern School*, p. 16); the original is Daoyuan, *Jingde chuandeng lu*, *T*, no. 2076, 51:219b.

25. See, respectively, Pei Cui (ca. 670–736), "Shaolin si bei" ("The Shaolin Monastery Stele") (728), in *Quan Tang wen*, ed. Dong Gao, 279.1253; and Gu Shaolian (fl. 800), "Song yue Shaolin xin zao chu ku ji" ("Record of the Reconstruction of the Song Mountain Shaolin Monastery's Kitchen and Storehouse") (798), in Fu Mei, *Song shu*, 20.13b.

26. This is Griffith Foulk's translation in his "Sung Controversies Concerning the 'Separate Transmission' of Ch'an," p. 246. The original is Daoyuan, *Jingde chuandeng lu*, *T*, no. 2076, 51:219b–c. The Shaolin stele that cites this text dates from 1346; see Wen Yucheng, *Shaolin fanggu*, p. 47.

27. The earliest stele in question dates from 1222; see Wen Yucheng, *Shaolin fanggu*, p. 49, and *Xin bian Shaolin si zhi*, p. 83.

28. See Daoyuan, *Jingde chuandeng lu*, *T*, no. 2076, 51:220b.

29. The earliest Shaolin stele of the Reed-Floating Bodhidharma dates from 1307, however earlier (thirteenth-century) paintings have been preserved elsewhere. See Lachman, "Why Did the Patriarch Cross the River?" The 1307 Shaolin stele is reproduced in *Zhongguo Shaolin si*, 2:75. I am not convinced by Lachman's argument (p. 255) that the stalk-riding motif might have existed as early as the eleventh century. Cao Shibang, at any rate, suggests that it originated during the 1129 Jin campaigns against the Southern Song. The latter's defenses of the Yangtze were said to be so weak that the enemy could "Cross the River on a Stalk of Reed." See Cao Shibang, "Yiwei dujiang yu chi roubiancai—liangge zhuming Chanzong gushi de lishi tanjiu."

30. See Shahar, *Crazy Ji*, pp. 30–45.

31. See Fu Mei, *Song shu*, 3.24b–25a; Wen Yucheng, *Shaolin fanggu*, pp. 169–172; and *Xin bian Shaolin si zhi*, pp. 39–42.

32. See Faure, "Relics and Flesh Bodies," p. 162.

33. See, for example, Du Mu's (1459–1525) account of his visit to the monastery in his *Jin xie linlang*, 20.8a. Compare also Du Mu, *You mingshan ji*, 1.18a–23a.

34. See Wen Yucheng, *Shaolin fanggu*, pp. 50–51.

35. See *Wei shu*, 114.3040; Ware, trans., "Wei Shou on Buddhism," pp. 155–156. Compare also Daoxuan, *Xu Gaoseng zhuan* (ca. 660), *T*, no. 2060, 50:551; and Pei Cui, "Shaolin si bei," in *Quan Tang wen*, 279.1252; Tonami Mamoru, *The Shaolin Monastery Stele on Mount Song*, pp. 32–33. See also Wen Yucheng, *Shaolin fanggu*, pp. 9–13.

The *Wei shu* and Pei Cui refer to Shaolin's founder as Batuo; Daoxuan refers to him as Fotuo. Some scholars have reconstructed his Sanskrit name as Buddhabhadra, assuming that his full Chinese name was Fotuobatuo.

36. Daoxuan alludes to a wall painting by Batuo, whose biography is included in Zhang Yanyuan's (fl. 850) *Lidai ming hua ji* (*Record of Famous Paintings Through the Ages*). See Daoxuan, *Xu Gaoseng zhuan*, *T*, no. 2060, 50:551b; and Acker, *Some T'ang and pre-T'ang Texts*, part 1, pp. 184–186, part 2, 7.93. See also Pelliot, "Notes sur quelques artistes des Six Dynasties et des T'ang," pp. 236–265.

37. See Daoxuan, *Xu Gaoseng zhuan*, *T*, no. 2060, 50:607b–608a and 50:484b–c; see also Wen Yucheng, *Shaolin fanggu*, pp. 34–37.

38. See Pei Cui, "Shaolin si bei," in *Quan Tang wen*, 279.1252, and *Da Tang da*

Cien si Sanzang fashi zhuan (688), by Huili and Yancong, *T,* no. 2053, 50:253c. See also Wen Yucheng, *Shaolin fanggu,* pp. 24–28. Another reason for Xuanzang's choice of the Shaolin Monastery was its proximity to his native village. See Daoxuan, *Xu Gaoseng zhuan, T,* no. 2060, 50:457c.

39. See Yang Hsüan-chih, *A Record of Buddhist Monasteries in Lo-yang,* pp. 5, 7. See also Ch'en, *Buddhism in China: A Historical Survey,* pp. 162–163.

40. This is Yi-t'ung Wang's translation (Yang Hsüan-chih, *A Record of Buddhist Monasteries in Lo-yang,* pp. 5–6).

41. For a general survey see Ch'en, *Buddhism in China: A Historical Survey,* pp. 170–177.

42. See Pei Cui, "Shaolin si bei," in *Quan Tang wen,* 279.1252.

43. See Gernet, *Buddhism in Chinese Society,* pp. 142–150.

44. The empress's letter concerning the "Incarnated Maitreya Buddha Stupa" ("Xiasheng Milefo ta") was engraved in 683 on a Shaolin stele. It is transcribed in Fu Mei, *Song shu,* 20.64a–b. The empress's poem was written when she was still Emperor Gaozong's consort. Titled "Cong jia xing Shaolin si" ("Following the Emperor's Carriage as he Graces the Shaolin Monastery"), it is included in *Quan Tang shi,* 5.58. On the empress and the Shaolin Monastery, see Wen Yucheng, *Shaolin fanggu,* pp. 87–90. On her Buddhist policies see Weinstein, *Buddhism under the T'ang,* pp. 37–47.

2. Serving the Emperor

1. See Harvey, *Introduction to Buddhist Ethics,* pp. 69, 94; and Demiéville, "Le Bouddhisme et la guerre," pp. 347–348.

2. See Vasubandhu's *Abhidharmakośaśāstra,* translated into Chinese by Xuanzang, *Apidamo jushe lun, T,* no. 1558, 29:86b, and into French by Louis de La Vallée Poussin, *L'abhidharmakośa de Vasubandhu,* 3:152.

3. See the fifth-century Mahāyāna code (which was probably compiled in China), *Fanwang jing, T,* no. 1484, 24:1004b, 1005c, 1007b; see also Demiéville, "Le Bouddhisme et la guerre," p. 353, and Harvey, *Introduction to Buddhist Ethics,* p. 254.

4. See respectively Huijiao, *Gaoseng zhuan, T,* no. 2059, 50:344c, trans. Robert Shih, *Biographies des moines éminents,* p. 153; and *Da Tang da Cien si Sanzang fashi zhuan, T,* no. 2053, 50:253b, discussed by Weinstein, *Buddhism under the T'ang,* p. 24.

5. See Daoxuan, *Xu Gaoseng zhuan, T,* no. 2060, 50:646c. See also Zhipan's allusion to monk Daoping (fl. 756), who voluntarily joined the war against An Lushan, earning the title Lord of the Imperial Insignia General in Chief (*Fozu tongji* (1271), *T,* no. 2035, 49:375c).

6. See *Zizhi tongjian,* 182.5686–5687, 186.5833–5834, 187.5858, 188.5904; see also Weinstein, *Buddhism under the T'ang,* pp. 154–155 n. 1.

7. *Zizhi tongjian,* 239.7716–7717; *Jiu Tang shu,* 15.454; *Xin Tang shu,* 213.5993. See also the biography of the regional military leader Li Hanzhi (842–899), who began his career as a wandering monk (*Xin Tang shu,* 187.5442–5445). On Chinese fighting monks see also Gu Yanwu, "Shaolin seng bing," in his *Rizhilu jishi,* 29.21a–22b; Demiéville, "Le Bouddhisme et la guerre," pp. 357–368, and Wen Yucheng, *Shaolin fanggu,* pp. 141–142.

8. See Hao Chunwen, *Tang houqi Wudai Song chu Dunhuang seng ni de shehui shenghuo*, p. 104.

9. See Feng Peihong, "P. 3249 bei 'jun ji can juan.'"

10. Weinstein, *Buddhism under the T'ang*, p. 5.

11. See Schopen, "Two Problems in the History of Indian Buddhism," p. 30.

12. Its authenticity has been verified by such careful historians as Du Mu (1459–1525), Gu Yanwu (1613–1682), Wang Chang (1725–1806), Niida Noboru (1904–1966), and Tonami Mamoru (1937–). See Du Mu, *Jin xie linlang*, 12.1a–8b; Du Mu, *You mingshan ji*, 1.18a–23a; Gu Yanwu, *Jinshi wenzi ji*, 2.29b–30a, 3.34b–35b; Gu Yanwu, "Shaolin seng bing," in his *Rizhilu ji shi*, 29.21a–22b; Wang Chang, *Jinshi cuibian*, 41.1a–7a, 74.1a–8b, 77.15a–23a; Niida Noboru, *Tō Sō hōritsu bunsho*, pp. 830–833; and Tonami, *The Shaolin Monastery Stele on Mount Song*. Tonami's monograph includes transcriptions, as well as English translations, of the inscriptions. The latter were made by Penelope Herbert with Tonami's aid. In the following I use my own translations, except where otherwise noted. See also the stele's excellent photographic reproductions in *Zhongguo Shaolin si, beike juan*, pp. 18–22.

13. See Howard J. Wechsler, "T'ai-Tsung"; Zhao Keyao and Xu Daoxun, *Tang Taizong zhuan*. On Li's military genius see David Graff, *Medieval Chinese Warfare*, pp. 169–177.

14. See *Zizhi tongjian* 189.5913–5924. See also Wang Shichong's and Dou Jiande's biographies in *Jiu Tang shu*, 54.2227–2243, and *Xin Tang shu*, 85.3689–3703. For general background, see Wechsler, "The Founding of the T'ang Dynasty: Kaotsu (reign 618–626)," pp. 162–167, and Zhao Keyao and Xu Daoxun, *Tang Taizong zhuan*, pp. 39–44. Graff (pp. 172–177) analyzes the Hulao military victory.

15. Wang Shichong ennobled Wang Renze as "Prince of Tang" (Tang Wang). See *Jiu Tang shu*, 54.2232.

16. Pei's history occupies one side of the stele. The remaining six texts were inscribed on its other side. On Pei, see *Jiu Tang shu*, 100.3128–3129; *Xin Tang shu*, 130.4487–4488; and Tonami, *The Shaolin Monastery Stele on Mount Song*, pp. 42–45, 50–52.

17. The Tang revolt began in 617 at Taiyuan, Shanxi.

18. Guangwu is situated near Hulao, where Li Shimin defeated Wang Shichong's ally, Dou Jiande.

19. My translation follows Wang Chang's transcription in his *Jinshi cuibian*, 77.16b–17b. Compare also *Quan Tang wen*, 279.1252, and Tonami, *The Shaolin Monastery Stele on Mount Song*, pp. 29–30.

20. Gernet, *Buddhism in Chinese Society*, p. 117.

21. On the Sui period origins of Shaolin's estate, see Pei Cui's history as transcribed in Wang Chang, *Jinshi cuibian*, 77.17a.

22. See *Taiping huanyu ji*, 5.7a.

23. See Ibid., 4.2a.

24. The fort is first mentioned in the *Jin History*, and according to Pei Cui it was established during that period. See *Jinshu*, 119.3011. See also *Song shu*, 45.1372; *Zhou shu*, 15.246; and *Zizhi tongjian*, 117.3694, 170.5291.

25. During the medieval period the Shaolin estate itself was sometimes referred to as Cypress Valley *Fort* (rather than Cypress Valley *Estate*). See for example Li Shimin's letter to the Shaolin monks (text 2 below).

26. The *Jiu Tang shu* (54.2234) refers to Huanyuan as a county (*xian*); Pei Cui, like the Shaolin government document of 632 (text 4 below), refers to it as a prefecture (*zhou*). Li Shimin's general Wang Junkuo passed through Huanyuan (i.e., through the Cypress Valley Estate) as early as October 620. However, he did not station troops there (compare *Jiu Tang shu*, 54.2234, and *Zizhi tongjian*, 188.5889). This enabled Wang Shichong to recapture the strategic mountain estate, which he consequently lost to the Shaolin monks, on May 23, 621.

27. See Wen Yucheng, *Shaolin fanggu*, pp. 357–360. On Fan Zhongxiu, see *Min'guo renwu da cidian*, p. 1392.

28. The date of the monks' victory is provided by the magistrate verdict of 632 (text 4 below).

29. Careful scholars such as Gu Yanwu (*Jinshi wenzi ji*, 2.30a), Niida Noboru (p. 833), and Tonami Mamoru (p. 3) have concluded that the autograph is Li Shimin's own.

30. The Buddhist eightfold path consists of right views, right intentions, right speech, right conduct, right livelihood, right effort, right mindfulness, and right concentration.

31. There is a typographical error in the inscription. Li Anyuan, who participated in several of Li Shimin's campaigns, was ennobled as commandery duke of Guangde (in today's Anhui), not Deguang. He also served as commander-in-chief at Luzhou (in today's Shanxi) and Prefect of Huaizhou (in today's Henan). See *Xin Tang shu*, 88.3746–3747.

32. My translation is based on an original rubbing, which I obtained when I visited the monastery in 2000. Compare also the transcriptions in Wang Chang's *Jinshi cuibian*, 41.1a–2a; Tonami, *The Shaolin Monastery Stele on Mount Song*, p. 11; *Shaolin si zhi* (1748), "*chenhan*" ("imperial writings"), 1b–2.2b; and *Quan Tang wen*, 10.44.

Li Shimin's letter, which shared the "Shaolin Monastery Stele" of 728 with six other texts, had also been inscribed on another Shaolin stele. A recently discovered Shaolin stele dating from ca. 689 carries the same letter, written in a different calligraphic style. The imperial signature is identical. See Cui Geng, "*Tang 'Qin wang gao Shaolin si jiao bei' kao*," pp. 88–90, and Tonami, *The Shaolin Monastery Stele on Mount Song*, pp. 12–14.

33. Li Shimin's extant prose is included in *Quan Tang wen*, 4.13–10.51, and his poetry in *Quan Tang shi*, 1.1–20. On his writing and calligraphy, see Zhao Keyao and Xu Daoxun, *Tang Taizong zhuan*, pp. 392–403.

34. See *Zizhi tongjian*, 189.5918.

35. See Daoxuan, *Xu Gaoseng zhuan*, T, no. 2060, 50:633c. See also Demiéville, "Le Bouddhisme et la guerre," p. 361.

36. See text 4 below.

37. The prohibition on monks receiving homage from their parents was re-

voked in 633. On Li Shimin's policy toward Buddhism, see Weinstein, *Buddhism Under the T'ang*, pp. 11–27, and Wechsler, "T'ai-Tsung," pp. 217–219.

38. See Wechsler, "T'ai-Tsung," p. 219.

39. See Niida Noboru, *Tō Sō hōritsu bunsho no kenkyū*, pp. 830–838.

40. Li Shimin's "instruction" is translated in Twitchett, "Monastic Estates in T'ang China," pp. 131–132, and Tonami, *The Shaolin Monastery Stele on Mount Song*. pp. 17–18. It is transcribed in *Jinshi cuibian*, 74.1a–2b; Niida, *Tō Sō hōritsu bunsho no kenkyū*, pp. 831–832; and Tonami, *The Shaolin Monastery Stele on Mount Song*, p. 16.

41. See Twitchett, "Monastic Estates in T'ang China," pp. 126–130; and Gernet, *Buddhism in Chinese Society*. p. 123. On similar Ming inscriptions, see Brook, *Praying for Power*, p. 174. According to Brook, the inscriptions were sometimes meant to prevent the *monks* from selling the estate.

42. See Gernet, *Buddhism in Chinese Society*. pp. 142–150.

43. In the former case the land was intended for the support of an individual monk, after whose death it reverted to the state; in the latter it was used for the upkeep of the monastery. See Niida, *Tō Sō hōritsu bunsho no kenkyū*, pp. 832–833; Twitchett, "Monastic Estates in T'ang China," pp. 133–134; and Gernet, *Buddhism in Chinese Society*. pp. 66–73, 133–134. Niida considers the 632 official letter as evidence that the *koufen tian* system had been implemented in seventh-century Henan.

44. The abbreviated forms *shang kaifu* and *yitong* stand respectively for the honorary titles *shang kaifu yitong da jiangjun* and *yitong da jiangjun*. See *Zhongguo lidai guanzhi da cidian*, pp. 51, 272.

45. This is Penelope Herbert's translation in Tonami, *The Shaolin Monastery Stele on Mount Song*, pp. 24–25 (slightly revised). The original is transcribed in Wang Chang, *Jinshi cuibian*, 74.5a–5b; and Tonami, *The Shaolin Monastery Stele on Mount Song*, p. 21.

46. The letters are transcribed and translated in Tonami, *The Shaolin Monastery Stele on Mount Song*, pp. 16, 18, 22, 25. The second is transcribed also in Wang Chang, *Jinshi cuibian*, 74.6a–b. Tonami (pp. 49–52) suggests that the renowned monk Yixing (673–727) contributed to Xuanzong's decision to support the monastery. Yixing, who is mentioned in the first letter (dated December 6, 723), was serving at the time as court astronomer.

47. See Zhang Yue's biography in *Xin Tang shu*, 125.4404–4412; see also Twitchett, "Hsüan-tsung (Reign 712–756)," pp. 338–340, 376–379, and 387–389.

48. Written in elegant clerical script (*lishu*) the caption reads "Taizong Wenhuang di yu shu" ("Emperor Taizong Wenhuang Imperial Letter").

49. The latter included Xu Jian (?–729) and Zhao Dongxi (fl. 720), whose signatures appear on the letter. Xu's and Zhao's respective biographies in the *Xin Tang shu* 199.5663 and 200.5702 attest that they worked under Zhang Yue in the Academy in the Hall of Elegance and Rectitude, which name was changed in 725 to the Academy of Scholarly Worthies (Jixiandian shuyuan). On Zhang Yue's directorship of the Academy, see *Xin Tang shu*, 125.4408.

50. Weinstein, *Buddhism Under the T'ang*, p. 51.

51. The confiscation order is included in the *Tang Hui Yao*, 59.1028. According to Pei Cui, the emperor expressly exempted the Shaolin Monastery from it; see his

inscription as transcribed in Wang Chang, *Jinshi cuibian*, 77.18b. See also Tonami, *The Shaolin Monastery Stele on Mount Song*, pp. 47–48.

52. Tonami, *The Shaolin Monastery Stele on Mount Song*, pp. 47–52.

53. Gu Shaolian's history is titled "Song yue Shaolin xin zao chu ku ji" ("Record of the Reconstruction of the Song Mountain Shaolin Monastery's Kitchen and Store-house"). It was inscribed on a Shaolin stele, which today is badly damaged. However, the text in full is transcribed in such late Ming sources as Fu Mei, *Song shu*, 20.13a–16b. Gu Shaolian's biography is available in *Xin Tang shu*, 162.4994–4995. Compare also *Jiu Tang shu*, 13.396.

54. The governor was accompanied by two lower ranking officials, Lu Yin and Yuan You. His visit is dated Huichang, fifth year, second month, twenty-sixth day. The visit was recorded on the narrow side of the same stele as Gu Shaolian's letter. I am grateful to A'de who pointed to me this inscription, which, to the best of my knowledge, is nowhere transcribed. On Wuzong's suppression of Buddhism, see Weinstein, *Buddhism Under the T'ang*, pp. 114–136.

55. My translation is based on an original rubbing. Compare also the transcriptions in Tonami, *The Shaolin Monastery Stele on Mount Song*, p. 22; and Xu Changqing, *Shaolin si yu Zhongguo wenhua*, p. 104.

56. As is evident from the usage of his posthumous temple name, Taizong.

57. Of the seven texts inscribed on the Shaolin stele, the list of thirteen monks appears last. Thus conceivably it could have been added to the stele at a later date. In particular, the reference to the Tang raises the suspicion that the list of thirteen monks might have been compiled after that period (all the other documents on the stele are dated by reign periods only). Nonetheless, late Ming scholars such as Du Mu and Gu Yanwu concluded that "thirteen monks had been recognized for their merit." See Du Mu, *You mingshan ji*, 19a; and Gu Yanwu, "Shaolin seng bing," in Gu Yanwu, *Rizhilu jishi*, 29.21b.

58. Daoxuan, *Xu Gaoseng zhuan*, T, no. 2060, 50:553c. According to Pei Cui, Sengchou served as Shaolin's abbot. See his "Shaolin si bei" as transcribed in Wang Chang, *Jinshi cuibian*, 77.16b.

59. The original has *jun*, which equals thirty *jin*. A Tang period *jin* equaled approximately one and a half English pounds.

60. *Chaoye qian zai*, 2.21–22. The story's relevance to Shaolin history has been pointed out by Kuang Wennan, "Shaolin xiwu de faduan ji zaoqi Daojiao wushu," p. 10; and A'de, "Jinnaluo wang kao," p. 99.

61. This is, for example, the typical iconography of the Four Lokapālas, divine guardians of the universe, also known as the Catur Mahārājas (Chinese: Hushi Si Tianwang). See Stein, *Serinida*, 2:870–876; Getty, *Gods of Northern Buddhism*, pp. 166–168; and Demiéville, "Le Bouddhisme et la guerre," pp. 375–376.

62. The Chinese "jin'gang" renders the Sanskrit's secondary meaning of "diamond." See Monier-Williams, *Sanskrit-English Dictionary*, p. 913; and "jin'gang" in *Foguang da cidian*, 4:3532–3533. Vajrapāṇi is sometimes identified with Indra. See Lamotte, "Vajrapāṇi in India," pp. 1–9. See also Frédéric, *Les dieux du Bouddhisme*, pp. 209–211; and Getty, *The Gods of Northern Buddhism*, pp. 50–53, 200.

63. See "kongō" and "kongōsyo," in Mochizuki Shinkō, *Bukkyō daijiten*, 2:1309 and 2:1333–1335 respectively. See also Frédéric, *Les dieux du Bouddhisme*, pp. 60–62.

64. See "Jin'gang lishi" and "Erwangzun" in *Foguang da cidian*, 4:3534–3535 and 1:190–191 respectively; see also Frédéric, *Les dieux du Bouddhisme*, pp. 247–249.

65. Stein, *Serinida*, 2:876.

66. Yu, *Journey to the West*, 2:167. The original is Wu Cheng'en, *Xiyou ji*, 36.412.

67. Strickmann, *Chinese Magical Medicine*, p. 67.

68. See "Naluoyan li chi jin'gang," "Naluoyantian," and "Jin'gang lishi" in *Foguang da cidian*, 3:3029–3030 and 4:3534–3535 respectively. See also "Nārāyaṇa" in Monier-Williams, *Sanskrit-English Dictionary*, pp. 536–537, and "Naraenkongō" in *Zengaku daijiten*, p. 967.

69. See *Tuoluoni ji jing*, compiled in China by the Indian monk Atikūṭa, *T*, no. 901, 18:880c–881a; on this sutra see Strickmann, *Mantras et mandarins*, pp. 133–163.

70. *Yiqie jing yinyi, T*, no. 2128, 54:340a.

71. See A'de's transcription in his "Jinnaluo wang kao," p. 99.

72. See Kieschnick, "Buddhist Vegetarianism in China"; Goossaert, *L'interdit du boeuf en Chine*, pp. 51–71; and ter Haar, "Buddhist-Inspired Options," pp. 129–137.

73. Chen Li-li, *Master Tung's Western Chamber Romance*, pp. 46–47. Compare also the play's thirteenth-century *zaju* version, Wang Shifu, *The Moon and the Zither: The Story of the Western Wing*, ed. and trans. Stephen H. West and Wilt L. Idema, pp. 232–234.

74. See Shahar, "Lucky Dog;" and Weller, *Resistance, Chaos and Control in China*, pp. 134–135.

75. See Kieschnick, "Buddhist Vegetarianism in China."

76. Shapiro, *Outlaws of the Marsh*, 1:75.

77. See Ching [Chen Xing Hua], "How Jet Li Saved the Shaolin Temple."

78. Bloch, *The Historian's Craft*, p. 45.

79. See Gene Ching's essays "The 'One' of the Top Ten: Shaolin Grandmaster Liang Yiquan," "13,000 Warriors of Taguo," and "In the Dragon's Den."

80. See Ching [Chen Xing Hua], "Shaolin Temple's Prodigal Son"; and Jakes, "Kicking the Habit." On other United States Shaolin Temples, see Ching, "Shaolin Brothers Go West," and Ching and Oh, "Shaolin's Second Wave."

81. See Gene Ching's essays "The World Heritage of Shaolin" and "United Nations, Divided Shaolin." See also Jakes, "Kicking the Habit."

82. The emperor's edict is included in the 1748 *Shaolin si zhi*, "chenhan," 4b–5a. See also Wen Yucheng, *Shaolin fanggu*, pp. 341–342; and Zhou Weiliang, "Ming-Qing shiqi Shaolin wushu de lishi liubian," pp. 8–9. On the Yongzheng emperor, see Zelin, "The Yung-Cheng Reign," p. 202.

83. See Huang Changlun, "Lüzong diyi daochang," pp. 53–54.

84. See Wang Shixing, *Yu zhi*, p. 6.

85. The magistrate's warning was engraved on a Shaolin stele, for which transcription I am indebted to A'de.

86. Ibid.

87. Quoted in *Kang Yong Qian shiqi chengxiang renmin fankang douzheng ziliao*, 2:619.

88. The warning was engraved on the back side of a stele, which contains a 1595 letter of patronage by the Dengfeng County magistrate. I am grateful to A'de for pointing it to me.

89. See Shahar, *Crazy Ji*, pp. 30–45; and Welch, *The Practice of Chinese Buddhism*, p. 16. On meat-eating monks, see also Kieschnick, *The Eminent Monk: Buddhist Ideals in Medieval Chinese Hagiography*, pp. 51–63; and Faure, *The Red Thread: Buddhist Approaches to Sexuality*, pp. 151–53.

90. The other guardian deity mentioned is Kapila (Jiapiluo shen). See *Guang hong ming ji*, *T*, no. 2103, 52:298a; and Soper, *Literary Evidence for Early Buddhist Art in China*, pp. 74, 229. I am grateful to Susan Bush for this reference.

3. Defending the Nation

1. See, for example, Zhu Guozhen (1557–1632), *Yongchuang xiaopin*, 28.673; *Zuixing shi* (ca. 1650), 12.101; and *Pingyao zhuan*, revised by Feng Menglong (1574–1646), 10.59.

2. See *Jin Ping Mei cihua*, 90.1244.

3. Yu Dayou, "A poem, with prologue, sent to the Shaolin monk Zongqing," in his *Zhengqi tang xuji*, 2.7a.

4. See Hou Anguo's preface to the *Shaolin gunfa chan zong*. On Cheng Zongyou see also Lin Boyuan, *Zhongguo tiyu shi*, p. 337.

5. Chen Jiru (1558–1639), for example, wrote the preface to Cheng's *She shi* (History of archery).

6. Huang Baijia's martial instructor, Wang Zhengnan (1617–1669), received no formal education and earned his livelihood as a manual laborer. See Huang Zongxi's epitaph for Wang in his *Nanlei wending*, 8.128–130; and Wile, *T'ai Chi's Ancestors*, pp. 55–57.

7. The titles of the other three manuals included are *Juezhang xin fa* (Essentials of the crossbow method); *Changqiang fa xuan* (Selections of the long spear method); and *Dandao fa xuan* (Selections of the broadsword method). Cheng's *Shaolin gunfa* is available also in an edition titled *Shaolin gun jue* (The Shaolin staff formulas), which carries a forged preface attributed to the earlier Yu Dayou (1503–1579).

8. Yu Dayou, "A poem, with prologue, sent to the Shaolin monk Zongqing," in his *Zhengqi tang xuji*, 2.7a.

9. A spear manual attributed to Hongzhuan and titled *Menglü tang qiangfa* is included in Wu Shu, *Shoubi lu*, pp. 113–124.

10. Cheng Zongyou, *Shaolin gunfa*, 1.1b–2b.

11. Mao Yuanyi, *Wubei zhi*, 88.1a.

12. Ibid., chapters 88–90.

13. See Cheng Zongyou, *Shaolin gunfa*, 2.1a, 3.8b. For the relevant conversions, see "Ming Weights and Measures," in *The Cambridge History of China*, vol. 7, p. xxi.

14. Cheng Zongyou, *Shaolin gunfa*, 3.8a–b.

15. Ibid., 1.5b–6b.

16. Ibid., 3.7b–8a.

17. Ibid., 1.1b–2b; 3.7b.

18. Tang Shunzhi, *Wu bian*, 5.39b. On Tang Shunzhi, see Goodrich, *Dictionary of Ming Biography*, 2:1252–1256.

19. See respectively Qi Jiguang, *Jixiao xinshu: shiba juan ben,* 14.229; Mao Yuanyi, *Wubei zhi*, chapters 88–90; and He Liangchen, *Zhenji*, 2.27. On Qi, see Huang, *1587 A Year of No Significance*, pp. 156–188; and Goodrich, *Dictionary of Ming Biography*, 1:220–224. On Mao, see Goodrich, *Dictionary of Ming Biography*, 2:1053–1054. On He, see Lin Boyuan, *Zhongguo tiyu shi*, pp. 319–320.

20. Wu Qiao, *Weilu shihua*.

21. See Wu Shu, *Shoubi lu*, pp. 109–111, for his initiation into the martial arts. On Wu and his teacher Shi Dian, see also Ma Mingda, *Shuo jian cong gao*, pp. 88–111; Lin Boyuan, *Zhongguo tiyu shi*, pp. 339–340; Matsuda Ryūchi, *Zhongguo wushu shilüe*, pp. 28–30; and "Shoubi lu," in *Siku da cidian*, p. 1633.

22. Wu Shu, *Shoubi lu*, preface, p. 1.

23. Ibid., p. 113.

24. See Goodrich, *Dictionary of Ming Biography*, 2:1616–1618.

25. Yu's *Jian jing* must have circulated as an independent volume prior to 1562, when Qi Jiguang quoted it in full in his *Jixiao xinshu: shiba juan ben*, 12.184–219. It is also available in Yu's collected writings, which were published in three installments between 1565 and the early 1580s under the titles *Zhengqi tang ji, Zhengqi tang xuji,* and *Zhengqi tang yuji.* The *Jian jing* is in the *yuji;* see the combined 1841 edition of all three installments. He Liangchen praises the *Jian jing* in his *Zhenji*, 2.27.

26. I am not sure of the reason for this usage in Yu's writings. Perhaps he applied the word "sword" for "staff" because the former had already appeared in the name of the staff method, Jingchu Long Sword (Jingchu changjian), which he studied. Cheng Dali suggests that "sword" signifies in this instance the entire martial arts tradition rather than the concrete weapon; see his *Zhongguo wushu*, pp. 121–123. In any event the text of Yu's *Sword Classic* leaves no doubt that it is concerned with staff fighting (rather than fencing), as indeed was clear to Yu's contemporaries Qi Jiguang and He Liangchen. See also Tang Hao, *Shaolin Wudang kao*, p. 42; Tang Hao, *Shaolin quanshu mijue kaozheng*, pp. 67–69; Lin Boyuan, *Zhongguo tiyu shi*, pp. 317–318; Lin Boyuan, "Tan Zhongguo wushu zai Mingdai de fazhan bianhua," pp. 67–68; and Matsuda Ryūchi, *Zhongguo wushu shilüe.* pp. 7–9, 52–53.

27. The Yin/Yang terminology figures in Yu's *Sword Classic*, as in the formula: "The Yin and the Yang should alternate, the two hands need be straight." See *Jian jing*, in *Zhengqi tang yuji*, 4.3b.

28. Yu Dayou, "A poem, with prologue, sent to the Shaolin monk Zongqing," *Zhengqi tang xuji*, 2.7a–8a. An almost identical account of Yu's visit to the monastery is found in his 1577 "Inscription on the Renovation of the Universal Chan Courtyard," *Zhengqi tang xuji*, 3.6a–7b.

29. Tang Hao located only one shared formula in Yu's and Cheng's manuals: "*jiu li lüe guo, xin li wei fa*" ("[Strike when] one surge of [your rival's] energy is largely over, and before another has been generated"). Compare Yu Dayou, *Jian*

jing, in *Zhengqi tang yuji*, 4.23a, and Cheng Zongyou, *Shaolin gunfa*, 3.4a. See also Tang Hao, *Shaolin quanshu mijue kaozheng*, pp. 65–66; and Matsuda Ryūchi, *Zhongguo wushu shilüe*, p. 53.

30. The Shaolin method of the "Hidden Hands" (Yinshou), discussed in Cheng's *Shaolin gunfa*, is already mentioned in Tang Shunzhi's *Wu bian, qianji* (5.39b), which was compiled approximately ten years prior to Yu's visit to Shaolin.

31. Wu Shu, *Shoubi lu*, p. 89.

32. Tang Hao, *Shaolin quanshu mijue kaozheng*, pp. 68–69. See also Matsuda Ryūchi, *Zhongguo wushu shilüe*, p. 54.

33. On these roles—religious, cultural, social, and political—see, among others, Yü Chün-fang, "Ming Buddhism"; Yü Chün-fang, *The Renewal of Buddhism in China*; and Brook, *Praying for Power*.

34. See Wu Shu, *Shoubi lu*, p. 109.

35. Included in Wu Shu, *Shoubi lu*, pp. 93–109. It is tempting to speculate that Cheng Zhenru belonged to the same extended family as Cheng Zongyou. The former's birthplace is given as Haiyang, by which old county name the latter sometimes refers to his native place in Xiuning, Anhui.

36. See Cheng's introduction to his *Emei qiangfa*, in Wu Shu, *Shoubi lu*, p. 93.

37. See, respectively, Wu Shu, *Shoubi lu*, pp. 14, 93, 110; Cheng Zongyou, *Shaolin gunfa*, 1.2a; and Sanqi Yougong's epitaph inscribed on his burial stupa and still extant in Shaolin's Stupa Forest (Talin). On Shaolin itinerant warriors see also Xie Zhaozhe (1567–1624), *Wu zazu*, 5.23a.

38. Cai Jiude, for instance, alludes to a Shaolin monk as a member of the "rivers and lakes." See Cai Jiude, *Wobian shilüe* (preface 1558), 1.9–10. Compare also Wu Shu, *Shoubi lu*, preface p. 1.

39. Yun Youke, *Jianghu congtan*, pp. 191–220.

40. See Chen Pingyuan, *Qiangu wenren xiake meng*, pp. 187–228.

41. See Needham and Yates, *Science and Civilization in China*, vol. 5, part VI, pp. 27–29.

42. Huang, *1587 A Year of No Significance*, p. 159.

43. See *Mingshi*, 91.2251–2252. See also Hucker, "Ming Government," p. 69.

44. For general background, see Geiss, "The Chia-ching Reign," pp. 490–505; Kwan-wai So, *Japanese Piracy in Ming China*; and Antony, *Like Froth Floating on the Sea*, pp. 22–28.

45. The "Seng bing shou jie ji" is in chapter 8b.

46. On Zheng, see Goodrich, *Dictionary of Ming Biography*, 1:204–208.

47. Compare Zheng Ruoceng, *Jiangnan jing lüe*, 8b.16b; Cai Jiude, *Wobian shilüe*, 1.9–10; and Wan Biao's epitaph in Jiao Hong (1541–1620), *Guochao xianzheng lu* 107.82b. On Wan, see Goodrich, *Dictionary of Ming Biography*, 2:1337–1339.

48. Three sixteenth-century gazetteers allude to the participation of "monastic troops" (*seng bing*) in this battle, even though none of them specifies to which monastery they belonged. See the 1561 *Zhejiang tongzhi* (chap. 60); the Jiajing period (1522–1566) *Ningbo fu zhi* (chap. 22); and the 1579 *Hangzhou fu zhi* (chap. 7). The relevant passages from all three gazetteers are reproduced in *Mingdai wokou shiliao*, 5:1831,

5:1976, and 5:2073 respectively. Compare also Cai Jiude, *Wobian shilüe*, 1.9–10. Zheng Ruoceng, *Jiangnan jing lüe*, 8b.17a, alludes to a monastic victory on Mount Zha, by which he is probably referring to Mount Zhe.

49. Compare Zheng Ruoceng, *Jiangnan jing lüe*, 8b.19a–23a, with Zhang Nai (*jinshi* 1604), *Wusong jia yi wo bian zhi*, 2.38b–39b. For locations in the Huangpu River delta, see *Shanghai lishi ditu ji*. I take it that Wengjiagang is today's Wengjia village, near Zhelin.

50. The four monks were Chetang, Yifeng, Zhenyuan, and Liaoxin. Their stupa is no longer extant. See Zhang Shutong, *Sheshan xiao zhi, Ganshan zhi*, p. 30. I am grateful to Yang Kun of the Songjiang Museum for this reference.

51. Zheng Ruoceng, *Jiangnan jing lüe*, 8b.21b.

52. Ibid., 8b.18a.

53. In this respect Zheng Ruoceng's chronicle illustrates the difficulty of separating historical and fictional martial arts narratives. It is noteworthy that another anecdote in Zheng's chronicle, concerning the monk Guzhou, was fictionally embellished within fifty years of its publication. Compare Zheng Ruoceng, *Jiangnan jing lüe*, 8b.16b–17a, with Zhu Guozhen, *Yongchuang xiaopin*, 28.673.

54. Zheng Ruoceng, *Jiangnan jing lüe*, 8b.22b.

55. See Xue Yu, *Buddhism, War, and Nationalism*, pp. 49–51, 55.

56. Two Dengfeng County documents confirm the participation of Shaolin monks in these campaigns. The documents, dated 1581 and 1595, were engraved in stone at the Shaolin Monastery, where they are still extant. See Wen Yucheng, *Shaolin fanggu*, pp. 292–293, 300–302; and Zeng Weihua and Yan Yaozhong, "Cong Shaolin si de ji fang bei ta mingwen kan Ming dai sengbing." The participation of monastic troops (*sengbing*) in the 1511 war with the Liu brothers is confirmed by Gu Yingtai, *Mingshi jishi benmo* (1658), 45.9b. Gu does not specify to which monastery they belonged. See also Robinson, *Bandits, Eunuchs, and the Son of Heaven*, pp. 136–137.

57. See Wen Yucheng, *Shaolin fanggu*, pp. 292–298, and Zeng Weihua and Yan Yaozhong, "Cong Shaolin si de ji fang bei ta mingwen kan Ming dai sengbing."

58. The poem is included in the *Shaolin si zhi*, 11.7a. It is quoted and discussed in Xu Changqing, *Shaolin si yu Zhongguo wenhua*. p. 228. See Cheng's biography in *Mingshi*, 242.6282–6283.

59. This passage is from the 1595 letter. The Liu bandits were active during the late Zhengde (1506–1521)—not the Jiajing—reign. I am grateful to A'de, who provided me with transcriptions of both letters. See also Wen Yucheng, *Shaolin fanggu*, pp. 300–302.

60. The edict is quoted in the *Shaolin si zhi*, "*chenhan*," p. 4a.

61. See Wen Yucheng, *Shaolin fanggu*, pp. 290–291. On Zhang, see Goodrich, *Dictionary of Ming Biography*, 1:111–113.

62. See Yang Tinghe (1459–1529), *Yang Wenzhong san lu*, 4.5b; and Wang Shizhen (1526–1590), *Yanshan tang bieji*, 97.1847.

63. See A'de, "Qianfo dian ji bihua kao"; *Shaolin si qianfodian bihua*, pp. 19, 104; and *Xin bian Shaolin si zhi*, pp. 27–28.

64. See *Ming shi lu*, Wuzong reign, 86.1851.

65. On Zhu Yuanzhang's early years at the monastery, see Wu Han, *Zhu Yuan-zhang zhuan*, pp. 11–16, and Mote, "The Rise of the Ming Dynasty, 1330–1367," pp. 44–45.

66. *Gushan Yongjue heshang guanglu*, 24.16a.

67. The hells of fire, blood, and knives.

68. *Gushan Yongjue heshang guanglu*, 24.16a–b.

69. Huang Zongxi, *Nanlei wending*, 8.130; and Wile, *T'ai-chi's Ancestors*, p. 56.

70. See Zheng Ruoceng, *Jiangnan jing lüe*, 8b.22b; He Liangchen, *Zhenji*, 2.27; and Wen Yucheng, *Shaolin fanggu*, p. 298.

71. See A'de, "Mingdai lamajiao yu Shaolin si." On the Tibetan monk's fight-ing techniques, see Cheng Zongyou, *Shaolin gunfa*, 1.1b.

72. See Cheng Zongyou, *Shaolin gunfa*, 1.1b; Fu Mei, *Song shu*, 9.33b–34; and Wen Yucheng, *Shaolin fanggu*, pp. 309–310.

73. See Cheng Zongyou, *Shaolin gunfa*, 1.1b.

74. See *Jizu shan zhi*, 6.6b–7a. The *Jizu shan zhi* erroneously has Bianqun in-stead of Biandun. It alludes to Vajrapāṇi by the sixteenth-century name he was given at the Shaolin Monastery: Jinnaluo, on which see chapter 4 below.

75. See Wu Shu, *Shoubi lu*, p. 110; and Ma Mingda, *Shuo jian cong gao*, p. 95.

76. Naquin, *Peking Temples and City Life*, p. xxxi.

77. Zhang Dai (1597–ca. 1670), *Langhuan wenji*, p. 37, translated by Wu Pei-Yi, "An Ambivalent Pilgrim to T'ai Shan," p. 77.

78. Yun Youke, *Jianghu congtan*, p. 201.

79. Huang Baijia, *Neijia quanfa*, p. 1b; and Wile, *T'ai-chi's Ancestors*, p. 58.

80. See Ma Mingda, *Shuo jian cong gao*, pp. 68–76.

81. See Xu Mengxin, *San chao bei meng huibian*, 48.8b–9a, 51.9b, and Ma Mingda, *Shuo jian cong gao*, pp. 68–69.

82. *Songshi*, 455.13382.

83. See *Shuihu quanzhuan*, 4.62 (Sidney Shapiro's translation, *Outlaws of the Marsh*, p. 65), and the two late Ming versions of the Yang Family Saga: *Yangjia jiang yanyi* (50 chapters), by Xiong Damu (fl. 1550), 25.118–26.125, 38.179–180, and *Yangjia jiang yanyi* (58 chapters) (Preface 1606), by Ji Zhenlun, 15.98–17.109; 31.189–191; 36.212–213; see also Ma Mingda, *Shuo jian cong gao*, pp. 71–73.

84. Both monks figure in a Southern Song list of subjects popular among story-tellers. See Luo Ye, *Xinbian zuiweng tanlu*, p. 4. Lu is referred to in the story by his nick-name "Tattooed Monk" (Hua Heshang).

85. See Wu Shu, *Shoubi lu*, pp. 93–109.

86. Tang Shunzhi, "Emei daoren quan ge," in Tang Shunzhi, *Jingchuan xian-sheng wenji*, 2.8b–9a.

87. Mt. Yu is in Changshu County, Jiangsu.

88. The "nobleman" was Zhang's friend Li Zhuyi, in whose house Li Lantian sojourned. Zhang's poem was authored for Li Zhuyi's manual of Li Lantian's style. See Ma Mingda, *Shuo jian cong gao*, pp. 206–211.

89. The "Six-Flowers Formation" (Liuhua zhen) was attributed to the renowned

Tang general Li Jing (571–649). See Sawyer, *The Seven Military Classics*, pp. 339, 341, 344–345.

90. Included in Yuan Xingyun, *Qingren shiji xulu*, 1:399.

91. The origins of the Sha Family Fist are obscure. It is possible, however, that the family in question was of Muslim descent. See Ma Mingda, *Shuo jian cong gao*, p. 210.

92. Mining fantasies assume surprising twists and turns. Nineteenth-century Russian and Chinese gold hunters on the banks of the Amur were believed to have created a communist republic there. See Gamsa, "How a Republic of Chinese Red Beards Was Invented in Paris."

93. Wang Shixing (1547–1598), *Yu zhi*, p. 6. The Ming suspicion of miners was not unfounded, as mine pilfering was common. See Tong, *Disorder under Heaven*, pp. 60, 64. As noted above, in 1522–1523, Shaolin monks were drafted to fight the miner turned bandit Wang Tang.

94. Zheng Ruoceng, *Jiangnan jing lüe*, 8b.22b. See also He Liangchen, *Zhenji*, 2.27; and *Mingshi*, 91.2252.

95. See *Song xian zhi*, p. 837; and *Yunyan si*, p. 16.

96. A'de wrote of our trip in his "Funiu shan xing ji."

97. "Funiu shan Yunyan si ji," transcribed in *Yunyan si*, pp. 38–40.

4. Staff Legends

1. See respectively Wu Shu, *Shoubi lu*, pp. 113–120; Tang Shunzhi, "Emei dao-ren quan ge," in Tang Shunzhi. *Jingchuan xiansheng wenji*, 2.8b; Zheng Ruoceng, *Jiangnan jing lüe*, 8b.18b; and Cheng Zongyou, *Shaolin gunfa*, 3.7b.

2. Zheng Ruoceng, *Jiangnan jing lüe*, 8b.16b. Guzhou might have been trained at a monastery other than Shaolin.

3. See Cheng Zongyou, *Shaolin gunfa*, 1.1b; Fu Mei, *Song shu*, 9.30b–31a; *Shunzhi Dengfeng xian zhi*; and *Henan fu zhi*. The legend was further elaborated in eighteenth-century sources such as Jing Rizhen, *Shuo Song*, 8.2b, 21.26a–27a; and *Shaolin si zhi*, 1.12a–b. See also *Kangxi Dengfeng xian zhi*, 8.8a.

4. The term *hufa* is usually applied to the four Lokapālas, who serve as protectors of the world (each guarding one quarter of space) and the Buddhist faith.

5. The inscription is still located at the monastery. It is transcribed in A'de, "Jinnaluo wang kao," pp. 100–101. For a biography of its author, Wenzai, see Fu Mei, *Song shu*, 9.32b–33b. Wenzai cites as his source the now-lost "Jingzhu ji" ("Admired Traces") by a monk Ziyong.

6. On the Red Turbans uprising, see Mote, "Rise of the Ming Dynasty," pp. 38–40, 42–43; and ter Haar, *White Lotus Teachings*, pp. 115–123. The movement's political mastermind was Liu Futong, and its religious leader was Han Shantong, who declared the imminent arrival of the Buddha Maitreya. Following Han's capture and execution, his son Han Liner was installed by Liu as emperor of a new Song dynasty.

7. Tang Hao, *Shaolin quanshu mijue kaozheng*, pp. 55–62.

8. The inscriptions, titled "Chong zhuang fo xiang bei" ("Stele Commemorating the [Gold] Re-Coating of the Buddha Images") and "Chongxiu fatang bei ming" ("Stele Inscription Commemorating the Renovation of the Dharma-Hall"),

are outlined in the *Shaolin si zhi*, 3.9a–b and 3.10b–11a respectively. The former provides 1371 as the renovation date. The two epitaphs, for the monks Jungong and Xungong, were inscribed on their respective stupas; the relevant passages are transcribed in Tang Hao, *Shaolin quanshu mijue kaozheng*, pp. 55–58, where he analyzes them in conjunction with the stele inscriptions.

9. Tang Hao, *Shaolin quanshu mijue kaozheng*, pp. 56–61.

10. See A'de's transcription of Zuduan's stele in "Jinnaluo wang kao," p. 99.

11. This is Leon Hurvitz's translation (slightly altered), *Scripture of the Lotus Blossom of the Fine Dharma*, p. 315. The original is *Miaofa lianhua jing*, *T*, no. 262, 9:57b. See also A'de, "Jinnaluo wang kao," pp. 98–99.

12. See Wenzai's 1517 version as transcribed in A'de, "Jinnaluo wang kao," pp. 100–101; Fu Mei, *Song shu*, 9.31a; and Jing Rizhen, *Shuo Song*, 21.26b.

13. On the evolution of the Guangong and Zhiyi legend, see Huang Huajie, *Guangong de renge yu shenge*, pp. 106–116. The legend is mirrored in the Ming period novel *Sanguo yanyi*, 77.617–618, where the monk's name is changed from Zhiyi to Pujing. See also Moss Roberts' translation, *Three Kingdoms*, pp. 585–586. On Guangong's Daoist aspect, see ter Haar, "The Rise of the Guan Yu Cult: The Taoist Connection."

14. In some monasteries Guangong shares the office of "guardian spirit" with other deities; see Prip-Møller, *Chinese Buddhist Monasteries*, pp. 204, 224.

15. See Shahar, *Crazy Ji*, pp. 30–45.

16. Yampolsky, *The Platform Sutra of the Sixth Patriarch*, pp. 128, 131–132.

17. See "*kinnara*" in Mochizuki Shinkō, *Bukkyō daijiten* 1:543–544. See also "*kinnara*," in Nakamura Hajime, *Bukkyōgo daijiten*, pp. 250–251. In China the Kiṃnaras were known as members of the Buddha's retinue, which was made up of eight types of divine beings, collectively called the "Eight Categories of Devas, Nāgas, [and Other Divine Beings]" (Tianlong babu). See *Miaofa lianhua jing*, *T*, no. 262, 9:12a; and Hurvitz, *Scripture of the Lotus Blossom of the Fine Dharma*, p. 56.

18. See A'de, "Jinnaluo wang kao," pp. 99, 103.

19. See *Miaofa lianhua jing*, *T*, no. 262, 9:2a; and Hurvitz, *Scripture of the Lotus Blossom of the Fine Dharma*, pp. 2–3.

20. Cheng Zongyou, *Shaolin gunfa*, 1.1b.

21. On the location of the "Imperial Fort," see *Shaolin si zhi*, 1.1b–2a. The name "Mt. Song" refers in this instance to the peak of this name, and not to the entire mountain range (of which Shaoshi is another peak).

22. Fu Mei, *Song shu*, 9.30b.

23. The earliest explicit references to a Kiṃnara Hall date from the eighteenth century. See Jing Rizhen, *Shuo Song*, 8.2b, 21.27a; *Shaolin si zhi*, 1.6a; and *Kangxi Dengfeng xian zhi*, 8.1b. However, it might have been erected much earlier. The fourteenth-century Shaolin stele "Epitaph for Chan Master Fenglin" ("Fenglin chanshi xingzhuang") already mentions a "Guardian Spirit Hall" (*qielan shen tang*), but it does not specify which deity was venerated there. See A'de, "Jinnaluo wang kao," p. 99.

24. See *Shaolin si zhi*, 1.6a.

25. See Shahar, *Crazy Ji*, p. 197.

26. On the twentieth-century vicissitudes of the Jinnaluo Hall, see *Xin bian Shaolin si zhi*, p. 23; and Ching, "Shaolin Temple Reincarnated."

27. See *Shangdang gu sai xiejuan shisi zhong jianzhu*, pp. 366–369.

28. On the dating of the Thousand Buddhas Hall and its wall painting, see *Shaolin si qianfodian bihua*, pp. 19, 104; and A'de, "Qianfo dian ji bihua kao," p. 51, where he argues that the painting must have been completed before 1623.

29. Compare arhat images in *Luohan hua* and in Kent, "Depictions of the Guardians of the Law."

30. Demiéville, "Le Bouddhisme et la guerre," p. 375.

31. See Harvey, *An Introduction to Buddhist Ethics*, pp. 137–138.

32. See Demiéville, "Le Bouddhisme et la guerre," pp. 380–381.

33. This is Mark Tatz's translation, quoted in Harvey, *An Introduction to Buddhist Ethics*, p. 137. See also Demiéville, "Le Bouddhisme et la guerre," pp. 379–380.

34. Zimmerman, "A Mahānist Criticism of ārthaśāstra; and Zimmerman, "War," in Buswell, *Encyclopedia of Buddhism*, pp. 893–897.

35. See, respectively, Victoria, *Zen at War*, esp. pp. 86–91, and Yu, *Buddhism, War, and Nationalism*, pp. 136–149. See also Sharf, "The Zen of Japanese Nationalism." On Japanese monk-warriors, see Adolphson, *The Teeth and Claws of the Buddha*.

36. See Cheng Zongyou, *Shaolin gunfa*, 1.4b.

37. Yu Dayou, *jian jing*, 4.3a. This passage is quoted by Qi Jiguang (*Jixiao xinshu* 12.184) and is echoed by Cheng Zongyou (*Shaolin gunfa*, 3.1a). See also Lin Boyuan, "Tan Zhongguo wushu zai Mingdai de fazhan," pp. 66–68.

38. On the evolution of the *Journey to the West* cycle, see Dudbridge, *Hsi-yu chi*; and Dudbridge, "The *Hsi-yu chi* Monkey and the Fruits of the Last Ten Years." On Sun Wukong's origins, see Shahar, "The Lingyin si Monkey Disciples." On his religious cult, see Sawada Mizuho, "Songokū shin"; and Elliot, *Chinese Spirit Medium Cults in Singapore*, pp. 74–76, 80–109, 170–171.

39. I suspect that the English renditions of *bang* as "club" or "cudgel" are misleading, for they suggest a short and heavy instrument, whereas the description of Sun Wukong's weapon in the novel—no less than its depiction in Ming woodblock prints—leaves no doubt that it is a long rod, similar to the Shaolin staff. More generally, an examination of Ming sources reveals that the terms *bang* and *gun* refer to the same weapon. In his *Wubei zhi* (104.1a), for example, Mao Yuanyi explains that "the *bang* and the *gun* are the same thing" (*bang yu gun yi ye*). In the sixteenth-century novel, Sun Wukong's "Ruyi jingu bang" is sometimes referred to as *gun*. See Wu Cheng'en, *Xiyou ji*, 27.310–311.

The difference between *gun* and *bang* is grammatical rather than semantical. Whereas the former can be used without a qualifying adjective, the latter commonly appears in compounds such as *tiebang* (iron *bang*), *ganbang* (wooden *bang*), and, of course, "Ruyi jingu bang."

40. Yu, *Journey to the West*, 1:108; the original is Wu Cheng'en, *Xiyou ji*, 3.30–31. I have changed Yu's "cudgel" to "staff" (see the preceding note).

41. Yu, *Journey to the West*, 1:167–168; Wu Cheng'en, *Xiyou ji*, 7.70.

42. Two slightly different versions of this Southern Song text survive. Both are

photographically reproduced in *Da Tang Sanzang fashi qu jing shihua*. Since both texts were originally discovered at the Kōzanji Monastery in Kyoto, they are sometimes called the "Kōzanji version." On their dating, see Dudbridge, *Hsi-yu chi*, pp. 25–29.

43. See Wang Shifu, *Xixiang ji*, 2.60–61; and Wang Shifu, *The Moon and the Zither*, pp. 232–234.

44. Chen Li-li, *Master Tung's Western Chamber Romance*, p. 58. The original is Dong Jieyuan, *Dong Jieyuan Xixiang*, 2.79. I have substituted "staff" for Chen Li-li's "cudgel" (see note 39 above).

45. See Chen Li-li, *Master Tung's Western Chamber Romance*, pp. 45–46; and Dong Jieyuan, *Dong Jieyuan Xixiang* 2.61–62; On the *jiedao*, see "tōsu" in Mochizuki Shinkō, *Bukkyō daijiten*, 4:3879–3880, and illustration no. 1147.

46. See Luo Ye, *Xinbian Zuiweng tanlu*, p. 4.

47. This is Sidney Shapiro's translation (slightly altered), *Outlaws of the Marsh*, 1:75–76. The original is *Shuihu quanzhuan*, 4.69–70.

48. See Wu Cheng'en, *Xiyou ji*, 22.245–255; and Yu, *Journey to the West*, 1:429–443. On "Sha Monk" and the "God of the Deep Sands," see Dudbridge, *Hsi-yu chi*, pp. 18–21, and Strickmann, *Chinese Magical Medicine*, pp. 110–111, 312 n. 47.

49. See *Zhongguo wushu da cidian*, pp. 103, 113, 195–196.

50. See *Yangjia jiang yanyi* (50 chapters), 38.179, and *Yangjia jiang yanyi* (58 chapters), 31.190–191. In the latter version (17.108) the monk is also armed with a sword.

51. See "Wulang wei seng," in Luo Ye, *Xinbian zuiweng tanlu*, p. 4.

52. Cheng Dali, *Zhongguo wushu*, p. 96.

53. Fayun, *Fanyi mingyi ji*, *T*, no. 2131, 54:1169b. On the ring staff, see Kieschnick, *The Impact of Buddhism on Chinese Material Culture*, pp. 113–115. See also "shakujō," in Mochizuki Shinkō, *Bukkyō daijiten*, 3:2152–2153; and "shakujō," in *Zengaku daijiten*, p. 469.

54. *Dedao ticheng xizhang jing*, *T*, no. 785, 17:724c, Kieschnick, *Impact of Buddhism on Chinese Material Culture*, p. 113. It was probably translated into Chinese during the Eastern Jin (317–420) period.

55. Liu Yanshi (fl. 800), in *Quan Tang shi*, 468.5328; Kieschnick, *Impact of Buddhism on Chinese Material Culture*, p. 115.

56. *Quan Tang shi*, 446.5006.

57. Originally from a temple in north China, this wall painting is currently at the Metropolitan Museum of Art, New York. See *The Metropolitan Museum of Art: Asia*, pp. 84–85.

58. See "Crosier," in *The Oxford Dictionary of the Christian Church*, p. 357.

59. On the religious and political significance of the staff in the ancient Near East, see "ma'teh" in *Encyclopedia Mikra'it*, 4:825–832.

60. Exodus 7:14.

61. I substitute "rattled" for Victor Mair's "shook." See his *Tun-huang Popular Narratives*, pp. 105, 107; the original is *Dunhuang bianwen ji*, pp. 730, 732.

62. See Teiser, *The Ghost Festival in Medieval China*; and Johnson, *Ritual Opera, Operatic Ritual*.

63. Compare de Groot, "Buddhist Masses for the Dead at Amoy," pp. 94–96; and Dean, "Lei Yu-sheng" ("Thunder Is Noisy"), pp. 54–57, 63–64.

64. Wang Qiao, who was the heir apparent to the Zhou dynasty king Ling, was reputed to ride a white crane. I have substituted "staffs" for "staves" in Mather's "The Mystical Ascent of the T'ient'ai Mountains," p. 242; the original is "You Tiantai shan fu" ("Poetic essay on roaming the Tiantai Mountains"), in *Wen xuan*, 11.499.

65. See respectively, Du Fu, in *Quan Tang shi*, 232.2565; and Liu Zongyuan, in *Quan Tang shi*, 352.3938.

66. Daocheng, *Shishi yaolan*, *T*, no. 2127, 54:298b.

67. Zanning, *Song Gaoseng zhuan*, *T*, no. 2061, 50:847a. See also the same legend in Daoyuan, *Jingde chuandeng lu* (1004), *T*, no. 2076, 51:259b–c.

68. *Da Tang Sanzang fashi qu jing shihua*, pp. 14, 24, 27, 31, 86–87, 96. In one instance, after subduing nine dragons with his magic ring staff, the monkey employs an "iron *bang*" (*tiebang*) to beat them up. Whereas the ring staff serves him for fighting, the "iron *bang*" is used to execute punishment (p. 32).

69. Sun Wukong's weapon is referred to in the Ming period *zaju* play *Journey to the West* as "golden *gun*" as well as "iron *bang*" (*tiebang*); see *Zaju Xiyou ji*, 11.48 and 19.87 respectively. (On the play's dating, see Dudbridge, *Hsi-yu chi*, pp. 76–80). Sun Wukong's elder brother, Tongtian Dasheng, is armed with an "iron *bang*" (*tiebang*) in the Ming period *zaju* play *Erlang Shen suo Qitian Dasheng*, 29:9b, 10b.

70. Wu Cheng'en, *Xiyou ji*, 3.28; and Yu, *The Journey to the West*, 1:105.

71. On the composite figure of Vaiśravaṇa and Mahābrahmā, see Dudbridge, *Hsi-yu chi*, pp. 32–35.

72. Dudbridge, *Hsi-yu chi*, p. 35; the original is *Da Tang Sanzang fashi qu jing shihua*, p. 27 (compare also pp. 31, 86–87).

73. See the sixteenth-century legend of monk Lianfeng, who transformed his ring staff into a purple dragon, *Huaicheng ye yu*, p. 304.

74. Exodus 7:8–12. I have substituted "staff" for "rod" in *The New Oxford Annotated Bible With the Apocrypha*, pp. 74–75.

5. Hand Combat

1. Tang Shunzhi, "Emei daoren quan ge," in Tang Shunzhi, *Jingchuan xiansheng wenji*, 2.8b.

2. Tang Shunzhi, *Wu bian, qianji*, 5.37a–5.39b.

3. Wang Shixing alludes to the Shaolin Monkey style of fighting; see his "Song you ji" (A journey to Mt. Song), in Wang Shixing, *Wuyue you cao*, 1.2b–3a. See also Gongnai, "Shaolin guan seng bishi ge" ("Watching the Shaolin monks compete"); Wen Xiangfeng, "You Shaolin ji" ("A Journey to Shaolin"), in *Shaolin si zhi*, 7.2a and 3.23a respectively; and Yuan Hongdao, "Songyou di yi" ("First account of a journey to Mt. Song"), in Yuan Hongdao, *Yuan Hongdao ji jian jiao*, 51.1475.

4. Cheng Zongyou, *Shaolin gunfa*, 3.7b.

5. See *Quan jing, Quan fa beiyao*, preface 1a–2a, 1.1, and 1.7, where Cao explains that Zhang Kongzhao's manual has been transmitted in his family for more than a century. Compare *Xuanji mishou*, preface 1a and 1.14a. Two other martial artists who

are mentioned in both manuals are Cheng Jingtao and Hu Wojiang; compare *Quan jing, Quan fa beiyao*, preface 1a; and *Xuanji mishou*, 1.3a. The latter manual alludes also to another military expert, Chen Songquan, who, Zhang Ming'e explains, was his teacher; see *Xuanji mishou*, preface 2a.

6. Compare *Quan jing, Quan fa beiyao*, 2.4a, 2.15a; and *Xuanji mishou*, illustrations 1.1a, 1.4a.

7. See Tang Hao and Gu Liuxin, *Taijiquan yanjiu*, p. 15; and Matsuda Ryūchi, *Zhongguo wushu shilüe*, pp. 34–35, 57–60.

8. See *Shaolin quanshu mijue*, p. 259, and Tang Hao, *Shaolin quanshu mijue kaozheng*, pp. 70–74, 99–138. The *Shaolin quanshu mijue* refers to Hongquan as Wuquan.

9. *Quan jing, Quan fa beiyao*, 1.1a. This is largely Douglas Wile's translation of the Qi Jiguang's passage that had served as the *Quan jing, Quan fa beiyao*'s source; see Wile, *T'ai Chi's Ancestors*, pp. 18–19.

10. In Qi Jiguang, *Jixiao xinshu: shiba juan ben*, 14.227–229; Wile, *T'ai Chi's Ancestors*, pp. 18–19.

11. Ming period lore attributed to Song Taizu also staff techniques, in which the historical emperor might have been versed; see Ma Mingda, *Shuo jian cong gao*, pp. 77–82. On contemporary Song Taizu practice, see Kash, "The Original Emperor's Long Fist System."

12. The stele is titled "Chongxiu Hengcuiting ji" ("Record of the suspended-emerald pavilion's reconstruction"). The 1677 Stupa Inscription of Shaolin's abbot Ningran Gaigong ("Ningran Gaigong taming beiji") alludes to Xuanji specifically as a "fighting monk" (*wu seng*). However, it writes his name *xuan* with the metal radical. I am grateful to A'de for both transcriptions.

13. Compare *Quan jing, Quan fa beiyao*, 1.2b; and *Xuanji mishou*, 1.16a–b.

14. *Quan jing, Quan fa beiyao*, 1.10b–13a.

15. *Xuanji mishou*, 1.11b–12a.

16. See Qi Jiguang, *Jixiao xinshu: shiba juan ben*, 14.229; He Liangchen, *Zhenji*, 2.26; Cheng Zongyou, *Shaolin gunfa*, 3.11a; and Tang Shunzhi, *Wu bian, qianji*, 5.37b. See also "*duanda*" in *Zhongguo wushu baike quanshu*, p. 171.

17. See Watson, *The Complete Works of Chuang Tzu*, 3.50–51.

18. *Xuanji mishou*, 1.3b.

19. See Shou-Yu Liang and Wen-Ching Wu, *Kung Fu Elements*, p. 363.

20. *Xuanji mishou*, 1.1a–b; where the terms are still being used, I consulted Shou-Yu Liang and Wen-Ching Wu, *Kung Fu Elements*.

21. See Strickmann, *Mantras et mandarins*.

22. Compare *Quan jing, Quan fa beiyao* 1.29a–31a; and *Xuanji mishou*, 1.10b–11b. See also "*zui quan*," in *Zhongguo wushu baike quanshu*, pp. 131–132.

23. See *Study of the Hong Kong Martial Arts Film*, p. 216.

24. *Quan jing, Quan fa beiyao*, 1.16b; compare *Xuanji mishou*, 1.9b.

25. Matsuda Ryūchi, *Zhongguo wushu shilüe*, p. 127.

26. See Matsuda Ryūchi, *Zhongguo wushu shilüe*, pp. 123–125. See also "Yanqing quan," in *Zhongguo wushu baike quanshu*, pp. 122–123; and Lee, "The Real Fists of Fury: The Artists and Artistry of Mizong Quan."

27. See Matsuda Ryūchi, *Zhongguo wushu shilüe*, p. 129.

28. See *Quan jing, Quan fa beiyao*, 1.18b, 2.19a. See also *Yihequan yundong qiyuan tansuo*, p. 89; "Meihua quan" in *Zhongguo wushu baike quanshu*, p. 122; and *Chuantong Shaolin quan taolu jiaocheng*, 1:409–453.

29. See *Yihequan yundong qiyuan tansuo*, pp. 83–88; and Zhou Weiliang, *Zhongguo wushu shi*, pp. 86–88.

30. The manual is reproduced in *Yihequan yundong qiyuan tansuo*, pp. 163–169. See also Esherick, *Origins of the Boxer Uprising*, p. 149.

31. See Naquin, *Millenarian Rebellion in China*, p. 31. See also Esherick, *Origins of the Boxer Uprising*, p. 149.

32. See *Yihequan yundong qiyuan tansuo*, pp. 83–102; Esherick, *Origins of the Boxer Uprising*, pp. 148–155; and Zhou Weiliang, *Zhongguo wushu shi*, pp. 86–88.

33. This is a reference to the ten principles of Shaolin close-range striking, which are elaborated in *Quan jing Quan fa beiyao*, 1.10b–13a.

34. This is an allusion to the *Zhuangzi*: "When Confucius was on his way to Ch'u, he passed through a forest where he saw a hunchback catching cicadas with a sticky pole as easily as though he were grabbing them with his hand." See Watson, *Complete Works of Chuang Tzu*, 19.199.

35. Yang Youji was a fabulous archer of the Spring-and-Autumn period state of Chu.

36. *Quan jing, Quan fa beiyao*, preface, 1a–2a.

37. This is a reference to the *Zhuangzi*: "To pant, to puff, to hail, to sip, to spit out the old breath and draw in the new, practicing *bear-hangings and bird-stretchings* (*xiong jing niao shen*), longevity his only concern—such is the life favored by the scholar who practices gymnastics (*daoyin*), the man who nourishes his body, who hopes to live to be as old as Pengzu." See Watson, *Complete Works of Chuang Tzu*, 15.167–168 (slightly altered).

38. Lin Qing, *Hong xue yinyuan tuji*, section 1. On Lin Qing, see Hummel, *Eminent Chinese of the Ch'ing period*, pp. 506–507.

39. Wen Yucheng (*Shaolin fanggu*, p. 355) speculates that Lin Qing's visit occasioned the mural's painting. Liu Baoshan's Taguo school of Shaolin fighting claims to teach only those forms that are shown in the fresco. See Ching, "13,000 Warriors of Taguo," p. 49.

40. Compare Qi Jiguang, *Jixiao xinshu: shiba juan ben*, 14.227–230; He Liangchen, *Zhenji*, 2.26–27; Zheng Ruoceng, *Jiangnan jing lüe*, 8a.3b–4a; and Tang Shunzhi, *Wu bian, qianji*, 5.37b. See also Cheng Dali, "Mingdai wushu," pp. 66–70.

41. Tang Shunzhi, *Wu bian, qianji*, 5.37b–39b.

42. See Cao Wenming's introduction to Qi Jiguang's *Jixiao xinshu: shiba juan ben*, pp. 4–5. On Qi Jiguang, see Goodrich, *Dictionary of Ming Biography*, 1:220–224; and Huang, *1587 A Year of No Significance*, pp. 156–188.

43. Wile, *T'ai-chi's Ancestors*, p. 19. The original is Qi Jiguang, *Jixiao xinshu: shiba juan ben*, 14.229.

44. Wile, *T'ai-chi's Ancestors*, p. 19. The original is Qi Jiguang, *Jixiao xinshu: shiba juan ben*, 14.229–230.

45. He Liangchen, *Zhenji*, 2.26.

46. Wile, *T'ai-chi's Ancestors*, pp. 12, 18. The original is Qi Jiguang, *Jixiao xinshu: shiba juan ben*, 14.227.

47. Wile, *T'ai-chi's Ancestors*, p. 12. The original is Tang Shunzhi, *Wu bian, qianji*, 5.37a.

48. Qi Jiguang, *Jixiao xinshu: shiba juan ben*, 14.227. Compare also Wile, *T'ai-chi's Ancestors*, p. 18. Eventually, the general added four chapters to his book. Nevertheless, he kept this comment, indicating that *Quan jing jieyao* was originally intended for the last.

49. See Qi Jiguang, *Jixiao xinshu: shisi juan ben*. See also Ma Mingda, *Shuo jian cong gao*, p. 310; and Wile, *T'ai-chi's Ancestors*, pp. 16–17.

50. Ma Mingda, *Shuo jian cong gao*, p. 311.

51. See *Jin Ping Mei cihua*, 90.1244.

52. The "Four-Levels" (*siping*) posture figured in late Ming armed and unarmed fighting alike. See Cheng Zongyou, *Shaolin gunfa*, 2.1b–2b; Tang Shunzhi, *Wu bian, qianji*, 5.37b; Qi Jiguang, *Jixiao xinshu: shiba juan ben*, 14.234–235; and Wile, *T'ai-Chi's Ancestors*, pp. 27–30.

53. This is Anthony Yu's translation (*Journey to the West*, 3:14–15) slightly altered; the original is Wu Cheng'en, *Xiyou ji*, 51:594. Compare also Wu Cheng'en, *Xiyou ji*, 2.22, and Yu, *The Journey to the West*, 1:97.

54. Wu Huifang, *Wanbao quanshu*.

55. See *Santai Wanyong zhengzong*, 14.1a–1b; and Wu Huifang, *Wanbao quanshu*, p. 346 and note 491. (The "Sand-Washing-Waves Fist" and "Spear-Seizing Fist" are mentioned in the 1607 edition.)

56. See Tang Hao and Gu Liuxin, *Taijiquan yanjiu*, pp. 179–183; Matsuda Ryūchi, *Zhongguo wushu shilüe*, pp. 81–83; and *Zhongguo wushu baike quanshu*, pp. 71, 91.

57. An influential Daoist classic, the *Scripture of the Yellow Court* (*Huangting jing*) (ca. third century CE) outlines respiratory techniques coupled with meditation on the body's internal divinities. See Paul Kroll's partial translation, "Body Gods and Inner Vision." See also below, chapter 6.

58. Quoted in Tang Hao and Gu Liuxin, *Taijiquan yanjiu*, p. 180.

59. See Tang Hao and Gu Liuxin, *Taijiquan yanjiu*, p. 15.

60. Matsuda Ryūchi, *Zhongguo wushu shilüe*, p. 88.

61. Zhou Weiliang, *Zhongguo wushu shi*, pp. 88–90. See also Naquin, *Millenarian Rebellion in China*, pp. 31, 88, 313.

62. See Matsuda Ryūchi, *Zhongguo wushu shilüe*, pp. 135–138; and Zhou Weiliang, *Zhongguo wushu shi*, p. 89.

63. See Ma Litang and Sun Yamin, "Xingyi shizu Ji Longfeng," pp. 36–37; and "Ji Jike" in *Zhongguo wushu baike quanshu*, p. 538.

64. The legend first appeared in Huang Baijia, *Neijia quanfa*, p. 1a. See also Wile, *T'ai-Chi's Ancestors*, p. 58.

65. See Matsuda Ryūchi, *Zhongguo wushu shilüe*, pp. 183–184. Compare also Shou-Yu Liang and Wen-Ching Wu, *Kung Fu Elements*, p. 447.

66. Chang Naizhou, *Chang Shi wuji shu*, trans. Wile, *T'ai-chi's Ancestors*, pp. 71–

188. See also Wells, *Scholar Boxer: Chang Naizhou's Theory of Internal Martial Arts*. Wang Zongyue's writings are included in *Taijiquan pu*, pp. 24–39. According to Tang Hao and Gu Liuxin (*Taijiquan yanjiu*, p. 183), Wang probably studied Chen Family Taiji Quan when he resided in nearby Luoyang and Kaifeng.

67. Their manuals are included in *Taijiquan pu*, pp. 245–275 and 276–339 respectively.

6. Gymnastics

1. See Chase, *Firearms: A Global History to 1700*, pp. 141–150.

2. *Neigong tushuo*, p. 2. Wang's scholarly works are listed in the *Qing shi gao*, 145.4262; 147.4334; 148.4417.

3. See *Neigong tushuo*, pp. 2–3. We have no way of knowing how accurate Wang's memory was. Pan's *Essential Techniques* might have differed from the *Illustrated Exposition* Wang had obtained at the Shaolin Temple. However, even if the manuals were textually diverse, it is likely that the techniques were largely similar. See Tang Hao, "Songshan Shaolin chuanxi de he huiji de ticao," pp. 26–27.

4. Dudgeon, "Kung-fu or Medical Gymnastics," pp. 521–522 (slightly revised); the original is *Neigong tushuo*, pp. 21–27. Dudgeon probably worked on an earlier edition of the same exercises: Pan Weiru's *Weisheng yaoshu* (1858). See Dudgeon, "Kung-fu or Medical Gymnastics," p. 503.

5. *Neigong tushuo*, pp. 1–2.

6. Watson, *The Complete Works of Chuang Tzu*, 15.167–168 (slightly altered).

7. See Harper, *Early Chinese Medical Literature*, pp. 125–142; 310–327.

8. See Ibid., pp. 310–327.

9. Engelhardt, "Longevity Techniques and Chinese Medicine," p. 101.

10. Needham and Lu, *Science and Civilization in China*, vol. 5, part V, p. 161; the original is *Sanguo zhi*, "Weishu," 29.804.

11. See Maspero, "Methods of 'Nourishing the Vital Principle,'" p. 469; and Needham and Lu, *Science and Civilization in China*, vol. 5, part V, p. 149. On *qi*, see also Kuriyama, *Expressiveness of the Body*.

12. Maspero, "Methods of 'Nourishing the Vital Principle,'" pp. 459–460; and Needham and Lu, *Science and Civilization in China*, vol. 5, part V, pp. 145–146.

13. Lau, *Lao Tzu: Tao Te Ching*, p. 116.

14. Maspero, "Methods of 'Nourishing the Vital Principle,'" pp. 465–484; Needham and Lu, *Science and Civilization in China*, vol. 5, part V, pp. 147–148.

15. See Despeux, "Gymnastics: The Ancient Tradition," p. 249; Dudgeon, "Kung-fu or Medical Gymnastics," pp. 494–500; and Needham and Lu, *Science and Civilization in China*, vol. 5, part V, p. 155.

16. *Chifeng sui*, 2.25a.

17. Consider for example the following statement from the "Inward Training" (*neiye*) chapter of the *Guanzi* (ca. fourth century BCE): "concentrate the *qi* as if a spirit (*ru shen*), and the myriad things will all reside within." See Puett, *To Become a God*, p. 115.

18. Needham and Ling, *Science and Civilization in China*, vol. 2, pp. 139–154; and Needham and Lu, *Science and Civilization in China*, vol. 5, part II, pp. 71–127.

19. See Maspero, "Methods of 'Nourishing the Vital Principle,'" pp. 445–448.

20. Maspero, quoted in Needham and Ling, *Science and Civilization in China*, vol. 2, p. 153.

21. Seidel, "Chronicle of Taoist Studies," p. 261.

22. See Engelhardt, "Longevity Techniques and Chinese Medicine," p. 77.

23. Needham and Lu, *Science and Civilization in China*, vol. 5, part V, p. 27. See also Seidel, "Chronicle of Taoist Studies," p. 264.

24. Kroll, "Body Gods and Inner Vision," pp. 153–154. On the *Scripture of the Yellow Court*, see also Robinet, *Taoist Meditation*, pp. 55–96.

25. See Engelhardt, "Longevity Techniques and Chinese Medicine," pp. 102–103; and Harper, *Early Chinese Medical Literature*, p. 110.

26. See Needham and Lu, *Science and Civilization in China*, vol. 5, part V, pp. 181–184; and Maspero, "Methods of 'Nourishing the Vital Principle,'" pp. 506–517.

27. Palmer, "Modernity and Millenarianism in China," p. 79.

28. Palmer, "Modernity and Millenarianism in China," pp. 79–109. See also Chen, *Breathing Spaces*, pp. 170–184; and Miura, "The Revival of Qi."

29. Tang Hao and Gu Liuxin, *Taijiquan yanjiu*, pp. 5–6.

30. Lin Boyuan, *Zhongguo tiyu shi*, pp. 378–379.

31. *Quan jing, Quan fa beiyao*, preface, 1b.

32. Tang Shunzhi, *Jingchuan xiansheng wenji*, 2.9a. See also Zhou Weiliang, *Zhongguo wushu shi*, p. 91.

33. *Quan jing, Quan fa beiyao*, preface, 1b.

34. Wile, *T'ai-chi's Ancestors*, pp. 100–101; the original is Chang Naizhou, *Chang Shi wuji shu*, 2.21–22.

35. Wile, *T'ai-chi's Ancestors*, p. 93; Chang Naizhou, *Chang Shi wuji shu*, 2.14.

36. Wile, *Lost T'ai-chi Classics*, p. 56; the original is transcribed in ibid., p. 133; the song is attributed to Li Yiyu (1832–1892).

37. *Qing bai lei chao*, 6:2906.

38. *Beijing lao Tianqiao*, p. 23.

39. See *Yijin jing*, in *Zhongguo chuantong yangsheng zhendian*, pp. 224 and 209 respectively.

40. Wu Jingzi, *Rulin waishi*, 51.492. The reference to *qi*, and to the *Yijin jing*, is in 49.475–476.

41. The Iron Cloth Shirt is the subject of an ironic Pu Songling (1640–1715) tale; see his "Tiebu shan fa," in *Liaozhai zhiyi*, 6.757.

42. Quoted in Esherick, *Boxer Uprising*, p. 105.

43. His name was Zhang Luojiao. See Cheng Dali, "Qingdai wushu," p. 72; Naquin, *Millenarian Rebellion*, p. 30; and Esherick, *Boxer Uprising*, pp. 96–98.

44. See Esherick, *Boxer Uprising*, pp. 104–109.

45. Esherick, *Boxer Uprising*, p. 225; the original memorial by magistrate Ji Guifen is in *Shandong jindaishi ziliao*, 3:192.

46. On magic and the late imperial martial arts, see Zhou Weiliang, *Zhongguo wushu shi*, pp. 92–93; and Hao Qin, "Lun wushu wenhua yu zhongguo minjian mimi zongjiao de guanxi," pp. 205–208.

47. *Qing bai lei chao*, 6:2965.

48. Wile, *T'ai Chi's Ancestors*, p. 54; the original is Huang Zongxi, *Nanlei wending*, 8.129. See also Huang Baijia, *Neijia quanfa*, 1b, trans. Wile, *T'ai Chi's Ancestors*, p. 59.

49. *Yijin jing*, in *Zhongguo chuantong yangsheng zhendian*, pp. 215–216.

50. *Xuanji mishou*, chapter 2.

51. *Quan jing, Quan fa beiyao*, preface, 1b.

52. See Wile, *T'ai Chi's Ancestors*, p. 55.

53. See respectively *Qing shi gao*, 505.13922; and Naquin, *Shantung Rebellion*, p. 38.

54. See Zhou Weiliang, *Zhongguo wushu shi*, p. 98; and *Zhongguo wushu baike quanshu*, pp. 18–21.

55. See Zhou Weiliang, *Zhongguo wushu shi*, p. 98.

56. Compare the *Xiwu xu*, in *Yihequan yundong qiyuan tansuo*, p. 168, with the *Yijing*, "*Xici shang*," XI. My translation follows Derk Bodde's in Fung Yu-Lan, *History of Chinese Philosophy*, 2:438. See also Zhou Weiliang, *Zhongguo wushu shi*, p. 98.

57. See Wang's writings in *Taijiquan pu*, pp. 24, 30. See also Tang Hao and Gu Liuxin, *Taijiquan yanjiu*, p. 184; Zhou Weiliang, *Zhongguo wushu shi*, p. 98; and *Zhongguo wushu baike quanshu*, p. 19.

58. Wile, *Lost T'ai-chi Classics*, p. 89; the original is transcribed in ibid., p. 153.

59. See Chang Naizhou, *Chang Shi wuji shu*, 3.35–36; and Wile, *T'ai-chi's Ancestors*, pp. 111–112. Chang has transmuting form (*xing*) into breath, rather than transmuting essence into breath. On the three stages of Daoist "inner alchemy," see Predagio and Skar, "Inner Alchemy," pp. 489–490. On "inner alchemy" and Xingyi Quan, see Cao Zhiqing, quoted in Liu Junxiang, *Dongfang renti wenhua*, pp. 254–255.

60. See Ware, *Alchemy, Medicine, Religion*, p. 294; Cheng Dali, *Zhongguo wushu*, pp. 117–118; Granet, *Danses et légendes de la Chine ancienne*, pp. 496–501; and Campany, *To Live as Long as Heaven and Earth*, pp. 70–72.

61. See Zhou Weiliang, *Zhongguo wushu shi*, p. 35; and Robinet, "Shangqing— Highest Clarity," p. 219. See also the beautiful reproductions of Daoist ritual swords in Little and Eichman, *Taoism and the Arts of China*, pp. 214–217.

62. See Lagerwey, *Taoist Ritual*, p. 93.

63. See *Yunji qiqian*, 84.7a, trans. Maspero, "Methods of 'Nourishing the Vital Principle,'" p. 447 n. 6; and Robinet, "Metamorphosis and Deliverance," pp. 60–61. During the early medieval period the staff could likewise serve as the Daoist's double; see Campany, *To Live as Long as Heaven and Earth*, pp. 69–70.

64. See, for example, Takuan Sōhō, *Unfettered Mind*.

65. *Wu Yue chunqiu zhuzi suoyin*, 9.41–42, trans. Douglas Wile, *T'ai Chi's Ancestors*, pp. 3–4. I have substituted "face-to-face combat" for Wile's "hand-to-hand combat," for it is clear that in this context *shouzhan* refers to fencing. See also "*shouzhan*," in *Hanyu dacidian*, 6:304–305. In its present form, the story might date from the Tang period, when the anthology was revised. See Lagerwey, "Wu Yüeh ch'un ch'iu," pp. 473–476.

66. *Taiping guangji*, 195.1464–1465, and James Liu's translation, *The Chinese Knight-Errant*, pp. 93–94.

67. *Hanshu,* 30.1761, 63.2760, 81.3336, and 87.3557. See also Ma Mingda, *Shuo jian cong gao,* pp. 46–67; and Zhou Weiliang, *Zhongguo wushu shi,* pp. 21–22. During the Han period, several wrestling forms called *juedi* (later known as *xiangpu*) were also practiced. Some apparently resembled modern Japanese sumo. See Zhou Weiliang, *Zhongguo wushu shi,* pp. 19–21, 31–33; and Cheng Dali, *Zhongguo wushu,* pp. 189–194.

68. The sentence is replete with Daoist technical terms for meditation: *mingxin* means clearing the mind of all thoughts; *wogu* means clenching the fist, usually by pressing the thumb against the middle finger's middle section, then wrapping it with the other fingers; *jingsi* is quiet visualization. See *Zhonghua Daojiao da cidian,* pp. 980 and 983 respectively. On *wogu,* see also Engelhardt, "Longevity Techniques and Chinese Medicine," p. 103.

69. Daoist cosmology identifies the head with the immortals' abode atop Mt. Kunlun in northwest China.

70. *Neigong tushuo,* pp. 8–12. My translation partially follows Dudgeon's ("Kung-fu or Medical Gymnastics," pp. 375–385) rendition of the set's source, The Eight-Exercises Brocade.

71. *Neigong tushuo,* p. 6.

72. Zeng Zao (fl. 1131–1155), *Dao shu;* Schipper, ed. *Concordance du Tao-tsang* (hereafter "*DZ*"), 1017, 35.17a (Zeng Zao, however, does not mention the name "Eight-Section Brocade"). See also Tang Hao et al., *Baduan jin,* p. 2; and *Zhongguo gudai tiyu shi,* p. 347.

73. Hong Mai, *Yijian zhi,* section *yi,* 9.65–66.

74. See Tang Hao et al., *Baduan jin;* and Chen Pengcheng and Feng Wu, "The Eight-Section Brocade." Contemporary Shaolin "Eight-Section Brocade" is outlined in *Chuantong Shaolin quan taolu jiaocheng,* 5:296–308.

75. See Gao Lian, *Zunsheng bajian,* 10.18b–22b, trans. Dudgeon, "Kung-fu or Medical Gymnastics," pp. 375–385; *Chifeng sui,* 1.45–56, trans. Despeux, *La moelle du phénix rouge,* pp. 112–126; and *Xiuzhen shishu, DZ,* 263, 19.1a–5b. On the *Shou shi chuan zhen* (which I have not seen), see Tang Hao, "Songshan Shaolin chuanxi de he huiji de ticao," pp. 26–27; and Tang Hao, "Wo Guo tiyu ziliao jieti," pp. 65–67.

76. The exercises are attributed to Zhongli Quan in *Xiuzhen shishu, DZ,* 263, 19.1a. Zeng Zao (fl. 1131–1155) alludes to Lü Dongbin in a comment that is included in the same work (23.1b): "Master Zhongli's 'Eight-Section Brocade' was written on a stone wall by the hand of Sir Lü [Dongbin]; thus were they passed on to the world." See Maspero, "Methods of 'Nourishing the Vital Principle,'" p. 547, note 16. On the literary corpus attributed to the two immortals see Predagio and Skar, "Inner Alchemy," p. 469.

77. *Neigong tushuo,* pp. 47–70, and Dudgeon's translation (which was made from the *Weisheng Yijin jing* (1875)), pp. 529–541. On the *Weisheng Yijin jing,* see appendix, edition no. 4.

78. See Prip-Møller, *Chinese Buddhist Monasteries,* p. 30, p. 34, plate 38. The mistranscription is Weituo instead of (Sai) Jiantuo for Skanda; see Noël Peri, "Le dieu Wei-t'ouo"; and Strickmann, *Chinese Magical Medicine,* pp. 218–227. See also Stein, "The Guardian of the Gate."

79. Weituo's exercises first appeared in the Daoguang (1821–1850) edition of the *Yijin jing*, 2.29b–39b (see appendix, edition no. 3). See also the modern edition *Yijin jing*, in *Zhongguo chuantong yangsheng zhendian*, pp. 225–236; and Tang Hao, "Songshan Shaolin chuanxi de he huiji de ticao," p. 28.

80. Appendix, edition 6, p. 37a. See also Tang Hao, "Jiu Zhongguo tiyu shi shang fuhui de Damo," part 1, p. 24; and Gong Pengcheng (who mistakenly has Songheng instead of Zongheng), "Damo Yijin jing lunkao," pp. 73, 80.

81. Zi ning daoren is not mentioned in Tiantai gazetteers such as the *Tiantai shan quan zhi* or the *Tongbai shizhi*.

82. See, among other entries, "*zijin*" and "*ningshen*" in the *Zhonghua Daojiao dacidian*, pp. 1221 and 1237 respectively.

83. Compare Appendix, edition 3, 1.8a–10a; Appendix, edition 6, 1.2b–3b; and *Zhongguo chuantong yangsheng zhendian*, pp. 213–214. The reference is to D. C. Lau, translator, *Mencius*, book II, part A, p. 77.

84. The term appears as early as section 5 of the *Daode jing* (ca. 400 BCE). The meditative technique is mentioned in the eleventh-century Daoist encyclopedia *Yunji qiqian*, 10.10a. It is detailed in Wu Shouyang's (1563–1644), *Xianfo hezong yulu*, 16b–21b.

85. Compare Appendix, edition 3, 1.11a–12a; Appendix, edition 6, 1.13a–14a; and *Zhongguo chuantong yangsheng zhendian*, p. 215. On the Daoist elements in the *Sinews Transformation Classic*, see Gong Pengcheng, "Damo Yijin jing lunkao," pp. 78–84.

86. See respectively, Chang Naizhou, *Chang Shi wuji shu*, p. 38; Wile, *T'ai Chi's Ancestors*, p. 113; and Wu Jingzi, *Rulin waishi*, 49.475–476.

87. See Gu Liuxin, "Wushu shishang de Gan Fengchi"; and He Zehan, *Rulin waishi renwu benshi kaolüe*, pp. 120–124, 136.

88. See Buswell, *Chinese Buddhist Apocrypha*.

89. The author confuses Emperor Xiaoming (reigned 516–528) with Emperor Xiaowen (reigned 471–499), who proclaimed the Taihe period.

90. The historical monk Pramiti issued in 705 a Chinese translation of the *Śūraṃgama-mahā-sūtra*. Therefore, as Xu Zhen (1898–1967) has pointed out, he could not possibly have been active as a translator some eighty years earlier, before this preface (dated 628) was presumably authored. See Xu Zhen, *Guoji lunlüe*, p. 14.

91. Where, according to Chinese mythology, the immortals reside. The 1884 edition has the Pure Realm of the Buddha Amitābha instead.

92. The Bushy-Bearded Hero (Qiuran ke) is the protagonist of the Tang period short story of the same name. The story had been attributed by some to Du Guangting (850–933). See Cyril Birch's translation, "The Curly-Bearded Hero."

93. The "Six-Flowers Formation" (*liuhua zhen*) is attributed to Li Jing in a military classic, *Questions and Replies Between Tang Taizong and Li Weigong*, that purports to record his conversations with Emperor Li Shimin. Most scholars, however, date the work to the Northern Song. See Sawyer, *Seven Military Classics*, pp. 339, 341, 344, 345.

94. Compare Appendix, edition 3, *xu*, 1a–3b; Appendix, edition 6, *xu*, 1a–3b; and *Zhongguo chuantong yangsheng zhendian*, pp. 206–208.

95. Ling Tingkan, *Jiaolitang wenji*, 25.17a. See also Zhou Zhongfu (1768–1831),

Zheng tang dushu ji, 68.335; Xu Zhen, *Guoji lunlüe*, pp. 14–15; Tang Hao, *Shaolin Wudang kao*, pp. 13–20; and Gong Pengcheng, "Damo Yijin jing lunkao," pp. 74–75, 79–80.

96. It is included in a Daoguang (1821–1850) edition (Appendix, edition 3).

97. See Morris, *Marrow of the Nation*, pp. 185–229.

98. See Matsuda Ryūchi, *Zhongguo wushu shilüe*, p. 135; Tang Hao et al., *Baduan jin*, pp. 1, 42; and "Yue Fei" in *Zhongguo wushu baike quanshu*, pp. 531–532.

99. Compare Appendix, edition 3, *xu*, 4a–5b; Appendix, edition 6, *shenyong xu*, 1a–2a; and *Zhongguo chuantong yangsheng zhendian*, pp. 208–209.

100. See Ling Tingkan, *Jiaolitang wenji*, 25.16b.

101. See, for example, the reference to the legend in the story "Maiyou lang du zhan Huakui" ("The Oil Vendor wins the Flower Queen"), in Feng Menglong, *Xingshi hengyan*, 3.33.

102. See *Shuihu quanzhuan*, 107.1621. Identified with the Buddhist deity Vaiśravaṇa (Chinese: Duowentian or Pishamen), Li Jing figures in the *Fengshen yanyi* (12.101–14.128) as Nezha's father. On his Song period cult, see Hansen, *Changing Gods*, pp. 112–113, 186, 191.

103. See, for example, Xu Hongke's portrayal in Chu Renhuo (fl. 1700), *Sui Tang yanyi*, 24.196–197. A third novel that featured Bodhidharma was the *Biographies of Twenty-Four Enlightened Arhats (Ershisi zun dedao luohan zhuan)* (1604). On the Indian patriarch in Ming fiction, see Durand-Dastès, *Le Roman du maître de dhyāna*, pp. 1–243.

104. See respectively Ching, "Black Whirlwind Axes"; and Leung and TC Media, "Wu Song Breaks Manacles."

105. See chapter 5.

106. See *Yunji qiqian*, 59.12b–15b; and *Songshi*, 205.5185, 205.5188. A third manual listed by the *Songshi* that might have been informed by Daoist beliefs is *Bodhidharma's Blood-Vessels Theory [as Recorded by] Monk Huike (Seng Huike Damo xuemai lun)*, except that an extant work with a very similar title bears no Daoist traces. See *Damo dashi xuemai lun (The great master Bodhidharma's blood vessel theory)*, (preface 1153), ZZ edition.

Another Daoist-inspired text that bears the saint's name is "Great Master Bodhidharma's Methods for Knowing the Time of One's Death" ("Damo dashi zhi siqi"), which was well-known in Japan by the twelfth century. Included, among other sources, in the Tendai encyclopedia *Keiran shūyō shū*, *T*, no. 2410, 76:781, it is translated and discussed by Faure, *Rhetoric of Immediacy*, pp. 184–187. The text is likely related to "The Collection of Returning to the Void" ("Guikong lun") that was dismissed as a forgery by the Yuan monk Pudu. See ter Haar, *White Lotus Teachings*, p. 103.

Some scholars have identified Bodhidharma in the Daoist diagram of internal circulation, the "Neijing tu," which was engraved in 1886 on a stele at the White Clouds Temple in Beijing. The stele features a "blue-eyed foreign monk," by which nickname the saint was sometimes referred to. See Needham and Lu, *Science and Civilization in China*, vol. 5, part V, p. 116. David Wang challenges the identification, suggesting that the "blue-eyed monk" is in this instance Milefo (Maitreya); see his "*Nei jing Tu*," pp. 146, 149.

107. ter Haar, *White Lotus Teachings*, pp. 101–106.

108. See Predagio and Skar, "Inner Alchemy," p. 490. See also Yao Tao-Chung, "Quanzhen-Complete Perfection," pp. 588–589.

109. See, for example, the Tang period *Shesheng zuanlu*, DZ, 578, pp. 2a–3a. See also Despeux, "Gymnastics," pp. 231–232. That *daoyin* predated the arrival of Buddhism in China poses a difficulty in assessing Indian influences. The tradition's main features, such as breathing, *qi* circulation, and limb movements, had been firmly established by the second century BCE; see Needham and Lu, *Science and Civilization in China*, vol. 5, part V, pp. 280–283.

110. See, respectively, *Neigong tushuo*, p. 70, and Tang Hao, "Jiu Zhongguo tiyu shi shang fuhui de Damo," part 2, pp. 27–37. Tang demonstrates that the earliest written association of the "Eighteen-Arhats Hand" with the Shaolin Temple was made by the *Shaolin Authentic Techniques* (*Shaolin zongfa*) of 1911, which had served as the source for the *Secret Formulas of the Shaolin Hand Combat Method* (*Shaolin quanshu mijue*) of 1915.

111. See Ching, "Bodhidharma's Legendary Fighting Cane." It remains to be investigated when the weapon was invented.

112. Liu T'ieh-yün (Liu E), *Travels of Lao Ts'an*, pp. 73, and 248, notes 4, 5. The Shaolin relevance was first noted by Henning, "Reflections on a Visit to the Shaolin Monastery," p. 100.

113. See Brook, "Rethinking Syncretism," p. 22; and Berling, *Syncretic Religion of Lin Chao-en*.

114. Compare *Zhongguo chuantong yangsheng zhendian*, p. 308; and Appendix, edition 6, pp. 36a–37b.

115. See Yü, *Renewal of Buddhism in China*, pp. 101–137.

116. See Yu, *The Journey to the West*, 1:79–93. I am grateful to Rania Huntington for suggesting the analogy. Note also Yu's comment, "It is quite remarkable how extensively the themes and rhetoric of Daoism appear in every part of the [*Journey to the West*]," (ibid., 1:36).

117. See Brook, "Rethinking Syncretism," pp. 20–23.

118. Wile, *T'ai Chi's Ancestors*, p. 53 (slightly altered); the original is Huang Zongxi, *Nanlei wending*, 8.128. Compare Huang Baijia, *Neijia quanfa*, p. 1a; and the biography of the martial artist Zhang Songxi in *Ningbo fu zhi*, 31.2289, both trans. Wile, *T'ai Chi's Ancestors*, pp. 58 and 68 respectively.

119. Wile, *T'ai Chi's Ancestors*, p. 58 (slightly altered); the original is Huang Baijia, *Neijia quanfa*, p. 1a.

120. See Seidel, "A Taoist Immortal of the Ming Dynasty," p. 504; and Lagerwey, "The Pilgrimage to Wu-tang Shan," p. 305. On the historical Zhang Sanfeng, see also Huang Zhaohan, *Mingdai daoshi Zhang Sanfeng kao*, pp. 36–37.

121. See Lagerwey, "The Pilgrimage to Wu-tang Shan," pp. 293–302.

122. Wile, *T'ai Chi's Ancestors*, p. 53 (slightly altered); the original is Huang Zongxi, *Nanlei wending*, 8.128. See also Seidel, "A Taoist Immortal of the Ming Dynasty," p. 506.

123. See Seidel, "A Taoist Immortal of the Ming Dynasty," pp. 485–496.

124. See Yang Lizhi, "Mingdai diwang yu Wudang daojiao guanli"; and Lager-wey, "The Pilgrimage to Wu-tang Shan," pp. 299–302.

125. Wile, *Lost T'ai-chi Classics*, p. 110; see also Wile, *T'ai-chi's Ancestors*, pp. 37–44.

126. Wile, *T'ai-chi's Ancestors*, pp. 55–57; the original is Huang Zongxi, *Nanlei wending*, 8.129–130. See also Tang Hao, *Neijia quan de yanjiu*, p. 14; Tang Hao, *Shaolin Wudang kao*, p. 77; and Huang's biography in Goodrich, *Dictionary of Ming Biography*, 1: 351–354.

127. Wile, *T'ai Chi's Ancestors*, pp. 65–66; the original is Huang Baijia, *Neijia quanfa*, p. 4a.

128. Wile, *T'ai Chi's Ancestors*, p. 39; and Wile, *Lost T'ai-chi Classics*, p. 110.

129. See Faure's structural interpretation of early Chan hagiography, "Bodhidharma as Textual and Religious Paradigm."

130. See Lévi-Strauss, *The Raw and the Cooked*.

131. See Huang Baijia, *Neijia quanfa*, pp. 5b–6a, trans. Wile, *T'ai-chi's Ancestors*, p. 67. See also Tang Hao, *Neijia quan de yanjiu*, p. 40.

132. See Wile, *Lost T'ai-chi Classics*, pp. 108–111.

7. Suspect Rebels

1. See Gu Yanwu, *Jinshi wenzi ji*, 2.29b–30a, 3.34b–35b, and his "Shaolin seng bing," in *Rizhilu jishi*, 29.21a–22b. Gu authored his poem on the monastery in the spring of 1679 (see Qian Bangyan, "Gu Tinglin xiansheng nianpu," p. 64a). However, it is possible that he had visited the monastery earlier as well.

2. See Peterson, "The Life of Ku Yen-wu (1613–1682), Part II: Ku's Traveling After 1657," p. 209, and Goodrich, *Dictionary of Ming Biography*, 2:422.

3. The Wuru Peak is situated behind the monastery to its north.

4. Gu Yanwu, "Shaolin si," in *Gu Tinglin shi ji huizhu*, 6.1212–1216. See also Xu Changqing's commentary in his *Shaolin si yu Zhongguo wenhua*, pp. 230–231.

5. See Wakeman, *Great Enterprise*, 2:777–781.

6. On the Heaven and Earth Society, see Ownby, *Brotherhoods and Secret Societies*; Murray and Qin, *Origins of the Tiandihui*; and ter Haar, *Ritual and Mythology of the Chinese Triads*.

7. See Murray and Qin, *Origins of the Tiandihui*, pp. 151–175, 197–228; ter Haar, *Ritual and Mythology of the Chinese Triads*, 368–388.

8. The connection to *Water Margin* is argued by Murray and Qin, *Origins of the Tiandihui*, pp. 169–172. Barend ter Haar (*Ritual and Mythology of the Chinese Triads*) analyzes the legend in the context of the late imperial messianic paradigm.

9. See ter Haar, *Ritual and Mythology of the Chinese Triads*, pp. 404–407. Whether a Southern Shaolin Temple did exist goes beyond the scope of this study. Currently at least three Fujian cities, Putian, Quanzhou, and Fuqing, boast the remains of what they claim had been the authentic Southern Shaolin Temple. The claims have been reviewed by Wen Yucheng and Zhou Weiliang. Both scholars consider the latter hypothesis the most plausible. A "Shaolin Cloister" (Shaolin yuan) had been situated in the western outskirts of Fuqing County since the Southern Song.

However, neither its relation to the Henan Temple nor its military history are clear. See Wen Yucheng, *Shaolin fanggu*, pp. 374–385; Zhou Weiliang, "Ming-Qing shiqi Shaolin wushu de lishi liubian," pp. 10–14; and the less critical *Fuqing Shaolin si*. The Quanzhou case is argued by Chen Sidong, *Xingyuan bigeng lu*, 1:201–281, and in *Quanzhou Nan Shaolin si yanjiu*.

The earliest novel celebrating the Southern Shaolin Temple was likely the late Qing *Shengchao ding sheng wannian qing* (*The sacred dynasty's tripods flourish, verdant for ten thousand years*). See Hamm, *Paper Swordsmen*, 34–38, 56.

10. See Weng Tongwen, "Kangxi chuye 'yi-Wan weixing' jituan yudang jianli Tiandihui," pp. 433–449; and He Zhiqing, *Tiandihui qiyuan yanjiu*. Barend ter Haar disputes the Changlin hypothesis in *Ritual and Mythology of the Chinese Triads*, pp. 407–416.

11. For a general survey, see Atwell, "The T'ai-ch'ang, T'ien-ch'i, and Ch'ung-chen Reigns," pp. 621–637; Des Forges, *Cultural Centrality and Political Change*, pp. 204–311; and Parsons, *Peasant Rebellions of the Late Ming Dynasty*. See also Mote, *Imperial China: 900–1800*, pp. 795–801.

12. See Ye Feng, "Shaolin si er shou," in *Shaolin si zhi, wuyanlü*, 12a–12b.

13. "Chongjian ciyun an beiji" ("Inscription on the Reconstruction of the Compassionate Clouds Hermitage"), in *Shaolin si zhi, beiji*, 28b.

14. See Shen Quan, "Shaolin si" in *Shaolin si zhi, wuyanlü*, 13a. See also Xu Changqing's annotations in his *Shaolin si yu Zhongguo wenhua*, p. 232.

15. Alluding to the Liangshan outlaws led by Song Jiang in *Water Margin*.

16. Songyang was the site of the renowned Northern Song Confucian Academy Songyang shuyuan.

17. Wang Jie, *Zhongzhou zazu*, 25.10b–11a. Stanley Henning drew attention to Wang's account in his "Reflections on a Visit to the Shaolin Monastery," p. 96.

18. *Mingshi*, 152.6517; 273.7004; 277.7105; *Ming shi lu*, Chongzhen reign, 16.490, 16.506; *Qing shi gao*, 4.107; Des Forges, *Cultural Centrality and Political Change*, pp. 216, 285; Wakeman, *Great Enterprise*, 1:413, 1:510. Several sources give the wrong character for *yu zhai*, hence mistakenly "Jade Fort" rather than "Imperial Fort."

19. After Li's execution, one of his lieutenants, Jiang Fa, sought refuge at the Chen household. Jiang was known for his martial skills; see Tang Hao and Gu Liuxin, *Taijiquan yanjiu*, p. 180. Compare also the account by Chen Wangting's descendant, Chen Xin (1849–1929), in *Taijiquan pu*, p. 358.

20. See *Mingshi*, 292.7489–7490. On Ma Shouying, see Rossabi, "Muslim and Central Asian Revolts," pp. 170, 189.

21. See Wu Shu, *Shoubi lu*, p. 14. The incident took place during the Chongzhen reign (1628–1644), but its exact date is not given.

22. On Ningran Liaogai, see Wen Yucheng, *Shaolin fanggu*, p. 276.

23. On Yang's campaign, see Parsons, *Peasant Rebellions of the Late Ming Dynasty*, pp. 68–83.

24. See Yu Dayou, "Xinjian Shifang Chan yuan bei" ("Inscription on the Renovation of the Universal Chan Courtyard") (1577), in his *Zhengqi tang ji*, 3.6a–7b. See also Wen Yucheng, *Shaolin fanggu*, p. 315.

25. The inscription is photographically reproduced in *Zhongguo Shaolin si*, p. 256.

26. See *Song xian zhi*, p. 837.

27. The course of events is outlined in a Ministry of Rites document dated 1657, which is included in the *Shaolin si zhi, buzha,* 1a–2a. See also Wen Yucheng, *Shaolin fanggu,* pp. 331–333, 343.

28. See Wen Yucheng, *Shaolin fanggu,* pp. 337–338, 343.

29. The ceremonies are recorded on a Shaolin stele dated 1654 that commemorates their completion; see *Zhongguo Shaolin si, beike juan,* p. 257. See also Wen Yucheng, *Shaolin fanggu,* pp. 332, 343.

30. See *Shaolin si zhi, chenhan,* 4b; and Wen Yucheng, *Shaolin fanggu,* p. 339.

31. See Wen Yucheng, *Shaolin fanggu,* pp. 347–349.

32. *Shaolin si zhi, chenhan,* 5a. In this edict the emperor does not mention the monks' military activities, of which we know he had been well aware from an earlier document. See his correspondence of 1726 with the governor of Henan, Tian Wenjing, in *Shizong Xian Huangdi zhupi yuzhi,* 9.9b.

33. Edict dated Qianlong fortieth year, fifth month, eighth day (June 15, 1775), in *Qianlong chao shangyu dang,* 7:878.

34. See ter Haar, *White Lotus Teachings.* On late imperial religion and rebellion, see also Naquin, *Millenarian Rebellion*; Naquin, *Shantung Rebellion*; Esherick, *Boxer Uprising*; Mann and Kuhn, "Dynastic Decline and the Roots of Rebellion."

35. Qianlong fourth year, tenth month, nineteenth day (November 19, 1739), in *Kang Yong Qian shiqi chengxiang renmin fankang douzheng ziliao,* 2:619.

36. Report by the Anyi County magistrate that was appended to a memorial dated Qianlong twenty-second year, third month, twenty-fourth day (May 11, 1757) by the Hedong salt commissioner, Na Jun; *Lufu zouzhe,* number 166/*juan* 9015/*hao* 66.

37. Document quoted in Zhou Weiliang, "Ming-Qing shiqi Shaolin wushu," p. 9. See also the memorial dated Jiaqing twentieth year, fifth month, ninth day (June 10, 1815) by the governor-general of Zhili, Nayancheng (1764–1833), in *Na wenyi gong zouyi,* 40.2b.

38. The warning was engraved on a Shaolin stele; see chapter 2.

39. Liu T'ieh-yün, *Travels of Lao Ts'an,* p. 73.

40. Lin Qing, *Hong xue yinyuan tuji,* section 1. See also chapter 5. On Wang, see chapter 6.

41. Morris, *Marrow of the Nation,* pp. 185–229. A martial arts demonstration was included in the 1936 Berlin Olympics; ibid., p. 179.

42. Mentioned as early as the Yuan period, the Northern Shaolin Temple was situated on Mt. Pan some forty miles east of Beijing; Wen Yucheng, *Shaolin fanggu,* pp. 230–233.

Conclusion

1. Mote, *Imperial China: 900–1800,* p. 81.

2. See Demiéville, "Le Bouddhisme et la guerre," pp. 375–376; Strickmann,

Mantras et mandarins, p. 41; Chou Yi-Liang, "Tantrism in China," pp. 305–306; and Hansen, "Gods on Walls," pp. 80–83.

    3. See Zhou Weiliang, *Zhongguo wushu shi*, pp. 86–88. See also the anthropological explorations of Amos, "A Hong Kong Southern Praying Mantis Cult"; and Boretz, "Martial Gods and Magic Swords."

Glossary

Authors and titles included in the Works Cited are not listed below. Place names and biographical names that are readily available in standard reference works are similarly omitted.

Baduan jin 八段錦
Bagua Zhang 八卦掌
Baigu shu 柏谷墅
Baigu zhuang 柏谷莊
Baima 白馬 Temple
Baiyi dashi dian 白衣大士殿
bang 棒
bang yu gun yi ye 棒與棍一也
Baoben 報本 Temple
baobiao 保鏢
Baofang 豹房
baozhang 寶杖
Batuo 跋陀
Bawang quan 霸王拳
Beifang Pishamen Dafan Tianwang 北
　方毗沙門大梵天王
Benda 本大
Bengquan 崩拳
bian 變
Biandun 匾囤
Bianqun 匾困
bianxing 變形
bing 兵
bingfa 兵法

bixi wusheng shenqi shou 鼻息無聲神氣守
bu 步
bu sha sheng 不殺生
Cao Zhiqing 曹志清
chan 禪
Changlin 長林
Changqiang fa xuan 長槍法選
changquan 長拳
changzhu sengtian 常住僧田
chan zhang 禪杖
Chen Changxing 陳長興
Chen Jiru 陳繼儒
Chen Songquan 陳松泉
Chen Wangting 陳王庭
Chen Xin 陳鑫
Cheng Jingtao 程景陶
cheng qi di xian 乘其地險
Cheng Shao 程紹
Cheng Yinwan 程胤萬
Cheng Zhenru 程真如
Cheng Long 成龍
Chenjiagou 陳家溝
Chetang 徹堂
chifu yunqi 吃符運氣

chong shang 重上
"Chongxiu fatang beiming" 重修法堂
　碑銘
"Chongxiu Hengcuiting ji" 重修橫翠亭
　記
"Chong zhuang fo xiang bei" 重裝佛像
　碑
Chuansuo 穿梭
Chuzu an 初祖庵
ci 慈
ci yi yong yang 慈以勇養
"Cong jia xing Shaolin si" 從駕幸少林
　寺
cunshen 存神
Da Jiangjun 大將軍
Damo 達摩
Damo chushen chuandeng zhuan 達摩出身
　傳燈傳
"Damo dashi zhi siqi" 達磨大師知死期
Damo zhang 達摩杖
Damuqianlianmingjian jiumu bianwen 大
　目乾連冥間救母變文
dan 丹
Dandao fa xuan 單刀法選
dantian 丹田
Daochang 道場Monastery
Daofu 道副
Daoji 道濟
Daoping 道平 (fl. 756)
Daoping 道憑 (488–559)
daoyin 導引
Daoyin tu 導引圖
Daoyu 道育
Daxiong Dian 大雄殿
Dazhi 達智
Dengfeng 登封
dexin yingshou 得心應手
dian seng 顛僧
die 跌 (throwing)
die 牒 (official letter)
Dizang pusa 地藏菩薩
Dongdu ji 東度記
Dongjia quan 董家拳
dongtian 洞天

Dou Jiande 竇建德
Du Guangting 杜光庭
Du Taishi 杜太師
duanda 短打
duanda sheng changquan 短打勝長拳
duanquan 短拳
dun 頓
Duowentian 多聞天
Duti 讀體
dutidian 都提點
duweina 都維那
E quan 囮拳
Emei 峨嵋 (Mt.)
"Emei daoren quan ge" 峨嵋道人拳歌
Emei qiangfa 峨嵋槍法
Ershisi zun dedao luohan zhuan 二十四尊
　得道羅漢傳
Erwangzun 二王尊
fa 法
Facong 法聰
fan Qing fu Ming 反清復明
Fan Zhongxiu 樊鍾秀
Fang Shouchou 方受疇
fangbian 方便
fangtou seng 房頭僧
Fanjing Tang 翻經堂
Faru 法如
fashi 法師
feixi 飛錫
feng heshang 瘋和尚
Feng Mingqi 鳳鳴岐
"Fenglin chanshi xingzhuang" 風林禪
　師行狀
fengshan 封禪
Fenxing waigong jue 分行外功訣
Foguang 佛光
Fotuo 佛陀
fudi 福地
Funiu 伏牛 (Mt.)
"Funiu shan Yunyan si ji" 伏牛山雲巖寺
　記
Gan Fengchi 甘鳳池
ganbang 桿棒
gangcha 綱叉

ge an jiu ye 各安舊業
Ge Hong 葛洪
gejue 歌訣
Gong Nai 公鼐
gouqiang 鉤槍
Gu Shaolian 顧少連
guan 管
Guang'an 廣按
Guangong 關公
Guanyin 觀音
Guanyin dashi 觀音大士
Guijie 鬼節
"Guikong lun" 歸空論
Guiyi jun 歸義軍
gun 棍
gun fa 棍法
guoshu 國術
Guzhou 孤舟
Haikuan 海寬
Haiyang 海陽
He Wei 何為
Heng 恒 (northern holy peak)
Heng 衡 (southern holy peak)
Hengquan 橫拳
Hongji 洪紀
Hongjin 紅巾
Hongjun 紅軍
Hongquan 洪拳
Hongzhuan 洪轉
Hou Anguo 侯安國
Hou quan 猴拳
Hou Xingzhe 猴行者
Hu Wojiang 胡我江
Hu Zongxian 胡宗憲
Hua 華 (Mt.)
Hua Heshang 花和尚
Hua Tuo 華佗
Huangjue 皇覺 Monastery
Huangting jing 黃庭經
Huanyuan 轘轅 (Mt.)
Huanxiu Changrun 幻休常潤
Huanzhou 轘州
hufa 護法
Huian 慧安

Huiguang 慧光
Huike 慧可
Huiming 惠明
Huineng 慧能
Huiyang 惠瑒
Hulao 虎牢
hun 魂
huo fa wu ding shi 活法無定勢
Huo Yuanjia 霍元甲
huogun 火棍
Hushi Si Tianwang 護世四天王
Ji Jike 姬際可
jian 堅
Jiang Fa 蔣法
jianghu 江湖
jiansi 監寺
jiao 醮
Jiao Hong 焦竑
Jiapiluo shen 迦毘羅神
jiazi 架子
Jidian 濟顛
jiedao 戒刀
jiehuo 劫火
jijian 擊劍
Jin Yong 金庸
jing 精
jin'gang chu 金剛杵
Jin'gang (shen) 金剛神
jin'gang yecha 金剛夜叉
Jingchu changjian 荊楚長劍
jingluo 經絡
jingsi 靜思
jingtu 淨土
"Jingzhu ji" 景躅集
jinhuan xizhang 金環錫杖
jinhuan zhang 金環杖
Jinnaluo (wang) 緊那羅 (王)
Jinzhong zhao 金鐘罩
jiu li lüe guo, xin li wei fa 舊力略過，
    新力未發
jiurou heshang 酒肉和尚
Jixiandian shuyuan 集賢殿書院
juedi 角抵
Juezhang xin fa 蹶張心法

jun 郡
Jungong 俊公
kou 寇
Kou Qianzhi 寇謙之
kouchi 叩齒
koufen tian 口分田
Langlitaosha quan 浪裏淘沙拳
"Lanling laoren" 蘭陵老人
Lao Huihui 老回回
Laoan 老安
Laocan youji 老殘遊記
Lenamoti 勒那摩提
Li Anyuan 李安遠
Li Changyun 李昌運
Li Hanzhi 李罕之
Li Jing 李靖
Li Jiyu 李際遇
Li Kui 李逵
Li Lantian 李藍田
Li Lianjie 李連杰
Li Shannuo 李善諾
Li Shidao 李師道
Li Shimin 李世民
Li Yiyu 李亦畬
Li Yuan 李淵
Li Zhuyi 李竹逸
Li Zicheng 李自成
Lianfeng 蓮峰
Liang Yiquan 梁以全
lianqi 練氣
Liaoxin 了心
Libu shangshu 吏部尚書
Lidai ming hua ji 歷代名畫記
Lin Zhaoen 林兆恩
ling 令
Lingta 靈塔
Liu Baoshan 劉寶山
Liu Dechang 劉德長
Liu duanda 劉短打
Liu Wengchong 劉翁重
Liu Yanshi 劉言史
Liu Zongyuan 柳宗元
Liubu quan 六步拳
Liuhua zhen 六花陣

Lixue ting 立雪亭
Lizhengdian xiushuyuan 麗正殿修書院
Longchang 隆昌
Lü Dongbin 呂洞賓
Lu Junyi 盧俊義
Lu Shiyi 陸世儀
Lu Yin 盧寅
Lu Zhen 盧真
Lu Zhishen 魯智深
lun 輪
luohan 羅漢
Luohan dao 羅漢刀
Luoyi 洛邑
lushi 路勢
Ma Shouying 馬守應
maiyi 賣藝
Meihua quan 梅花拳
Meihua quan jiao 梅花拳教
Menglü tang qiangfa 夢綠堂槍法
Mian Zhang duanda 綿張短打
Milefo 彌勒佛
mingxin 冥心
Miquan 迷拳
Mizong quan 迷蹤拳 (Confounding
    Track Fist)
Mizong quan 秘宗拳 (Tantric Fist)
Mulian 目連
na 拿
Na Jun 那俊
"Naluoyan shen hufa shiji" 那羅延神護
    法示跡
Naluoyan (tian) 那羅延天
Nayancheng 那彥成
neidan 內丹
neigong 內功
neijia 內家
"Neijing tu" 內經圖
neili 內力
neizhuang 內壯
Nezha 哪吒
ninggu 凝固
Ningran Gaigong 凝然改公
Ningran Liaogai 凝然了改
Niu Gao 牛皋

Nizong quan 狔猔拳

Pai gun 排棍

Pan Weiru 潘蔚如

Paoquan 炮拳

Pei Cui 裴漼

Pingcheng 平城

Piquan 劈拳

Pishamen 毘沙門

po 魄

Poluomen daoyin 婆羅門導引

Pucong 普從

Pudu 普度

Pu'en 普恩

Pujing 普靜

Putidamo taixi jue 菩提達磨胎息訣

Putiliuzhi 菩提留支

Puxian 普賢

Puzhao 普照

qi 氣

Qianfo dian 千佛殿

qianqi neiyun 潛氣內運

qielan shen 伽藍神

Qigong 氣功

qihelan 耆賀濫

Qimen quan 奇門拳

Qin Wang 秦王

Qinggong 輕功

Qingqiang quan 擒鎗拳

Qiunabatuoluo 求那跋陀羅

Qiuran ke 虯髯客

quan 拳

Quan jing jieyao 拳經捷要

quan you wei shengxing hainei 拳猶未盛行海內

quanhui 拳會

quanjiao 拳教

Quanzhen 全真

Renjia duanda 任家短打

rou sheng gang 柔勝剛

Ruan Zutang 阮祖棠

ruo di qiang 弱敵強

Ruo jingcheng qidao, duo huo shen li ye 若精誠祈禱，多獲神力也

Ruyi jingu bang 如意金箍棒

sai 賽

(Sai) Jiantuo (塞) 揵馱

Sanjiao heyi 三教合一

Sanqi Yougong 三奇友公

sanmei 三昧

sansi 三司

seng bing 僧兵

"Seng bing shou jie ji" 僧兵首捷記

"Seng bing tan" 僧兵嘆

Seng Huike Damo xuemai lun 僧慧可達磨血脈論

Seng Putidamo cunxiang fa 僧菩提達磨存想法

Sengchou 僧稠

Sengjia huguo shi 僧伽護國史

Sengyan 僧彥

sengzheng 僧正

Sha Heshang 沙和尚

shang kaifu yitong da jiangjun 上開府儀同大將軍

shang zhuguo 上柱國

shangzuo 上座

Shanhu 善護

Shaolin 少林

Shaolin nanzong 少林南宗

"Shaolin seng bing" 少林僧兵

"Shaolin si bei" 少林寺碑

"Shaolin si duanda shen fa tong zong quan pu" 少林寺短打身法統宗拳譜

Shaolin wushu jie 少林武術節

Shaolin yuan 少林院

Shaoshi 少室 (Mt.)

"Shaquan ge" 沙拳歌

shen 身 (body)

shen 神 (spirit)

shen gun 神棍

Shen Quan 沈荃

Shengchao ding sheng wannian qing 聖朝鼎盛萬年青

shenli 神力

shengxian 聖賢

shengzhang 聲杖

Shensha shen 深沙神

shenzhi 神智

shi 勢

Shi Dian 石電 (*hao*: Jingyan 敬巖)

Shi Shangzhao 師尚詔.

Shi Xiaolong 釋小龍

Shi Yousan 石友三

Shiba Luohan shou 十八羅漢手

shiba wu 十八物

Shier duan jin 十二段錦

Shifang Chan Yuan 十方禪院

Shou shi chuan zhen 壽世傳真

shoubo 手搏

shouzhan 手戰

shouzhong 守中

shuinian 水碾

Sida ming shan 四大名山

Sima Chengzhen 司馬承禎

siping 四平

sizhu 寺主

Song 嵩(Mt.)

Song Jiang 宋江

"Song yue Shaolin xin zao chu ku ji" 嵩
    嶽少林新造廚庫記

Songyang shuyuan 嵩陽書院

sui 髓

sujia dizi 俗家弟子

Sun Chuo 孫綽

Sun Tong 孫通 (style: Li Kuan 李寬)

Sun Wukong 孫悟空

Sunjia pigua quan 孫家披掛拳

Tai 泰 (Mt.)

Taiji Quan 太極拳

Taiji tu 太極圖

Taishi太室 (Mt.)

taixi 胎息

"Taizong Wenhuang di yu shu" 太宗文
    皇帝御書

Talin 塔林

Tang Wang 唐王

Tanglang Quan 螳螂拳

Tanran Pinggong 坦然平公

Tanzong 曇宗

Tian Wenjing 田文鏡

Tiandihui 天地會

Tianlong babu 天龍八部

Tiantong 天童Monastery

Tianwang Dian 天王殿

Tianyuan 天員

Tianzhu anmo 天竺按摩

tiebang 鐵棒

Tiebu shan 鐵布衫

Tiefo 鐵佛 Temple

Tongtian Dasheng 通天大聖

Tongzi bai guanyin shen quan 童子拜
    觀音神拳

tui 腿

tuna 吐納

Wan Biao 萬表 (*hao*: Luyuan 鹿園)

wan xing 萬行

Wan'an Shungong 萬庵順公

Wanbao quanshu 萬寶全書

Wang Junkuo 王君廓

Wang Lang 王朗

Wang Lun 王倫

Wang Renze 王仁則

Wang Shichong 王世充

Wang Shijun 王士俊

Wang Tang 王堂

Wang Zhengnan 王征南

Wanyong zhengzong 萬用正宗

Weisheng yaoshu 衛生要術

Weituo xian chu 韋馱獻杵

wen 文

Wen Xiangfeng 文翔鳳

Wenjia quan 溫家拳

Wenshu 文殊

Wenzai 文載

wogu 握固

wokou 倭寇

wu 武(military)

wu 塢 (fort)

Wu Hanying 武漢英

wu seng 武僧

Wu Song tuo kao 武松脫銬

Wu yue zhen xing shan tu 五嶽真形山圖

Wubai luohan 五百羅漢

wubian li 無邊力

wuchan 武禪

Wudang 武當(Mt.)

Wuhu lan 五虎攔
"Wulang wei seng" 五郎為僧
Wuquan 五拳
wushang puti 無上菩提
Wutai 五臺 (Mt.)
wuxia xiaoshuo 武俠小說
Wuyi 無依
Wuyue 五嶽
xi 膝
Xi Lu 西魯
xiake 俠客
xian 仙
xiang bing 鄉兵
xianglong bang 降龍棒
xiangpu 相撲
xiangyao zhang 降妖杖
xiaoyao xue 笑腰穴
"Xiasheng Milefo ta" 下生彌勒佛塔
xiejiao 邪教
Xincheng 心誠
xinfa 心法
Xingyi Quan 形意拳
Xinyi Liuhe Quan 心意六合拳
xiong jing niao shen 熊經鳥伸
xiqiluo 隙棄羅
Xisui jing 洗髓經
Xiwu xu 習武序
xixi 錫錫
xizhang 錫杖
xu 虛
Xu Hongke 徐鴻客
Xu Ji 徐績
Xu Jian 徐堅
Xu Ji'an 徐濟庵
Xu Quanlai 徐全來
Xuanwu 玄武
Xuanzang 玄奘
xuedao 穴道
Xungong 訓公
Yaertu 雅爾圖
Yan Qing 燕青
Yanfu 閻浮
Yang Bing 楊炳
Yang Kefa 楊可發

Yang Kun 揚坤
Yang Sichang 楊嗣昌
Yang Wulang 楊五郎
Yang Ye 楊業
Yang Youji 養由基
Yangjia qiang 楊家鎗
yangsheng 養生
Yanming 延明
Yanqing quan 燕青拳
Yanshi 偃師
yao 搖
Yaoshi 藥師
Ye Feng 葉封
ye heshang 野和尚
yecha 夜叉 (*yakṣa*)
yi 意
yi da yi jie 一打一揭
Yifeng 一峰
Yihe quan 義和拳
Yijing 易經
Yinfeng 隱峰
Yinshou 陰手
Yinshu 引書
yinxiang 印相
Yinyuan 隱元
yiren 異人
yitong da jiangjun 儀同大將軍
Yixing 一行
yong 勇
Yongtai 永泰
Yongxin 永信
Yongyu 永玉
"You Tiantai shan fu" 遊天台山賦
Youji jiangjun 游擊將軍
Yu 虞 (Mt.)
Yuan You 元繇
Yuanjing 圓淨
yuanqi 元氣
Yuanxian 元賢
Yuanzhou 轅州
Yue Fei 岳飛
Yuejia duanda 樂家短打
Yuekong 月空
yueya 月牙

Yulanpen 盂蘭盆

yunqi 運氣

Yunyan 雲巖 Temple

Yuzhai 御寨

zan 讚

zei 賊

zengzhang shen li 增長身力

zhang 掌

Zhang Daoling 張道陵

Zhang Fei shen quan 張飛神拳

Zhang Luojiao 張洛焦

Zhang Sanfeng 張三丰(峰)

Zhang Siming 張思明

Zhang Songxi 張松溪

Zhang Xianzhong 張獻忠

Zhang Yanyuan 張彥遠

Zhang Yichao 張議潮

Zhang Yong 張永

Zhang Yongquan 張永銓

Zhang Yue 張說

Zhang Zhonglüe 張仲略

Zhao Dongxi 趙冬曦

Zhao Taizu changquan 趙太祖長拳

Zhao Xiaozai 趙孝宰

zhen 振

Zhenbao 真寶

Zheng 鄭

Zhenhua 震華

Zhenwu 真武

Zhenyuan 真元

Zhicao 志操

Zhiyi 智顗

Zhongli Quan 鍾離權

zhongshu ling 中書令

Zhongyue miao 中嶽廟

Zhongyue si 中嶽寺

zhou 肘 (elbow)

zhou 咒 (spell)

Zhou Bin 周斌

Zhou Jiafu 周嘉福

Zhu Hong 袾宏

Zhufang Cangong 竺方參公

Zi ning daoren 紫凝道人

Zisheng 茲聖

Ziyong 子用

Zizai 自在

Zongchi 總持

Zongdai 宗岱

Zongheng 宗衡

Zongqing 宗擎

Zongxiang 宗想

Zou 鄒

Zuanquan 鑽拳

Zuduan 祖端

Zui baxian quan 醉八仙拳

Zui quan 醉拳

Works Cited

Abbreviations

SKQS	*Wenyuange siku quanshu*
T	*Taishō shinshū daizōkyō*
DZ	Schipper, Kristofer, ed. *Concordance du Tao-tsang*
ZZ	*Dai Nihon zokuzōkyō*

(Editions of the *Yijin jing* (*Sinews Transformation Classic*) are listed in the Appendix)

Acker, William R. B. *Some T'ang and pre-T'ang Texts on Chinese Paintings.* Vol. 2, *Chang Yen-yuan, Li tai ming hua chi.* Leiden: Brill, 1974.

A'de 阿德. "Funiu shan xing ji" 伏牛山行記 (Record of an expedition to Mt. Funiu), *Chanlu* 禪露 24 (2002): 28–33.

———. "Jinnaluo wang kao" 緊那羅王考 (A study of King Jinnaluo). In *Shaolin gongfu wenji* (q.v.).

———. "Mingdai lamajiao yu Shaolin si" 明代喇嘛教與少林寺 (Ming period Tibetan Buddhism and the Shaolin Monastery). In *Shaolin gongfu wenji* (q.v.).

———. "Qianfo dian ji bihua kao" 千佛殿暨壁畫考 (The Thousand Buddhas' Hall wall painting). *Chanlu* 禪露 13 (1999): 48–51.

Adolphson, Mikael S. *The Teeth and Claws of the Buddha: Monastic Warriors and Sōhei in Japanese History.* Honolulu: University of Hawai'i Press, 2007.

Amos, Daniel M. "A Hong Kong Southern Praying Mantis Cult." *Journal of the Asian Martial Arts* 6, no. 4 (1997): 31–61.

Antony, Robert J. *Like Froth Floating on the Sea: The World of Pirates and Seafarers in Late Imperial South China.* China Research Monograph 56. Berkeley: Institute of East Asian Studies, University of California, 2003.

Apidamo jushe lun 阿毘達磨俱舍論 (Abhidharmakośaśāstra). By Vasubandhu. Translated by Xuanzang 玄奘. *T*, no. 1558.

Atwell, William. "The T'ai-ch'ang, T'ien-ch'i, and Ch'ung-chen Reigns, 1620–1644."

In *The Cambridge History of China*, vol. 7, 585–640. Cambridge: Cambridge University Press, 1988.

Beijing lao Tianqiao 北京老天橋 (The old Tianqiao District of Beijing). General Editor Wang Lixing 王立行. Beijing: Wenjin, 1993.

Berling, Judith A. *The Syncretic Religion of Lin Chao-en.* New York: Columbia University Press, 1980.

Birch, Cyril, trans. "The Curly-Bearded Hero." In *Classical Chinese Literature: An Anthology of Translations*. Vol. 1, *From Antiquity to the Tang Dynasty*, edited by John Minford and Joseph S. M. Lau. New York: Columbia University Press, 2000.

Bloch, Marc. *The Historian's Craft.* Translated by Peter Putnam. New York: Knopf, 1953.

Boretz, Avron A. "Martial Gods and Magic Swords: Identity, Myth, and Violence in Chinese Popular Religion." *Journal of Popular Culture* 29, no. 1 (1995): 93–109.

Brook, Timothy. *Praying for Power: Buddhism and the Formation of Gentry Society in Late-Ming China.* Harvard-Yenching Institute Monograph Series, 38. Cambridge, Mass.: Council on East Asian Studies, Harvard University, 1993.

———. "Rethinking Syncretism: The Unity of the Three Teachings and their Joint Worship in Late-Imperial China." *Journal of Chinese Religions* 21 (Fall 1993): 13–44.

Buswell, Robert E., ed. *Chinese Buddhist Apocrypha.* Honolulu: University of Hawai'i Press, 1990.

Cai Jiude 采九德. *Wobian shilüe* 倭變事略 (Outline of the pirates' upheaval). Preface 1558. Congshu jicheng edition. Shanghai: Shangwu, 1936.

Campany, Robert Ford. *To Live as Long as Heaven and Earth: A Translation and Study of Ge Hong's Traditions of Divine Transcendents.* Berkeley: University of California Press, 2002.

Cao Shibang 曹仕邦. "Yiwei dujiang yu chi roubiancai—liangge zhuming Chanzong gushi de lishi tanjiu" 「一葦渡江」與「喫肉邊菜」—兩個著名禪宗故事的歷史探究 ("Crossing the River on a Stalk of Reed" and "Eating Vegetables Cooked with Meat": A historical survey of two well-known Chan stories). *Zhonghua foxue xuebao* 中華佛學學報 13 (2005): 267–280.

Chang Naizhou 萇乃周. *Chang Shi wuji shu* 萇氏武技書 (The martial arts writings of Chang Naizhou). Edited by Xu Zhen 徐震. 1932. Reprint. Taibei: Yiwen, 1996.

Chaoye qian zai 朝野僉載 (The complete stories of the court and the people). Attributed to Zhang Zhuo 張鷟 (ca. 660–741). Congshu jicheng chubian edition. Beijing: Zhonghua, 1985.

Chase, Kenneth. *Firearms: A Global History to 1700.* Cambridge: Cambridge University Press, 2003.

Chavannes, Edouard. *Le T'ai chan; essai de monographie d'un cult Chinoise.* Paris: Ernest Leroux, 1910.

Ch'en, Kenneth K. S. *Buddhism in China: A Historical Survey.* Princeton, N.J.: Princeton University Press, 1964.

Chen Li-li, trans. *Master Tung's Western Chamber Romance.* Cambridge: Cambridge University Press, 1976.

Chen, Nancy N. *Breathing Spaces: Qigong, Psychiatry, and Healing in China.* New York: Columbia University Press, 2003.

Chen Pengcheng and Feng Wu. "The Eight-Section Brocade of General Yue Fei." *Kung Fu Tai Chi,* part 1 (January 2004): 102–105, part 2 (April 2004): 102–105.

Chen Pingyuan 陳平原. *Qiangu wenren xiake meng* 千古文人俠客夢 (The scholars' ancient knight-errant dream). 1992. Reprint, Taibei: Maitian, 1995.

Chen Sidong 陳泗東. *Xingyuan bigeng lu* 幸園筆耕錄 (A life of writing at Xingyuan). 2 vols. Quanzhou: Lujiang, 2003.

Cheng Dali 程大力. "Mingdai wushu" 明代武術 (Ming martial arts). In *Zhongguo wushu baike quanshu* (q.v.).

———. "Qingdai wushu" 清代武術 (Qing martial arts). In *Zhongguo wushu baike quanshu* (q.v.).

———. *Zhongguo wushu: lishi yu wenhua* 中國武術: 歷史與文化 (The Chinese martial arts: history and culture). Chengdu: Sichuan daxue, 1995.

Cheng Zongyou 程宗猷 (Style: Chongdou 沖斗). *Shaolin gunfa chan zong* 少林棍法闡宗 (Exposition of the original Shaolin staff method). In Cheng Zongyou, *Gengyu shengji* 耕餘剩技 (Techniques for after-farming pastime). 1621 edition. (Copies at the Beijing Library and the Shanghai Library). The *Shaolin gunfa chan zong* is available also in an edition titled *Shaolin gun jue* 少林棍訣 (The Shaolin staff formulas), which carries a forged preface attributed to the earlier Yu Dayou 俞大猷 (1503–1579). (Copy at the Naikaku Bunko Library).

———. *She shi* 射史 (History of archery). 1629 edition. (Copy at the Beijing Library).

Chifeng sui 赤鳳髓 (The red phoenix's marrow). Preface 1578. Compiled by Zhou Lüjing 周履靖. Congshu jicheng edition. Shanghai: Shangwu, 1939.

China Statistical Yearbook 2000. Compiled by the National Bureau of Statistics, People's Republic of China. Beijing: China Statistics Press, 2000.

Ching, Gene. "Battling to be Shaolin's best." *Kung Fu Tai Chi* (December 2003): 40–45.

———. "Black Whirlwind Axes: The Legend of Li Kwei." *Kungfu Qigong* (August 2000): 10–13.

———. "Bodhidharma's Legendary Fighting Cane." *Kungfu Qigong* (February 2002): 65–66.

——— [Chen Xing Hua]. "How Jet Li Saved the Shaolin Temple." *Kungfu Qigong* (January 1999): 62–65.

———. "In the Dragon's Den: Grandmaster Chen Tongshan and his Superstar Son, the Little Dragon, Shi Xiaolong." *Kung Fu Tai Chi* (December 2003): 50–53.

———. "The 'One' of the Top Ten: Shaolin Grandmaster Liang Yiquan." *Kung Fu Tai Chi* (December 2003): 54–57, 103.

———. "Shaolin Brothers Go West: Shi De Shan and Shi Xing Hao, Two Shaolin Temple Monks Begin Teaching in America." *Kungfu Qigong* (December 1999): 50–57.

——— [Chen Xing Hua]. "Shaolin Temple's Prodigal Son: Monk Shi Yanming's

Return to Shaolin after His Defection." *Kungfu Qigong* (Spring 2000): 76–80.

———. "Shaolin Temple Reincarnated." *Kung Fu Tai Chi* (June 2005): 24–28.

———. "13,000 Warriors of Taguo." *Kung Fu Tai Chi* (December 2003): 46–49.

———. "United Nations, Divided Shaolin." *Kung Fu Tai Chi* (December 2003): 10–13, 36–37.

———. "The World Heritage of Shaolin: Interview with Venerable Shi Yongxin, Abbot of Shaolin Temple." *Kung Fu Tai Chi* (December 2003): 24–35.

Ching, Gene, and Gigi Oh. "Shaolin's Second Wave." *Kung Fu Tai Chi* (February 2004): 78–80.

Chou Yi-Liang. "Tantrism in China." *Harvard Journal of Asiatic Studies* 8.3/4 (March 1945): 241–332.

Chu Renhuo 褚人獲 (fl. 1700). *Sui Tang yanyi* 隋唐演義 (Romance of the Sui and Tang). Changsha: Yuelu, 1997.

Chuanfa baoji 傳法寶記 (Precious record of the Dharma's transmission). Compiled by Du Fei 杜朏. *T*, no. 2838.

Chuantong Shaolin quan taolu jiaocheng 傳統少林拳套路教程 (Shaolin gong-fu: a course in traditional forms). 5 vols. Edited by Liu Haichao 劉海超. Zhengzhou: Henan keji, 1994–1997.

Cole, Alan. "It's All in the Framing: Desire and Innocence in Early Chan Narratives—A Close-Reading of the Biography of Chan Master Fa Ru." (Unpublished paper.)

Cui Geng 崔耕. "*Tang 'Qin wang gao Shaolin si jiao bei' kao*" (A study of the inscribed Tang Qin prince letter to the Shaolin Monastery) 唐《秦王告少林寺教碑》考. *Zhongyuan wenwu* 中原文物 (1983.3): 88–90.

Dai Nihon zokuzōkyō 大日本續藏經 (The great Japanese continuation of the Buddhist canon). 750 *ce*, in 150 cases. Kyoto: Zōkyō shoin, 1905–1912.

Damo dashi xuemai lun 達磨大師血脈論 (The great master Bodhidharma's blood vessels theory). Preface Ren Zhe 任哲 (1153). ZZ edition.

Daocheng 道誠. *Shishi yaolan* 釋氏要覽 (Buddhist essentials). Preface 1020. *T*, no. 2127.

Daoxuan 道宣. *Xu Gaoseng zhuan* 續高僧專 (Continuation of the biographies of eminent monks). *T*, no. 2060.

Daoyuan 道原. *Jingde chuandeng lu* 景德傳燈錄 (Jingde period record of the transmission of the lamp). *T*, no. 2076.

Da Tang da Cien si Sanzang fashi zhuan 大唐大慈恩寺三藏法事傳 (Biography of the great Tang master of the law, Sanzang of the great Cien monastery). By Huili 慧立 and Yancong 彥悰. *T*, no. 2053.

Da Tang Sanzang fashi qu jing shihua 大唐三藏法師取經詩話 (The poetic tale of the master of the law, Tripitaka of the great Tang, procuring the scriptures). Beijing: Wenxue guji, 1955.

Dars, Jacques, trans. *Au bord de l'eau*. Authors given as Shi Nai-an and Luo Guanzhong. 2 vols. Paris: Gallimard, 1978.

Dean, Kenneth. "Lei Yu-sheng ("Thunder Is Noisy") and Mu-lien in the Theatrical and Funerary Traditions of Fukien." In *Ritual Opera, Operatic Ritual,* edited by David Johnson (q.v.).

Dedao ticheng xizhang jing 得道梯橙錫杖經 (The Sutra of attaining the way through the ladder steps of the ring staff). *T,* no. 785.

de Groot, J. J. M. "Buddhist Masses for the Dead at Amoy." In *Actes du sixième congrès international des orientalistes.* Leiden: Brill, 1985.

de La Vallée Poussin, Louis, trans. *L'abhidharmakośa de Vasubandhu.* 1923. Reprint. Mélanges Chinois et Bouddhiques, vol. XVI. 6 vols. Bruxelles: Institut Belge des Hautes Études Chinoises, 1971.

Demiéville, Paul. "Le Bouddhisme et la guerre: post-scriptum à l'histoire des moines guerriers du Japon de G. Renondeau." Reprinted in his *Choix d'etudes Bouddhiques.* Leiden: E. J. Brill, 1973.

Des Forges, Roger V. *Cultural Centrality and Political Change in Chinese History: Northeast Henan in the Fall of the Ming.* Stanford, Calif.: Stanford University Press, 2003.

Despeux, Catherine. "Gymnastics: The Ancient Tradition." In *Taoist Meditation and Longevity Techniques,* edited by Livia Kohn (q.v.).

———. *La moelle du phénix rouge: santé et longue vie dans la Chine du XVIe siècle.* Paris: Guy Trédaniel, 1988.

Dong Jieyuan 董解元. *Dong Jieyuan Xixiang* 董解元西廂 (Master Dong's story of the western wing). Annotated by Tang Xianzu 湯顯祖. Ming edition, photographic rpt., Taiwan: Shangwu, 1970.

Dudbridge, Glen. *The Hsi-yu chi: A Study of Antecedents to the Sixteenth-Century Chinese Novel.* Cambridge: Cambridge University Press, 1970.

———. "The Hsi-yu chi Monkey and the Fruits of the Last Ten Years." *Hanxue yanjiu* 漢學研究 6.1 (June 1988): 463–486.

Dudgeon, John. "Kung-fu or Medical Gymnastics." *Journal of the Peking Oriental Society* 3, no. 4 (1895): 341–565.

Dumoulin, Heinrich. *Zen Buddhism: A History.* Translated by James W. Heisig and Paul Knitter. New York: Macmillan, 1988.

Du Mu 都穆. *Jin xie linlang* 金薤琳琅 (Calligraphic gems). Ming edition. (Copy at the Beijing Library). (Also a SKQS edition.)

———. *You mingshan ji* 遊名山記 (Record of journeys to famous mountains). Preface 1515. In *Baoyantang miji* 寶顏堂秘笈. Edited by Chen Jiru 陳繼儒. 1606–1620 edition. (Copy at the Harvard-Yenching Library.)

Dunhuang bianwen ji 敦煌變文集 (Collection of *bianwen* from Dunhuang). Edited by Wang Chongmin 王重民. Beijing: Renmin wenxue, 1957.

Durand-Dastès, Vincent. "Le Roman du maître de dhyāna: Bodhidharma et Ji-le-Fou dans le roman Chinois en langue vulgaire du XVIIe siècle." Thèse de doctorat. Institut national des langues et civilisations orientales, 2000.

Elliot, Allan J. A. *Chinese Spirit Medium Cults in Singapore.* 1955. Reprint. Taibei: Southern Materials Center, 1981.

Encyclopedia Mikra'it (Encyclopedia Biblica). 9 vols. Jerusalem: Mosad Bialik, 1962.

Engelhardt, Ute. "Longevity Techniques and Chinese Medicine." In Kohn, *Daoism Handbook* (q.v.).

Erlang Shen suo Qitian Dasheng 二郎神鎖齊天大聖 (Erlang Shen captures Qitian Dasheng). In vol. 29 of *Guben Yuan Ming Zaju* (q.v.).

Ershisi shi jiaodian ben 二十四史校典本 (Collated edition of the "twenty-four histories"). 241 vols. Beijing: Zhonghua shuju, 1974.

Esherick, Joseph W. *The Origins of the Boxer Uprising*. Berkeley: University of California Press, 1987.

Fanwang jing 梵網經. (The Brahmā's net sutra). *T*, no. 1484.

Faure, Bernard. "Bodhidharma as Textual and Religious Paradigm." *History of Religions* 25, no. 3 (February 1986): 187–198.

———. *The Red Thread: Buddhist Approaches to Sexuality*. Princeton, N.J.: Princeton University, 1998.

———. "Relics and Flesh Bodies: The Creation of Ch'an Pilgrimage Sites." In *Pilgrims and Sacred Sites in China*, edited by Susan Naquin and Chün-fang Yü (q.v.).

———. *The Rhetoric of Immediacy: A Cultural Critique of Chan/Zen Buddhism*. Princeton, N.J.: Princeton University Press, 1991.

———, trans. *Le Traité de Bodhidharma: Première anthologie du bouddhisme Chan*. Paris: Le Mail, 1986.

Fayun 法雲. *Fanyi mingyi ji* 翻譯名義集 (Translated Buddhist terminology). Preface 1157. *T*, no. 2131.

Feng Menglong 馮夢龍. *Xingshi hengyan* 醒世恒言 (Constant words to awaken the world). Taibei: Dingwen, 1978.

Feng Peihong 馮培紅. "P. 3249 bei 'jun ji can juan' yu Guiyi jun chuqi de sengbing wuzhuang" P. 3249 背《軍籍殘卷》與歸義軍初期的僧兵武裝 (The "damaged military document" on the back of P. 3249 and armed monastic troops in the early stages of the "Return to Allegiance Army"). *Dunhuang yanjiu* 敦煌研究56 (1998, no. 2): 141–147.

Fengshen yanyi 封神演義 (Investiture of the gods). Author given as Xu Zhonglin 許仲琳. Edited by Li Guoqing 李國慶. 2 vols. Beijing: Beijing tushuguan, 2001.

Foguang da cidian 佛光大辭典 (The big dictionary of the Buddha light). General Editor Ci Yi 慈怡. 8 vols. Gaoxiong: Foguang, 1988.

Foulk, T. Griffith. "Sung Controversies Concerning the 'Separate Transmission' of Ch'an" In *Buddhism in the Sung*, edited by Peter N. Gregory and Daniel A. Getz. Kuroda Institute Studies in East Asian Buddhism 13. Honolulu: University of Hawai'i Press, 1999.

Frédéric, Louis. *Les dieux du Bouddhisme*. Paris: Flammarion, 2006.

French, Howard W. "So Many Paths. Which Shaolin Is Real?" *New York Times*, February 10, 2005.

Fu Mei 傅梅. *Song shu* 嵩書 (The Song Mountain book). Preface 1612. (Copy at the Naikaku Bunko library). (Those *Song shu* chapters that are relevant to the Shaolin Monastery's history have been reprinted under the title *Songshan*

Shaolin si ji zhi 嵩山少林寺輯志 in series no. 2, vols. 23–24 of *Zhongguo fo si shi zhi hui kan* 中國佛寺史志彙刊. Taibei: Mingwen, 1980 (q.v.).

Fung Yu-Lan. *A History of Chinese Philosophy*. Translated by Derk Bodde. 2 vols. Princeton, N.J.: Princeton University Press, 1953.

Fuqing Shaolin si 福清少林寺 (The Fuqing Shaolin Temple). Edited by Fuqing Shaolin si Bianzuan Weiyuanhui 福清少林寺編纂委員會. Fuzhou: Fujiansheng ditu, 1996.

Gamsa, Mark. "How a Republic of Chinese Red Beards Was Invented in Paris." *Modern Asian Studies* 36, no. 4 (2002): 993–1010.

Gao Lian 高濂. *Zunsheng bajian* 遵生八牋 (Eight treatises on guarding life). 1591 edition. Photographic reprint in vol. 61 of *Beijing tushuguan guji zhenben congkan* 北京圖書館古籍珍本叢刊 (Ancient rare books from the Beijing Library collection). Beijing: Shumu wenxian, 1988.

Geiss, James. "The Chia-ching Reign, 1522–1566." In *The Cambridge History of China*, vol. 7, 440–510. Cambridge: Cambridge University Press, 1988.

Gernet, Jacques. *Buddhism in Chinese Society: An Economic History from the Fifth to the Tenth Centuries*. Translated by Franciscus Verellen. New York: Columbia University Press, 1995.

Getty, Alice. *The Gods of Northern Buddhism: Their History, Iconography and Progressive Evolution through the Northern Buddhist Countries*. 1928. Reprint. New Delhi: Munshiram Manoharlal, 1978.

Gong Pengcheng 龔鵬程. "Damo Yijin jing lunkao" 達摩易筋經論考 (A study of Bodhidharma's "Yijin jing"). *Pumen xuebao* 普門學報 5 (September 2001): 73–100.

Goodrich, L. Carrington, ed. *Dictionary of Ming Biography 1368–1744*. 2 vols. New York: Columbia University Press, 1976.

Goossaert, Vincent. *L'interdit du boeuf en Chine. Agriculture, éthique et sacrifice*. Bibliothèque de l'institut des hautes études Chinoises, vol. 36. Paris: Collège de France, 2005.

Graff, David A. *Medieval Chinese Warfare, 300–900*. London: Routledge, 2002.

Granet, Marcel. *Danses et légendes de la Chine ancienne*. 1926. Reprint. Paris: Presses Universitaires de France, 1959.

Guang hong ming ji 廣弘明集 (The enlarged collection of spreading the Dharma and enlightening the people). Compiled by Daoxuan 道宣. *T*, no. 2103.

Guben Yuan Ming Zaju 孤本元明雜劇 (Rare editions of Yuan and Ming *zaju*). Shanghai: Hanfenlou, 1941.

Gu Liuxin 顧留馨. "Wushu shishang de Gan Fengchi" 武術史上的甘鳳池 (The historical martial artist Gan Fengchi). In *Zhongguo tiyushi cankao ziliao* 中國體育史參考資料 (Research materials on the history of Chinese physical education), vol. 5, 17–23. Beijing: Renmin tiyu, 1958.

Gushan Yongjue heshang guanglu 鼓山永覺和尚廣錄 (The comprehensive records of monk Yongjue [Yuanxian] from Mt. Gu). Edited by Dao Pei 道霈. In *Mingban Jiaxing Dazang jing* 明版嘉興大藏經 (Ming period Jiaxing edition of the Buddhist canon). Wanli edition. Photographic reprint. Taibei: Xinwenfeng, 1987.

Gu Shiquan 谷世權. *Zhongguo tiyu shi* 中國體育史 (A history of Chinese physical education). Vol. 2, *Jin xian dai* 近現代 (The modern and contemporary periods). Beijing: Beijing tiyu xueyuan, 1989.

Gu Yanwu 顧炎武. *Gu Tinglin shi ji huizhu* 顧亭林詩集彙注 (Gu Yanwu's collected poetry with collected annotations). Annotated by Wang Qucheng 王蘧常. Collated by Wu Piji 吳丕績. 2 vols. Shanghai: Shanghai guji, 1983.

———. *Jinshi wenzi ji* 金石文字記 (Records of writings on metal and stone). SKQS edition.

———. *Rizhilu jishi* 日知錄集釋 (Collected notes on record of knowledge gained day by day). Edited by Huang Rucheng 黃汝成. 1834 edition. Photographic reprint. Shanghai: Shanghai guji, 1984.

Gu Yingtai 谷應太. *Mingshi jishi benmo* 明史紀事本末 (The complete record of Ming history). 1658. SKQS edition.

Hamm, John Christopher. *Paper Swordsmen: Jin Yong and the Modern Chinese Martial Arts Novel.* Honolulu: University of Hawai'i Press, 2005.

Hanan, Patrick. *The Chinese Short Story: Studies in Dating, Authorship, and Composition.* Cambridge, Mass.: Harvard University Press, 1973.

———. *The Chinese Vernacular Story.* Cambridge, Mass.: Harvard University Press, 1981.

Hansen, Valerie. *Changing Gods in Medieval China, 1127–1276.* Princeton, N.J.: Princeton University Press, 1990.

———. "Gods on Walls: A Case of Indian Influence on Chinese Lay Religion?" In *Religion and Society in T'ang and Sung China,* edited by Patricia Buckley Ebrey and Peter N. Gregory. Honolulu: University of Hawai'i Press, 1993.

Hanshu 漢書 (History of the [Former] Han). Compiled by Ban Gu 班固. In *Ershisi shi jiaodian ben* (q.v.).

Hanyu dacidian 漢語大詞典 (The big dictionary of the Chinese language). Edited by Luo Zhufeng 羅竹風 et al. 13 vols. Shanghai: Hanyu dacidian, 1991.

Hao Chunwen 郝春文. *Tang houqi Wudai Song chu Dunhuang seng ni de shehui shenghuo* 唐后期五代宋初敦煌僧尼的社會生活 (The social life of monks and nuns at Dunhuang in the late Tang, Five Dynasties, and early Song periods). Beijing: Zhongguo shehui kexue, 1998.

Hao Qin 郝勤. "Lun wushu wenhua yu zhongguo minjian mimi zongjiao de guanxi" 論武術文化與中國民間秘密宗教的關係 (On the relations between martial arts culture and Chinese popular religious sects). In *Zhongguo wushu yu chuantong wenhua* 中國武術與傳統文化 (Chinese martial arts and traditional culture). Beijing: Beijing tiyu, 1990.

Harper, Donald J. *Early Chinese Medical Literature: The Mawangdui Medical Manuscripts.* Sir Henry Wellcome Asian Series. London: Kegan Paul, 1998.

Harvey, Peter. *An Introduction to Buddhist Ethics: Foundations, Values and Issues.* Cambridge: Cambridge University Press, 2000.

He Liangchen 何良臣. *Zhenji* 陣紀 (Records of military tactics). Congshu jicheng edition. Shanghai: Shangwu, 1939.

Henan fu zhi 河南府志 (Gazetteer of Henan Prefecture). Edited by Zhu Mingkui 朱明魁 and He Bairu 何柏如. 1661 edition. (Copy at the Shanghai Library.)

Henning, Stanley E. "Reflections on a Visit to the Shaolin Monastery." *Journal of Asian Martial Arts* 7, no. 1 (1998): 90–101.

He Zehan 何澤翰. *Rulin waishi renwu benshi kaolüe* 儒林外史人物本事考略 (Draft study of the protagonists' origins in the "unofficial history of the scholars"). Shanghai: Gudian wenxue, 1957.

He Zhiqing 赫治清. *Tiandihui qiyuan yanjiu* 天地會起源研究 (Research into the origins of the Tiandihui). Beijing: Shehui kexue wenxian, 1996.

Hong Mai 洪邁. *Yijian zhi* 夷堅志 (Stories heard by Yijian). 8 vols. Congshu jicheng chubian edition. Shanghai: Shangwu, 1936.

Huang Baijia 黃白家. *Neijia quanfa* 內家拳法 (Internal school fist method). In *Zhaodai congshu bieji* 昭代叢書別集 (Second installment of the collected books of a bright era). 1876 edition. (Copy at the Harvard-Yenching Library.)

Huang Changlun 黃常倫. "Lüzong diyi daochang: Baohuashan Longchangsi" 律宗第一道場——寶華山隆昌寺 (The *vinaya* school foremost temple: Longchang monastery on Mt. Baohua). *Fayin* 法音 165 (1998, no. 5): 51–54.

Huang Huajie 黃華節. *Guangong de renge yu shenge* 關公的人格與神格 (Guangong's human and divine personality). Taibei: Shangwu yinshuguan, 1967.

Huang, Ray. *1587 A Year of No Significance: The Ming Dynasty in Decline*. New Haven, Conn.: Yale University Press, 1981.

Huang Zhaohan 黃兆漢. *Mingdai daoshi Zhang Sanfeng kao* 明代道士張三丰考 (A study of the Ming period Daoist master Zhang Sanfeng). Taibei: Xuesheng shuju, 1988.

Huang Zongxi 黃宗羲. *Nanlei wending* 南雷文定 (Selected writings by Huang Zongxi). Congshu jicheng edition. Shanghai: Shangwu, 1936.

Hucker, Charles O. "Ming Government." In *The Cambridge History of China*, vol. 8, 9–105. Cambridge: Cambridge University Press, 1998.

Huijiao 慧皎 (497–554). *Gaoseng zhuan* 高僧傳 (Biographies of eminent monks). *T*, no. 2059.

Hummel, Arthur W., ed. *Eminent Chinese of the Ch'ing period (1644–1912)*. 2 vols. Washington: Library of Congress, 1943–1944.

Hurvitz, Leon, trans. *Scripture of the Lotus Blossom of the Fine Dharma*. New York: Columbia University Press, 1976.

Irwin, Richard Gregg. *The Evolution of a Chinese Novel: Shui-hu-chuan*. Harvard-Yenching Institute Studies, no. 10. Cambridge, Mass.: Harvard University Press, 1953.

Jakes, Susan. "Kicking the Habit." *Time* (Asia edition), November 19, 2001, 42–45.

Jiao Hong 焦竑 (1541–1620). *Guochao xianzheng lu* 國朝獻徵錄 (Record of our dynasty's documents). 1616 edition. Photographic reprint in *Mingdai zhuanji congkan* 明代傳記叢刊 (Collected biographical works of the Ming dynasty). Taibei: Mingwen 1991.

Jing Rizhen 景日昣. *Shuo Song* 說嵩 (On Mt. Song). Preface 1721. (Copy at the Harvard-Yenching Library.)

Jin Ping Mei cihua 金瓶梅詞話 (The poetic story of the plum in the golden vase). 4 vols. Hongkong: Mengmei guan, 1993.

Jinshu 晉書 (History of the Jin dynasty). Edited by Fang Xuanling 房玄齡 et al. In *Ershisi shi jiaodian ben* (q.v.).

Jiu Tang shu 舊唐書 (Old history of the Tang dynasty). Edited by Liu Xu 劉昫 et al. In *Ershisi shi jiaodian ben* (q.v.).

Jizu shan zhi 雞足山志 (Gazetteer of Mt. Jizu). By Qian Bangzuan 錢邦纂. Revised by Fan Chengxun 范承勳. 1692 edition. Photographic reprint in series no. 3, vol. 1 of *Zhongguo fo si shi zhi hui kan* (q.v.).

Johnson, David, ed. *Ritual Opera, Operatic Ritual: Mu-lien Rescues His Mother in Chinese Popular Culture*. Publications of the Chinese Popular Culture Project 1. Berkeley, Calif.: Institute of East Asian Studies Publications, 1989.

Kangxi Dengfeng xian zhi 康熙登封縣志 (Kangxi period (1662–1722) Dengfeng County gazetteer). Compiled by Jing Rizhen 景日昣 and Zhang Shenggao 張聖誥. Revised by Shi Yizan 施奕簪 and Jiao Ruheng 焦如蘅. 1696. Revised edition 1745. (Copy at the Beijing Library).

Kang Yong Qian shiqi chengxiang renmin fankang douzheng ziliao 康雍乾時期城鄉人民反抗斗爭資料 (Materials on urban and agricultural popular revolts and conflicts of the Kangxi, Yongzheng, and Qianlong reigns). Edited by Zhongguo renmin daxue qingshi yanjiusuo 中國人民大學清史研究所. 2 vols. Beijing: Zhonghua, 1979.

Kash, David E. "The Original Emperor's Long Fist System." *Kung Fu Tai Chi* (February 2004): 10–19.

Katz, Paul R. *Images of the Immortal: The Cult of Lü Dongbin at the Palace of Eternal Joy*. Honolulu: University of Hawai'i Press, 1999.

Keiran shūyō shū 溪嵐拾葉集 (Collection of leaves from mountain streams). By Kōshū 光宗 (1276–1350). *T*, no. 2410.

Kent, Richard K. "Depictions of the Guardians of the Law: Lohan Painting in China." In *Latter Days of the Law: Images of Chinese Buddhism 850–1850*, edited by Marsha Weidner. Lawrence, Kan.: Spencer Museum of Art, 1994.

Kieschnick, John. "Buddhist Vegetarianism in China." In *Tripod and Palate: Food, Politics, and Religion in Traditional China*, edited by Roel Sterckx. New York: Palgrave Macmillan, 2005.

———. *The Eminent Monk: Buddhist Ideals in Medieval Chinese Hagiography*. Kuroda Institute Studies in East Asian Buddhism, no. 10. Honolulu: University of Hawai'i Press, 1997.

———. *The Impact of Buddhism on Chinese Material Culture*. Princeton, N.J.: Princeton University Press, 2003.

Kohn, Livia, ed. *Daoism Handbook*. Leiden: Brill, 2000.

———, ed. *Taoist Meditation and Longevity Techniques*. Michigan Monographs in Chinese Studies, vol. 61. Ann Arbor, Mich.: Center for Chinese Studies 1989.

Kroll, Paul W. "Body Gods and Inner Vision: The Scripture of the Yellow Court." In *Religions of China in Practice*, edited by Donald S. Lopez. Princeton, N.J.: Princeton University Press, 1996.

———. "Verses from on High: The Ascent of T'ai Shan." *T'oung Pao* LXIX, 4–5 (1983): 223–260.

Kuang Wennan 曠文楠. "Shaolin xiwu de faduan ji zaoqi Daojiao wushu" 少林習武的發端及早期道教武術 (The origins of Shaolin martial practice and the early Daoist martial arts). *Tiyu wenshi* 體育文史 (1994, no. 4): 9–11.

Kuriyama, Shigehisa. *The Expressiveness of the Body and the Divergence of Greek and Chinese Medicine.* New York: Zone Books, 1999.

Lachman, Charles. "Why Did the Patriarch Cross the River? The Rushleaf Bodhidharma Reconsidered." *Asia Major* third series, 2, no. 2 (1993): 237–268.

Lagerwey, John. "The Pilgrimage to Wu-tang Shan." In Naquin and Chün-fang Yü, *Pilgrims and Sacred Sites in China* (q.v.).

———. *Taoist Ritual in Chinese Society and History.* New York: Macmillan, 1987.

———. "Wu Yüeh ch'un ch'iu." In *Early Chinese Texts: A Bibliographical Guide*, edited by Michael Lowe. Berkeley, Calif.: The Society for the Study of Early China, and the Institute of East Asian Studies, 1993.

Lamotte, Étienne. "Vajrapāṇi in India." Translated by Sara Boin-Webb. *Buddhist Studies Review* 20, no. 1 (2003): 1–30.

Lau, D. C., trans. *Mencius.* London: Penguin Books, 1970.

———, trans. *Lao Tzu: Tao Te Ching.* Middlesex: Penguin Books, 1963.

Lee, Hon K. "The Real Fists of Fury: The Artists and Artistry of Mizong Quan." *Kung Fu Tai Chi* (February 2004): 48–53.

Leung, Chan Kai, and TC Media. "Wu Song Breaks Manacles." *Kungfu Qigong* (August 2002): 16–20, 25–28.

Lévi-Strauss, Claude. *The Raw and the Cooked.* Translated by John and Doreen Weightman. New York: Harper and Row, 1964.

Liangshanbo Li Kui fu jing 梁山泊李逵負荊 (Li Kui of Liangshanbo shoulders thorns). In *Yuan qu xuan* 元曲選 (Collection of Yuan plays). Edited by Zang Jinshu 臧晉叔. Beijing: Zhonghua, 1979.

Lin Boyuan 林伯原. "Tan Zhongguo wushu zai Mingdai de fazhan bianhua" 談中國武術在明代的發展變化 (On the evolution and transformation of the Chinese martial arts during the Ming period). In *Zhonghua wushu luncong* 中華武術論叢 (Essays on the Chinese martial arts). Beijing: Renmin tiyu, 1987.

———. *Zhongguo tiyu shi* 中國體育史 (A history of Chinese physical education). Vol. 1, *gudai* 古代 (Classical period). Beijing: Beijing tiyu xueyuan, 1987.

Lin Qing 麟慶. *Hong xue yinyuan tuji* 鴻雪因緣圖記 (Illustrated record of goose life's traces in the snow). 1849. Photographic reprint. Beijing: Beijing guji, 1984.

Ling Tingkan 凌廷堪 (1757–1809). *Jiaolitang wenji* 校禮堂文集 (Collected prose from the Investigating the Rites Hall). 1812 edition.

Little, Stephen, and Shawn Eichman, eds. *Taoism and the Arts of China.* Chicago: Art Institute of Chicago, 2000.

Liu, James J. Y. *The Chinese Knight-Errant.* Chicago: The University of Chicago Press, 1967.

Liu Junxiang 劉峻驤. *Dongfang renti wenhua* 東方人體文化 (The eastern body culture). Shanghai: Shanghai wenyi, 1996.

Liu T'ieh-yün (Liu E). *The Travels of Lao Ts'an.* Translated by Harold Shadick. Ithaca, N.Y.: Cornell University Press, 1952.

Lufu zouzhe 錄副奏摺 ([[Grand council archives] memorial reference copies). Stored at the Zhongguo diyi lishi dang'an guan 中國第一歷史檔案館 (The Chinese first historical archives), Beijing.

Luohan hua 羅漢畫 (Arhat paintings). Edited by Guoli gugong bowuyuan bianji weiyuanhui. Taibei: Guoli gugong bowuyuan, 1990.

Luo Ye 羅燁. *Xinbian zuiweng tanlu* 新編醉翁談錄 (Newly edited notes of the drunken old man). Shanghai: Gudian wenxue, 1957.

Lu Zhishen xishang huanghua yu 魯智深喜賞黃花峪 (Lu Zhishen enjoys yellow flower valley). In *Guben Yuan Ming zaju* (q.v.).

Mair, Victor H. *T'ang Transformation Texts.* Harvard-Yenching Institute Monograph Series, 28. Cambridge, Mass.: Council on East Asian Studies, Harvard University, 1989.

————. *Tun-huang Popular Narratives.* Cambridge: Cambridge University Press, 1983.

Ma Litang 馬禮堂 and Sun Yamin 孫亞民. "Xingyi shizu Ji Longfeng" 形意始祖姬龍峰 (Xingyi founder Ji Longfeng). *Wulin* 武林 84 (1988, no. 9): 36–38.

Ma Mingda 馬明達. *Shuo jian cong gao* 說劍叢稿 (Draft essays on the sword). Lanzhou: Lanzhou daxue, 2000.

Mann, Susan, and Philip A. Kuhn. "Dynastic Decline and the Roots of Rebellion," *Cambridge History of China*, vol. 10, 107–162. Cambridge: Cambridge University Press, 1978.

Mao Yuanyi 茅元儀. *Wubei zhi* 武備志 (Treatise on military preparations). 1621 edition. Photographic reprint in vols. 27–36 of *Zhongguo bingshu jicheng* (q.v.).

Maspero, Henri. "Methods of 'Nourishing the Vital Principle' in the Ancient Taoist Religion." In Henri Maspero, *Taoism and Chinese Religion*. Translated by Frank A. Kierman. Amherst: University of Massachusetts, 1981.

Master Tung's Western Chamber Romance. Translated by Chen Li-li. New York: Columbia University Press, 1994.

Mather, Richard B. "The Mystical Ascent of the T'ient'ai Mountains: Sun Ch'o's 'Yu-t'ien-t'ai-shan fu.'" *Monumenta Serica* 20 (1961): 226–245.

Matsuda Ryūchi 松田隆智. *Zhongguo wushu shilüe* 中國武術史略 (A brief history of the Chinese martial arts). (Translation of *Zusetsu Chūgoku bujutsu shi*). Taibei: Danqing tushu, 1986.

McRae, John R. *The Northern School and the Formation of Early Ch'an Buddhism.* Kuroda Institute Studies in East Asian Buddhism, no. 3. Honolulu: University of Hawai'i Press, 1986.

The Metropolitan Museum of Art: Asia. New York: Metropolitan Museum of Art, 1987.

Miaofa lianhua jing 妙法蓮華經 (Scripture of the lotus blossom of the fine Dharma). Translated by Kumārajīva (344–413). *T*, no. 262.

Mingdai wokou shiliao 明代倭寇史料 (Materials on the Ming period pirates). Edited by Zheng Liangsheng 鄭樑生. 5 vols. Taibei: Wenshizhe, 1987.

Mingshi 明史 (History of the Ming). Compiled by Zhang Tingyu 張廷玉 et al. In *Ershisi shi jiaodian ben* (q.v.).

Ming shi lu 明實錄 (Ming veritable records). Manuscript edition. Photographic reprint. 133 vols. Taibei: Zhongyang yanjiuyuan, 1961–1966.

Min'guo renwu da cidian 民國人物大辭典 (The big dictionary of Republican period biographies). General editor Xu Youchun 徐友春. Shijiazhuang: Hebei renmin, 1991.

Miura, Kunio. "The Revival of Qi: Qigong in Contemporary China." In Kohn, *Taoist Meditation and Longevity Techniques* (q.v.).

Mochizuki Shinkō 望月信亨, ed. *Bukkyō daijiten* 佛教大辭典 (The big dictionary of Buddhism). 3d. ed. 10 vols. Kyoto: Sekai seiten kankō kyōkai, 1954–1971.

Monier-Williams, Monier. *A Sanskrit-English Dictionary, Etymologically and Philologically Arranged With Special Reference to Cognate Indo-European Languages.* 1899. Reprint. Oxford: Clarendon Press, 1979.

Morris, Andrew D. *Marrow of the Nation: A History of Sport and Physical Culture in Republican China.* Berkeley: University of California Press, 2004.

Mote, Frederick W. *Imperial China: 900–1800.* Cambridge, Mass.: Harvard University Press, 1999.

———. "The Rise of the Ming Dynasty, 1330–1367." In *The Cambridge History of China,* vol. 7, 11–57. Cambridge: Cambridge University Press, 1988.

Murray, Dian H., and Qin Baoqi. *The Origins of the Tiandihui: The Chinese Triads in Legend and History.* Stanford, Calif.: Stanford University Press, 1994.

Nakamura Hajime 中村元, ed. *Bukkyōgo daijiten* 佛教語大辭典 (The big dictionary of Buddhist terminology). Tokyo: Tōkyō shoseki, 1981.

Naquin, Susan. *Millenarian Rebellion in China: The Eight Trigrams Uprising of 1813.* New Haven, Conn.: Yale University Press, 1976.

———. *Peking Temples and City Life, 1400–1900.* Berkeley: University of California Press, 2000.

———. *Shantung Rebellion: The Wang Lun Uprising of 1774.* New Haven, Conn.: Yale University Press, 1981.

Naquin, Susan, and Chün-fang Yü, eds. *Pilgrims and Sacred Sites in China.* Berkeley: University of California Press, 1992.

Na wenyi gong zouyi 那文毅公奏議 (The collected memorials of Nayancheng). 1834 edition.

Needham, Joseph, and Wang Ling. *Science and Civilization in China.* Vol. 2, *History of Scientific Thought.* Cambridge: Cambridge University Press, 1956.

Needham, Joseph, and Lu Gwei-Djen. *Science and Civilization in China.* Vol. 5, part II, *Spagyrical Discovery and Invention: Magisteries of Gold and Immortality.* Cambridge: Cambridge University Press, 1974.

———. *Science and Civilization in China.* Vol. 5, part V, *Spagyrical Discovery and Invention: Physiological Alchemy.* Cambridge: Cambridge University Press, 1983.

Needham, Joseph, and Robin D. S. Yates. *Science and Civilization in China.* Vol. 5, Part VI, *Military Technology: Missiles and Sieges.* Cambridge: Cambridge University Press, 1994.

Neigong tushuo 內功圖說 (Illustrated exposition of internal techniques). Preface by Wang Zuyuan 王祖源. 1882 edition in *Tianrangge congshu* 天壤閣叢書 (Collected books from the Heaven and Earth Hall). Photographic reprint in *Congshu jicheng chubian* 叢書集成初編. Shanghai: Shangwu, 1936.

The New Oxford Annotated Bible With the Apocrypha. Edited by Herbert G. May and Bruce M. Metzger. New York: Oxford University Press, 1973.

Niida Noboru 仁井田陞. *Tō Sō hōritsu bunsho no kenkyū* 唐 宋法律文書の研究 (The critical study of legal documents of the T'ang and Sung eras). Tokyo: Toōhō bunka gakuyin, 1937.

Ningbo fu zhi 寧波府志 (Gazetteer of Ningbo Prefecture). 1735. Edited by Cao Bingren 曹秉仁. 1846 edition. Photographic reprint. Taibei: Zhonghua congshu weiyuanhui, 1957.

Ownby, David. *Brotherhoods and Secret Societies in Early and Mid-Qing China: The Formation of a Tradition.* Stanford, Calif.: Stanford University Press, 1996.

The Oxford Dictionary of the Christian Church. Edited by F. L. Cross. London: Oxford University Press, 1958.

Palmer, David A. "Modernity and Millenarianism in China: Qigong and the Birth of Falun Gong." *Asian Anthropology* 2 (2003): 79–110.

Parrinder, Geoffrey. *Witchcraft.* Bristol: Penguin Books, 1958.

Parsons, James Bunyan. *Peasant Rebellions of the Late Ming Dynasty.* 1970. Reprint. The Association for Asian Studies Monograph and Occasional Papers, no. 26. Ann Arbor, Mich.: Association for Asian Studies, 1993.

Pelliot, Paul. "Notes sur quelques artistes des Six Dynasties et des T'ang." *T'oung Pao* 22 (1923): 215–291.

Peri, Noël. "Le dieu Wei-t'ouo." *Bulletin de l'École Francaise d'Extrême-Orient* 16, no. 3 (1916): 41–56.

Peterson, Willard J. "The Life of Ku Yen-Wu (1613–1682)." Parts 1–2. *Harvard Journal of Asiatic Studies* 28 (1968): 114–156; 29 (1969): 201–247.

Pingyao zhuan 平妖傳 (Suppressing the demons' revolt). Revised and enlarged by Feng Menglong 馮夢龍 (1574–1646). Taibei: Shijie shuju, 1982.

Predagio, Fabrizio, and Lowell Skar. "Inner Alchemy (Neidan)." In Kohn, *Daoism Handbook* (q.v.).

Prip-Møller, J. *Chinese Buddhist Monasteries: Their Plan and Its Function As a Setting For Buddhist Monastic Life.* 1937. Reprint. Hong Kong: Hong Kong University Press, 1967.

Pu Songling 蒲松齡. *Liaozhai zhiyi huijiao huizhu huiping ben* 聊齋志異會校會注會評本 (The complete collated and annotated Liaozhai's records of the strange). Edited by Zhang Youhe 張友鶴. 2 vols. Shanghai: Shanghai guji, 1986.

Puett, Michael J. *To Become a God: Cosmology, Sacrifice, and Self-Divinization in Early China.* Harvard-Yenching Institute Monograph Series, 57. Cambridge, Mass.: Harvard University Asia Center, 2002.

Qi Jiguang 戚繼光. *Jixiao xinshu: shiba juan ben* 紀效新書十八卷本 (New treatise on military efficiency: eighteen chapters edition). Annotated by Cao Wenming 曹文明 and Lü Yingshi 呂穎慧. In *Qi Jiguang yanjiu congshu* 戚繼光研究叢書 (Collected scholarly materials on Qi Jiguang). Beijing: Zhonghua, 2001.

———. *Jixiao xinshu: shisi juan ben* 紀效新書十四卷本 (New treatise on military efficiency: fourteen chapters edition). Annotated by Fan Zhongyi 范中義. In *Qi Jiguang yanjiu congshu* 戚繼光研究叢書 (Collected scholarly materials on Qi Jiguang). Beijing: Zhonghua, 2001.

Qian Bangyan 錢邦彥. "Gu Tinglin xiansheng nianpu" 顧亭林先生年譜 (Chronology of Mr. Gu Yanwu). In *Tianxia junguo libing shu* 天下郡國利病書 (Advantages and disadvantages of the provinces and prefectures of the empire), by Gu Yanwu 顧炎武. Congshu jicheng edition. Shanghai: Shangwu, 1936.

Qian Ceng 錢曾 (1629–1701). *Pengcheng shijia shugutang tushu ji* 彭城世家述古堂圖書記 (Catalogue of the Shugu family library at Pengcheng). In vol. 277 of the history section of the *Siku quanshu cunmu congshu* 四庫全書存目叢書 (All the books in the "Siku quanshu" catalogue). Tainan: Zhuangyan, 1996.

———. *Yeshiyuan cang shumu* 也是園藏書目 (Catalogue of books stored at the Yeshiyuan). Conshujicheng xubian edition. Taibei: Xinwenfeng, 1989.

Qianlong chao shangyu dang 乾隆朝上諭檔 (Archive of the Qianlong reign imperial edicts). Edited by Diyi lishi dang'anguan 第一歷史檔案館. 18 vols. Beijing: Dang'an chubanshe, 1991.

Qing bai lei chao 清稗類鈔 (Classified anthology of Qing anecdotes). Edited by Xu Ke 徐珂. 13 volumes. Beijing: Zhonghua, 1986.

Qingpingshan tang huaben 清平山堂話本 (Huaben stories from the Qingpingshan Hall). Complied by Hong Pian 洪楩. Edited by Shi Changyu 石昌渝. Jiangsu: Jiangsu guji, 1990.

Qing shi gao 清史稿 (Draft history of the Qing). Edited by Zhao Erxun 趙爾巽 (1844–1927) et al. 48 volumes. Beijing; Zhonghua, 1977.

Quan jing, Quan fa beiyao 拳經拳法備要 (Hand combat classic, collection of hand combat methods). Authors given as Zhang Kongzhao 張孔昭 (style: Hengqiu 橫秋) and Cao Huandou 曹煥斗 (style: Zaidong 在東). In *Miaoyuan congshu* 邈園叢書 (Collected books from the remote garden). Shanghai: Chanyin lu, 1936. Photographic reprint. Congshu jicheng xubian edition. Taibei: Xinwenfeng, 1988.

Quan Tang shi 全唐詩 (The complete poetry of the Tang). 25 vols. Beijing: Zhonghua, 1960.

Quan Tang wen 全唐文 (The complete prose of the Tang). 1814 edition. Photographic reprint. 5 vols. Shanghai: Shanghai guji, 1990.

Quanzhou Nan Shaolinsi yanjiu 泉州南少林寺研究 (Research into the Quanzhou Southern Shaolin Temple). Compiled by Quanzhou Nan Shaolinsi yanjiuhui 泉州南少林寺研究會. Hong Kong: Huaxing, 1993.

Roberts, Moss, trans. *Three Kingdoms: A Historical Novel*. Attributed to Luo Guanzhong. Berkeley: University of California Press, 1991.

Robinet, Isabelle. "Metamorphosis and Deliverance from the Corpse in Taoism." *History of Religions* 19, no. 1 (1979): 37–70.

———. "Shangqing—Highest Clarity." In Kohn, *Daoism Handbook* (q.v.).

———. *Taoist Meditation: The Mao-Shan Tradition of Great Purity*. Translated by Julian F. Pas and Norman J. Girardot. Albany: State University of New York, 1993.

Robinson, David. *Bandits, Eunuchs, and the Son of Heaven: Rebellion and the Economy of Violence in Mid-Ming China*. Honolulu: University of Hawai'i Press, 2001.

Rossabi, Morris. "Muslim and Central Asian Revolts." In *From Ming to Ch'ing: Conquest, Region, and Continuity in Seventeenth-Century China*, edited by Jonathan D. Spence and John E. Wills. New Haven, Conn.: Yale University Press, 1979.

Russell, Jeffrey Burton. *Witchcraft in the Middle Ages*. Ithaca, N.Y.: Cornell University Press, 1972.

Sanguo yanyi 三國演義 (Romance of the three kingdoms). Author given as Luo Guanzhong 羅貫中. Beijing: Renmin wenxue, 1972.

Sanguo zhi 三國志 (History of the three kingdoms). By Chen Shou 陳壽 (233–297). In *Ershisi shi jiaodian ben* (q.v.).

Santai Wanyong zhengzong 三台萬用正宗 (Santai [publishing] all-purpose correct way). 1599 edition. Photographic reprint in *Chūgoku nichiyō ruisho shūsei* 中國日用類書集成 (Collection of Chinese encyclopedias for everyday use), edited by Sakai Tadao 酒井忠夫, Sakade Yoshihiro 坂出祥伸, and Ogawa Yōichi 小川陽一. Tokyo: Kyūko, 2000.

Sawada Mizuho 澤田瑞穗. "Songokū shin" 孫悟空神 (The deity Sun Wukong). 1979. Reprint in his *Chūgoku no minkan shinkō* 中國民間信仰 (Chinese popular beliefs). Tokyo: Kōsaku sha, 1982.

Sawyer, Ralph D., trans. *The Seven Military Classics of Ancient China*. Boulder. Colo.: Westview Press, 1993.

Schipper, Kristofer, ed. *Concordance du Tao-tsang: Titres des ouvrage*. Publications de l'Ecole Francaise d'Extrême-Orient, no. 102. Paris: Ecole Francaise d'Extrême-Orient, 1975.

Schopen, Gregory. "Two Problems in the History of Indian Buddhism: The Layman/Monk Distinction and the Doctrines of the Transference of Merit." In Gregory Schopen, *Bones, Stones, and Buddhist Monks: Collected Papers on the Archeology, Epigraphy, and Texts of Monastic Buddhism in India*. Honolulu: University of Hawai'i Press, 1997.

Seidel, Anna. "Chronicle of Taoist Studies in the West 1950–1990." *Cahiers d'Extreme-Asie* 5 (1989–1990): 223–347.

———. "A Taoist Immortal of the Ming Dynasty: Chang San-feng." In *Self and Society in Ming Thought*, edited by William Theodore de Bary. New York: Columbia University Press, 1970.

Shahar, Meir. *Crazy Ji: Chinese Religion and Popular Literature*. Harvard-Yenching Institute Monograph Series, 48. Cambridge, Mass.: Harvard University Asia Center, 1998.

———. "The Lingyin si Monkey Disciples and the Origins of Sun Wukong," *Harvard Journal of Asiatic Studies* 52, no. 1 (June 1992): 193–224.

———. "Lucky Dog." *Free China Review* 41, no. 7 (July 1991): 64–69.

Shandong jindaishi ziliao 山東近代史資料 (Materials on modern Shandong history). Edited by Zhongguoshi xuehui jinan fenhui 中國史學會濟南分會. 3 vols. Ji'nan: Shandong renmin, 1957–1961.

Shangdang gu sai xiejuan shisi zhong jianzhu 上黨古賽寫卷十四種箋注 (Fourteen annotated ancient *sai* manuscripts from Shangdang (Shanxi)). Edited by Yang Mengheng 楊孟衡. Minsu quyi congchu. Taibei: Shihezheng jijinhui, 2000.

Shanghai lishi ditu ji 上海歷史地圖集 (Historical atlas of Shanghai). Edited by Zhou Zhenhe 周振鶴 et al. Shanghai: Shanghai renmin, 1999.

Shaolin gongfu wenji 少林功夫文集 (Studies on the Shaolin martial arts). Edited by Yongxin 永信. 2 vols. Henan: Shaolin shuju, 2003–2004.

Shaolin quanshu mijue 少林拳術秘訣 (Secret formulas of the Shaolin hand combat method). 1915. Reprint in *Shaolin si ziliao ji* (q.v.).

Shaolin si qianfodian bihua 少林寺千佛殿壁畫 (The wall painting at the Thousand Buddhas Hall of the Shaolin Monastery). Edited by Henan sheng gudai jian-zhu baohu yanjiusuo 河南省古代建筑保護研究所. Zhengzhou: Henan mei-shu, 1986.

Shaolin si shike yishu 少林寺石刻藝術 (The Shaolin Monastery's stone carving art). Edited by Su Siyi 蘇思義 et al. Beijing: Wenwu, 1985.

Shaolin si zhi 少林 寺志 (History of the Shaolin Monastery). Preface 1748. Compiled by Ye Feng 葉封 et al. Revised by Shi Yizan 施奕簪 et al. (Copy at the Harvard-Yenching Library.)

Shaolin si ziliao ji 少林寺資料集 (Compilation of materials on the Shaolin Monastery). Edited by Wu Gu 無谷 and Liu Zhixue 劉志學. Beijing: Shumu wen-xian, 1982.

Shaolin si ziliao ji xu bian 少 林寺資料集續編 (Supplement to the compilation of ma-terials on the Shaolin Monastery). Edited by Wu Gu 無谷 and Yao Yuan 姚遠. Beijing: Shumu wenxian, 1984.

Shapiro, Sidney, trans. *Outlaws of the Marsh.* Authors given as Shi Nai'an and Luo Guanzhong. 4 vols. Beijing: Foreign Languages Press, 1988.

Sharf, Robert H. "The Zen of Japanese Nationalism." In *Curators of the Buddha: The Study of Buddhism Under Colonialism,* edited by Donald S. Lopez. Chicago: The University of Chicago Press, 1995.

Shesheng zuanlu 攝生纂錄 (Collected records of protecting life). *DZ*, 578.

Shih, Robert, trans. *Biographies des moines éminents (Kao seng tchouan) de Houei-Kiao.* Bibliothèque du Muséon, no. 54. Louvain: Université de Louvain, 1968.

Shizong Xian Huangdi zhupi yuzhi 世宗憲皇帝硃批諭旨 (The Yongzheng emperor's vermillion responses to official memorials). Compiled in 1738. SKQS edition.

Shou-Yu Liang and Wen-Ching Wu. *Kung Fu Elements: Wushu Training and Martial Arts Application Manual.* Edited by Denise Breiter-Wu. East Providence, R.I.: Way of the Dragon, 2001.

Shuihu quanzhuan 水滸全傳 (Water margin). 3 vols. Beijing: Renmin wenxue, 1954. Reprint. 2 vols. Taibei: Wannianqing shudian, 1979.

Shunzhi Dengfeng xian zhi 順治登封縣志 (Shunzhi period (1644–1661) Dengfeng County gazetteer). Compiled by Zhang Chaorui 張朝瑞, and Jiao Fuheng 焦復亨. Preface 1652. (Copy at the Beijing Library.)

Siku da cidian 四庫大辭典 (The big dictionary of Chinese bibliography). Edited by Li Xueqin 李學勤 and Lü Wenyu 呂文郁. 2 vols. Changchun: Jilin daxue, 1996.

So, Kwan-wai (Su Chün-wei 蘇均煒). *Japanese Piracy in Ming China During the 16th Century.* East Lansing: Michigan State University Press, 1975.

Song shi 宋史 (History of the Song). Edited by Tuotuo 脫脫 (1313–1355) et al. In *Er-shisi shi jiaodian ben* (q.v.).

Song shu 宋書 (History of the [Liu] Song). Edited by Shen Yue 沈約 (441–513). In *Ershisi shi jiaodian ben* (q.v.).

Song xian zhi 嵩縣志 (Song County gazetteer). Songxian: Henan renmin, 1990.

Song yue wenxian congkan 嵩岳文獻叢刊 (Collected writings on Mt. Song). Edited by Zhengzhou tushuguan bianji weiyuanhui 鄭州圖書館編輯委員會. 4 vols. Zhengzhou: Zhongzhou guji, 2003.

Soper, Alexander Coburn. *Literary Evidence for Early Buddhist Art in China*. Ascona: Artibus Asiae, 1959.

Stein, Aurel. *Serinida: Detailed Report of Explorations in Central Asia and Westernmost China*. 5 vols. Oxford: Oxford University Press, 1921.

Stein, Rolf. "The Guardian of the Gate: An Example of Buddhist Mythology from India to Japan." In *Asian Mythologies*, edited by Yves Bonnefoy, translated under the direction of Wendy Doniger by Gerald Honigsblum et al. Chicago: University of Chicago Press, 1993.

Strickmann, Michel. *Chinese Magical Medicine*. Edited by Bernard Faure. Asian Religions and Cultures. Stanford, Calif.: Stanford University Press, 2002.

———. *Mantras et mandarins: Le Buddhism Tantrique en Chine*. Paris: Gallimard, 1996.

A Study of the Hong Kong Martial Arts Film: The 4th Hong Kong International Film Festival (Xianggang gongfu dianying yanjiu 香港功夫電影研究). Presented by the [Hong Kong] Urban Council. Hong Kong: Urban Council, 1980.

Taijiquan pu 太極拳譜 (Taiji Quan manuals). By Wang Zongyue 王宗岳 et al. Collated by Shen Shou 沈壽. Zhonghua wushu wenku guji bu. Beijing: Renmin tiyu, 1991.

Taiping guangji 太平廣記 (Extensive records compiled during the Taiping period). Edited by Li Fang 李昉 (925–996). Beijing: Renmin wenxue, 1959.

Taiping huanyu ji 太平寰宇記 (Geography of the world compiled during the Taiping period). Edited by Yue Shi 樂史 (fl. 980). 1803 edition. Photographic reprint. Taibei: Wenhai, 1963.

Taishō shinshū daizōkyō 大正新脩大藏經 (The great Buddhist canon compiled during the Taishō period). 100 vols. Tokyo: Taishō issaikyō kankōkai, 1924–1932.

Takuan Sōhō. *The Unfettered Mind: Writings of the Zen Master to the Sword Master*. Translated by William Scott Wilson. Tokyo: Kodansha International, 1986.

Tang Hao 唐豪. "Jiu Zhongguo tiyushi shang fuhui de Damo" 舊中國體育史上附會的達摩 (The unfounded association of Bodhidharma with the ancient history of Chinese physical education). Parts 1, 2. In vol. 4 and vol. 6 of *Zhongguo tiyushi cankao ziliao* 中國體育史參考資料 (Research materials on the history of Chinese physical education). Beijing: Renmin tiyu, 1958.

———. *Neijia quan de yanjiu* 內家拳的研究 (A Study of the internal school fist). 1935. Reprint. Taibei: Hualian, 1971.

———. *Shaolin quanshu mijue kaozheng* 少林拳術秘訣考証 (Research on the *Shaolin quanshu mijue*). Shanghai: Shanghai guoshu xiejinhui, 1941. (Copy at the Shanghai Library.)

———. *Shaolin Wudang kao* 少林武當攷 (Shaolin and Wudang research). 1930. Photographic reprint. Hong Kong: Qilin tushu, 1968.

———. "Songshan Shaolin chuanxi de he huiji de ticao" 嵩山少林傳習的和匯輯的體操 (The gymnastic exercises transmitted and assembled at the Mt. Song Shaolin Monastery). In vol. 5 of *Zhongguo tiyushi cankao ziliao* 中國體育史參考資料 (Research materials on the history of Chinese physical education). Beijing: Renmin tiyu, 1958.

——— [Style name Fan Sheng 范生]. "Wo guo tiyu ziliao jieti" 我國體育資料解題 (Exposition of sources on our nation's physical education). In vol. 5 of *Zhongguo tiyushi cankao ziliao* 中國體育史參考資料 (Research materials on the history of Chinese physical education). Beijing: Renmin tiyu, 1958.

Tang Hao 唐豪 and Gu Liuxin 顧留馨. *Taijiquan yanjiu* 太極拳研究 (Research into Taijiquan). 1964. Reprint. Hong Kong: Yixin, 1970.

Tang Hao 唐豪 et al. *Baduan jin* 八段錦 (The eight-section brocade). Beijing: Renmin tiyu, 1957.

Tang Hui Yao 唐會要 (Essential regulations of the Tang). Compiled by Wang Pu 王溥 (922–982). 3 vols. Beijing: Zhonghua, 1955.

Tang Shunzhi 唐順之. *Jingchuan xiansheng wenji* 荊川先生文集 (Collected writings of Mr. Jingchuan [Tang Shunzhi]). Wanli edition. Photographic reprint. Sibu congkan. Shanghai: Shangwu, 1922.

———. *Wu bian* 武編 (Treatise on military affairs). Wanli edition. Photographic reprint in vols. 13–14 of *Zhongguo bingshu jicheng* (q.v.).

Teiser, Stephen F. *The Ghost Festival in Medieval China*. Princeton, N.J.: Princeton University Press, 1988.

ter Haar, Barend J. "Buddhist-Inspired Options: Aspects of Lay Religious Life in the Lower Yangzi from 1100 until 1340." *T'oung Pao* 87, no. 1–3 (2001): 92–152.

———. "The Rise of the Guan Yu Cult: The Taoist Connection." In *Linked Faiths: Essays on Chinese Religions and Traditional Culture in Honour of Kristofer Schipper*, edited by Jan A. M. de Meyer and Peter M. Engelfriet. Sinica Leidensia, vol. XLVI. Leiden: Brill, 2000.

———. *Ritual and Mythology of the Chinese Triads: Creating an Ideology*. Leiden: Brill, 1998.

———. *The White Lotus Teachings in Chinese Religious History*. Leiden: Brill, 1992.

Tiantai shan quan zhi 天台山全志 (The complete history of Mt. Tiantai). Edited by Zhang Lianyuan 張聯元. 1717 edition.

Tonami Mamoru. *The Shaolin Monastery Stele on Mount Song*. Translated and annotated by P. A. Herbert. Edited by Antonino Forte. Italian School of East Asian Studies Epigraphical Series, no. 1. Kyoto: Italian School of East Asian Studies, 1990.

Tong, James W. *Disorder under Heaven: Collective Violence in the Ming Dynasty*. Stanford, Calif.: Stanford University Press, 1991.

Tongbai shizhi 桐柏史志 (History of the Paulownia Temple). Edited by Zhao Zilian 趙子廉. Tiantai: Tonbai guan, 1999.

Tuoluoni ji jing 陀羅尼集經 (Sutra of the assembled charms). Compiled by Atikūṭa (Chinese: Adiquduo 阿地瞿多) (fl. 654). *T*, no. 901.

Twitchett, Dennis. "Hsüan-Tsung (Reign 712–756)." In *The Cambridge History of China*, vol. 3, 333–436. Cambridge: Cambridge University Press, 1979.

———. "Monastic Estates in T'ang China." *Asia Major*, n.s., 5, no. 2 (1956): 123–146.

Victoria, Brian (Daizen) A. *Zen at War*. New York: Weatherhill, 1997.

Wakeman, Frederick. *The Great Enterprise: The Manchu Reconstruction of Imperial Order in Seventeenth-Century China*. 2 vols. Berkeley: University of California Press, 1985.

Wang Chang 王昶 (1725–1806). *Jinshi cuibian* 金石萃編 (Collection of inscriptions on metal and stone). 1805 edition.

Wang, David Teh-Yu. "*Nei jing Tu*, a Daoist Diagram of the Internal Circulation of Man." *The Journal of the Walters Art Gallery* 49/50 (1991–1992): 141–158.

Wang Jie 汪价. *Zhongzhou zazu* 中州雜俎 (Henan miscellany). Qing Dexingtang manuscript edition. (Copy at the National Central Library, Taibei.)

Wang Shifu 王實甫. *Xixiang ji* 西廂記 (The story of the western wing). Annotated by Wang Jisi 王季思. Beijing: Zhonghua shuju, 1959.

Wang Shifu. *The Moon and the Zither: The Story of the Western Wing*. Edited and translated by Stephen H. West and Wilt L. Idema. Berkeley: University of California Press, 1991.

Wang Shixing 王士性. *Wuyue you cao* 五嶽遊草 (Draft account of journeys to the five mountains) 1593 edition. (Copy at the National Central Library, Taibei.)

———. *Yu zhi* 豫志 (Report from Henan). Congshu jicheng edition. Shanghai: Shangwu, 1936.

Wang Shizhen 王世貞 (1526–1590). *Yanshan tang bieji* 弇山堂別集 (Other writings of Wang Shizhen). Beijing: Zhonghua, 1985.

Ware, James R., trans. *Alchemy, Medicine, Religion in the China of A.D. 320: The N'ei P'ien of Ko Hung (Pao-p'u tzu)*. Cambridge, Mass.: MIT Press, 1966.

———. "Wei Shou on Buddhism," *T'oung Pao* 30 (1933): 100–181.

Watson, Burton, trans. *The Complete Works of Chuang Tzu*. New York: Columbia University Press, 1968.

Wechsler, Howard J. "The Founding of the T'ang Dynasty: Kao-Tsu (Reign 618–26)." In *The Cambridge History of China*, vol. 3, 150–187. Cambridge: Cambridge University Press, 1979.

———. *Offerings of Jade and Silk: Ritual and Symbol in the Legitimation of the T'ang Dynasty*. New Haven, Conn.: Yale University Press, 1985.

———. "T'ai-Tsung (Reign 626-49) The Consolidator." In *The Cambridge History of China*, vol. 3, 188–241. Cambridge: Cambridge University Press, 1979.

Weinstein, Stanley. *Buddhism Under the T'ang*. Cambridge: Cambridge University Press, 1987.

Wei shu 魏書 (History of the Wei). Compiled by Wei Shou 魏收 (506–572). In *Ershisi shi jiaodian ben* (q.v.).

Welch, Holmes. *The Practice of Chinese Buddhism, 1900–1950*. Cambridge, Mass.: Harvard University Press, 1967.

Weller, Robert P. *Resistance, Chaos and Control in China: Taiping Rebels, Taiwanese Ghosts, and Tiananmen*. Seattle: University of Washington Press, 1994.

Wells, Marnix. *Scholar Boxer: Chang Naizhou's Theory of Internal Martial Arts and the Evolution of Taijiquan.* Berkeley, Calif.: North Atlantic Books, 2005.

Weng Tongwen 翁同文. "Kangxi chuye 'yi-Wan weixing' jituan yudang jianli Tiandihui" 康熙初葉「以萬為姓」集團餘黨建立天地會 (The establishment of the Tiandihui by the remnants of the groups who took the surname Wan in the early Kangxi period). In vol. 3 of *Zhonghua xueshu yu xiandai wenhua congshu* 中華學術與現代文化叢書 (Chinese learning and modern civilization series). Taibei: Huagang, 1977.

Wen xuan 文選 (Literary anthology). Compiled by Xiao Tong 蕭統. 6 vols. Shanghai: Shanghai guji: 1986.

Wenyuange Siku quanshu 文淵閣四庫全書 (All the books from the four treasuries stored at the Wenyuan Hall). 1782 manuscript edition. Photographic reprint. 1500 vols. Taiwan: Shangwu, 1983–1986.

Wen Yucheng 溫玉成. *Shaolin fanggu* 少林訪古 (Visiting the past at the Shaolin Monastery). Tianjin: Baihua wenyi, 1999.

Wile, Douglas. *Lost T'ai-chi Classics from the Late Ch'ing Dynasty.* Albany: State University of New York Press, 1996.

———. *T'ai Chi's Ancestors: The Making of an Internal Art.* New City: Sweet Ch'i Press, 1999.

Wu Cheng'en 吳承恩. *Xiyou ji* 西遊記 (Journey to the west). 2 vols. Beijing: Zuojia, 1954.

Wu Han 吳晗. *Zhu Yuanzhang zhuan* 朱元璋傳 (Biography of Zhu Yuanzhang). Shanghai: Shenghuo dushu xinzhi sanlian shudian, 1949.

Wu Huifang 吳蕙芳. *Wanbao quanshu: Ming Qing shiqi de minjian shenghuo shilu* 萬寶全書: 明清時期的民間生活實錄 (The "Complete book of myriad treasures": veritable records of common people's lives during the Ming-Qing period). Zhengzhi daxue shixue congshu, no. 6. Taibei: Zhengzhi daxue, 2001.

Wu Jingzi 吳敬梓. *Rulin waishi* 儒林外史 (The unofficial history of the scholars). Edited by Zhang Huijian 張慧劍. Beijing: Renmin, 1985.

Wu Liu xianzong quanji 伍柳仙宗全集 (The complete immortality teachings of Wu and Liu). Edited by Deng Huiji 鄧徽績. 1897 edition. Photographic reprint. Taibei: Zhenshanmei, 1962.

Wu Pei-Yi. "An Ambivalent Pilgrim to T'ai Shan in the Seventeenth Century." In Naquin and Chün-fang Yü, *Pilgrims and Sacred Sites in China* (q.v.).

Wu Qiao 吳喬 (Other name Wu Shu 吳殳). *Weilu shihua* 圍爐詩話 (Poetic conversations around the fireplace). Congshu jicheng edition. 2 vols. Shanghai: Shangwu, 1939.

Wu Shouyang 伍守陽 (1563–1644). *Xianfo hezong yulu* 仙佛合宗語錄 (Recorded sayings of the common tradition of Daoism and Buddhism). In *Wu Liu xianzong quanji* (q.v.).

Wu Shu 吳殳 (other name: Wu Qiao 吳喬). *Shoubi lu* 手臂錄 (Arm exercises). Preface 1678. Congshu jicheng edition. Shanghai: Shangwu, 1939.

Wu Yue chunqiu zhuzi suoyin 吳越春秋逐字索引 (Word-by-word concordance of the "annals of Wu and Yue"). Edited by Liu Dianjue 劉殿爵 (D. C. Lau) et al.

Xian Qin liang Han guji zhuzi suoyin congkan shibu, no. 5. Hong Kong: Shangwu, 1993.

Xie Zhaozhe 謝肇淛. *Wu zazu* 五雜組 (Five assorted offerings). 1618 edition. Photographic reprint. Taibei: Xinxing 1971.

Xin bian Shaolin si zhi 新編少林寺志 (Newly edited history of the Shaolin Monastery). Edited by Dengfeng xianzhi bangongshi 登封縣志辦公室. Beijing: Zhongguo luyou, 1988.

Xin Tang shu 新唐書 (New history of the Tang). Edited by Ouyang Xiu 歐陽修 and Song Qi 松祁. In *Ershisi shi jiaodian ben* (q.v.).

Xiuzhen shishu 修真十書 (Ten compilations on cultivating perfection). *DZ*, 263.

Xuanji mishou xuedao quan jue 玄機秘授穴道拳訣 (Xuanji's secret transmission of acupuncture points' hand combat formulas). Preface by Zhang Ming'e 張鳴鶚. Shanghai: Guoji xueshe, 1927. (Copy at the Shanghai Library.)

Xu Changqing 徐長青. *Shaolin si yu Zhongguo wenhua* 少林寺與中國文化 (The Shaolin Monastery and Chinese culture). Zhengzhou: Zhongzhou guji, 1993.

Xu Mengxin 徐夢莘 (1124–1205). *San chao bei meng huibian* 三朝北盟會編 (Collected materials on the three reigns' northern treaties). 1194. SKQS edition.

Xu Zhen 徐震 (Style: Zhedong 哲東). *Guoji lunlüe* 國技論略 (Summary of the Chinese martial arts). 1929 edition. Photographic reprint in series no. 1, vol. 50 of *Minguo congshu* 民國叢書 (Collected works from the Republican period). Shanghai: Shanghai shudian, 1989.

Yampolsky, Philip, ed. and trans. *The Platform Sutra of the Sixth Patriarch*. New York: Columbia University Press, 1967.

Yang Hsüan-chih. *A Record of Buddhist Monasteries in Lo-yang*. Translated by Yi-t'ung Wang. Princeton. N.J.: Princeton University Press, 1984.

Yangjia jiang yanyi 楊家將演義 (Romance of the Yang family generals). 50 chapters. By Xiong Damu 熊大木 (fl. 1550). Shanghai: Shanghai guji, 2000.

Yangjia jiang yanyi 楊家將演義 (Romance of the Yang family generals). 58 Chapters. Preface by Ji Zhenlun 紀振倫 (1606). Taibei: Sanmin shuju, 1998.

Yang Lizhi 楊立志. "Mingdai diwang yu Wudang daojiao guanli" 明代帝王與武當道教管理 (Ming emperors and the administration of Wudang Daoism). *Shijie zongjiao yanjiu* 世界宗教研究 (1988, no. 1): 86–95.

Yang Tinghe 楊廷和 (1459–1529). *Yang Wenzhong san lu* 楊文忠三錄 (Yang Tinghe's three collected records). SKQS edition.

Yang Xuanzhi 楊衒之. *Luoyang qielan ji* 洛陽伽藍記 (Record of Buddhist monasteries in Luoyang). Shanghai, Shanghai shudian, 2000.

Yao Tao-Chung. "Quanzhen-Complete Perfection." In Kohn, *Daoism Handbook* (q.v.).

Yihequan yundong qiyuan tansuo 義和拳運動起源探索 (An exploration into the origins of the Boxer movement). Edited by Lu Yao 路遙 et al. Ji'nan: Shandong daxue, 1990.

Yiqie jing yinyi 一切經音義 (Dictionary of the Buddhist canon). By Huilin 慧琳. *T*, no. 2128.

Yu, Anthony, trans. *The Journey to the West*. 4 vols. Chicago: University of Chicago Press, 1977–1983.

Yü, Chün-fang. "Ming Buddhism." In *The Cambridge History of China*, vol. 8, 893–952. Cambridge: Cambridge University Press, 1998.

———. *The Renewal of Buddhism in China: Chu-hung and the late Ming synthesis*. New York: Columbia University Press, 1981.

Yu Dayou 俞大猷. *Jian jing* 劍經 (The sword classic) in Yu Dayou, *Zhengqi tang yuji* (q.v.).

———. *Zhengqi tang ji* 正氣堂集 (Collected writings from the Upright Spirit Hall). With two sequels: *Zhengqi tang xuji* 續集 (More writings from the Upright Spirit Hall), and *Zhengqi tang yuji* 餘集 (Other writings from the Upright Spirit Hall). Combined 1841 edition. (Copy at the Harvard-Yenching Library.)

Yu, Xue. *Buddhism, War, and Nationalism: Chinese Monks in the Struggle against Japanese Aggressions, 1931–1945*. New York: Routledge, 2005.

Yuan Hongdao 袁宏道. *Yuan Hongdao ji jian jiao* 袁宏道集箋校 (An annotated and collated edition of Yuan Hongdao's writings). Annotated by Qian Bocheng 錢伯城. 3 vols. Shanghai: Shanghai guji, 1981.

Yuan Xingyun 袁行雲, ed. *Qingren shiji xulu* 清人詩集敘錄 (Survey of Qing poetic anthologies). 3 vols. Beijing: Xinhua, 1994.

Yunji qiqian 雲笈七籤 (Seven slips from a cloudy satchel). Compiled by Zhang Junfang 張君房 (fl. 1015). Ming Daoist canon edition. Photographic reprint. Sibu congkan. Shanghai: Shangwu, 1929.

Yunyan si 雲巖寺 (The Yunyan Monastery). Edited by Wu Jianshe 吳建設. Songxian, 1999.

Yun Youke 雲游客. *Jianghu congtan* 江湖叢談 (Collected talks on the rivers and lakes). Beijing: Zhongguo quyi, 1988.

Zaju Xiyou ji 雜劇西遊記 (Zaju-style journey to the west). Edited by Shionoya On 鹽谷溫. Tokyo: Shibunkai, 1928.

Zanning 贊寧. *Song Gaoseng zhuan* 宋高僧傳 (Biographies of eminent monks, compiled during the Song period). *T*, no. 2061.

Zelin, Madeleine. "The Yung-Cheng Reign." In *The Cambridge History of China*, vol. 9, 183–229. Cambridge: Cambridge University Press, 2002.

Zeng Weihua 曾維華 and Yan Yaozhong 嚴耀中. "Cong Shaolin si de ji fang bei ta mingwen kan Ming dai sengbing" 從少林寺的幾方碑塔銘文看明代僧兵 (An Examination of the Ming period monastic troops on the basis of several Shaolin stele and stupa inscriptions). *Shanghai shifan xueyuan xuebao (shehui kexue)* 上海師範學院學報(社會科學) (1984, no. 2): 75–77.

Zeng Zao 曾慥 (fl. 1131–1155). *Dao shu* 道樞 (The pivot of the way). *DZ*, 1017.

Zengaku daijiten 禪學大辭典 (The big dictionary of Zen studies). Edited by Zengaku Daijiten Hensanjo 禪學大辭典編纂所. 3 vols. Tokyo: Taishūkan, 1978.

Zhang Dai 張岱. *Langhuan wenji* 瑯嬛文集 (Collected writings from an immortal realm). Shanghai: Shanghai zazhi, 1935.

Zhang Nai 張鼐 (*jinshi* 1604). *Wusong jia yi wo bian zhi* 吳淞甲乙倭變志 (Record of the 1554–1555 pirate upheaval in Wusong). Shanghai zhang'gu congshu 上海掌故叢書, no. 2. Shanghai: Zhonghua, 1936.

Zhang Shutong 張叔通. *Sheshan xiao zhi, Ganshan zhi* 佘山小志干山志 (A short his-

tory of Mt. She, and a history of Mt. Gan). 1936. Reprint. Shanghai: Shang-
haishi xinwen, 1994.

Zhao Keyao 趙克堯 and Xu Daoxun 許道勳. *Tang Taizong zhuan* 唐太宗傳 (Biography of the Tang emperor Taizong). Beijing: Renmin, 1995.

Zheng Ruoceng. 鄭若曾. *Jiangnan jing lüe* 江南經略 (The strategic defense of the Jiangnan region). Preface 1568. SKQS edition.

Zhipan 志磐. *Fozu tongji* 佛祖統紀 (Record of the lineages of Buddhas and patriarchs). *T*, no. 2035.

Zhongguo bingshu jicheng 中國兵書集成 (Collection of Chinese books on warfare). 50 vols. Beijing: Jiefangjun, 1987.

Zhongguo chuantong yangsheng zhendian 中國傳統養生珍典 (Rare classics of Chinese
traditional methods for nourishing life). Edited by Ding Jihua 丁繼華 et al.
Beijing: Renmin tiyu, 1998.

Zhongguo fo si shi zhi huikan 中國佛寺史志彙刊 (Collection of Chinese Buddhist
temple histories) Series no. 1–2, 80 vols. Taibei: Mingwen, 1980. Series no. 3,
30 vols. Taibei: Danqing tushu, 1985.

Zhongguo gudai tiyu shi 中國古代體育史 (History of traditional Chinese physical education). Edited by the Guojia tiwei tiyu wenshi gongzuo weiyuanhui 國家體
委體育文史工作委員會. Beijing: Tiyu xueyuan, 1990.

Zhongguo jindai tiyu shi 中國近代體育史 (History of modern Chinese physical education). Edited by Guojia tiwei tiyu wenshi gongzuo weiyuanhui 國家體委體
育文史工作委員會. Beijing: Tiyu xueyuan, 1989.

Zhongguo lidai guanzhi da cidian 中國歷代官制大辭典 (The big dictionary of Chinese officialdom through the ages). Edited by Lü Zongli 呂宗力 et al. Beijing: Beijing chubanshe, 1994.

Zhongguo Shaolin si 中國少林寺 (China's Shaolin Monastery). Edited by Yongxin 永
信 et al. 3 vols. Beijing: Zhonghua, 2003.

Zhongguo wushu baike quanshu 中國武術百科全書 (The complete encyclopedia of
the Chinese martial arts). Beijing: Zhongguo dabaike quanshu, 1998.

Zhonghua Daojiao da cidian 中華道教大辭典 (The big dictionary of Chinese Daoism).
Edited by Hu Fuchen 胡孚琛 et al. Beijing: Zhongguo shehui kexue, 1995.

Zhou shu 周書 (History of the Zhou). Edited by Linghu Defen 令狐德棻 (583–661).
In *Ershisi shi jiaodian ben* (q.v.).

Zhou Weiliang 周偉良. "Ming-Qing shiqi Shaolin wushu de lishi liubian" 明清時期
少林武術的歷史流變 (The historical evolution of the Shaolin martial arts
during the Ming-Qing period). In *Shaolin gongfu wenji* (q.v.)

———. *Zhongguo wushu shi* 中國武術史 (History of the Chinese martial arts). Beijing: Gaodeng jiaoyu, 2003.

Zhou Zhongfu 周中孚 (1768–1831). *Zheng tang dushu ji* 鄭堂讀書記 (Bibliographic
studies from the solicitude hall). Beijing: Zhonghua: 1993.

Zhu Guozhen 朱國禎 (1557–1632). *Yongchuang xiaopin* 湧幢小品 (Springing pavilion trifles). Beijing: Zhonghua 1959.

Zimmerman, Michael. "A Māhānist Criticism of Ārthaśāstra: The Chapter on Royal
Ethics in the Bodhisattva-gocaropāya-viṣaya-vikurvaṇa-nirdeśa-sútra." In *An-*

nual Report of the International Research Institute for Advanced Buddhology at Soka University for the Academic Year 1999. Tokyo, 2000.

————. "War." In *Encyclopedia of Buddhism,* edited by Robert E. Buswell et al. New York: Macmillan Reference, 2004.

Zizhi tongjian 資治通鑑 (Comprehensive mirror for the aid of government). By Sima Guang 司馬光. 20 vols. Beijing: Zhonghua, 1995.

Zuixing shi 醉醒石 (The sobering stone). Shanghai: Shanghai guji, 1992.

Index

About the Author

Meir Shahar received his doctorate in East Asian Languages and Civilizations from Harvard University. He is the author of *Crazy Ji: Chinese Religion and Popular Literature* (1998) and coeditor (with Robert Weller) of *Unruly Gods: Divinity and Society in China* (1996). He is currently associate professor of Chinese studies in the Department of East Asian Studies, Tel Aviv University.

Production Notes for Shahar / *The Shaolin Monastary*

Jacket design by April Leidig-Higgins.

Text design by University of Hawai'i Press Production Staff
with text in New Baskerville and display in Minion Bold Condensed

Composition by inari information services